ANDREW SINCLAIR

AN ANATOMY
OF TERROR

A HISTORY OF TERRORISM

PAN BOOKS

First published 2003 by Macmillan

This paperback edition published 2004 by Macmillan
an imprint of Pan Macmillan Ltd
Pan Macmillan, 20 New Wharf Road, London N1 9RR
Basingstoke and Oxford
Associated companies throughout the world
www.panmacmillan.com

ISBN 0 330 49260 8

3 5 7 9 8 6 4 2

A CIP catalogue record for this book is available from
the British Library.

Typeset by SetSystems Ltd, Saffron Walden, Essex
Printed and bound in Great Britain by
Mackays of Chatham plc, Chatham, Kent

To Sonia
who has always been the
anatomy of harmony
in my life

They said this mystery never shall cease:
The priest promotes war, & the soldier peace.

William Blake.

Contents

List of Illustrations

Introduction

This book is called *An Anatomy of Terror* because I cannot deal with so indiscriminate a subject without dissecting and examining its various parts. Nearly all of those who have taken over nation states have terrorist acts to their discredit. They are usually judged by the scale of these crimes. For every country in its wars is guilty of some terror tactics. The degree of blame lies in the count of the dead. How many were killed? How were they killed? How long did they take to die?

The philosophers of terrorism, from Machiavelli to Robespierre, from Lenin to Hitler, advocated its limited use, until the state was taken over. All terrorist groups were forgiven, once they had become the government; in the pursuit of power, success leaves few enemies. The horror of modern times, however, has been the scale of the use of state terror, which has managed to massacre in the last century more than 100,000,000 people.

No account of terror may be inclusive. That would take many volumes. I have tried to keep this brief history in proportion, although I have included short studies of clandestine societies that have used terror in their search for influence: the Knights Templars, the Assassins, the Thuggees, the Mafia and the Ku Klux Klan. If these groups are less well known than the anarchists and the Bolsheviks, they seem to me more illuminating and worthy of revelation. I have also tried to balance the history of terror in the West against the East, although the present global war against terrorism is more directed towards the rising sun and the crescent moon.

Ten principles of Terror have emerged:

Terror is warfare by extreme means.

Terror is the lifeblood of tyranny.

Terror is the weapon of the outlaw against the oppressor.

Terror is murder on the cheap.

Terror is the lash on the back of the refugee.

Terror is victory by stealth for the few.

Terror is defeat by cowardice for the crowd.

If we are terrorized, we may become terrible to those who make us fear.

Terror is measured by the scale of its victims, not the merit of its cause.

Tolerance of terror is no virtue.

1. ANCIENT TERRORS

In the ancient Greek myths, terror was a way of seizing power. The infamous Medea was said to have persuaded the daughters of King Pelias to cut him up and boil him in a cauldron of supposed regeneration, which killed him. She poisoned a contender for the throne of Corinth, which went to her husband Jason, who had taken the Argonauts to the Golden Fleece. She also served up their dismembered sons in a stew when Jason betrayed her with a Theban princess, who was dispatched by an early form of napalm from heaven. Zeus himself was meant to have fallen in love with Medea. Such a bloodthirsty woman was a role model for early Greek society.

The three great sagas, the *Iliad* and the *Odyssey* and the *Aeneid*, featured the destruction of two of the leading cities of their day, Troy and Carthage. With these epics, legend became history. One fascination in Homer's poem about the Greek penetration of Asia Minor was its revelations about the cruelty and deceit of Bronze Age societies. Women and young men were raped and enslaved, traitors were stoned, the poisoned arrows of Heracles slowly killed. Two incidents were particularly horrific. The first was the treatment of the corpse of the Trojan hero Hector by Achilles. The second was the slaughter of the suitors and the straying maids by Odysseus after his ten years' voyage home to Ithaca.

On their final encounter outside the walls of Troy, Hector ran away and begged Achilles to allow him a proper burial, if he should be killed. Achilles scorned the advice of the gods and refused such mercy. He was still mad with rage over the death of his beloved Patroclus. Once he had thrown his spear through Hector's throat, he swore he would leave his enemy's body to the dogs and the birds. The rest of his Greek supporters came and mutilated the stripped corpse. Then Achilles cut the tendons of both of Hector's feet at the heel, pulled strips of oxhide through them, attached them to the back of his chariot, and dragged the naked flesh round the walls of Troy, also round the funeral pyre of his male lover (see plate 1).

We do not believe in the Greek gods any more. They are often described as the divine expressions of psychological guilt and fatalism. In modern terms, the unconscious caused Achilles to return the corpse of Hector to his father King Priam for a ritual burning. Certainly, the citizens of Troy were terrorized by such treatment of their fallen hero. The downfall of the great city was presaged by the desecration of Hector's remains. The Trojans did not believe the dire and correct prophecies of Priam's daughter Cassandra, who knew their days were numbered, as they were.

In the *Odyssey*, when Odysseus returned in a beggar's disguise to his kingdom in Ithaca, he sought a savage revenge, approved by his society. When he had slaughtered all the suitors of his wife Penelope with his deadly arrows, piling up their corpses as fish from the nets gasping for their lives, he called in his maids who had slept with his rivals. They were made to cleanse all the blood which spattered the great hall, which was purged with sulphur and fire. Then the women were hanged from a ship's cable:

> As when thrushes with long wings or doves
> Are meshed in a snare, set in a copse –
> They are flying to roost, but grim is the branch –
> So the women's heads were fastened in a row
> With nooses round their necks for their sad end.
> Briefly their feet twitched, but not for very long.

Odysseus then had a jeering goatherd castrated. His nose and ears and hands and feet were cut off and fed to the dogs. Such was his return to Ithaca and his wife's bed.

The most illuminating use of terror in Greek tragedy would become a fulcrum of Freudian psychiatry, the myth of Oedipus. He solved the riddle of the horrible man-eating Sphinx: the answer was 'Mankind'. This response delivered his city Thebes from catastrophe. Oedipus then killed his father by mistake, became King of Thebes, married his mother Jocasta unknowingly, and had children by her. These acts sickened the whole realm with divine vengeance, as would the plagues in Egypt during the time of Moses. Informed of the crimes of his ignorance, Oedipus tore out his eyes and was hounded by the Furies towards a final forgiveness and mercy from heaven. What the Sphinx had really told him was that humanity would suffer terribly, unless it pursued a just way.

The shock of the fall of Troy was retold by Virgil, who also forecast in the *Aeneid* the obliteration of Carthage. In his escape from his burning homeland, the Trojan prince Aeneas confessed to being 'surrounded by a savage terror'. Reaching Carthage with his companions, he drove Queen Dido mad with love, before escaping to found Rome. She killed herself, and her funeral pyre seemed to set her whole capital alight.

> Screams and weeping rose to heaven from the city
> As if Carthage were invaded by the enemy.
> As if the ancient place lay in ruins, and flames
> Devoured the houses of men and divine temples.

Before the Latin epic was written, Rome had already wiped out Carthage by a process as lethal as the firestorm of Dresden in the Second World War. Driven to extremes of fear by Hannibal's attacks from North Africa on the mainland of Italy, the Romans had listened to Cato crying, *Delenda est Carthago* – Carthage must be destroyed. After a siege which lasted for three years, the city burned for seventeen days. One-tenth of a population of half a million survived and were enslaved or exiled. The rubble was ploughed and sown with salt. The general Scipio was afraid that a like fate might reach Rome, as it would when the Goths sacked the city in AD 410. Then, as the British monk Pelagius would record, 'Every household was grieving. A common terror gripped us. The same spectre of death strode before us all.'

In the city states of Greece and Rome, law and treaty usually ruled the relationships between civilized communities, although not barbaric ones. Sparta might use a secret police known as the Krypteia which carried out selected murders on suspicion to keep down the helot serfs, but in dealing with Athens, the oracles of the gods and the methods of diplomacy were observed. In the long Peloponnesian War, the Athenians used tactics of deterrence to quell revolts in their spread empire. In the notorious case of Mytilene in 427 BC, the whole adult male population was condemned to death, the women and children to slavery. A trireme was sent out to enforce the judgement of the Athenian Assembly, which then changed its mind, after Diodotus argued that such a severe punishment would make any future rebels fight to the last useless ruin of their city. A second trireme overtook the first, and the island of Lesbos was saved. The late surrender of Melos, however, led to what Mytilene was spared: the male defenders were executed, the women and children turned into slaves, the place colonized by Athenian settlers. Another terrible retribution took place with the failure of the Athenian expedition against Syracuse in 413 BC, when 7,000 prisoners were worked to death in winter in the open dungeons of the Sicilian stone quarries.

A later tyrant of Syracuse, Agathocles, was admired for his cruelty by Niccolò dei Machiavelli in *The Prince*, that supreme guide for Renaissance rulers. Agathocles used assassination and the massacre of his rivals to seize power. He maintained himself by fear, yet he did liberate Sicily from the Carthaginians. Machiavelli declared that Agathocles would never be named among the most famous men because of his 'barbarous cruelty and inhumanity together with his countless atrocities'. Even so, his regime and policy were admired for the security of his long reign in Syracuse without civil strife. He provided an example for any intriguer who sought supremacy. 'In taking a state, the conqueror must arrange to commit all his cruelties at once.' Then he should grant a better life for all in morsels, so that the times were thought to be slowly improving.

In the Roman Empire, deterrence was always a factor. Terror certainly matched counter-terror in AD 66 in the province of Judaea. Organized as holy warriors after the example of Judas Maccabaeus and his revolt, the Zealots (the Sicarii), an extreme group of Pharisees, rose up; their cry was, 'No god but God, no tax but to the Temple!' The Roman garrison in the Antonia fortress in Jerusalem was massacred. Faced with the loss of Judaea, the Emperor Nero sent his leading general Vespasian with his son Titus to subdue the province with his legions. On Nero's death, Vespasian became the Roman Emperor and left Titus to retake Jerusalem. After many assaults and a siege, his troops burst into the city and washed the walls of the Temple with Zealot blood and left the holy places in heaps of rubble. A final heroic stand by the Sicarii at Masada took thirty months of blockade to reduce its thousand defenders to the necessity of mass suicide. 'Let us go from the world,' their leader Eleazer said in the record of Josephus, 'together with our children and our wives, in a state of freedom. This is what our laws command us to do.'

Sixty years later, the rabbi Akiva inspired the last revolt which would obliterate Jerusalem. In the Talmud of Babylon, he is said to have seen with two comrades a jackal run from the fallen stones of the Tabernacle, which had once housed the lost Ark of the Covenant. He smiled while the others wept, for he knew of the prophets who had foretold the utter destruction of Jerusalem, but also its restoration in glory. As the first prophecy had happened under Titus, so the second would be fulfilled.

An even greater destruction would take place after another war of independence, provoked in part by the rabbi Akiva. Led by the rebel leader Bar Kochba, who stamped on his coins the

facade of a third Temple which he hoped to build again, the
Jews resisted the decrees of the Emperor Hadrian that aimed
to extirpate all traces of their religion from the Holy City. For
three years, this guerrilla leader defeated the Roman troops and
their mercenaries before turning on Jerusalem and destroying the
Tenth Legion there (see plate 2). Hadrian himself had to bring
out a large army to quell the rebellion, which ended in Bar
Kochba and the rabbi Akiva being tortured to death. What was
left of the killing streets of Jerusalem was crushed into level
ground between its Mounts. Only the Western Wall still stood.
Upon the broken stones was built a new city named Aelia Capi-
tolina, from which all Jews were barred under penalty of death.
Judaea was named Palaestina, a name that would replace Israel
as the country of the Jews, now in exile or a minority in their
homeland.

In Britain, after her flogging and the rape of her daughters by
Roman tax gatherers, Boudicca repaid the invaders' insolence
with the ravage of Colchester and St Albans and London. The
Roman historian Tacitus described her and her army's strategy
as 'slaughter, the gibbet, fire, and the cross'. The Greek historian
Dio Cassius wrote of the fate of Roman women in the groves of
the Celtic goddess Andrasta: 'their breasts were cut off and
stuffed in their mouths, so that they seemed to be eating them,
then their bodies were skewered lengthwise on sharp stakes.'
Tacitus thought that such atrocities were a way of exacting
vengeance in advance, a form of blood oath binding everybody
to fight to the death before an inevitable defeat. Her vast and
unruly forces gutted by the stabbing swords of the disciplined
Roman legions, Boudicca took poison as Cleopatra chose the asp.
Neither queen would be dragged in triumph through the avenues
of Rome.

The processions of victory were not free of blood. The glitter
of the uniforms and the chariots and the spoils of war were
followed by the strangling of the enemy leaders at the foot of the
Capitoline Hill. Slavery and punishment were always weapons of

law and order. The Roman lictors' symbol of the fasces, later adopted by Mussolini's regime, was a bound pack of twelve rods containing an axe, used for beheading captives or criminals. Throwing enemies to the lions or public executions were deterrents to any subversion of the Roman Empire. Loss in battle or siege meant a life of servitude. Only the Christian faith was emerging to question these methods of government.

St Augustine defined a 'just war' before the collapse of the Roman Empire. He was building on the existing distinction between a *guerra*, against outlaws and pirates, now called a guerrilla war, and a *bellum*, against legitimate rulers of other countries. This latter 'just war' was an armed conflict, which might be governed by rules accepted by both sides, able to restrain the behaviour of their troops and even claim a divine purpose in the fight. But no holds were barred in the *guerra* against bandits or warlords or barbarian chieftains such as Boudicca. As Aristotle had declared, anyone who lived in the wilderness was near to a beast and should be treated bestially, or enslaved.

The Celtic rites of human sacrifice, which are still displayed on the Gunderstrup Cauldron in Denmark, had appalled the Romans themselves (see plate 3). Although revered as a defender of French liberty against Julius Caesar, Vercingetorix sent his mounted Gauls into battle with the severed heads of their enemies tied together around the necks of their horses. Yet however justified the cause of any freedom fighters, the use of tactics of horror must repel, when the object of the rebels should be to attract the mass of the people behind them.

Terror is a two-edged sword, which deters foe and friend alike. The tortures inflicted on opponents may appal future subjects. Agathocles had been prudent in seizing power by horror, then easing security measures to allow for popular support. In his tortuous approval of a 'just war', St Augustine allowed Christians to massacre pagans after the example of Joshua in the Old Testament, but such violence should not be through hatred.

It should be a parent's cruelty in punishing his child for its own good. Certainly, the sack of Rome during Augustine's lifetime appeared as the triumph of evil over good, and religious wars now became necessary for the Christian faith.

2. THE TEXTS OF
HOLY TERROR

Of the three seminal religions of the Near East, Judaism and
Christianity and Islam, the Jews founded Israel by a form of
genocide. Moses said that the Lord had ordered the annihilation
and subjugation of the original inhabitants of Canaan in a holy
war. As Deuteronomy stated:

> When the Lord thy God shall bring thee into the land
> whither thou goest to possess it, and hath cast out many
> nations before thee, the Hittites, and the Girgashites, and
> the Amorites, and the Canaanites, and the Perizzites, and the
> Hivites, and the Jebusites, seven nations greater and mightier
> than thou;
>
> And when the Lord thy God shall deliver them before
> thee; thou shalt smite them, and utterly destroy them; thou
> shalt make no covenant with them, nor shew mercy unto
> them . . .
>
> For thou art an holy people unto the Lord thy God: the
> Lord thy God has chosen thee to be a special people unto
> Himself, above all people that are upon the face of the earth.

Joshua had particularly practised a policy of ethnic cleansing,
as can be read in the biblical account of his reign, when he killed
the population of Ai, men and women together to the number of
12,000, and burned the town. 'For Joshua drew not his hand
back, wherewith he stretched out the spear, until he had utterly
destroyed all the inhabitants of Ai . . . And Joshua burnt Ai, and

made it an heap for ever, even a desolation unto this day.' He exterminated king after king and tribe after tribe, particularly in Hebron. 'And they took it, and smote it with the edge of the sword, and the king thereof, and all the cities thereof, and all the souls that were therein; he left none remaining'.

While Israel became more humane, with King David sparing the Jesubite citizens of his new Jerusalem, the Jewish faith always kept a militant streak. Yet revenge was taken on the Jews for their early annihilation of their enemies by King Tiglath-Pileser III of Assyria with his armies. The ten tribes of northern Judaea were conquered and enslaved and disappeared, never to be seen again except in the later fantasies of the British Israelites and American fundamentalist preachers.

The second disaster to hit Judaea was the razing of the Temple of Solomon and the deportation of the remaining two tribes of Israel to Babylon in 589 BC after the destruction of Jerusalem. They were allowed, however, to live in the first ghettos and practise their religion. Then the Medes and the Persians conquered the pagan city, and Cyrus allowed the Jews to return to their homeland and rebuild their Temple, which they did with a sword in one hand and a trowel in the other – an inspiration to the Freemasons to come.

In contrast to the aggressive Jewish faith, the paradox of Christianity was that Jesus had suffered from state terror. He was crucified as a sacrifice and intermediary between a cruel earth and a merciful heaven. Equally, the paradox of Islam was that the Prophet Muhammad was a general, who occupied pagan Mecca at the critical moment, when it might have fallen to a Christian Abyssinian army and gone to another faith.

Christianity began as a victim culture, suffering barbaric tortures. It was also organized as a secret society with cells, which later became chapels. It had code words such as the sign of the fish, the meaning of *Ichtheos* in Greek letters, otherwise trans-lated as an acronym for 'Jesus Christ, Son of God, Saviour'. The Roman governments thought of missionary Christianity as a heresy against the state religion of the Emperor, who was divine among other gods. The spread of the cult among the slave population encouraged revolts, such as that of Spartacus, who was also crucified with many of his followers.

Yet the subversive Christians seemed to be driven on by a martyr complex. Even if faced with torture or a rending by the beasts in the Circus Maximus, the Christians saw their self-sacrifice as an expiation on the way to heaven. Their suffering was their victory. They were soldiers of Christ, who had died so horribly in the holy war against the enemies of God.

As with Judaism and Islam, the great problem of any religion is when it passes from poverty to power. When the faithful are persuaded that they now rule through the leaders, a terrible revenge is exacted against those who disagree. Although old Rome fell to the barbarians, the Second Rome of Byzantium rose, later to be called Constantinople after its first Christian Emperor, Constantine. The heirs of the rebel apostles became the bishops and saints of the new power, which bridged Europe and Asia. Their worst barbarities were now inflicted on those who split hairs over the nature of the communion or the Trinity. Doctrinal differences became the material of massacre. When a revolutionary group takes over the state, it will persecute other rebel groups to preserve the fruits of the first revolution.

During the spread of early Christianity, there was a multitude of interpretations of what the Torah and the Gospels meant. Many of these Gnostic texts were excluded from the final Bible. One of them, 'The Epistle to Rheginos', began by stating that there were some who wanted to learn much, but they were occupied with questions which had no answers. They had not stood within the Word or Logos of Truth. They sought their own solution, which could only come through Jesus Christ, who had denied death, which was the law of humankind. 'Those who are living shall die. How do they live in an illusion? The rich have become poor and the kings have been overthrown, everything has to change. The cosmos is an illusion.' All was a process, the transformation of things into newness, which would create a heaven from a corrupt society.

The authors of the Gnostic texts chose insight rather than the sermons of early Christian bishops to interpret the Gospels and reach revelation. On this count they were denounced in the late second century by St Irenaeus, the Bishop of Lyon, for 'inventing something new every day'. His chief target was Justin Martyr, who had been a Stoic and a Platonist before becoming a Christian philosopher. Justin praised the heresies of Simon Magus, the magician and enemy of St Paul, while Christ was treated as the Logos or Word, who mediated between the sinful earth and the light of paradise.

These inspirations were called Gnosis, which now came to mean a personal vision, a direct and individual perception of truth. The first appearance of Jesus to Mary Magdalene in the garden after His Crucifixion was interpreted in her apocryphal Gospel as no actual event or even a spiritual flash; she saw Him in her mind. This vision she reported to His disciples. They could now see the risen Christ as she had; any believer could see Him.

Of course, the direct approach to Christian revelation put in doubt all religious authority. Why listen to a bishop if an inner voice told you what Christ wanted you to do? In St Mark's Gospel, it was stated that Jesus had given the disciples the secret of the kingdom of God, while He spoke to the rest of the world in parables. While Saints Peter and Paul professed to pass on these secrets to the Churches later established in Rome and Byzantium, the Gnostic Gospels claimed that the living Jesus could at any time reveal His hidden mysteries to a woman who was not a disciple, to a Mary Magdalene, who represented the ancient female principle of generation, and the Sophia, the goddess of Wisdom. He should show Himself to the person who was fit to see and hear the divine message.

For the Gnostics, there were two distinct worlds, split by a war zone and a veil between heaven and earth. On the shining and dividing screen were the pictures of things, created by the

Logos or Word and interpreted by Christ. Flaming walls separated wisdom from matter with angels as messengers across the horizon between sky and sea and land. The problem of evil allowed by a just God was solved, for life below was already hell.

While the Christians were still secret sects persecuted by the Roman Empire, such heresies could flourish among a larger heresy. Yet after Constantine established Christianity as the official faith, these subversive cults which declared that authority was evil had to be extirpated, although even the Byzantine Emperor would call his new basilica Sancta Sophia, not after any saint, but the wise goddess. The more extreme of these sects were persecuted – the Orphites, who worshipped the wise Serpent; the Adamites, who held their ceremonies in the nude; and the Cainites, who cast aside all civil authority to venerate Cain carrying out the divine will by killing his brother Abel, as well as Judas, who was forced to denounce Jesus. As Irenaeus wrote of the teaching of the Gnostic 'Gospel of Judas', 'He alone was acquainted with the truth as no others were, and so accomplished the mystery of betrayal. By him all things, both earthly and heavenly, were thrown into dissolution.'

These doctrines of the personal revelation of a secret knowledge and of a continuing revolution were to be the motive forces of sacred terror movements within Christianity for two thousand years. Every state and each Church had to reject the rebellion of the cults. Once the Bible was defined within the limits of the Old and the New Testaments, allowing only the messianic and apocalyptical Book of Revelation inside its covers, all deviations from that holy norm might be pursued with fire and sword. The so-called heretics would be terrified into dissolution. Fear will drive men to any extreme, as George Bernard Shaw noted – as faith will, too.

The Islamic creed was revealed to a tribal Arab war leader. In the seventh century, Muhammad was born in Mecca, then a pagan city with a cube, the Ka'aba, as a centre of worship.

Inspired by the Angel Gabriel to form a new religion, Muhammad was ejected with his disciples to the nearby city of Medina. In his absence, Christian Abyssinian armies assaulted Mecca, but were turned back by disease. Muhammad began ambushing caravans and won a victory against superior forces at Badr, then he regained Mecca without a fight. As Christ had done with the money-changers in the Temple at Jerusalem, the Prophet cast out all the idols from the Ka'aba except one, a black meteorite still kissed and revered in the hajj, the holy pilgrimage.

As did the Jews and the later Christians, Muhammad saw the reason for his victory in the hand of God or Allah. In the records of his sayings, the Qur'ān, he told his followers after Badr: 'It was not you but Allah who slew them. It was not you who smote them. Allah smote them so that He might richly reward His faithful. He hears and knows all. He will surely destroy the designs of the unbelievers.'

The inspiration of conquering Islam, which spread quickly over North Africa and the Near East after the death of the Prophet in 632, was his revelations, set down in the Qur'ān. As the ruler of Mecca, he had time to make laws and war and peace. He declared that he was the messenger of Allah, called to earth to form the missionary Umma, the global community of the Islamic faith. The divine purpose was to spread the Prophet's revelation to the far corners of the earth.

Like the Torah and the Bible, the Qur'ān was an ambiguous text, misused for political purposes by its various believers. The small groups of desert Bedouin who took over large areas in two continents had to practise tolerance towards other faiths, particularly Christians and Jews, in order to stay in power. Thus they preached texts from the Qur'ān such as: 'Truth is from Allah, therefore you shall not doubt. Every sect has a certain tract of heaven to which they turn themselves in prayer; but do you strive to run after good things.' And as a just and holy nation, the Arabs were commanded to pray towards the Ka'aba at Mecca. 'The direction of Allah is the true direction.'

Equally, other texts in the Qur'ān inspired a merciless war against all infidels.

> The Jews say, the Christians are grounded on nothing; and the Christians say, the Jews are grounded on nothing; yet they both read the scriptures. [*Indeed, the name of Jesus is mentioned ninety-three times in the Qur'ān.*] . . . But Allah shall judge between them on the day of the resurrection.
>
> Therefore the curse of Allah shall be upon the infidels. For a vile price they have sold their souls, that they should not believe in that which Allah has sent down.
>
> Fight for the religion of Allah against those who fight against you, but transgress not by attacking them first, for Allah loves not the transgressors. And kill them wherever you find them, and turn them from where they have dispossessed you. For temptation to idolatry is more grievous than slaughter.

Tragically, in modern times, Osama bin Laden convinced himself from the Qur'ān that the corruption of the United States and the continual conflicts over modern Israel were attacks on Islam, which justified his orders to kill the infidels, wherever his guerrilla pilots or suicide bombers found them. As a very wealthy man, he would certainly follow the Prophet's declaration: 'Contribute out of your substance toward the defence of the religion of Allah.' All sacred texts are misused, particularly by bellicose states or rebel terrorists, to justify the horrors which they perpetrate on civilian societies.

Most significant for Islam, however, was the eventual split between the Sunni rulers of Mecca and the Shi'ite refugees towards Persia. Within that enduring faith, a schism and a victim culture were created. Quarrels over the succession to the Prophet within Muhammad's family led to the murder of his son-in-law Ali and the martyrdom of his rebel grandson Husain at the hands of the Umayyad caliphs. In 680, the massacre of Husain and his followers at Karbalā became a holy day of expiation in the Shi'ite regions of Persia. This observance gave these refugee Muslims a sense of persecution and self-sacrifice that has endured to this time.

Curiously enough, the focal point of war for the trio of great faiths, the city of Jerusalem, was not mentioned in the Qur'ān. A later tradition ascribed Muhammad's ascent to the seventh heaven from the rock on the Temple Mount, which had been razed by the Romans. That stone was also sacred to Abraham, whose holy influence was revered by all three faiths. When the Caliph Omar took Jerusalem six years after the death of the Prophet, he spared its Christian population and the Church of the Holy Sepulchre. Later, Byzantine and Greek architects would construct the Dome of the Rock over the sacred stone on the Mount, so preventing the building of a third Temple, and creating a site of future religious strife.

The Muslim term jihad described the endless struggle to achieve virtue and follow God's will. It was the effort to make society more just and to spread Islam through preaching as well as the armed fist. Muslim scholars emphasized that jihad might be fulfilled by the heart and the tongue and the hands as well as by the sword. Its object was to spread the Muslim faith over all peoples by persuasion and aggression, discipline and diplomacy, in order to create a perfect community, the Umma. And yet, in the words of the Prophet himself, reported in the 101st sura, or chapter, jihad was an endless mission that could only terminate with the Day of the Last Judgement – similar to the faith of the later crusaders. This was a millennial and apocalyptic message:

> That which strikes!
> What is that which strikes?
> Ah, who will convey to you what the Striking is?
> The day mankind shall become like scattered moths,
> And the mountains like tufts of carded wool.
> Then those whose scales weigh heavy shall enter Paradise,
> And those whose scales are light shall enter the Abyss.
> And who shall convey to you what the Abyss is?
> A raging fire!

The Torah and the Bible and the Qur'ān with the suras are the sacred sagas of a spiritual journey towards one God. Their differences over who was the Messiah or Prophet resulted in horrific carnage over two millennia. The Christians also produced quasi-religious texts in the Middle Ages, which exposed their brutality. For those who could listen, if they could not read, their favourite recitals were the Lives of the Saints and the Grail romances about King Arthur and Charlemagne.

These were the Grand Guignol of a pious and barbarous age. St Catherine, beloved by the crusaders, was broken on the wheel; St Sebastian was skewered with arrows; St Lawrence, who sent a Grail to northern Spain, was charbroiled on a gridiron. Such tortures were accompanied by the mass veneration of holy relics such as the severed head of St John the Baptist, particularly holy to the Knights Hospitallers and the Templars, who expected to suffer a similar sacred sacrifice in their defence of the Holy Land of Palestine against Islam.

Despite the Grail romances of the loves of Tristan and Iseult, of Lancelot and Guinevere, many of these sagas were testaments to the accepted terror of the time. Extremely bloodthirsty were the *Peredur* and the *Perlesvaus*, said to be written by Joseph of Arimathea himself on the dictation of an angel, as Gabriel had instructed the Prophet Muhammad to set down the Qur'ān. In the *Perlesvaus*, King Arthur was cured from a long depression by the sister of Perceval, who was followed by a bald maiden with a cart containing the heads of 150 knights sealed in caskets of gold and silver and lead.

Lancelot then took up the Quest for the Grail. The brutality of the period intruded on the story. Martyrdom was presented to Lancelot in the guise of mutilation. He sat with the lady of a castle:

The first course was brought in by knights in chains who had their noses cut off. The second by knights in chains who had their eyes put out, so that squires led them. The third course was brought in by knights with one hand and chained. After that, other knights with one foot brought in the fourth course. And with the fifth course came tall and fair knights, each with a naked sword used to cut off their heads, now given to the lady.

Perceval resumed the Quest, carrying his azure and silver shield with the red cross of Joseph of Arimathea. Meeting his sister, he learnt of the disappearance of the Grail. The Lord of the Moors had taken Camelot from his mother. In delivering that castle from Islam, Perceval showed himself more a pagan Celtic knight than a crusader. His killing of the Muslim chief and his warriors was a scene of ritual slaughter, even worse than the beheading inflicted on the Templars by Saladin after his victory at the Horns of Hittīn, which would lead to the recapture of Jerusalem.

The cult of the sacred head was even more sanguinary in the eponymous Welsh romance *Peredur*. Witnessing a horrific Grail procession, Peredur saw two youths carrying 'a spear of huge size, and three streams of blood running along it from the socket to the floor'. All present were crying out in grief. And then 'two maidens came in holding a great platter between them, with a man's head on the platter bathed in blood'. This version of the Grail procession was a Celtic blood ritual, commemorating the sacred head of Bran, as well as alluding to the gory death of St John the Baptist. At the same time, in a startling confusion between pagan and Christian beliefs, the spear symbolized the Holy Lance of Longinus at the foot of the Cross and the platter represented the Holy Vessel of the Last Supper.

The great epic of Charlemagne's counterattack on the Moors, *The Song of Roland*, was already being sung at the time of the First Crusade. It gave the best contemporary insight into the barbaric, cruel and proud temperament of the Frankish knight. Recalling a defeat of the Holy Roman Emperor in his campaign against the Ummayads in Spain, the destruction of his rearguard

in a Basque ambush at Roncesvalles was translated int
slaughter of the Muslim hordes and the sacrifice of a
martyr through betrayal. This legendary epic was shot
with the silk and blood of the period. It was a declara ᴐn of
a holy war against Islam, in which a smatter of chivalry was
restricted to the knights on both sides while there was no mercy
for the rest of humanity.

The Song of Roland presaged the disaster which would befall
the later Christian Kingdom of Jerusalem, which was born in the
confused ideal of a crusade, and condemned by the pride and
treachery of the actual rulers of the expeditionary force that was
to occupy Palestine. In the romance, the Franks were the Chosen
People of God, and their enemies were doomed to hell or the
sword unless they accepted conversion. When Charlemagne
seized Córdoba and razed its walls, the poet took it as a matter
of course that 'all infidels in the city had been slain / Or else
converted to the Christian faith.' The Holy Roman Emperor
himself held court in the great garden or paradise there, created
by the Moorish King, 'the foe of God, who served Muhammad
and to Apollyon prayed'.

The massacre of the unbelievers who resisted a forced conversion to Christianity was advocated as a habitual strategy in
the counterattack of Europe on Islam. To die in such a holy war
would be to enter the heavenly gates with warrior angels as a
guide. When Count Roland prayed with his dying words for
the remission of his sins, he offered up to God the mailed glove
on his right fist, and St Gabriel took it from his hand. And so he
died:

> To him God sent angels and Cherubim
> Along with Saint Michael of the Peril;
> And with them came down Saint Gabriel
> To carry the Count's soul up to paradise.

As these inspirational texts showed, massacre and terror were
acceptable at every level in these early sacred wars. Death by

mutilation was expected, if a knight were seized and could not pay a ransom. The price of defeat was literally his head. In the medieval Islamic sharia law, still practised by the Taliban and the Saudis, maiming was the penalty for theft or adultery. The loss of a hand or a foot was the retribution for some acts, which were said to be sins.

3. THE HORROR OF THE CRUSADES

The original armed bands which set off on the First Crusade of 1096 began their barbarities in Europe. The rabble led by Peter the Hermit committed atrocities in Hungary on the way to Constantinople, where the Emperor Alexius Commenus shipped them over the Bosphorus to be massacred by the Turks in Asia Minor. Other German crusaders in three parties, led by Peter's disciple Gottschalk and the obscure Volkmar and Emich, decided to attack and plunder the Jews in their homeland before setting off for the East. These early pogroms appeared an easy way of financing the journey as well as avenging the blood of Christ. The Bishops of Speyer and Worms, and the Archbishop of Mainz, tried to protect the Jewish communities, but dozens of ghettos were attacked. Volkmar had all the Jews he could find in Prague massacred. All three German bands of fanatics and bigots were in turn destroyed by the Christian King of Hungary and his forces, who could not tolerate such an armed rabble within their territory. To their journey to Jerusalem, the First Crusade added a popular wave of anti-Semitism and the persecution of the first builders of the Holy City.

During the siege of Antioch, the expelled Christian citizens were suspected by the crusaders of collaboration with the occupying Muslim forces, and condemned to a double penalty. They had to join the ranks of the extraordinary Tafurs, a group of poor marauders led by a penniless knight, who terrorized the surrounding Muslim communities and were accused of every atrocity, including cannibalism. At Ma'arra, even the Frankish chronicler Albert of Aix agreed with the Arab horror stories, writing: 'Not only did our troops not shrink from eating dead Turks and Saracens; they also ate dogs.'

At the siege of Jerusalem, the Sudanese and Egyptian garrison desecrated crosses and shouted obscenities at the Christians out- side. So when the enraged crusaders broke through the walls, only the garrison in the Tower of David was spared. Such wise mercy was the prelude to an orgy of destruction which shamed Christendom and led to jihad against the crusaders. There was a slaughter of the Muslims who had taken refuge in the al-Aqsa mosque, 'more than seventy thousand of them', according to the Islamic historian Ibn al-Qalanisi, although he exaggerated the numbers of the victims. And all the Jews who crowded into their synagogue were burned alive inside. Mistaking the al-Aqsa mosque for the Temple of Solomon, Raymond of Aguilers wrote a notorious account of what he had observed:

> Wonderful sights were to be seen. Some of our men – and this was more merciful – cut off the heads of their enemies; others shot them with arrows, so that they fell from the towers; others tortured them longer by casting them into the flames. Piles of heads, hands and feet were to be seen in the streets of the city. It was necessary to pick one's way over the bodies of men and horses. But these were small matters compared to what happened at the Temple of Solomon, a place where religious services are normally chanted. What happened there? If I tell the truth it will exceed your powers of belief. So let it be enough to say this much, at least, that in the Temple and porch of Solomon, men rode in blood up to their knees and bridle reins. Indeed it was a just and splendid judgement of God that this place should be filled with the blood of the unbelievers since it had suffered so long from their blasphemies.

Another historian of the crusade, William of Tyre, did show disquiet, writing that 'the city offered such a spectacle of the massacre of enemies, such a deluge of bloodshed, that the victors themselves could not help but be struck with horror and disgust.' Certainly, the crusaders tried to kill all the Muslims and Jews in the Holy City, although enough of them did escape to found a suburb in Damascus. And in this religious cleansing of Jerusalem, the crusaders did not feel too much horror and disgust, but mainly thankfulness. Albert of Aix spoke of the joy of the victors at their success, which they saw as the triumph of God. The Holy City would be exclusively Christian. Those of other faiths were eliminated and would be excluded.

Such massacres by the crusaders made them infamous to Islam throughout history. Yet the savage and looting knights could also shock their fellow Christians. When the Fourth Crusade sacked Constantinople in 1204, the Franks and the Venetians pillaged the greatest city in Europe. Libraries were plundered, the Church of the Holy Apostles and the imperial tombs and Sancta Sophia were robbed, nuns were violated, and the sacred relics were stolen. 'Since the world was created,' the historian Villehardouin noted with his usual hyperbole, 'never had so much booty been taken in any city!' The Byzantine Niketas Choniates contrasted the good behaviour of the Muslims under Saladin at the recapture of Jerusalem in 1187 with the savagery of these 'forerunners of the Anti-Christ' at the ruin of Constantinople seventeen years later.

The crusades were becoming a form of Christian self-destruction. The precedent for sending expeditions to fight the heretics or the pagans or the infidels outside Palestine was to prove fatal to the concept of a Christian holy war. In Provence and the Languedoc, where so many of the troubadours of the Grail romances had chanted their bloodthirsty knightly sagas, a Gnostic secret sect of the *cathari*, or pure ones, had won a mass following by preaching the ancient heresy of the direct approach of the believer to God through Cathar priests, called *perfecti*. There was no need to pray within a corrupt state or Church. A return was needed to the early rebel days of Christianity.

e heresy of the Languedoc had caused concern in Rome for
y years; but the provocation of open war lay in the assassi-
tion in 1208 of the papal legate by a servant of the comte de
Toulouse. Pope Innocent III declared the murdered man to be a
holy martyr. A crusade was declared against people the Holy See
called heretics, 'worse even than the Saracens'. Just as the split
between the Sunnis and the Shi'ites had bedevilled Muslim unity,
so now the division between the Church of Rome and its reformers, inspired by puritan beliefs from the Near East, threatened the
cohesion of Christendom.

The first city to be invested on this crusade, Béziers, fell
immediately. The butchery was as savage as at the capture of
Jerusalem. Hardly a citizen escaped; the buildings were looted
and burned. In a notorious remark, Abbot Arnald Almaric
answered the question of distinguishing good Catholics from
heretics with the words, 'Kill them all: God will look after His
own.' He boasted after the massacre that 20,000 people had been
slain by the sword, regardless of age or sex. This outrage was
both an excessive reaction to Church propaganda that damned
the people of the Languedoc as children of Satan and a deliberate
policy of terror. As William de Tudela wrote, the leaders of the
crusade agreed that any place which refused to surrender should
have all its defenders killed, 'thinking that afterwards no man
would dare to stand out against them because of widespread fear
when it was seen what they had already done.'

In recognition of his ruthlessness as well as his martial quali-
ties, the crusader Simon de Montfort was charged by Rome with
extirpating all heresy in the south of France, and he followed
this charge with grim persistence. To some Catholics, he seemed
like the flail of the Almighty, a second Judas Maccabaeus; to
the Cathars and the Church reformers he appeared proof that the
Devil did rule the earth. He continued a policy of terror, blinding
and cutting off the noses of the defenders of Bram and sending
them under the guidance of a one-eyed man to deter the occupiers
of a neighbouring castle. And he was in charge of three mass

burnings of the *perfecti*, who gladly suffered the stake and the flame in their martyrdom. They would rather char than recant.

This was the beginning of the Inquisition, which became the holy terror of the Catholic Church. The new order of the Dominicans were the judges of the penalties inflicted on the heretics. Even the bones of previous Cathars were condemned, exhumed and burned. Systematic persecution drove the rebels underground, but they maintained their organization in the forests and the mountains (see plate 4). And at the castle of Montségur, they had their headquarters on an inaccessible rock outcrop with colonies of adherents living in the caves and village below.

The Dominicans referred to the citadel as the Synagogue of Satan, the very term used by the Cathars to describe the Church of Rome. Then a band of knights from Montségur assassinated seven monks who were serving as Inquisitors. This was a declaration of open war on Rome. After a long siege of nine months, Montségur capitulated and its obdurate Cathar defenders were burned alive and became the stuff of legend.

Most of the Cathar knights who escaped the slaughter at Montségur were received into the military order of the Knights Templars, which was already permeated with puritan and Oriental influences. Although Catharism was officially persecuted from existence in the Languedoc, its spirit remained to burst out again in the religious civil wars of the sixteenth century. The apparent victory of Rome did not extinguish the embers of the revolt against it.

The memory of a misdirected holy war is a sour heritage. The bitter grapes sown in the name of a particular Church set the children's teeth on edge for generation after generation. As the massacre at Jerusalem still lodges in Muslim minds, so that of Béziers still irritates the Languedoc. The wound of an unjustified faith which is suppressed never heals. As a Cathar poet wrote ironically about the crusade of Simon de Montfort, who was himself dispatched by a stone on his head that fell from the walls of Toulouse:

> If, to kill men and splatter their blood,
> To lose their souls and connive in murder,
> To believe in perverse advice, to light up burnings,
> To destroy the barons and dishonour their rank,
> To seize lands and support Arrogance,
> To swell evil and suppress the good,
> To massacre women and kill their children,
> Or if, for all that, a man may,
> In this world, so conquer Jesus Christ,
> Then that one has the right to the crown
> And to shine in glory in the sky.

In 1252, the papal bull *Ad Extirpanda* encouraged the torture of heretics by the Inquisition, which was developing as the Knights Templars were into a self-perpetuating secret society. Inquisitors were allowed to absolve each other of acts of violence committed against the accused. They were appointed for life and could condemn the least critic to the stake. The Catholic notables of southern Europe paid gangs of enforcers to quell any deviance or hint of peasant revolt, and to deliver the victims into the hands of the invulnerable Inquisition, now the most fearful instrument of the Christian sacred wars to come.

Nothing much has changed in condemning deviants and nonconformists. Medieval communities and the Inquisition and the Puritans at Salem accused the unorthodox of witchcraft. Surely, there were some herbal healers or deluded Satanists, who believed that they could cast spells. Yet usually those burned at the stake were nearer to Joan of Arc than Beelzebub. If witchcraft has largely died away outside Africa, the modern state merely persecutes its outsiders by psychiatric torture. The mental hospital still serves as the punishment for protesters in Russia. Mind-altering drugs and electric-shock treatment were the new correctives of the tyrannies of the second millennium.

4. THE OLD MAN OF THE MOUNTAINS

Marco Polo travelled through northern Persia or Iran near the Caspian Sea on his way to China, and brought back to Europe the legend of the training of a primary cadre of political killers. He wrote that there was a fortified valley between two mountains, where the Sheikh or Old Man of the Mountains had planted a beautiful garden in which grew every fruit in the world (see plate 31). The garden was watered with streams of wine, milk and honey. As in the Prophet Muhammad's paradise, on which it was modelled, it held gilded palaces, houris, dancers, musicians and singers. And it was seen only by those who were to be converted into Assassins.

Young men who had been trained in combat at the Old Man's court were drugged, taken to the hidden garden, and initiated into its delights. They lived there in luxury for a few days, convinced that their leader had transported them back to paradise. When they were suddenly doped again and taken back to his court, they were eager to risk their lives for him in order to return. 'Away they went,' concluded Polo, 'and did all they were commanded. Thus it happened that no man ever escaped when the Sheikh of the Mountain desired his death.' The Assassin leader was Hassan Ibn al-Sabbah, a poet and a scientist, who moulded in the thirteenth century a Shi'ite and Ismaili sect of Hashshīshīn. To impress other warlords, he would order his acolytes to stab themselves or to leap to their deaths from the castle walls on his orders. They always obeyed. Their instant sacrifice scared all opponents.

As we learn from the followers of modern Islamic terrorism, the same divine rewards are promised to all fanatical killers. The toppling of the World Trade Center was a ticket to paradise. Self-immolation is salvation. Equally, long ago, at his castle and gardens at Alamut, Hassan indoctrinated young men to go out and murder his enemies, usually at the cost of their own lives. From these suicide squads derived the word 'fedayeen', still used of Palestinian guerrillas.

The heretic Assassins found the Christian military order of the Knights Templars were willing allies in the destruction of the Sunni rulers of Syria and other Arab states, as well as converts to some of the secrets of their organization. As the permanent standing army of the Kingdom of Jerusalem, a few hundred Templar Knights held the Holy City and a broken necklace of castles across Palestine. Any combination of the Muslim leaders against them would have been their end. So they were particularly influenced by the subversive sect of the Assassins, immune in their mountain strongholds. Diplomacy and ruthlessness made up for lack of manpower. Whatever the differences of doctrine, the enemy of enemies was a friend.

The Ismaili sect held that Muslim law and scriptures contained an inner meaning which was known only to the imams. They taught that there were seven prophets: Adam, Noah, Abraham, Moses, Jesus, Muhammad and the Imam Ismail. In the order of creation, the prophets stood at the level of Universal Reason, second only to God. Last in the sevenfold chain of creation stood man. Though God Himself was unknowable, a man could work through these grades as far as Universal Reason, and a new aspect of the teaching would be revealed to him at each level.

Because such views were heretical, every Ismaili initiate was required to conceal his beliefs in accordance with the Shia demand of secrecy and to conform, outwardly, to the state religion. Central to Ismaili writings was the quest of an obsessed wanderer like Perceval in search of the Holy Grail. The initiate sought truth through trial and suffering until he was at last accepted into the faith by an imam, who revealed to him the true meaning of Muslim law and scriptures.

Such a quest was described by Hassan Ibn al-Sabbah. In his memoirs, he told of how he pursued spiritual strength by means of political power and transformed the role of the Ismaili believer by turning him into a murderer for the faith. At the same time, he modified the grades of initiation. The only descriptions of these mysteries were written by later European scholars, who saw the Ismaili hierarchy itself as mere brainwashing. According to their accounts, the teaching given at each level negated anything that had been taught before. The innermost secret of the Assassins was that Heaven and Hell were the same, all actions were indifferent, and there was no good or evil except the virtue of obeying the master of the sect.

Little is known of the Assassins' secrets, because their books of doctrine and ritual were burned in 1256 when Hulagu and the Mongols sacked their surrendered fortress at Alamut among the Persian peaks, after immolating the 700,000 citizens of Baghdad (see plates 31 and 32). Hassan emphasized the Shia doctrine of obedience and made changes in the Ismaili hierarchy. Tradition had it that below Hassan, who was the chief *da'i* or Grand Master, came the senior *da'is*, the ordinary *da'is*, the *rafiqs* or companions, the *lasiqs* or laymen, and the *fidais* or devotees who committed the murders. The division of the Templars under their Grand Master into grand priors, priors, knights, esquires and lay brothers followed this order closely, as do the modern cells of terrorism.

In his asceticism and singleness of purpose, Hassan was an ideal revolutionary leader and conspirator. He is said to have remained continuously within his home in his fortress for more than thirty years, going out only twice and appearing twice more on his roof. His invisibility increased his power. From his seclusion, he strengthened the defences of Alamut, purged the ranks of his followers, putting to death two of his own sons, and he continued with his strategy of seizing hill positions as centres of local subversion.

Hassan elevated his authority to absolute command. The will of the Old Man of the Mountains was the unspoken will of his Shi'ite caliph and thus the will of God. By winning over garrisons and assassinating local governors, he occupied strongpoints and terrorized the Sunni believers – Persian and Turk alike. The conspiracy of the determined few, as usual, met little resistance from the fearful many. On the model of Muhammad himself, who had fled to Medina to rally support and reconquer Mecca and all Arabia, Hassan hoped to take over the caliphate of Baghdad.

By the authority of his rank and by the use of drugs, Hassan trained *fidais* in such blind obedience that, like the Japanese suicide pilots of the Second World War, they welcomed death during an attempt at assassination. They preferred the dagger as a weapon, and the court or the mosque as a place of execution. They scorned the use of poison and backstairs intrigue, for their code was that of soldiers rather than of harem murderers. Legend tells of one *fidai*'s mother who rejoiced when she heard that her son had died in an attempt on a ruler's life, then put on mourning when he returned alive.

Rather like the later Mafia, the Assassins operated from their strongholds a drug trade and a protection racket under threat of death. Their techniques helped to undermine the Arab states and to fragment the Islamic world even further. Suspicion ran riot, and murder was a normal method of princely government. Thus the crusaders, coming to the Holy Land, found only a divided enemy, disorganized by the Assassins. Hassan may not have intended to aid the Christian invaders; but he did help the crusaders to entrench themselves in the Levant.

The founder of the Templars, Hugues de Payens, knew of the Assassins when he formed his organization, and the Christian and Muslim military orders were aware of each other in Syria before 1128 when the Templar Rule was written. Even the colours worn by the knights, a red cross on a white ground, were the same as those of the Assassin *rafiqs*, who wore red caps and belts and white tunics. Some claimed that the Templars adopted the Assassin 'hues of innocence and blood, and of pure devotion and murder', only because the rival Knights Hospitallers wore black. However that might be, the function of the Templars was virtually the same as that of the Assassins – to serve as an independent power on the side of their religious faith.

When the Assassins murdered the Count of Tripoli, the Templars forced the Syrian branch to pay them a yearly tribute. And when the Shi'ite caliphate of the Fatimids finally fell in Egypt in 1169, the Assassins in Syria were in such despair that they offered to convert to Christianity. The Templars, however, were reluctant to lose their income and they had the Assassin envoys killed as they returned from their interview with the King of Jerusalem – an action which spelt the end of cooperation between the two warrior orders of Christianity and Islam.

Three years earlier, the Andalusian traveller Ibn Jubayr had noted the complete understanding and respect that Christians and Muslims had for each other's rights and commerce in Palestine. Yet this was doomed, for the great Kurdish general Saladin had succeeded in uniting the divided Muslim states in jihad against the infidels after the Franks had raided the trade routes in the Red Sea and the pilgrim caravans to Mecca. In 1187, he sent a reconnaissance force of 7,000 cavalry under safe conduct, but they were attacked by the Templar and Hospitaller Knights, who were decimated. The survivors berated the King of Jerusalem for dealing with the Muslims, as they had done themselves for ninety years. They persuaded him to march out and fight Saladin's united army.

At the Horns of Hittīn, the Christian army was trapped without water and cut to pieces. For once, Saladin gave up his usual policy of mercy to punish infidel perfidy. All his prisoners from the military orders of knights were beheaded by their Muslim equivalents, the Sufis. Yet in contrast to the Christians' massacre of the citizens of Jerusalem during the First Crusade, Saladin spared the sacred place. The leader of the resistance,

Balian of Ibelin, threatened to destroy the holy city, including the Dome of the Rock, unless the defenders were ransomed, and Saladin accepted the terms. He even put guards in the Christian places of worship and refused to raze the Church of the Holy Sepulchre in retaliation for the brutality of the Christians, when they had taken Jerusalem. The Templar headquarters, the al-Aqsa mosque, became an Islamic shrine again after its walls were sprinkled with rose-water.

The Muslims had already fought the Christians for control of the Mediterranean for more than five hundred years. They would continue fighting until the next millennium and longer. The question was, what would be the means? So far, the terror of waging war included slaughter, rape, torture, fire, starvation, slavery and imprisonment. Yet these were open threats to human existence. Would the next eight hundred years assume the hidden daggers of the Assassins? Would the future murderers of the peace use covert methods – indoctrination, infiltration, drugs and stealth?

The Knights Templars were the most dangerous and successful sacred secret society in Western Europe. Their methods of organization were passed on to generations of later revolutionaries. Yet they had become too clandestine and powerful for their own survival. After the loss of Jerusalem, they were driven from their remaining fortresses. Caught between the fearsome Mongols and the Turks and the Egyptians under Sultan Baybars, they lost stronghold after stronghold. No more effective help came from Europe, which used its knights increasingly in its own quarrels; the Kingdom of Jerusalem was written off after the failure of so many crusades. The Pope himself wanted to bring back crusaders from the Levant to help him against the Holy Roman Emperor. The troubadour Oliver the Templar despaired: 'Crazed is the man who wants to fight the Turks, since Jesus Christ is no longer fighting them. They have conquered – they will conquer, that lies heavy on me – Franks and Tartars, Armenians and Persians. They know that every day they will humiliate us, for God sleeps.'

In 1291, Tripoli fell and Acre was assaulted by the Egyptian armies. After a desperate siege, which united at last the rival Frankish warlords and the military orders, the Mameluks forced the walls of the port by the Accursed Tower. This last Templar stronghold was mined, and the city razed to the ground. The population was slaughtered or sold into slavery; the price of a girl in the Damascus slave-market fell to one drachma. The Templars had lost their function as the police of the routes of the Holy Land, for there was no Holy Land left to police. Not until 1917 would another Christian army enter Jerusalem, and then the tombs of the Templars in London would be crowned with laurel.

Their wealth, arrogance and secrecy made the Knights Templars a marked order. With the rise of the new nation states, the European monarchs would not tolerate an army within the army and a state within the state, especially as the order now served more as an international bank than a defender of pilgrims. By the thirteenth century, the Templars had 15,000 lances and 9,000 manors across Europe, all of which were free of taxes and provided security for the storage and transport of bullion. Although in the Middle Ages usury was forbidden by the Church, the Templars added to the money they held or transported by paying back an agreed sum less than the original amount, while a debtor returned more than his debt. The Paris Temple became the centre of the world's money market.

The European kings were always short of funds. They regularly turned on their bankers, Italians and Jews; they defaulted on their loans and expelled their creditors. The Templars were particularly vulnerable to such treatment. They had lost the Holy Land, their pride was almost royal, while their secrecy provoked slander. To these sins, the Templars added hidden rituals and Oriental diplomacy, which increased the envy and hatred of princes and people. They were seen both as the poor knights of Christendom and as rich conspirators against the state and public welfare. When King Philip of France imprisoned more than 600 of the 3,000 Templars in the country in 1307, according to Inquisition records, their interrogation and torture produced confessions that corroborated medieval superstitions, but were the result of applying force and pain. They were not the evidence of truth.

Few Templars were strong enough to hold out against the racks and screws and whips of Philip's torturers. Following the example of their Grand Master Jacques de Molay, most of the knights confessed to what the examiners wished them to confess. Yes, the Templars were homosexuals, forced to kiss the mouth, navel, and anus of their initiator. Yes, novices were made to spit on the Cross. Yes, the knights had worshipped the devil Baphomet, which was a jewelled skull or a wooden phallus. They also worshipped the devil in the form of a cat, in the presence of young virgins and female devils. Thirty-six of the Paris Templars died under torture within a few days of their arrest, and the remainder were only admitting to a hotchpotch of the diabolical and sexual fantasies of their age. Above all, the Templars were made the scapegoat for the loss of the Holy Land. They were accused of selling to the Muslims what they had fought to hold.

Jacques de Molay ended by retracting his admissions and denying all the evil he had spoken of his order. In 1314, when he was brought out onto a scaffold in front of Notre Dame to receive his sentence, he declared: 'I confess that I am indeed guilty of the greatest infamy. But the infamy is that I have lied. I have lied in admitting the disgusting charges laid against my Order. I declare, and I must declare, that the Order is innocent. Its purity and saintliness have never been defiled. In truth, I had testified otherwise, but I did so from fear of horrible tortures.' He was burned alive the following day (see plate 30).

So ended the legitimate Templars, the victims of the greed of kings and of their own pride and wealth. The Assassins, curiously enough, survive to this day in India as part of the Ismaili sect whose spiritual head is the Aga Khan. But the Templars have gone the way of all secret societies whose power seems to constitute a threat to the state. As a contemporary poet asked:

> The brethren, the Masters of the Temple,
> Who were well stocked and ample
> With gold and silver and riches,
> Where are they? How have they done?
> They had such power once that none
> Dared take from them, none was so bold;
> Forever they bought and never sold . . .

Until they were sold to satisfy the greed of kings, in whom the state was sovereign and indivisible.

Yet some knights of the military order escaped to pass on their practices under other cloaks. Although King Philip's seizure and destruction of Jacques de Molay and the French Templars was as efficient an operation as Hitler's purge of Röhm and his Brownshirts, there is no record of his finding the Templar treasure in Paris or its secret archives or its fleet, which was based mainly at La Rochelle. Much evidence and some tradition points to the removal of the treasure and most of the archives by ship, with refugee Templars taking them to Portugal and to the west and east coasts of Scotland, where they were welcomed. Acting on warnings, de Molay had already had many records recalled and burned. One of the confessions extorted from the French knights and recorded by the Inquisition was the testimony of John de Châlons of Poitiers. According to his statement, Gerard de Villiers, the Preceptor of the Order, knew in advance of the mass arrests and fled the Temple in Paris with fifty knights, whom he commanded to put to sea in eighteen Templar galleys.

In other European countries, the Templars merged with the Knights Hospitallers or left their order and went underground. In Germany, where the Teutonic Knights were carving out an empire to the east, the Templars joined their ranks and accepted a slightly different ritual. Most of the sea-borne French refugee Templars reached Scotland. According to one French Masonic tradition, the records and wealth were taken on nine vessels to the Isle of Mey in the Firth of Forth. Others held that these vessels went to Ireland and then to Mull and the Western Isles of Scotland. When the authorities burst into the Irish Templar presbyteries, they found them stripped of ornaments, while Robert the Bruce was receiving new supplies of weapons before the Battle of Bannockburn – to the cost and complaint of King Edward II of England.

Robert the Bruce, of Norman and Scottish royal ancestry, had been excommunicated for the murder of John Comyn, who had defeated three English armies in one day, but had later recognized the sovereignty of England and the Church of Rome. After this apostasy, the Scottish patriot and guerrilla leader, William Wallace, had been captured and horribly executed by the English. Now Bruce was making his stand against King Edward II and his army at Bannockburn, three months after Jacques de Molay was burned at the stake.

The battle took place near Stirling Castle on St John's Day in June 1314, a significant date for the military orders which venerated the Baptist. Bruce's army was outnumbered by at least three to one, 6,000 men pitted against 20,000. His deficiency lay in mounted knights. There were some 3,000 in the English army, while the Scots could muster only 500 poorly armed cavalrymen. Accounts of the conflict are sparse and fragmentary, yet they testify to two strange events. Following a charge by mounted soldiers against the English archers from a reserve kept back by Bruce, a fresh force of horsemen appeared with banners flying once all the troops were engaged, and routed the enemy. This new squadron struck terror in the English, who recognized the force of their foe and probably their chequered war banner, *Beauséant*.

Wishing eventually to make his peace with the Church so that a crusade could not be declared against Scotland as it had been against the heretic Cathars of the Languedoc, Robert the Bruce required the Templars to become a secret organization, which was to give rise to the Ancient Scottish Rite of Masonry. According to an old tradition, Bruce established the Royal Order of Scotland to reward the courage of the Templars at Bannockburn. The Sovereign Grand Master was the King of Scotland, and the office remained a royal appointment, existing to this day in its secret power. Although the order was not combined with the Templars, many prominent members became members of the Royal Order, including its Grand Master in Scotland.

The Templars' contribution to the Ancient Scottish Rite of the later rebellious Freemasons was organization and ceremony. To this day, the Masons' hierarchy is modelled on Templar and Assassin precedents, as are the oaths of secrecy. The symbols of the skull and the noose, the twin pillars of the Temple, the Ark of the Covenant, the serpent on the Tau cross, and the black-and-white tessellated pavement that is a copy of *Beauséant*, all were transmitted to the Ancient Scottish Rite, as can still be seen on the fifteenth-century Kirkwall Scroll in Orkney, the surviving proof of the Templar connection.

Most significantly, the Cathar and Templar belief in a direct approach to divine wisdom in opposition to a corrupt and oppressive Church and state was bequeathed to the medieval crafts and guilds, which would later emerge as the Freemasons. In the Civil War in England, and in the American and French Revolutions, clandestine Lodges acted as military operations centres in the manner of the old Templar commanderies. And the original heresy of personal holy revelation inspired the bloodiest centuries of sacred terror in European history, the two hundred years after the coming of the Reformation and its persecutions.

5. THE ANABAPTISTS AND MILLENNIAL TERROR

During the Reformation and the revolt from Rome, the Anabaptists were the extremists in an age of the extreme. As millennial radicals, their heritage derived from the Manicheans and the Gnostics, but they took their practices beyond the tolerable in a most intolerant time. One of their first leaders, Felix Manz, was the bastard son of a Zurich preacher. He was a disciple of the important and early Swiss evangelist Ulrich Zwingli, whose teachings helped in the establishment of the Church of England. Manz preached that the baptism of an adult or child ensured their direct passage to the grace of God without the need for an intervening state and Church. As the radical *Chronicle of the Hutterite Brethren* declared of the Anabaptist ceremony: 'Therewith began the separation from the world and its evil works.'

By 1526, the preachers of the cult were practising mass baptisms in the rivers of Germany and Switzerland. Zwingli turned against them, accusing them of early Christian socialism. 'There should not be any magistrates,' he wrote of their teaching. 'All things should be held in common.' Felix Manz was led from a Zurich prison, bound on a hurdle and thrown into the Limmat River, where he drowned. His death, however, did not stop his message reaching a revolutionary organizer, Thomas Müntzer, in the growing German Peasants' Revolt. He had met the other inspired leader of the Reformation, Martin Luther, but they turned on one another with Luther branded as a hog and a master liar.

Müntzer was an early Babeuf and Bakhunin, founding a revolutionary group named the League of the Elect, directed against the dukes and princes who ruled Germany. Authority was his goal: the rural insurgents were his fodder. Soon Luther counterattacked. He had won what he wanted, the support of the local lords for the Reformation on his terms, so in 1525 he issued a pamphlet, *Against the Murderous and Thieving Mobs of Peasants*; he declared that nothing could be more poisonous or harmful or satanic than a rebel. As a mad dog with rabies must be killed, so the revolt had to be put down, or it would strike at everybody and the whole land.

Soon Müntzer was captured, tortured and beheaded. Yet just as early Christianity spread among the slaves of Rome, so Anabaptist doctrine was revealed to the deprived country people of northern Europe in a message of hope. From Poland to Holland there were minor uprisings and executions. While some Anabaptist preachers recommended the non-violence taught by Jesus Christ, others were centred on creating a new heaven on earth. In Haarlem, a baker named Jan Matthys married a beautiful nun, Divara, during the revolt of the Anabaptists against Rome. He brought to Münster in Westphalia a radical society aiming at changing the conditions all over Europe.

A charismatic personality in disturbed times, Matthys converted most of the 12,000 citizens there to his version of the Christian faith. An election led to an Anabaptist city council. The cathedral was sacked. Mass baptism took place every day. Those who refused their initiation ceremony to a direct God were driven out of the walls with iron pikes and wooden clubs. The local German bishop responded by a siege of the heretic city. Confusing himself with Christ, Jan Matthys gave a Last Supper, kissed his disciples and sallied out to die with twenty of them. He was hacked to pieces.

Another Dutch prophet took over in Münster. Jan Beukels was a Puritan and a hedonist. He condemned to death all those who were guilty of blasphemy and adultery, of fraud and any subversion of what he held to be true. He then married the lovely widow Divara and fourteen other young women. An insurrection within the walls led to the public beheading of fifty-eight of the conspirators. Beukels declared himself the reincarnation of King David of Israel and was crowned as the King of All the World. Faced with starvation, the terror in Münster became a series of executions for hoarding food or even for a wife who denied her husband in bed. The quarters of the victims were nailed on trees. The Elect ruled and their verdicts were justice. As a follower wrote: 'Revenge without mercy must be inflicted on all who are not marked with the Sign.'

The Sign was that only the 144,000 saints mentioned in the Book of Revelation would be redeemed, of all the population of the planet. The citizens and converts of Münster were not spared when the city fell; another slaughter of sacred terror took place. Nearly all the men and half the women and children were killed. When Beukels was asked why he had declared himself to be the King of Münster and All the World, he replied that he had been called by God and the prophets. A direct revelation was his justification, as it would be for so many messianic cult leaders after his example. He was bound with an iron collar to a stake, tortured with red-hot pincers, had his tongue torn out, and then stabbed to death. The cage in which his corpse was exhibited still hangs outside the rebuilt tower of the Church of St Lamberti, a patron saint of the revolutionary city.

For Luther, the elimination of the Anabaptists was a just war, as were the current pogroms against the Jews in Germany. Although it might be cruel to punish these heretics with fire and sword, it was more cruel that they condemned the ministry of the Word of God, and so undermined the social order. Paradoxically, the Dutch Anabaptists taught the doctrine of adult baptism to the Mennonites, who passed it on to the Baptists and the Quakers with their pacifist creeds. These sects believed in the ancient heresy of a good heaven and a corrupt earth, where all the same the faithful might live and let live with any bad government. They held themselves to be the messengers of God by direct contact through Jesus with the Lord. But unlike the Anabaptists, they chose non-violence as their method of resistance to tyranny.

The finest moment of these Nonconformist faiths came during the Napoleonic Wars, when pressure on Parliament put an end in 1807 to the lucrative British slave trade, and the supply of black Africans to the Caribbean sugar plantations. And so a radical and terrorist spiritual movement resulted in a vast emancipation. If this would not be heaven on earth, it would serve as progress.

6. SACRED TERROR AND THE FRENCH RELIGIOUS WARS

'Therefore it is necessary for a prince,' Niccolò dei Machiavelli wrote, 'who wishes to maintain himself, to learn how not to be good, and to use this knowledge and not use it, according to the necessity of the case.' The proper study of the prince was war in the interest of his government. In Machiavelli's opinion, the most admirable prince of Renaissance times in Italy was Cesare Borgia, the son of Pope Alexander VI, who then ruled the Ecclesiastical States around Rome. The succession of Cesare to power in the Romagna in 1501 was opposed by the powerful Orsini and Colonna parties. The heads of these families were invited by Cesare to a peace conference at Sinigaglia, where they were all strangled.

With his leading rivals eliminated, Cesare proceeded to a quick reign of terror in the disaffected Romagna. He appointed as his chief of police the ruthless Remirro de Orco, who reduced the population to fear and loathing and obedience. This agent of frightfulness was then cut in half and displayed in the public square at Cesena. The ferocity of the spectacle satisfied and amazed the people, who now thought Cesare might be a saviour against the horror he had unleashed.

As with Agathocles in Syracuse, Cesare Borgia committed his worst crimes on his rise to power. His trembling competitors and subjects now found themselves living in a religious state, backed by the Church as well as force, and promising security in this life and the next. If his father had not died, if a new pope, Julius II, had not been elected, and if illness had not laid him low, Cesare Borgia might have united all Italy. For Machiavelli, he was certainly the exemplar of the use of terror in seizing the state and maintaining his power after the coup. As Cesare told his biographer, he had never thought that at his father's death he would be dying himself.

So Machiavelli held up Cesare Borgia as the peerless model of those who wished to rule:

> Whoever thought it necessary in his new state to secure himself against enemies, to gain friends, to conquer by force or fraud, to make himself beloved and feared by the people, followed and reverenced by the soldiers, to destroy those who can and may injure him, introduce innovations into old customs, to be severe and kind, magnanimous and liberal, suppress the old militia, create a new one, maintain the friendship of kings and princes in such a way that they are glad to benefit him and fear to injure him, such a one can find no better example than the actions of this man.

These principles of power were demonstrated in the French Wars of Religion. They began in 1562, when the Regent and Queen Mother Catherine de' Medici issued the Edict of St-Germain, which recognized within the Catholic state the rebellious Protestant Huguenots. The Parlement of Paris remonstrated, quoting the Gospel of Matthew: 'Every kingdom divided against itself is brought to desolation.' The Huguenots were branded as 'beggars from everywhere, mixed with criminals, thieves and trouble-makers, who live and plunder under the pretext of religion.'

The Catholic leader, the duc de Guise, provoked a civil war by massacring a Protestant congregation inside the town of Vassy. The Protestant leader, the prince de Condé, then called to arms the fearful and persecuted Huguenots. This breakdown of law and order in the name of religion was exploited by ambitious nobles and disaffected peasants. There were social scores to settle as well as religious ones. Several hundred Calvinist and Catholic peasants cut off the comte de Fumel's head and plundered his castle. The rural nobles seized the chance of gaining more power and ending taxes in the collapse of central authority.

Using the cell-and-chapel system of early Christianity, the prince de Condé raised a revolt in many of the cities and districts of France. Le Havre and Rouen, Orléans and Lyon, Poitiers and Bourges, and the old Cathar strongholds of Béziers and Montpellier in the Languedoc fell to internal coups by armed Huguenot bands. In Rouen, altars and fonts and holy relics were smashed in an orgy of desecration, which led to the flight of many of the Catholic citizens. Such was the early reign of terror advocated by Machiavelli, if power were to be grabbed.

Regular warfare by the Catholic generals favoured by Catherine de' Medici soon led to the recapture of Rouen, Poitiers, Bourges and other insurrectionary cities. After a year of fighting, Guise was dead and Condé a prisoner, and a truce was arranged at Amboise, leaving most of the old heretic lands of the Languedoc in Huguenot hands. This was the prelude for a series of horrific religious wars that lasted for seventy more years, until the devastation of the Thirty Years War in Germany put any Gallic atrocities in the shade. Although the later rural revolts of the Fronde against the Ancien Régime and the Vendée against the French Revolution produced many massacres and countless cruelties, in its baths of bigotry this conflict shed more blood.

Three inconclusive civil wars between the Catholics and the Huguenots were fought during the next ten years before the notorious Massacre of St Bartholomew's Day. This slaughter was Machiavellian in its plotting. Condé had died, and the leading Protestant was Admiral Gaspard de Coligny. On 22 August 1572 he was shot in the arm by a sniper in a Paris street after a meeting in the Louvre with the young King, whose mother, Catherine de' Medici, was the probable conspirator behind the assassination attempt. Two days later, Coligny was murdered in his bed by the heir of the duc de Guise, along with fifty other Huguenot nobles;

such was the tactic used by Cesare Borgia when he killed off the Orsinis and the Colonnas at Sinigaglia.

These executions led to an explosion of violence by the Catholic mob within the city. Vengeance was inflicted on 2,000 and more of the heretics in the name of God's will. Fear and envy were translated into a duty to butcher horribly. Coligny's corpse had its head and hands and genitals cut off. Women were impaled on spits as Boudicca had done to the Romans in London. Severed limbs littered the streets, gutters ran with gore, and drowned bodies stained the Seine. The victims were degraded and treated as beasts. Their houses were looted, then purified by fire.

The rioters continued their orgy of violence for three days and nights. The crown seemed to approve, while there was no condemnation from the pulpits or the priests. This ethnic cleansing spread to a dozen provincial cities, including Lyon and Rouen, Bourges and Orléans, which had suffered Huguenot coups in the past against a frightened Catholic majority. With their leadership dead, many of the surviving Huguenots recanted and rejoined the Catholic faith, while others became refugees in their citadel of La Rochelle, or else fled abroad to Geneva and London.

In the succeeding decades, assassination and terror tactics became the sinews of war. King Henri III had the duc de Guise murdered, and then was struck down himself by Jacques Clément, a fanatical Jacobin monk. When Henri de Navarre besieged Paris in 1590, the first of many radical committees which would control the capital, the Sixteen, came to power by a purge of their enemies, until they themselves were hanged when aristocratic forces under the duc de Mayenne relieved the city. That phase of the religious wars was only ended with the astute conversion to Catholicism of Henri de Navarre, as King Henri IV. He even appeased peasant revolts in Périgord by easing taxes and saying that if he had not been born to be king, he would have joined the rural rising himself.

By the Edict of Nantes of 1598, a measure of religious toleration was established, even if the Huguenots were only allowed to practise their faith in certain areas under their control. Although there was a final religious conflict in the twenty years after 1610, the wisdom of Henri IV had put an end to the worst of the massacres. He had restored royal authority over the provinces and the ambitious princes. His policies were continued by the great centralizer, Cardinal Richelieu, who bolstered the King's command by finally ending the last vestiges of the independence of the Huguenots, who were seen as subversives as well as heretics. As Richelieu advised his master, King Louis XIII:

> It is certain that as long as the Huguenot party exists in France, the King will not be absolute in his kingdom, and he will not be able to establish the order and rule, which is the duty of his conscience and the necessity of his people. It is also necessary to destroy the pride of the great nobles.

Machiavelli could not have expressed this obligatory strategy more clearly. And any means must be used to secure the state, through blood and fire and poison, if necessary.

7. BEAST AND PEST:
THE ORIGINS OF BIOTERROR

When we were wild in caves and woods, we feared the beast and the pest. The bear and the tiger and the wolf were the terror of primitive societies. There was no immunity to the epidemics that degraded or wiped out many early civilizations. The Asiatic rat carrying the bubonic flea decimated the population of Europe time and again. The virus was always deadlier than the sword or the spear.

Plagues killed more than armies. Marauding ships and troops on the march carried pestilence with them. The typhus louse was the lethal weapon of crews of pirates and squadrons of soldiers. Smallpox aided Cortés and Pizarro in conquering the Aztec and the Inca empires. That contamination laid low superior forces far more brutally than terror tactics on the field. Disease was the ally of victory by other means. As Leviticus had declared in a message from the Lord God: 'I will even appoint over you terror, consumption, and the burning ague, that shall consume the eyes, and cause sorrow of heart: and ye shall sow your seed in vain, for your enemies shall eat it.'

The plagues which afflicted ancient Egypt and allowed the departure of the tribes of Israel related in Exodus suggest bioterror. The Lord God commanded the High Priest Aaron to take his rod and smite the waters. These were turned into blood, the fish died, the river stank with pollutants. Then plagues of frogs and lice appeared, carrying more disease from Aaron's rod striking the dust. These were followed by swarms of flies, which corrupted the land. Cattle disease now laid low the herds of Egypt, while the beasts of the Jews were immune. Then a bubonic plague of boils broke out, followed by fire and hail from heaven, and then plagues of locusts and a long eclipse and the death of the firstborn in Egypt. With these serial disasters, the Pharaoh let Moses lead his people over the Red Sea towards their Promised Land. The Egyptian ruler pursued them to his own destruction, seeing in these horrors the work of man as well as the hand of God.

However true these biological weapons described in Exodus, certainly the spread of disease in the hordes of Xerxes allowed the survival of Greek civilization by battle and dysentery. In 428 BC, during the siege of Plataea, the Spartans produced poison gas by burning wood infused with pitch and sulphur under the walls of the city. The later development of the original napalm by the Hellenic fleets under the name of 'Greek fire' was also the first use of flaming projectiles in naval warfare. Plagues devastated the armies of Carthage before Syracuse and led to the eventual Roman victory against the Punic city, when every building was destroyed and salt ploughed into the ruins. Then Rome itself was consumed more by bacteria than barbarian invaders. As Gibbon wrote of the imperial fall, 'Pestilence and famine contributed to fill up the measure of the calamities of Rome.'

The question was, who caused the epidemics? Were they the result of human agents or divine justice? Judaism preached that plagues were the vengeance of Jehovah for transgressions on earth. The early Christians also believed that these infections were a heavenly retribution for their sins. And the Muslims were fatalistic about disease; their date of death was ordained by Allah.

In legend, smallpox saved Mecca from the Christians in AD 569 in the 'Elephant War'. Then the Abyssinian general Abraha and his army of 60,000 men had been afflicted by a flock of birds, dropping the stones of contagion on the retreating invasion force. So the Prophet Muhammad became the ruler of Mecca and could pursue his holy wars. Yet not so horribly as the Christians in the First Crusade. They indicted the Jews in Europe of what the Pharaoh had believed of Aaron. They were accused of spreading the plague by poisoning the wells. In Mayenne alone, more than 12,000 Jews were burned alive, for their property as much as their heresy.

Bioterror brought the Black Death to Europe. In 1346, the Genoese occupied the fortress of Kaffa in the Crimea to profit from the silk and fur trade as far as China. Besieged by the Tartars under Janibeg Khan, the Genoese watched their enemies struck down by the bubonic plague, caught by fleas from the Asiatic rat. The Khan was enraged. He had the black and swollen corpses of his men loaded into siege guns and blasted as missiles into the stronghold. 'Thus mountains of the dead were shot at us,' an Italian historian wrote. 'Nor could the Christians hide or flee or escape such a disaster . . . Soon all the air was infected and the water poisoned, corrupt and putrefied, and a great stench increased.'

The Genoese caught the plague and decided to abandon Kaffa on their galleys. They rowed to Constantinople, where they infected the Byzantines and the coast of the Mediterranean. The surviving Genoese sailed on to Sicily, and left the epidemic there before proceeding to their home port in northern Italy, from where the disease spread over the whole country. 'When was such a disaster ever seen or heard of?' Petrarch lamented. 'What records can we read to show houses deserted, cities abandoned, acres untilled, fields heaped with corpses, and a vast dreadful solitude over the whole world?' Only the rich could flee the Black Death, as did the Florentines from their stricken city in the *Decameron* by Boccaccio. Half the people of Western Europe perished.

As in the time of the First Crusade, the Jews were accused of spreading the epidemic, and 50,000 were massacred in Burgundy alone. In many German cities, they were burned alive in their synagogues: in Speyer, they were torn to pieces by an insane mob and their body parts were stuffed in barrels to float down the Rhine. They were allegedly infecting the wells, while, in fact, as the Jews were the leading apothecaries of the period, they were advising their neighbours not to touch contaminated water (see plates 5 and 6). They suffered for their reputation as Christ-killers and for their riches, as much as for their good advice.

The German people did not believe in any medical treatment for the plague. Current sayings declared that the epidemic had no fear of the doctor. Once it was in the house, it stayed there for a long time. 'The plague attacks first those who are most afraid' – a proverb which Camus would use to inform his modern master-piece on the subject. 'The plague lasted seven years, but nobody died before his time.' Yet still the best defence against the Black Death was flight, 'a pair of new boots worn until they have no soles.'

The priests saw the Black Death as divine retribution for the sins of the people. An answer was the mortification of the flesh, before the epidemic began its own mortification. The extraordi-nary pilgrimages of the Flagellants arose. They scourged them-selves with flails and cats-o'-three-tails. A French chronicler reported in 1349 that 80,000 of these masochists were on the march in Hainault and Brabant. This cult of repentance was their version of purgatory on earth. Forerunners of the Protestant rebels, they sang hymns and believed in direct divine inspiration without the need of the Catholic Church, which used the Inqui-sition to suppress this dangerous movement.

Ironically, the Flagellants carried the plague with them. When Strasbourg caught the disease, the Flagellants then accused the Jews of being the poisoners once more. Actually, the villains of the piece were the gravediggers, often recruited from criminal gangs and excluded from the cities as if they were lepers. They were infected, indeed, with avarice as well as sickness. Their victims were blackmailed and robbed and raped and even mur-dered, before being thrown on the corpse carts, dead or still barely alive.

Poison had always been the terror of rulers, the stealthy method of their removal, far cheaper than a revolt. The venom from the viper and the water-snake was used in Egypt to poison arrows. Cleopatra tried out the fangs of her asp on her slaves before using it on her breast. Often the heirs to a throne used toxins to hurry up their inheritance, so much so that Mithridates, the King of Pontus in the second century BC, became famous for dying old. His research on pharmacology derived from the influence of Greek medicine on Egyptian civilization. He studied antidotes to snakebite; again he experimented on slaves to discover the right dosage. His life-saving remedy was a mixture of sixty-three ingredients, including the flesh of vipers. In the Middle Ages, a variant called theriac was supposed to serve as a cure for poison attacks. This became treacle, a name later applied to molasses. Such an ineffective early antibiotic ended as a spring tonic, the sulphur and treacle mixture crammed down the throats of the Victorian young. How many rulers actually died from poisoning by the notorious Borgias or Catherine de' Medici, before the age of forensic science, will never be known.

At the time of the religious struggles between Protestants and Catholics after the Reformation, the true spreaders of infection were the many armies fighting in civil strife. During the Thirty Years War in Germany, half the population died in a horrific series of campaigns of torture and terror, yet these ravaged millions of Germans fell less to war bands living on loot and the land than to the lice the soldiers carried on their skins and uniforms. Wallenstein's troops spread typhus and dysentery across Pomerania and Saxony, Gustavus Adolphus and the Swedes took disease from Bavaria to Poland. Even for Brecht's Mother Courage with her travelling cart, bacteria were more deadly than the bayonet.

In the European conquest of the Americas, smallpox was among the engines of destruction. Where Columbus landed in the Caribbean islands, whole native populations were wiped out. Only one-tenth of the inhabitants of Mexico and Peru survived the import of transatlantic diseases. That did not mean that the usual tactics of terror in warfare were not used: in Alvarado's massacre of the sacred dancers in Tenochtitlán, now Mexico City, the Aztec chroniclers recorded the terrible slashing of the iron.

The Spaniards 'attacked the man who was drumming and cut off his arms. They then cut off his head, and it rolled across the floor.' They assaulted all the dancers, 'stabbing them, spearing them, striking them with their swords. They hacked some of them from behind and these fell instantly to the ground with their entrails hanging out.' Others were beheaded or had their skulls split into pieces. The Spaniards 'struck others in the shoulders, and their arms were torn from their bodies. They wounded some in the thigh and some in the calf.' More dancers had their stomachs cut open. 'Some attempted to run away, but their intestines dragged as they ran. They seemed to tangle their feet in their own entrails. No matter how they tried to save themselves, they could find no escape.'

The Spaniards in their turn had to watch the sacrifice of their fellows by the obsidian knives of the Aztecs (see plate 14). Once fifty-three Spanish prisoners and four of their horses were cut open by the Mexican priests, who removed their hearts and set their heads on pikes facing the sun, the horses' heads below the men's. An Aztec sacrificial pyramid seemed enough to confirm the righteousness of Christian conquest. Gómara, who was later Cortés' secretary and biographer, claimed that the skulls of 136,000 sacrificial victims were exposed near the great pyramid of Tenochtitlán. The door of that temple was carved 'in the form of a serpent's mouth, diabolically painted, with fangs and teeth exposed, which frightened those who entered, especially the Christians.' Every chapel inside the temple was crusted with blood and stank with human sacrifice.

Although iron vanquished the stone empires of Mexico and Peru, the use of the animals of Europe, the horse and the dog, induced the most horror in the American Indians. When Ponce de León was putting down a revolt in Puerto Rico, he had a fierce hound called Bezerrillo, which tore open the Indians and knew 'which of them were in war, and which in peace, like a man'. The Puerto Ricans were more afraid of ten Spaniards with Bezerrillo than of one hundred without it, and Bezerrillo received its share of the spoils with the rest of the soldiers. Cieza de León once met a Portuguese 'who had the quarters of Indians hanging on a porch to feed his dogs with, as if they were wild beasts'.

The riposte from the American Indian to biological and bestial terror was the poisoned arrow. The curare on the points of the blowpipe missiles from the forest tribes of the Amazon had been foretold in the Greek legends of Heracles, who had killed the centaur Nessus with a poisoned arrow to stop the man-horse ravishing his wife. In return, Heracles was put to death by the centaur's infected shirt, the method that the Puritans later used to murder the Indians in Massachusetts. The Greek hero's bow and inescapable arrows, indeed, carried by the envenomed Philoctetes, shot Paris in the heel and led to the fall of Troy.

The Pilgrim Fathers used smallpox to destroy the tribes in Massachusetts. They saw themselves as the Children of Israel and the instruments of God on their colonial mission. When the Indians were ravaged by the infection, brought across the Atlantic in the *Mayflower* in 1620, King James I of England hailed 'the wonderful plague among the savages' as a divine blessing. In fact, it was a form of biological warfare. These first colonists only survived due to the ruthlessness of their military Captain Miles Standish who terrified the Indians by ambush and massacre and hanging anyone he thought dangerous. The severed head of one tribal leader was exhibited stuck on a pole in Plymouth for twenty years.

When Governor John Winthrop arrived in Boston, he declared: 'We shall find that the God of Israel is among us, when tens of us shall be able to resist a thousand of our enemies, when He shall make us a praise and a glory.' The holy struggle against the Indian tribes was to be pursued by gunpowder and axe and genocide. Only the exiled Roger Williams at Providence objected to following 'that pattern of Israel', which would lead to 'bloody, irreligious and inhuman oppressions and destructions' in the name of Christ.

Yet in the Pequot War, which ethnically cleansed much of New England outside the townships of 'praying Indians', the stake and the noose, torture and even cannibalism were employed by the Puritans and their Indian allies. This was David's War, one commander declared, for Saul had killed in his thousands, but David in his tens of thousands. When a people was grown to such 'a height of blood and sin' against man and God, He 'harrows them, and saws them, and puts them to the sword'.

Some of the Pequot prisoners were sold into slavery, and African slaves were brought for the first time to New England. After the later and bloodier 'King' Philip's War with his Indian federation, his head and hands were cut off, his body quartered and hung from trees. And in the most threatening internal rebellion in Virginia, in 1676, Nathaniel Bacon had the backing of almost all the colony against Governor Berkeley in his desire to 'ruin and extirpate all Indians in general, and all manner of trade and commerce with them'.

By the middle of the eighteenth century, when rules of combat were observed in many European encounters, savagery was still the staple of the French and Indian War on the frontiers of the thirteen colonies. With French help, Pontiac combined the border tribes to take back the Ohio Valley and Great Lakes region. The British General Amherst wanted the Indians hunted down by dogs, as the Spanish had pursued the Aztecs. The enemy should be poisoned by blankets infested with smallpox 'to extirpate this execrable race'. Ironically, the Indian practice of scalping their foes and hanging the hairy trophies on their belts transmitted toxic agents carried by the European immigrants far better than contaminated cloth, or the spores of anthrax in the modern mail.

As the colonists spread across North America, so the Four Horsemen of typhus and smallpox, measles and influenza decimated the tribes ahead of them. Although the Sioux and their allies defeated General Custer at the Battle of the Little Big Horn, they could never subvert the virulence brought to their virgin land. Epidemic followed epidemic. As one specialist on the spread of diseases wrote in *Armies of Pestilence*, 'This was genocide on a grand scale and fit to rank with dreams of Hitler and Himmler.' The counter-terror of biological warfare in the modern American city was still a nightmare to come.

8. THE OUTLAW AND THE GUERRILLA

Terror can be the blackmail of the many by the few. When the dragon crests of the Viking longships appeared before monastery or town, fear of the savage Norsemen produced only token resistance and much plunder. Yet as with the payment of ransoms to kidnappers or hijackers today, any Danegeld extracted to keep off invaders only encouraged more Danish fleets to arrive in England and pick up more silver pieces. From the early Baltic pirates to the Mafia, tribute has been exacted most plentifully from the most afraid. Bribery is always the worst policy against the bandits. They will come back for more.

Four types of outlaw became local or folk heroes. There was the country bandit who rose to lead a national insurrection, from Hereward the Wake after the Norman Conquest to Pancho Villa in northern Mexico. Then there was the social bandit, forced by injustice to campaign against greedy landowners and priests on behalf of the downtrodden. After these came the transport bandit, from Barbary pirates through Bonnie and Clyde to the hijackers of aeroplanes. And then there were the urban exploiters, who moved from their rural heartlands into the jungles of the slums, as the Mafia did in Chicago. The Bolsheviks even recruited their early cadres from such city criminals, converting bank robbers into proletarian vanguards.

An Anglo-Saxon leader against Norman tyranny, Hereward fought a guerrilla war from the forests which then covered most of England. He was followed by a legendary outlaw from the woods,

Robin Hood, another prototype of rural resistance to urban menace, as was the mountaineer William Tell in Austria. These folk heroes inspired the later leaders of Peasant Revolts, such as Wat Tyler and Jack Cade, who represented the revolt of the cultivators against the exactions of the aristocracy and the church. They broke the law only to redress the balance between the rich and the poor. They were inspirational, but they had no success.

In the Peasants' Revolt of 1381, mass violence did not take place until the arrival of the mobs in London. They burned down the Savoy and the Temple and St John's Monastery. The Archbishop of Canterbury, also Lord Chancellor, and the Royal Treasurer, were dragged from the Tower to their execution, their heads later exhibited on pikes. According to Henry Knighton, 'the victims voluntarily and without protesting, offered themselves like lambs to the shearer: barefooted, with their heads uncovered and their belts laid aside, they went freely to their deaths as if they were murderers or thieves and deserved this fate.' This role of martyr was curiously taken over by the rebel leader, Wat Tyler, who was cut down while acting as an intermediary between the young King Richard II and the thousands of peasant followers, who then were dispersed into retribution.

The spiritual leader of the rural revolt, John Ball, was commemorated in a short play in four acts, possibly written by George Peele and called *The Life and Death of Jack Straw*, another rebel leader. Ball put forward the continuing plea of the Christian poor against their masters:

Neighbours, neighbours, the weakest nowadays goes to the wall,
But mark my words, and follow the counsel of John Ball,
England is grown to such a pass of late,
That rich men triumph to see the poor beg at their gate.
But I am able by good scripture before you to prove,
That God does not this dealing allow or love,
But when Adam delved and Eve span,
Who was then a gentleman?

Shakespeare himself was most circumspect about mob violence in an age of royal authority. From *King Henry the Sixth, Part Two* to *Coriolanus*, he refined the outlaw's philosophy, finally damning it through Jack Cade's mouth, once the rebel chief had taken London in 1450 and had begun his campaign of urban terror:

> CADE: Go and set London Bridge on fire; and, if you can, burn down the Tower too ... Pull down the Savoy; others to the Inns of Court; down with them all ... Away, burn all the records of the realm; my mouth shall be the parliament of England ... And henceforward all things shall be in common.

The historical Cade failed in his nihilistic campaign of destruction and vainglory (see plate 9), but in the north of Britain, William Wallace became the medieval hero of Scots resistance to the English government. As a sixteenth-century ballad sang:

> There is no story that I can hear,
> Of John or Robin Hood,
> Nor yet of Wallace which but were
> That methinks half so good.

The outlaw with his robber band became the symbol for the people's resistance against alien oppression. In Ireland, it was particularly so. The nationalist societies which emerged in the eighteenth century were Catholic terrorist groups resisting the Anglo-Irish Protestant ruling minority. The condition of the Catholic poor was desperate. A severe penal code denied them all civil rights and left them at the mercy of the immigrants, while the very words 'Irish landlord' suggested extortion and oppression. In the south, the peasants had no remedy for despair and a potato diet, except to drink and plot against the English rulers and their regiments. The peasants in Ulster in the north, however, were Dissenters who had crossed from Scotland and hated the Papists even more than they hated their own landlords. Like the poor whites in the southern states of America, who tolerated the planter because he made them feel superior to the black slaves, the Ulstermen tolerated the landlord because he made them feel superior to their Catholic neighbours.

While the English administration of Ireland was distinguished by its toughness and ruthlessness, Irish Catholic resistance was significant through its tenacity. John Mitchel's contemporary *History of Ireland* summed up the situation:

> In Ireland they found themselves face to face, not two classes, but two nations; of which the one had substantially the power of life and death over the other. When we add to this that one of these two nations had despoiled the other of those very lands which the plundered race were now glad to cultivate as rackrented tenants; and also that the dominant nation felt bound to hate the other, both as 'rebels' who needed only the opportunity to rise and cut their masters' throats, and as Papists who clung to the 'damnable idolatry' of the Mass, we can easily understand the difficulty of the 'landlord and tenant question' in Ireland.

The Irish have always shown a talent for clandestine organization, particularly at the village or ward level; Irish immigrants to the United States were to make the Tammany political machine in New York the model of urban boss politics. By the 1780s, when the American Revolution was setting the example for the successful overthrow of British rule, both northern and southern Ireland had already had experience of organized resistance outside the law. In the north, the Oakboys and Steelboys had sworn oaths of secrecy, slaughtered cattle, carried arms, and burned houses in defiance of compulsory road-building and rent increases. In the south, the Whiteboys had attacked landlords armed with scythes and clubs and swords. For them, terror was the tactic of the victim against the oppressor, the only way for the poor to defy an army of occupation. Random violence cost little and frightened much by snare and ambush.

After the Battle of the Boyne in 1689, the Irish resistance fighters called the Wild Geese fled to fight for France, while tens of thousands more left for America. The massacres committed by the Protector Cromwell at Drogheda and King William III's forces at Limerick were never forgotten; but equally, the atrocious murders in Ulster of 12,000 immigrant Scots Protestants at the beginning of the Irish rebellion of 1641 were consigned to oblivion, although not by their descendants. Fighting for the French, the Irish Brigade at the Battle of Fontenoy in 1745 defeated the Duke of Cumberland and the English with a ferocious charge, shouting, 'Remember Limerick!' 'Butcher' Cumberland was then recalled to Scotland to slaughter the Highlanders at Culloden. His revenge against the Celts was a brutal victory. 'There is good reason to believe they will soon be dispersed or destroyed,' he wrote back to Lord Granville before the conflict in a letter still preserved in its green dispatch case in the Royal Archives at Windsor, 'and that a little *case of examples* will restore this Country to a perfect state of tranquillity.'

That little case of examples involved military executions and ordering Lord Loudon and his cavalry to 'drive the Cattle, turn the Plough and destroy what you can belonging to all such as are or have been in the Rebellion by burning the Houses of the Chiefs' all the way to the north and Fort Augustus. This scorched-earth policy still worried Cumberland, for later he wrote back to the Duke of Newcastle, 'All the good we have done is a little blood-letting, which has only weakened the madness, not cured it.' He trembled for fear 'that this vile spot may still be the ruin of this island and our family.' But the old clan system was destroyed by forts and roads and sheep, its chieftains bought by the chance to turn clan land into personal property. The American Revolution changed ancient wrongs and grudges into a battle for liberty, reflected in the struggle between the independent mountain men – mainly Scots and Irish in ancestry – and the tidewater plantation owners, loyal to King George III and Britain.

In the highlands of Scotland and in Ireland, there was much

support for the Declaration of American Independence. 'Here are none but rebels,' a clergyman of the Church of Ireland wrote back in 1775 to the Under-Secretary for the Colonies in London on the eve of the American Revolution. 'All our newspapers abound with intelligence favourable to the rebels. The King is reviled, the ministry cursed, religion trampled under foot.' Early in the struggle, the young Lieutenant Ridsdale informed the *Hibernian Magazine* that the troops which 'kept up the spirit and life of the rebellion were totally Scotch and Irish'. And as Ebenezer Wild noticed in Valley Forge, St Patrick's Day produced a noticeable change in camp, a celebration by the Irishmen born in America or settlers there, reinforced by deserters from the British lines.

Although Scottish regiments under British officers fought their fellow-countrymen in the colonial war, as did some of the Loyalist Volunteers of Ireland, there were six mutinies among Scottish troops raised for America, which resulted in the discharge of the levies. Without doubt, the declaration of American Independence provoked strong support from the Gaelic nations. 'Here we sympathize more or less with the Americans,' an Irish Member of Parliament wrote from Dublin. 'We are in water colour what they are in fresco.'

'England's difficulty is Ireland's opportunity' had long been a political maxim. In 1778, when France entered the American War, the Protestant Irish had raised a militia called the Volunteers, a force of 80,000 men who were well armed and officered by the Protestant gentry. The British government, alarmed by the possibility of an Irish revolt for something suspiciously similar to the American demand of 'No taxation without representation', granted a form of home rule to the Irish Parliament. Yet this concession merely meant that 1,000,000 Protestants now ruled 3,000,000 unrepresented Catholics in Ireland. The historian Lecky described the system as government through rotten boroughs 'by the gentlemen of Ireland, and especially by its landlord class'. As Theobald Wolfe Tone, the leader of the first nationalist secret society in Ireland, later wrote: 'It was a Revolution which, while at one stroke it doubled the value of every boroughmonger in the kingdom, left three-quarters of our countrymen slaves . . . and the Government of Ireland in the base and wicked and contemptible hands, who had spent their lives in degrading and plundering her.'

Under this shadow of independence, the Volunteers began to enlist working-class Catholic recruits and gradually disintegrated. In 1785, Henry Grattan, the Protestant leader in the Irish Parliament, protested: 'The old, the original Volunteers had become respectable because they represented the property of the nation, but attempts had been made to arm the poverty of the kingdom. They had originally been the armed property; were they to become the armed beggary?' Here, as in the United States, independence was not to mean social revolution. The Volunteers broke up into groups of armed men, including the Protestant Peep o' Day Boys and the Catholic Defenders.

In the 1790s, the creed and example of the French Revolution gave fresh inspiration to the Irish Catholics. They found a leader in the young barrister and pamphleteer Wolfe Tone, who declared: 'To subvert the tyranny of our execrable Government, to break the connection with England . . . and to assert the independence of my country – these were my objects. To unite the whole people of Ireland . . . to substitute the common name of Irishman, in place of the denominations of Protestant, Catholic, and Dissenter – these were my means.' So Wolfe Tone formulated the method by which nationalism might be used to win freedom for an oppressed and divided country. In Belfast, he drafted the resolutions for the founding of the Society of United Irishmen, which demanded Catholic emancipation in a united Ireland ruled by a reformed Parliament. To the Belfast declaration, the Dublin branch of the society added a pledge to press for a reformed Parliament through 'a brotherhood of affection, an identity of interests, a communion of rights, and a union of power among Irishmen of all religious persuasions.'

In 1793, Britain entered the war against revolutionary France with the Irish Parliament's support, and the Dublin leaders of the United Irishmen were jailed. The society then dropped its ideas of constitutional reform in favour of treasonable and revolutionary action; it built up a resistance movement which could assist a French invasion. Within two years, the leaders of the insurrection at village, county and provincial levels had become field officers in a guerrilla movement, so that there was, as the historian Philip Harwood wrote, 'a sort of pyramidical hierarchy of sedition, with an infinite number of small local societies for the base, and gradually towering up, through the nicely fitted gradations of baronial, county, and provincial committees, to the apex of a national executive directory.' Having adopted subversion as its method, the society became secret. There was a minimum of time-wasting ritual; at initiation, a new member simply swore an oath of secrecy on the New Testament. The password was merely, 'I know U', to which the reply was, 'I know N', and so on through all the letters of the words 'United Irishmen'.

Wolfe Tone put to his recruits a most significant political catechism, based on the oaths sworn in the rebel Masonic Lodges, which were such a force in both the American and the French Revolutions.

Question: Are you straight?
Answer: I am.
Question: How straight?
Answer: As straight as a rush.
Question: Go on then.
Answer: In Truth, in Trust, in Unity and in Liberty.
Question: What have you got in your hand?
Answer: A green bough.
Question: Where did it first grow?
Answer: In America.
Question: Where did it bud?
Answer: In France.

> *Question*: Where are you going to plant it?
> *Answer*:   *In the Crown of Ireland.*

Members of the United Irishmen were armed and drilled, and by 1796 the society was ready for revolt. But its supporters, armed only with pikes, needed French regular troops to engage the British army with its cannon and muskets. Wolfe Tone and the Anglo-Irish revolutionary leader Lord Edward Fitzgerald made many trips to France, trying to persuade successive French governments to attack Ireland; the French navy actually made three invasion attempts. The first was defeated by storms, the second was intercepted, and the third ended in quick disaster, for the French troops were slaughtered soon after landing by those of Lord Cornwallis, then the viceroy, but also the military commander who had surrendered Yorktown, and so ensured the success of the American Revolution. The United Irishmen failed to coordinate their rising with any of these assaults (see plates 21, 34 and 35). They made one attempt in May 1798, but the organizers, including Lord Edward Fitzgerald, were arrested before the event, and the rebel army of 20,000 men was defeated by British troops.

Ulster did not rise in support of the United Irishmen, which had become an overwhelmingly Catholic organization. In fact, Ulster threw up a counter-structure, the Orangemen, to resist attacks from Catholic guerrillas. Armed landlords, the Yeomanry and the Orangemen joined with the British troops in suppressing the Catholic rebellion. Fitzgerald died of wounds in jail during the rising. Tone, who was arrested in the same year on board a French ship, received the death sentence in November and committed suicide. The United Irishmen ceased to be an active revolutionary force.

The Masonic Lodges deriving from the Ancient Scottish Rite had contributed to the success of the American Revolution as well as the failure of the United Irishmen. The wall chart of the Boyne Society, which was set up in 1690 to buttress the

Protestant victory of King William III, is still preserved in the Ulster Museum in Belfast. It showed off Gnostic, Templar and medieval guild symbols from Scotland – signs which became the teaching aids for members of those later aggressive forces, the Orange and Arch Purple and Black Orders, which would dominate politics in Ulster in the nineteenth and twentieth centuries. The Boyne Society became the 1st Loyal Orange Boyne Society, Armagh, dedicated to the Union with Great Britain and the British monarchy.

Equally, the organization of the Knights Templars and of the Masonic lodges influenced the secret societies of the Irish Catholic rebels and refugees. In 1761, the Grand Lodge of France appointed Stephen Morin as the Grand Inspector of the New World, with the power of instituting lodges according to the Ancient Scottish Rite. In 1769, the St Andrew's Lodge of Boston conferred a new Knights Templars degree. Certainly, the Scottish Rite was important in the American War of Independence, especially for the colonial lodges of Boston at their celebrated tea party. Another important Catholic Mason was the marquis de Lafayette, who brought over the French forces to aid George Washington until the final American victory at Yorktown.

Washington himself and his influential Irish Secretary of War McHenry were leading Masons. When he became President of his new nation, Washington stamped Templar and Masonic symbols on the currency, which survive to this day. On the dollar bill, the eye enclosed in the triangle echoed the apocalyptic visions of the medieval seer Joachim de Fiore, the three Ages evolving to that of the Spirit, while the pyramid, left unfinished, suggested that the pinnacle of human wisdom and achievement had not been reached. These Masonic symbols were also millennial, for the American Revolution was inspired by the hope and belief in building a heaven on earth as well as a better society.

The Freemasons became the exponents of revolution in France and Europe in the next generation. In America, the Scots and the Irish lodges had been founded on the hatred of state armies and government. The successes of the American freedom fighters against the redcoats and the Hessians were not those of set-piece engagements, but of guerrilla attacks. Their endurance and refusal to accept reverses had led to the triumph of American independence. And yet, when that independence was won, the first threat to the United States was another rebellion against taxation. A former Revolutionary officer, Daniel Shays, led a group of farmers in western Massachusetts against the state militia. Four of Shays' men were killed in the fighting, and the shudder of internal revolt helped to scare the representatives of the thirteen states into a Constitutional Convention. While that gathering felt obliged to guarantee the right of the people to bear arms because of its republican fear of standing armies, it only approved of a 'well-regulated Militia' or a National Guard, not of private squads of potential rebels and outlaws.

The paradox of a government born in a revolution is that it must conserve the fruits of the revolution. Radicalism congeals. 'The pursuit of happiness' demanded by the Declaration of Independence became the defence of 'property' written in the Constitution. But already there was social tension between those who had the bulk of the possessions in the mercantile Atlantic cities or in the coastal plantations and the pioneers, often Scots and Irish, in the mountains and the forests. New waves of immigration came from the dispossessed of Britain, the Highlanders sent away in the Clearances and the Irish farmers, starving after the Great Hunger. These people became the settlers of Canada and the United States, the people of the mountains and the fields who led the pushing of the frontiers to the Far West and the Pacific Ocean and the robbing of the prairies from the Indian tribes. After the soldiers of Scotland and Ireland came the farmers and the pioneers, who won the freedom that they had lost at home.

9. THE ILLUMINATI AND THE FRENCH REVOLUTION

After the Stewart defeat in 1715 in Scotland, the flight to France of the Jacobites resulted in a revival of the Scottish Knights Templars. A mystic and tormented figure played the role of another St John the Baptist in this resurrection. Andrew Michael, the Chevalier de Ramsay, was born in Ayr in 1686 and studied at Edinburgh, Leyden and Oxford. Elected as a Fellow of the Royal Society, he nonetheless wrote: 'All my ambition is, that I should be forgotten.'

This fate was not to be. As a young man, he campaigned in Flanders with the Duke of Marlborough's victorious armies against the French forces and their supporting Jacobite contingents. Attracted to the spiritual teachings of Archbishop François de Fénelon of Cambrai, Ramsay changed sides and became Fénelon's pupil until his death. The seminary had become a hospital for the war-wounded and the starving. Charity and chivalry were foremost in Fénelon's teaching. There Ramsay met James Francis Edward Stewart, the Old Pretender, who chose him as the tutor to his four-year-old son, Prince Charles Edward Stewart, and his younger brother Henry, afterwards to be appointed by the Pope as Cardinal of York. Ramsay revived the Military Order of the Scottish Knights Templars and became Grand Master of its Grand Lodge in Paris. In 1736, he made a speech to a sympathetic group of Catholic aristocrats:

At the time of the crusades in Palestine many princes, lords and citizens associated themselves, and vowed to restore the Temple of the Christians in the Holy Land. They agreed upon several ancient signs and symbolic words drawn from the mysteries of the faith in order to recognize each other in bringing back the architecture of the Temple to its first institution.

The fatal religious discords which embarrassed and tore Europe in the sixteenth century caused our order to degenerate from the nobility of its origin. Many of the rites and usage that were contrary to the prejudices of our times were changed, disguised, suppressed. Thus it was that many of our brothers forgot, like the ancient Jews, the spirit of our laws and only retained the letter and the shell. The beginnings of a remedy have already been made. It is only necessary to continue until at last, everything be brought back to the original institution.

Recollecting the ancient wisdom of the military orders brought from Scotland to France, perhaps through the royal order instituted by Robert the Bruce, Ramsay went on to allude enigmatically to a high degree or caste of knightly priests and princes in a revived Order of Melchizedek, who sought to follow the example of the sacred King of Israel.

The word Freemason must therefore not be taken in a literal, gross or material sense, as if our founders had been simple workers in stone, or merely curious geniuses who wished to perform the arts. They were not only skilful architects, desirous of consecrating their talents and goods to the construction of material temples; but also religious and warrior princes who designed to enlighten, edify, and protect the living Temples of the Most High.

Pope Clement XII soon forbade Catholics from becoming Freemasons under threat of excommunication, out of the usual fear that like the Knights Templars they might form a state within the state. Two years before the rebellion of the Young Pretender, the Chevalier Ramsay died – fortunately for him, since many of the Jacobites met their end in that failed adventure. His legacy, however, was left to Karl Gotthelf, Baron von Hundt, who revived in Germany the Ancient Order of the Temple, once the defeat at Culloden and the harrying of the Highlands had extinguished all Stewart hopes.

Von Hundt's diary states that in 1742 he was initiated into the Templar Order in Paris in the presence of Lord Kilmarnock – soon to be executed by the English for treason – and that he later met Prince Charles Edward Stewart, the Young Pretender. Von Hundt was a Protestant as well as a Mason; nevertheless he revived this old order, signing on twelve German princes, led by the Duke of Brunswick, to join the resurrected body. This resurrection was opposed by a rival Swedish order, which also held to the Ancient Scottish Rite of the Young Pretender as handed down to King Gustav III of Sweden.

Whatever the truth of the schism, the Jacobite connection was maintained in northern Europe. The early work of Nicolas de Bonneville during the French Revolution testified to the importance of the Ancient Scottish Rite. For him, 'the secret of the Freemasons is explained by the history of the Knights Templars.' He told of secret ceremonies, including the exchange of blood by sword-point for the initiate, then used in lodges of the ancient Swedish Rite. The novice Mason received a white apron and gloves, the colour of the Cistercian monks and the Templars. The three pillars of Masonry were Jachin, Boaz and Mac-Benac, making up the initials JBM or Jacq. Burg. Molay, the name of the martyred last Grand Master of the Order. Mac-Benac was also the pseudonym of Aumont, the Templar leader of those knights who had fled to Scotland.

De Bonneville also recognized that the Templars, as did the Muslims, worshipped a single God or Divine Creator and Intelligence. This led to their wrongful condemnation for denying the divinity of Jesus and spitting on the Cross. He even spoke of

a secret tradition among the Templars that the great Saladin
before his conquest of Jerusalem had been received into the order
by the knight Hugo of Tiberias. The cry of 'Yah-Allah' was a
recognition of an affinity with Islam, while the worship of the
head may have sprung from ancient Gnostic Orphite rites involv-
ing the dragon serpents which guarded the Greek paradise, the
Garden of Hesperides. Above all, the Masonic ceremony of
venerating the image of a skeleton in a coffin was derived from
the Templars, the skull being separate and representing the
beheaded St John the Baptist.

For the radicals of the time, however, the most important use
of Templar principles was through Frederick the Great, then
Crown Prince of Prussia. Through Voltaire, he had become interested in the revived order of the Knights Templars as a means of
subverting the Franco-Austrian alliance against his kingdom. In
1761, he was acknowledged as the European head of the Ancient
Scottish Rite. In the thirtieth degree of the revived Templar Order,
the Knight Kadosch, the knights wore Teutonic crosses and the
throne was surrounded by the double-headed eagle of Prussia. In
the top thirty-third degree, the Sovereign Grand Commander
Frederick wore the jewel of the two-headed predatory bird, as did
his lieutenant, the duc d'Orléans, the Grand Master of the Grand
Orient, and an intriguer in the Revolution to come.

For the Chevalier de Ramsay, the illumination of the mind
towards universal truth was important for the revived Templars.
'All the Grand Masters in Germany, England, Italy, and elsewhere
exhort all the learned men and all the artisans of the Fraternity
to unite to furnish the materials for a Universal Dictionary of all
the liberal arts and useful sciences; excepting only theology
and politics.' His two exceptions were ignored by the authors
of the *Encyclopédie*, an inspiration of the French Revolution.
Freemasons always specified the organization of their lodges and
the *Encyclopédie* as the seeds of the downfall of the Bourbon
dynasty. At the Congress of the Grand Orient in 1904, the
Freemason Bonnet declared:

Liberty, Equality, Fraternity. The Revolutionary seed quickly germinated among this elite of illustrious Freemasons. D'Alembert, Diderot, Helvetius, d'Holbach, Voltaire, Condorcet completed the evolution of minds and prepared the new era. And when the Bastille fell, Freemasonry had the supreme honour of giving to humanity the charter (the Declaration of the Rights of Man), which it had elaborated with devotion.

Bonnet went on to claim that the Constituent Assembly at the beginning of the French Revolution had 300 Masonic members, and that the Declaration of the Rights of Man was the work of the hero of the American Revolution, the marquis de Lafayette, who presented the key of the Bastille to the American President George Washington. Actually the Rights of Man was also derived from another major aristocratic contributor to the *Encyclopédie*, the marquis de Condorcet. He was a utopian and a pioneer in moral science, whose views on history improving the lot of society through successive changes would influence the positivism of Auguste Comte and the dialectic of Hegel and Marx.

After the Revolution, Condorcet did not succeed. Unlike the comte de Mirabeau and the marquis de Lafayette, he joined too late the triumphant Jacobins. He worked with Thomas Paine, who had written *The Rights of Man*, and yet his *Plan for a Constitution* was gutted, and when he protested, he was condemned. In hiding, he wrote a historical sketch on the progress of the human spirit. He affirmed the laws of nature and morality. He still believed in social betterment even during what would be called the 'Terror'. 'How welcome to the philosopher is this picture of humanity, freed from all its chains, released from the domination of chance and from that of the enemies of its progress, advancing with a firm and sure step in the path of truth, virtue and happiness!' Whatever his hopes, Condorcet to flee from Paris in women's clothes, then he was denied shelter by his friends, before dying in prison of unexplained causes, possibly of poison. His last protector, Madame de Vernet, was said to have said of him: 'Sir, the Convention may declare you outside the law, but not outside humanity.'

The comte de Mirabeau was a key player in the Constituent Assembly. In his papers, he admitted to being a Freemason, influenced by the mysterious Rosicrucians and the Bavarian Illuminati, whom he praised in his *History of the Prussian Monarchy*. He said that the Illuminati were modelled on the Jesuits in their secrecy and double logic, while opposing faith in God for faith in Reason. They wished to abolish royalty and serfdom and unjust taxation and superstition, while bringing in liberty of the press and universal toleration for all religions. Two later socialist thinkers, Louis Blanc and George Sand, attested to the success of the European conspiracy of the mystic Illuminati from Germany, and particularly to its brilliant organization.

Its founder, the inspired intriguer, Adam Weishaupt, drew an ancient diagram of the secret society organized in cells (see plates 17 and 18). A hierarchical system led upwards to a grand master, whose will was supreme. Yet no lieutenant or cell communicated with each other. As a commentator on Weishaupt wrote:

> He knew how to take from every association, past and present, the portions he required and to weld them all into a working system of terrible efficiency – the disintegrating doctrines of the Gnostics and Manicheans, of the modern philosophers and Encyclopaedists, the methods of the Ismailis and the Assassins, the discipline of the Jesuits and Templars, the organization and secrecy of the Freemasons, the philosophy of Machiavelli, the mystery of the Rosicrucians – he knew, moreover, how to enlist the right elements in all existing associations as well as isolated individuals and turn them to his purpose.

So strong was the influence of the Illuminati that the geniuses of German literature, Goethe and Lessing, became members of the Society. Percy Bysshe Shelley even wrote a bad novel, *St Irvyne or the Rosicrucian*, about a Protestant Brotherhood of the Rosy Cross opposing the Habsburg Emperors: Elizabeth Barrett Browning called it 'boarding-school idiocy'. Shelley also presumed that the Assassins and their vision of paradise had inspired the Illuminati, while Mary Shelley set the home of Victor Frankenstein in Ingoldstadt, the spiritual centre of the cult. The disruption caused by the man-made monster, meant to be beautiful, was a commentary on the Illuminati strategy of destroying the social and political and religious institutions, which shackled the individual in the chains which Rousseau in his *Social Contract* wanted to cast off.

By 1789, there were 2,000 lodges in France affiliated to the Grand Orient with some 100,000 members. Most of the leading radicals in the Constituent Assembly were informed by Illuminati beliefs in a social revolution. These included the duc d'Orléans, the marquises de Condorcet and de Lafayette, the comte de Mirabeau, and also their later opponents, Danton and Desmoulins, Marat and Robespierre himself. They used the techniques of conspiracy, cells and lodges and summary judgement, to overthrow the government and rule the people with a series of revolutionary groups, similar to the Sixteen in Paris during the religious wars. These plotters practised an internecine struggle against each other in order to acquire the levers of power for their hidden purposes. That this blood-letting by the Jacobins ended in a regime of fear was merely another demonstration of the problem: 'After the Revolution, who shall win the Revolution?'

10. THE TERROR

Until the French Revolution, terror had lacked definition. It was a method of using atrocities to frighten rulers and their subjects in order to plunder and seize and maintain power. Its only philosopher had been Machiavelli, who admired the techniques of Cesare Borgia and described his crimes for the benefit of future princes. Yet with the 'Terror', instituted by the Jacobins in France after 1792, the politics of revolutionary violence were exposed. They informed the conspiracies of the next two centuries, leading to the downfall of the two major tyrannies of Russia and China as well as dozens of other governments. A history of 'Terror' could be dated, in the manner of the history of Europe, not Before and After Christ, but Before and After Robespierre.

For the Académie française, terror was primarily an emotion caused by the approach of an evil or peril. It was a shock, a great fear. But secondarily, terror was violence and crime systematically committed with the purpose of frightening groups of individuals. These terms differentiated between the terrorized and the terrorists, who regulated the amount of their violence, sometimes confined to the mere propaganda of menace or the assassination of selected targets; but it could result in mass fury, as at the Massacre of St Bartholomew's Day. The objective was to provoke the degree of fright among the people necessary for the conspirators to achieve their political ends.

The 'Terror' of the French Revolution was distinguished from all previous reigns of fear by its rationale and planning, however deranged. There were no precursors for such a new ideology – the supremacy of Reason, the unlimited power of the Will, and the indefinite change of society through unceasing action. Yet in 1789, when the Revolution began, the aims of the Masonic leaders of the Third Estate were little more than the eventual goals of the American revolutionary leaders, the pursuit of liberty, not too much equality, and the security of property.

The loss of control by the Third Estate began in 1789 with the Great Fear of brigands and aristocratic conspirators, which led to the arming of a rural and urban militia. Some hold was kept on these numerous armed bands, until a series of defeats of the improvised revolutionary armies by the monarchical powers of Austria and Prussia and Spain led to a general scare of a coup from loyal royal groups, particularly in the south of France.

As the English historian Froude wrote, 'Fear is the parent of cruelty.' A secure society with a legitimate ruler had little need of severe measures. But when a fresh French radical government was trembling from the threat of enemies both outside and within the gates, the 'Terror' was a planned response, whether logical or not. For as the Roman Sallust had observed in his *Catalina*, 'Terror closes the ears of the mind.'

During the Revolution and for the next two hundred years, a fierce debate raged about the necessity for the vicious tactics of Robespierre and the Jacobins. Those who wrote about these actions said they were either necessary or indefensible. 'Every harvest needs its scythe,' Alphonse Esquiros declared. 'The French Revolution needed the Terror.' He was contradicted by the Encyclopédiste and philosopher Benjamin Constant, whose purpose was 'to show that the Republic was saved in spite of the Terror.'

To Joseph de Maistre, the aristocrats rumbling on carts to the guillotine and the use of summary justice by denunciation without trial were functional. The dreadful sight was good for morale. The poor were now prepared to volunteer to fight at the front and crush any counter-revolution. The Terror was an improvised response to foreign invasion and conspiracy at home; it became the organized instrument of victory. Albert Sorel saw the successful contradictions: 'A scaffold and so an army, a government which exterminates and so heroes who give their lives.'

Under Robespierre and the Committee of Public Safety, atrocity became part of the arsenal of defence – an inseparable aspect of warfare. The first mass murders of the September Massacres in Paris in 1792 were the consequence of the fall of Verdun to foreign forces. There was a collapse of radicalism, a contagion of fear. The Jacobins denounced 'the partisans of tyranny and federation and the enemies of liberty'. Thousands of privileged detainees were shot or guillotined. The White Terror of the counter-revolutionaries extended from Maçon through Lyon to Marseille along the Rhône, where bandits and criminals joined the refugee nobles to justify their depredations in the cause of the Bourbon King, soon to lose his head himself with his Queen, Marie Antoinette.

Terror breeds terror, indeed, yet Robespierre's deliberate policy of atrocity did appear to stiffen the resistance of the revolutionary armies, which began to push back their foes from France and within their country. The victorious fighters of the Vendée in the west were massacred, and the rebels in Lyon and Marseille, Toulon and Bordeaux were exterminated. The rival and colleague of Robespierre, Marat – himself a later victim of assassination – created a 'tyranny of liberty', or a 'dictatorship of national defence'. Pushed on by the measures recommended by the sans-culottes and a radical group of *Enragés* led by Jacques Roux with his slogan, 'Death to the monopolists', a Revolutionary Tribunal was instituted with total powers for the requisition of supplies and price control as well as the expropriation of the property of all suspects. Hoarding food now became a capital crime.

Outperforming Machiavelli as the philosopher of state terror, Robespierre spoke to the Convention on the principles of political morality, which should guide its decisions. 'The mainspring of popular government in time of war is both *virtue and terror*: virtue without which terror is fateful: terror without which virtue is helpless. Terror is nothing but prompt, severe and inflexible justice: it is thus an emanation of virtue.' This fearsome speech negated any rule of law in favour of every ruthlessness to keep the revolutionary government in power. The Rights of Man were abrogated for the invisible and assumed Will of the People.

During the heyday of the Terror, some 400,000 victims were detained, and 17,000 of them were executed. These numbers seem minimal set against the atrocities of the twentieth century, when tens of millions of innocent people died in what were miscalled 'class wars'. More thousands of counter-revolutionaries were slaughtered in 1793 among the rebels of the Vendée. The infamous Carrier told the Committee of Public Safety that he had given orders to burn all and exterminate even the women for aiding the enemy. Many of the prisoners were shot, while thousands more were drowned in the *noyades* at Nantes, with Carrier boasting, 'What a revolutionary torrent is the Loire!' Eight hundred more were executed in Toulon for collaborating with the British occupation. Yet in all, the massacres at home during the Terror were only a small proportion of those who died in the imperial wars of Napoleon.

The factions which ran the Terror fed on themselves, as a snake eating its own tail. Against the Committee of Public Safety, already fracturing apart, stood the moderate forces of the Convention, more and more concerned with incipient socialist assaults on property. An internal coup in the new Republican month of Thermidor put Robespierre and his group under arrest and had them executed (see plates 19 and 20). The success of the wars against foreign invaders and internal rebels had made retribution less necessary. This was the time to turn on the advocates of a social revolution. The purgers should now be purged.

The Jacobins had been organized in the widespread radical model of lodges and committees all over the nation, as had other revolutionary clubs. They represented a threat to the middle-class bourgeois majority in the Convention, which was setting up a new liberal Constitution. Economic hardship and a falling bread

ration in 1795 led in Paris to a brace of popular insurrections,
which were soon dispersed by the loyal National Guard, which
had grown from the earlier militias, also by a revised national
army corps. A military commission sentenced thousands of the
sans-culottes and their last leaders to execution or imprisonment.
After that, the new Constituent Assembly held power for four
precarious years until driven out in the final coup of Brumaire
1799 by General Napoleon Bonaparte, who created himself an
Emperor in 1804.

For Marat, revolutionary violence was justified. It was the
weapon of the sovereign people to gain and defend their liberty
against tyranny. Resistance to oppression was one of the Rights
of Man. 'Sacred insurrection' was a duty, as was a continuing
revolution. 'The political mechanism can only ever be rewound
by violent shaking.'

This ideology was the inspirational change in the French
Revolution, which led to three more major insurrections in Paris
in the next century. Later socialist thinkers thought the failed
rebel 'Gracchus' Babeuf the herald of the class warfare to come.
In his *Tribun du peuple* and his *Manifesto of the Equals* of 1796,
Babeuf advocated the abolition of private property and the
establishment of a form of communism. Yet his doctrines owed
more to Christian millennialism than to the sparks of socialism.
'The moment of great measures has arrived,' he declared. 'Evil is
at its peak; it covers the face of the earth. Chaos, under the name
of politics, reigns after too many centuries. All things must return
to order and take their place.'

More attuned to the later powerful movement of the anarchists, Babeuf wanted the rights to the land and its fruits restored
to local communities. He desired the abolition of private property
to ensure the fair distribution of produce. 'Perish, if they must,
all the arts,' he went so far as to declare, 'as long as real equality
remains ours!' His principles were both utopian and destructive,
but hardly attractive to the displaced workers in the age of the
coming Industrial Revolution. This was proved by the collapse

of his 'Conspiracy of the Equals' in 1796, when he led a group of Jacobin clubs and militant cells in an effort to rouse the apathetic sans-culottes and grasp power in Paris. He and his followers were betrayed by a police spy. Thirty of the rebels were shot without trial, while Babeuf was put on trial and went to the guillotine.

More progressive for future French revolutions was the reformer Louis Blanc, who reckoned that the concentration of capital and competition divided the wealthy from the bourgeois, who were driven to ruin along with the poor. 'I know of a tyranny,' Blanc wrote, 'much more inexorable, much more difficult to elude or aid than that of a Tiberius or a Nero, and that is the tyranny of things.' This materialism produced a corrupt social order, which needed to be prodded to ensure the fair distribution of all goods. Blanc searched for a process of historical reconstruction, the findings of 'laws of progress', the later dialectic of Hegel and Marx which would lead to fundamental social change. This was the duty of the revolutionary, the search for the truths which would bring about positive action for the good of the people.

11. NATIONALIST
SECRET SOCIETIES

Alien or minority rule, imposed by conquest, is the most common of the conditions that tend to produce the nationalist secret society. Opposition to such rule usually begins in the form of an open cultural society, set up as a club for the leaders of the oppressed majority. This club progresses from considerations of culture to demands for reform from the occupying power. When these are resisted, the club either splits between the moderates and the extremists or goes underground. At this point the nationalist secret society is formed. Its aim is insurrection, its organization military, and it often relies on mass urban revolt. The British historian Sir Lewis Namier, in his acute examination of the causes of the European revolutions of 1848, found that the revolutionaries were almost exclusively middle-class intellectuals who capitalized on popular outbursts, many of which originated in the crowded slums of capital cities.

The French Revolution set the pattern of the urban rebellions. In the capital of France, conspirators plotted, rose to power, and were overthrown. As Paris went, so went the nation. The Terror before the time of Napoleon Bonaparte proved that a small and determined body of men, such as the Jacobins, could seize power and hold on to it briefly by using their agents and levies to put down opposition at home and abroad. The 'Conspiracy of the Equals', Babeuf's failed rising in 1796, ushered in the age of the professional revolutionary – of men like Filippo Buonarroti and Auguste Blanqui. These men, in love with revolution and its preparation and its ritual, made the small secret society an instrument of nationalism.

The policy of the urban revolutionary was clear-cut. He aimed to form a group of militants, to cause unease by terrorist activity, and to use the support of army officers of liberal sympathies. He would wait until famine or depression made the urban mob restive, and then foment a riot. He would seize the strategic points of a city such as the parliament, the palace, and the newspaper offices. He would declare his group of revolutionaries to be the provisional government, and suppress any attempt at a counter-revolution. The beauty of the method was that it needed few militants and little, if any, mass support.

The professional revolutionaries generally regarded government as a sort of conspiracy of the rich against the people, who were supposed to be ignorant or passive. As self-appointed plotters for the poor, they sought to supplant the clique of the rich. After the revolution they would educate the workers to understand that they, the revolutionaries, were indeed their leaders. Blanqui himself coined the term 'the dictatorship of the proletariat', in an attempt to justify the period following a successful revolution, when the expert revolutionaries, not yet having won the support of the nation, would dictate to the people.

Although its ritual was often ludicrous, the nationalist secret society of the early nineteenth century was probably the most important agent of political change. Its effectiveness was unquestionable in times of disorder. In various countries, particularly Italy, the Masonic lodges had become the instruments of the political awakening of the middle classes. The most famous of the nationalist secret societies on the Continent, that of the Carbonari of the early nineteenth century, was heavily influenced and penetrated by Freemasons. Yet the Carbonari, though they adopted much of the ritual of the older brotherhoods, were essentially a political organization dating from the period of Napoleonic rule in Italy. Their first lodges were founded in Capua between 1802 and 1810 by a group of republican officers in the

French army who were hostile to the development of Bonapart-
ism. The function of these early lodges was to stir up political
opposition to the French, and to press for constitutional guaran-
tees; they found many recruits among Italian army officers,
landowners and officials.

The Carbonari borrowed their name, and much of their ritual,
from the mutual-aid societies of charcoal-burners which had
flourished since the Middle Ages and had later been influenced
by Freemasonry. Their initiation ceremony was a hotchpotch of
traditional rites, with ordeals by blindfold and fire, confrontation by Cross and axe. Their oath was modelled on that of the
Masons. With his hand resting on an axe, the initiate swore 'upon
this steel, the avenging instrument of the perjured, scrupulously
to keep the secret of Carbonarism; and neither to write, engrave,
or paint anything concerning it, without having obtained a written permission. I swear to help my Good Cousins in case of need,
as much as in me lies, and not to attempt anything against the
honour of their families. I consent, and wish, if I perjure myself,
that my body may be cut in pieces, then burnt, and my ashes
scattered to the wind, in order that my name be held up to the
execration of the Good Cousins throughout the earth.'

The oath of the Carbonari was not overtly political; it contained 'not a word of the purpose', as the revolutionary Mazzini
noted 'with surprise and suspicion' when he was initiated into the
society. But as the Carbonari were recruited from the ambitious
middle classes, they wanted political advancement for that social
level. Their lodges spread from France to Spain, from Italy to
Greece, and even to Russia. Everywhere they represented the
cause of liberalism against the Holy Alliance set up to control
Europe after the defeat of Napoleon.

In a series of insurrections beginning in 1820, the Carbonari
won constitutions in Spain and some of the Italian states, and
independence for Greece. They were most effective where they
attached to their cause young army officers who were popular
enough with the troops to be able to incite them to rebellion. The

reactionary powers of Europe, however, soon put down the new constitutional governments, and with the collapse of the last coup inspired by the Carbonari, the Decembrist rising against the Tsar Nicholas I of Russia in 1825, the heyday of the bourgeois quasi-Masonic secret society was over.

The social model of the Carbonari was the constitutional regimes of Britain and the United States; though international in organization, they were nationalist in their aims. They never attracted mass support. But they did show that conspiracies of the rising middle classes against the old regimes of Europe could force concessions from reactionary governments, if the army was disaffected. A successful pattern of conspiracy had been set to be imitated. In the revolutions of 1830, when mass support was forthcoming for risings in Paris, Belgium, Poland, Spain, and various parts of Germany, Italy and Switzerland, the secret societies were no longer isolated groups of conspirators. Those who plotted to win concessions for the middle classes found themselves, almost willy-nilly, the chiefs of nationalist agitation.

They became the leaders of the people, particularly where large areas speaking with one language were split up into a series of petty principalities, as in Germany and Italy, or where many different language-groups were forced together in an uneasy union, as in the Austro-Hungarian Empire. The result of the revolutions of 1830 was the creation of one new European nation, Belgium, and of several liberal constitutions on the Continent. Perhaps the most significant after-effect was to split the moderates in certain countries, such as France, from the radicals. Once the middle class of a principality or a nation or an empire had won a share in the legislative power, it showed as much zeal in suppressing radical secret societies as any aristocratic regime.

In 1848, when revolution spread through Europe like a contagion until hardly a capital was free from mob violence and hardly a suppressed nation failed to revolt, the divergent social aims of the emerging nationalist leaders became only too clear. Those who had plotted for a constitution were suspicious of those who had plotted for separatism, and both were afraid of those who had plotted for a social revolution. In such dangerous and anarchic situations, authoritarian regimes can often regain control, because they represent the only known stability. There are usually at least two revolutions in any given radical situation: the first displaces the established regime, the second decides which of the revolutionary groups shall dominate the others and form the new government.

The incoherent July Revolution in Paris of 1830 had put middle-class liberals in power, backed initially by the urban mob, and maintained by the marquis de Lafayette and the National Guard. The monarchy was retained under a new Orléanist constitutional king, Louis-Philippe. Although there were two outbreaks among the weavers of Lyon and other cities, these were crushed by royal troops. In 1832, an insurrection of the Parisian sans-culottes was quickly suppressed at the cost of 800 dead and wounded, as was another attempt two years later, when dozens of protesters died on the barricades.

Auguste Blanqui, the hero of these new insurrectionaries, was in jail. But in 1837 his followers engaged in a conspiracy against the government, assuming that they had the mass support of the French workers, though they had done little to secure it. They plotted in a void, and Blanqui himself was silly enough to divide his *Société des Saisons* of fellow conspirators into Months, Weeks, and Days, led by a committee of the four Seasons. Nearly a century later, this uprising inspired the best of the fantasy novels of G. K. Chesterton, the anarchist thriller *The Man Who Was Thursday: A Nightmare*.

About 1,200 of these calendar conspirators did manage to seize the Hôtel de Ville in Paris in May 1839, but they failed to incite the Parisians on their Sunday walk to join them. They were easily captured with little resistance. They were unable to liquidate the aristocracy of the nouveaux riches, who now ruled society. 'They are in the social body what cancer is to the human body,' the Blanquist manifesto declared. 'The first condition of

return to health is to extirpate the cancer.' Yet that journey back
to the Terror and the rolling of the dung carts loaded with the
aristocrats towards the guillotine was postponed until the next
uprising.

In the other capitals of Europe, the urban mobs found that
the liberal nationalists they had helped into office turned on their
own supporters for fear of a second revolution. In the last resort,
the middle classes preferred any stable regime, even an authoritarian one, to a regime that was liberal but weak. The leaders of
the new governments came from the constitutional and cultural
clubs. Various political groups rose briefly to power during
the revolutions of 1848, but religious divisions, allied with the
irrational hatreds of nationalism, brought them into conflict and
dissipated their success. Teutonic peoples and Slavs could no
more agree than Irish Catholics and Orangemen; the result was
that both the Austro-Hungarian Empire and British control of
Ireland were able to survive.

The early nineteenth century saw the rise of the vanguard of
the radical middle class, which often had to go underground to
win concessions from aristocratic regimes and to gain representation in a parliament. After 1848, however, the nationalist
secret society in Europe changed its nature. Once the wealthier
bourgeois were accepted within the framework of aristocratic
European governments, the secret society became a focus
of petty-bourgeois or proletarian discontent. Blanqui's League of
the Just and the League of Outlaws, a secret society of German
working men in Paris, served as the forerunners of the Communist League of Marx and Engels, which dropped the ritual
paraphernalia of the older brotherhoods – what Marx described
as 'superstitious authoritarianism'. The era of the anarchists and
the Bolsheviks was on hand in their search for an international
revolution.

As Talmon wrote in his *Political Messianism*, a growing
religion of revolution was inspired by belief in a permanent
revolution. 'The right and duty to maintain the state of revolt,

and with it civil war, was ... in the very nature of things, in the existence of evil.' Terror was the only means by which the deprived rebels might take on the rich and corrupt state. The priests of the religion of revolution owned no obedience to law or authority. Their guide was their faith in the will of the people, which was revealed to them. Their duty was the over-throw of existing institutions. Their strategy was the use of all means of destruction, which came into their hands.

In 1848 King Louis-Philippe of France abdicated, and power fell into the hands of a Provisional Government nominated by a National Assembly and supported by a democratized National Guard. One of its leaders, Lamartine, refused to proclaim a revolutionary republic backed by a popular vote. When asked by the mob why he and his fellow conspirators had seized 'the government of the people', he replied: 'By the right of the blood that runs, the fire that devours our buildings, the nation without a chief, the people without a guide, without orders and tomorrow without bread perhaps! ... Come and take part, you are the masters, but do not prolong your terrible inquisition, which is impossible in the midst of blood and fire.'

So Lamartine asserted that he who seized power first with sufficient force would hold on to office, if he could resist other radical groups. Some of his rivals set up a revolutionary secret police, which wore workers' blouses. Yet no new Committee of Public Safety was conjured into being by post-Jacobin leaders, and Blanqui failed to have the Red Flag substituted for the Tricolour. Moderate Republicans set up a working-class Garde Mobile to counter any new radical uprising, while the National Guard rose to 190,000 men, whose officers were elected by the Guards. Already, the government was blowing cool on any more change and certainly on socialist and communist attacks on property. Even an old rebel and conspirator like Raspail could write: 'The Terror of 1793 today in 1848! It has no more meaning; it would be no more than atrocious folly, a drama conceived by a Nero, fire put to Rome in order to translate the fire of Troy into action. Terror against whom? Against ourselves indeed, since we all think the same.'

So far, there had been a revolution without a revolution of terror. But the new Minister of the Interior was the radical Ledru-Rollin, and he appointed *Commissaires* to run the country instead of the old prefects of the previous regime. What were their powers? 'They are unlimited,' Ledru-Rollin said. 'Agents of a revolutionary authority, you are also revolutionaries.' The sovereign people had given them the power to act as they thought best for the public safety. As for the other forces of the Revolution, mistakes had been made. The owners of property were still armed, while the workers were not. As Blanqui warned, 'He who has iron, has bread.'

National elections were held without fraud at the ballot box. In spite of several hundred paid agitators and socialist agents, there was a large conservative and liberal majority sent to the National Assembly. An insurrection of several thousand workers led by Blanqui was easily dispersed by the alerted National Guard before the Hôtel de Ville. The reaction began, as the radical Proudhon put it, 'beneath the roll of the drums of capital and privilege'. At Rouen, some anarchists led mobs of workers onto the streets and into the guns, and there was another massacre. By now, Lamartine was being accused of starting as an arsonist and ending as a fireman, dousing the flames he had lit.

Those such as Baudelaire and George Sand who had joined the radical clubs were disillusioned by the reaction. As the polemical Sand wrote in her diary: 'In Paris a person is a trouble-maker if a socialist; in the provinces, someone becomes a communist as soon as being a republican; and if by chance somebody is a republican socialist, then he feeds on human blood, kills small infants, beats his wife, drinks too much, and is a bankrupt and a thief.' Such demonizations of the parties on the Left led to a second victory for a Bonaparte. Marx branded the adventurer Louis Napoleon as a caricature of the first Napoleon, a case of farce following tragedy. But when he won the plebiscite for the post of President of the Republic, he received 5,500,000 votes against only 2,000,000 for all his rivals: the old leader Lamartine polled 17,000 ballots in all.

In December 1851, Louis Napoleon carried out a classic coup d'état on the model of the Carbonari. Yet this was a conspiracy of the state against the state. There were arrests at night without warrants by the new secret police. All strategic points and communications were occupied by selected army units. The munitions of the National Guard were sabotaged, rendering it unable to resist. Six hundred protesters were shot down in the streets. A proclamation by the President of the Republic, who would soon declare himself an Emperor, asserted that the National Assembly had 'ceased to exist'. It had tried to weaken the authority of Louis Napoleon, 'which I hold from the nation as a whole.' A plebiscite approved the President's coup by a majority of eleven to one. The revolution for the people was dead in a counter-conspiracy, wholly approved by the people.

The fourth Revolution in Paris was different from the previous three: the foreign enemies were literally at the gates. When the sick Emperor Louis Napoleon surrendered to Prussian forces at Sedan in 1870, there was a republican uprising and a Government of National Defence, which recruited 350,000 volunteers for a National Guard to defend the French capital against a siege. Led by a new Danton, Léon Gambetta, the Parisians faced a winter of starvation. Edmond de Goncourt heard a girl whisper to him in the Bois de Boulogne: 'Mister, will you mount me for a crust of bread?'

The city was bombarded for several hours over twenty-three nights. There were 400 civilian casualties, terrible for those times. The old revolutionaries emerged as salivating jackals into the fray. Led by the enduring Blanqui with his new journal, *La Patrie en danger*, radical leaders twice tried to take over the Hôtel de Ville and began to cobble together revolutionary governments, but they were again put down by democratic troops. Other uprisings in Lyon and Marseille and Toulouse were also contained.

Gambetta had to accept an armistice with the Prussian army, and then he was forced to resign. A new National Assembly was elected to make peace. A few of the ageing revolutionaries were elected, including Louis Blanc and Ledru-Rollin, along with the novelist Victor Hugo, but they were pushed out of office. The refugee Blanqui was sentenced to death in his absence. But a rebellion by the National Guard put a revived Commune in power with leaders from the followers of Blanqui and Proudhon and the anarchists and the Socialist First International.

Another Committee of Public Safety was instituted on the previous model of a regime of Terror. A second siege of Paris began, this time from other republican forces, which still controlled the remnants of the defeated French army. Growing in strength, the regulars took on the Parisian street fighters and battled them for seven days through the boulevards and alleys of the capital. Buildings were burned to clear lines of fire, including the Tuileries. All prisoners were executed, a final 147 Communards against a wall in the cemetery of Père-Lachaise.

This became the bloody archetype of many urban revolutions. Some 20,000 rebels had been slaughtered, perhaps only 1,000 of their professional attackers. The conspirators, particularly the Bolsheviks, would have to learn how to penetrate the army as well as the factory, to infiltrate the supply system as well as the proletariat, if they wanted any chance in the revolutions to come.

12. THE EARLY ART AND LITERATURE OF TERROR

William Blake was the visionary poet and artist par excellence of the French Revolution. From *Songs of Innocence* through to *America* and *Europe: A Prophecy*, his art illuminated the hopes of the time. He had watched in London the fall of its Bastille in 1780, the storming of Newgate Jail by the Gordon rioters. He wrote of terror in 1783 in his *Poetical Sketches*; the scene was an attack on Gwin, the King of Norway:

> The god of war is drunk with blood,
> The earth doth faint and fail;
> The stench of blood makes sick the heavens;
> Ghosts glut the throat of hell!

In his *Europe*, Blake took his fears across the Channel during the Terror:

And in the vineyards of red France appear'd the light of his fury.
The sun glow'd fiery red!
The furious terrors flew around
On golden chariots raging with red wheels dropping with blood!
The Lions lash their wrathful tails!
The Tigers couch upon the prey & suck the ruddy tide . . .

Curiously enough, the opponent of the Terror in Paris, Edmund Burke, had brought the word into prominence in the

English language. When he had written his early *Philosophical Enquiry into the Origin of our Ideas on the Sublime and Beautiful*, he had put forward an aesthetic of terrorism, which he denied in his anti-Jacobin *Reflections on the Revolution in France*. William Blake was himself ecstatic about the violence of rebellious Paris. He showed his passion in the dynamic lines of his engravings of the period, when

> Albion's Angel stood beside the Stone of night, and saw
> The terror like a comet . . .

In the frontispiece of *Europe*, Blake also drew a giant serpent enveloping the hopes of any unity between the squabbling nations (see plate 33). And indeed, he considered the loss of the American colonies to be the revenge of God on England's green and pleasant land, as Jehovah had struck Egypt with the plagues to make the Pharaoh let the Jewish peoples go.

> Then the Pestilence began in streaks of red
> Across the limbs of Albion's Guardian; the spotted plague
>   smote Bristol's
> And the Leprosy London's Spirit, sickening all their bands:
> The millions sent up a howl of anguish and threw off their
>   hammer'd mail,
> And cast their swords & spears to earth, & stood, a naked
>   multitude . . .
> The plagues creep on the burning winds . . .
> And by the fierce Americans rushing together in the night,
> Driven o'er the Guardians of Ireland, and Scotland and
>   Wales.
> They, spotted with plagues, forsook the frontiers, & their
>   banners, sear'd
> With fires of hell, deform their ancient heavens with shame
>   & woe.

The French Revolution and its consequences were best shown by Jacques-Louis David in his *Marat, Assassinated* (see plate 35), the prelude to the wind-blown *Napoleon crossing the Alps*. The shock of the killing of the terrorist leader in his bath was an indictment of terror itself: deceived by his murderers, Marat was not immune from the revenge of the persecuted. The tyranny he espoused in the name of the Will of the People, as David suggested, ended in the despotism of Napoleon, riding to imperial glory and eventual humiliation.

The defeat of Napoleon in Spain inspired Francisco de Goya to invent the modern description of horror in warfare. The peasant risings after 1808 against the French occupation liberated the Iberian peninsula, aided by the forces of the Duke of Wellington, who put paid to his rival at Waterloo. *Los desastres de la guerra*, a series of drawings by Goya, showed the consequences of a revolution for liberty, which was corrupted into a fierce tyranny. The Spanish freedom fighters were brutally executed in their mistaken belief that the French had come to deliver them, not to conquer them (see plate 34). In the painter's sleep, one sketch of his *Caprichos* showed the dream of Reason producing monsters. Indeed, it did; Goya's contemporaries had tried to reconcile 'the fraternity of the scaffold, the equality of the grave, the liberty of death'.

After Goya, an English painter of genius recognized the going down of the other Great Terror of the time. In 1840, J. M. W. Turner painted *The Slave Ship* or *Slaves Throwing Overboard the Dead and Dying – Typhoon Coming On*. The picture represented a true incident, when sixty years before a ship's captain had thrown overboard his cargo of sick Africans to claim the insurance. The last of the slaves had jumped of their own choice into the freedom of the furious seas.

In the painting, the strong waves and the gory sunset predominate, although sharks feed on the chained limbs of a black corpse. The slaves and the ship are almost swallowed up in the outrage of nature. The cruelty of humanity has offended the heavens, which rage at man's injustice to man. John Ruskin once owned the picture, declaring that Turner's immortality would be founded on it; but he sold it to an American because it was too distressing to live in front of such a spectacle of human suffering.

Such recognition of evil and repugnance at past cruelty, in which the sharks represented the whites feeding on their shackled prey, and divine anger threatened all in a typhoon of wrath, was disguised as a storm in the ocean. Victorian sensibility would accept just so much, as in Géricault's *Raft of the Medusa*. In that picture, the gloom overhanging the survivors was withdrawn in his distress, while the rescue ship sailed indifferently by. A code governed the horrors that could be depicted. Conscience was left to interpolate what was only suggested to the eye.

In literature, the terror of the time was translated to Gothic fantasy. In 1816, Mary Shelley conceived *Frankenstein* under the influence of her husband, Percy Bysshe Shelley, and Lord Byron. While a novel of horror, *Frankenstein* was also a penetrating analysis of the revolt from Reason, of the conflict between the Satanic urge for the outer limits of freedom and the need for the restraints of society. The hero Count Frankenstein was himself a compound of Shelley and Byron, and he sought the origins of life and human nature. He created a monstrous image, who was a foul caricature of his desires.

> His limbs were in proportion, and I had selected his features as beautiful. Beautiful! – Great God! His yellow skin scarcely covered the work of muscles and arteries beneath; his hair was of a lustrous black, and flowing, his teeth of a pearly whiteness; but these luxuriances only formed a more horrid contrast with his watery eyes, that seemed almost of the same colour as the dun white sockets in which they were set, his shrivelled complexion and straight black lips.

In fact, Count Frankenstein had created the terrible and distorted version of himself, the fiend of the inward dream. This monster raged away, and yet he was innocent. Created by a man, he looked for the company of men, who could not bear his sight. His distorted features predetermined their fears. Yet

Frankenstein's monster did not choose to be deformed. He was created abhorrent to men.

When the monster later confronted Count Frankenstein on the wild summit of a Swiss mountain, he was full of bitter anguish, disdain and malignity. His unearthly ugliness was almost too horrible for human eyes, and yet he rightly complained to his master: 'Remember, that I am thy creature; I ought to be thy Adam; but I am rather the fallen angel, whom thou drivest from joy for no misdeed. Everywhere I see bliss, from which I alone am irrevocably excluded. I was benevolent and good; misery made me a fiend. Make me happy, and I shall again be virtuous.'

The monster put the case of those who were doubly deformed, the first time by creation, the second time by society. What of the black slave, whose colour made him seem evil to his white masters, and whose work on an American plantation denied him family life? What of the slave of the new mines or factories, made filthy and broken by his toil with wages too low even to keep himself? What of the convict, condemned by his character as well as his crime to wear out his life in a cell or the Australian desert? The monster forced Count Frankenstein to make him an equally monstrous mate, or else he would smash the engines of science which had made him so deformed. If he got a mate, they would go to the vast spaces of South America where the beasts would be their only companions.

The Count began to make a female monster in the desolate Orkneys. Then he considered that her creation could breed a race of devils which might make 'the very existence of the species of man a condition precarious and full of terror'. If science created the damned of the earth, they would revolt and destroy the society that damned them. At the last moment, Frankenstein cut up the female monster, and in revenge, the monster destroyed Frankenstein's own wife and his best friend. Now Frankenstein felt compelled to hunt his monster to the uttermost ends of the earth and destroy him 'as a beast of prey'. His need for revenge devoured his soul. He died in vain in the wastes of the north, while his monster mourned him and left to kill himself on a funeral pyre.

The later hold of the Frankenstein legend on the mass mind through the dream machine of the cinema paid tribute to its original prophecy of the conflict between the demands of the industrial age and the atavistic urges of passion. The monster was the noble, warped self-sacrifice in the heart of Count Frankenstein himself. His Promethean urge to discover the secrets of human life merely loosed the wild in his soul. He believed the origins of existence lay in light and Adam, but the flaws in his own nature released a demon of the dark. He learnt too late that the conflict between human and engine, mercy and massacre, good and evil, science and terror, must be fought to the final destruction or to life without end, amen.

A late Victorian horror novel also captured the mass imagination of the centuries to come – Bram Stoker's *Dracula*, based on Balkan history and superstition. King Vlad III Dracula or the Impaler of Wallachia, a Romanian state stuck between the Danube and the Carpathian mountains, had established his control by killing 20,000 people and then spitting them on stakes (see plate 13). These were the families of the native Boyars, the local warlords, who had also been put down by the Tsar Ivan the Terrible.

Vlad III Dracula repeated his campaign of terror twice more. After the murder of his brother, in an earlier St Bartholomew's Day Massacre of 1460, he perpetrated a slaughter at Amlas. According to a contemporary German account: 'All those that he could gather together he ordered to be thrown, one on top of the other, like a hill, and to be shredded like cabbage with swords and knives. And their chaplain and the others whom he did not kill immediately, he took back to his country, and there he had them hanged.' He ordered the place, and everything in it, to be burned. Then from other dissident areas, 'he took people and brought them to Wallachia, men, women and children, and he ordered that all of them be impaled.'

To the scorched-earth policy of previous warlords Vlad added mass torture to his terror tactics against the Turkish advance of the Ottoman Empire. He set out his own subjects as mutilated living scarecrows to deter the Sultan from going forward (see plate 13). As the Byzantine chronicler Chalcondyles recorded, a field of stakes over a square mile met the Sultan. 'And there were large stakes on which he would see the impaled bodies of men, women and children, about 20,000 of them.' This spectacle deterred the Sultan 'and the other Turks, seeing so many people impaled, were scared out of their wits. There were babies clinging to their mothers on the stakes, and birds had made nests out of their breasts.'

This absolute ferocity worthy of Hulagu shocked even late medieval opinion. The gory details led to the vampire legends, in which Vlad III Dracula was resurrected by Bram Stoker as the fanged blood-drinker of the modern cinema. His recreation was helped by the actual memory of the Hungarian countess Elizabeth Bathori, who had drained the blood from 650 young girls so that she could bathe in fresh redness and keep herself forever young. Adding to Transylvanian mountain legends of blood-sucking creatures, who only lived as corpses by their nightly injections from the throats of the breathing, Stoker wrote a tale of imaginary terror, which still horrifies the world.

These primary examinations of the psychology of fear were enhanced by two superlative novels by Joseph Conrad, the examiner of British imperialism at the end of the century. *The Secret Agent*, 1907, was his lesser work. Based on a failed anarchist attempt to blow up the Greenwich Observatory, it was meant to expose 'the criminal futility of the whole thing, doctrine, action, mentality.' As he said of his appalling hero Verloc, he was 'a brazen cheat exploiting the poignant miseries and passionate credulities of a mankind always so tragically eager for self-destruction.' Verloc himself was 'a man blown to bits for nothing even most remotely resembling an idea, anarchistic or other. As to the outer wall of the Observatory, it did not show as much as the faintest crack.'

Conrad's masterpiece, *Heart of Darkness*, began with his narrator Marlow considering the London docks, 'one of the dark places of the earth.' As the brooding gleam of the monstrous city by day changed to its lurid glare by night, Marlow remembered that the darkness had lain on the Thames 'yesterday'. What had the commander of a Roman trireme thought of the twisting river – 'sand-banks, marshes, forests, savages . . . cold, fog, tempests, disease, exile, and death.' From detesting the unknown, however, the Roman would have begun to surrender to 'the fascination of the abomination'. Even his disgust would have made him powerless to resist an escape.

So Conrad set his story with the suggestion that the heart of darkness lay in the European city and in the past as well as specifically in primitive lands. His hero had always craved to explore a great river in Central Africa, and at last he was appointed by a giant imperial trading company to captain a steamboat out there. Reaching the African river, Marlow found black chain-gangs condemned for the crimes they could not understand, building a railway which would rust before it worked. Other black contract labourers waited to die of sickness in an unnecessary pit. He met an immaculate accountant who had resisted 'the great demoralization of the land'. He heard of the remarkable trader Kurtz, who kept the ivory coming from the depths of the interior, and who was reputed to be a prodigy of pity and science and progress.

Marlow then marched to a station 200 miles upriver and found his steamboat sunk. He began getting hungry and ferocious himself as the months passed while he repaired the boat, surrounded by 'a taint of imbecile rapacity . . . like a whiff from some corpse.' All seemed unreal at the river station. 'The silent wilderness surrounding this cleared speck of the earth struck me as something great and invincible, like evil or truth, waiting patiently for the passing away of this fantastic invasion.'

At last the steamboat was repaired and Marlow took it up the great snake of the river. The crew were cannibals and lived on rotten hippo meat. The passengers were foolish, pink, irrelevant European pilgrims. The grimy beetle of the ship crawled on 'deeper and deeper into the heart of darkness'. Nothing could be understood by Marlow on this journey back to the hidden roots of civilization and the human heart.

When the boat reached Kurtz's station in the interior, it was stacked with ivory from slaughtered elephants. Its invisible master seemed to be the favourite of the wilderness which 'had taken him, loved him, embraced him, got into his veins, consumed his flesh, and sealed his soul to its own by the inconceivable ceremonies of some devilish initiation.' To achieve such riches, how many of the powers of darkness now claimed Kurtz for their own? He must have taken a high seat among the devils of the forest. He had even written a report on how to suppress the customs of the Africans, in which he claimed that Europeans should appear as supernatural beings and do good by the power of their will. Yet his report ended with the scrawled words, 'Exterminate all the brutes!'

Soon Kurtz himself appeared on a stretcher, as emaciated as an ivory carving of death. He was surrounded by his tribe of black killers. They stayed on the bank, leaving him to come on board the steamboat, now piled with his elephant tusks. He staggered back to a last unspeakable native ceremony, only to be stopped by Marlow who tried to break the spell over him, 'the heavy, mute spell of the wilderness – that seemed to draw him to its pitiless breast by the awakening of forgotten and brutal instincts, by the memory of gratified and monstrous passions.'

Marlow took the dying Kurtz back down the river on the steamboat, while 'both the diabolic love and the unearthly hate of the mysteries it had penetrated fought for the possession of that soul satiated with primitive emotions, avid of lying fame, of sham distinction, of all the appearances of success and power.' The banks of the river slipped monotonously past the dirty boat that was the forerunner of change, of conquest, of trade, of massacre, of blessings. Kurtz died with an expression of intense and hopeless despair on his face and the words, 'The horror! The horror!'

Conrad's *Heart of Darkness* remains the best analysis of that jumble of instinct and fear with which Victorian men confronted the terror inside themselves and which they met on their travels. No Englishman could deny the fact that Boudicca had impaled the population of Roman London on stakes or burned her captives in giant wicker men. The Victorians were not removed from barbarians by many centuries. They tried never to show the violence within by rigid codes of behaviour.

The truth was the horror, which Kurtz saw at the base of all human desire and mission – the outcast's urge to be both god and beast, to rend, hoard, kill, dominate, indulge, pursue, satisfy and die at the limits of power and lust. Such an escape into terror and the black forests of Germany and the human self was the final solution for the prodigies of Europe such as Kurtz. Their weaker followers were left to tell the little lies of civilization and to forget the horror that lay at the root of all instinctive action in men. In the words of Arthur Rimbaud, poet and traveller in East Africa: 'We have faith in poison. We know how to surrender our whole selves every day. Now comes the time of the assassins.'

13. BLACK TERROR

In ancient Egypt, the Nubians of the Sudan were despised and brutalized. The Greeks preferred to enslave barbarians, who did not speak their language; but sometimes they put their own people in chains, whatever the sheen of their skins. In the Roman Empire, slaves were merely taken from any defeated race: Greek philosophers themselves were so degraded. The unfortunate legacy, however, of the Arabs to the Europeans was racial bondage, along with the benefits of algebra and mathematics and medicine.

The Arabs and Berbers and Persians invented the continental slave trade which drove tens of millions of African captives across the Sahara by caravan or to the Red Sea by dhow. While scholars insisted that Islam was an all-embracing faith, they pronounced that all prisoners of any ethnic origin could be lawfully enslaved after jihad. Using the name of *abd*, however, the Arabs confused the word 'black' with 'slave', although this did not stop them from enslaving millions of white people, mostly from Spain and the Balkans and Russia, in the centuries to come. Even the supreme medieval historian of the Mediterranean, Ibn Khaldūn, designated the black tribes below the African deserts as not essentially human with 'attributes which are quite similar to those of dumb animals'.

As Islam had seen its jihad as a religious duty, so Portugal began the European slave trade as a Christian mission. In 1441, Henry the Navigator, the Prince of Portugal and the Grand Master of the refugee Templar Order called the Knights of Christ, looked on the first black slaves seized from Arab Mauritania. His chronicler declared that Prince Henry 'reflected with great pleasure upon the salvation of those souls that before were lost'. Yet the horror of inflicting more slavery upon Africa had less to do with God than with commerce. During the five centuries that followed, the transportation of some 24,000,000 men and women and children across the Atlantic to serve in bondage was the greatest crime ever perpetuated by Western civilization on other people before the advent of Nazi Germany.

Some 9,000,000 of the black victims died on the voyage across the Atlantic, while 15,000,000 survived to toil in the Americas. The very mass of the slaves involved in the trade degraded their individuality and their condition. As in the later case of the Jews in the Nazi concentration camps, the size of the operation reduced its victims to the status of animals. 'Markets of men are here kept,' a slaver wrote from West Africa, 'in the same manner as those of beasts with us.'

So they were. The African captives were snared like game, physically examined as closely as horses, bought and branded like cattle, herded in barracoons like pigs, chained below decks like wild beasts, then penned and led out to labour in the American fields under the whip like donkeys until they were worn to death. Slavery, as Voltaire said, might have been as ancient as war, and war as human nature. Yet even the Arabs had never subjected the ancient institution so stringently to the laws of commerce.

The mechanisms of Europe, from the account book to the design of the between-decks of the slaveship, from the drunken haggling with the Kings of Bonny to the auction in Charleston, were designed to degrade man's view of man. The Protestant slavers did not baptize as the Portuguese had. There was no mission now in Africa, only money to be made. The white crews of the slaveships were the refuse of the docks, for they were as likely to die of disease in the stinking holds as they were to be abandoned penniless and sick in the West Indies. They were themselves servants to a system that counted men's work only in ledgers. The economic basis of slavery corrupted all those it touched and freed through wealth only some thousands of citizens in a few European cities and on plantations in the Americas.

For slavery in Africa was not a process for the accumulation of capital. There was no local method of doing this. Among the Ashanti, for instance, the number of slaves possessed by a man represented his place in society, not his wealth. Slaves were allowed to keep their personal property and the hard-working slave enriched himself, not only his master.

As Dr Johnson fulminated in his introduction to a collection of voyages of discovery: 'The Europeans have scarcely visited any coast but to gratify avarice, and extend corruption; to arrogate domination without right, and practise cruelty without incentive.' In the European system, economic robbery was added to personal servitude. Once the slave was considered as a mere unit of production, arguments could be held seriously in Jamaica about the return on capital if slaves were worked to death quickly and new imports bought, as opposed to the profit when slaves were worked to death slowly and bred their own replacements. In investment terms, treating people as beasts made the calculations simpler.

Yet Africa was no Utopia when the Europeans reached its coasts. Old Calabar on the Niger Delta, for example, was rightly notorious as a slaving centre. The local Efik people and the Ibibios were loathed by the rest of the coast tribes. They had an indifference to human beings and a wish for death that made them ghastly to other West Africans. Their ruling secret society, called Egbo, or Leopard, flogged and killed to keep order; its followers appeared with sword and whip, hidden behind a demonic mask with long raffia hair.

At the funerals of kings, wives were strangled and followers beheaded or buried alive. The journal of a slave-trader described the death of a local town chieftain in these words: 'So we got ready to cut heads off, and at five o'clock in the morning we began to cut slaves' heads off, fifty heads in that one day . . . and there was play in every yard in town.' With such contempt for life dominant in Old Calabar, the captains of the slaveships could feel merciful as well as commercial. They were, after all, taking the blacks from what the evangelist and explorer Mary Kingsley called 'the steady kill, kill, kill' of West Africa.

The vested interests of the trade made it of interest to all. As another slaver wrote, its benefits outweighed its real or pretended mischiefs. 'It will be found, like all other earthly advantages, tempered with a mixture of good and evil.' The European traders made money, the Africans escaped to regular work and possible Christianity, the southern planters secured a labour force strong enough to cultivate sugar and tobacco and cotton and rice. After all, economics were paramount, and as the enslaved American Indians had largely died off, labour had to be secured from somewhere. White convicts and servants were more trouble and less productive than black people, who were acclimatized to the heat of the tropics.

The political economy of slavery did not raise the slaves from savagery to a Christian culture. Many of them did not come from herding or forest cultures, but from farming or even town societies. The black people from West Africa were not Neolithic, but already worked in copper and tin, while using iron hoes. While certain of the forest tribes of Africa were still at a primitive stage of civilization, the people of Ashanti and Dahomey, the Fulanis and the Yorubas, already had complex systems of trade and government, agriculture and the division of labour before they met Muslim or European influence.

The continual rapes of slavery, which brought the forest and village peoples of Africa to the plantations of America, also brought out the beast in their new white masters, whose violence and sexual fear could make them practise barbarities inhuman even to Old Calabar. In Jamaica in the seventeenth century, rebellious blacks were nailed to the ground and burned slowly to death limb by limb up to the head. They were castrated or flayed or slit open with pepper dropped into their wounds. In the southern United States of the nineteenth century, the lynchings of black men were a commonplace in fearful times, the bodies burning alive as they hung screaming from a tree. The master's horror of the alien and his fear of its revolt unleashed the violence within him. His effort to subjugate his fellow men for his gain and to treat them as beasts discovered the brute in himself.

Yet the slave revolts of those like Nat Turner in the Americas did not end the barbarous system. The white French Revolution, and not the American, spread the ideas of liberty and equality beyond continental Europe. Its message of emancipation was translated to the sugar and coffee colony of San Domingo, now called Haiti. This rich part of the Gallic empire, known as the Pearl of the Antilles, was infected by the rhetoric of the Jacobin Republic in Paris. An uprising of the half-million slaves and Creole peoples against their 40,000 French overlords began under Toussaint L'Ouverture. In response, the Convention abolished slavery in 1794, a decree later rescinded. This brought no end to the civil butchery in Haiti, where the free Creoles still needed black slaves to work the plantations. As in France, the bourgeois wanted to control the peasants and the workers.

Toussaint L'Ouverture was captured and died in a Swiss prison. The expeditionary forces sent from France were eventually slaughtered in a war of exceptional ferocity. Haiti declared its black independence in 1804: three years later, the evangelical Christians led by William Wilberforce in the Parliament at Westminster abolished the slave trade, a prohibition enforced by the British Navy.

Haiti had led the way to right this ancient wrong, but the appalling tyrannies which followed its epic victory for its oppressed peoples ruined its initiative. The self-styled Emperor Jacques Dessalines ruled for only two years before being hacked to death. The murderous King Henri Christophe, who was his successor, was forced into suicide after thirteen years of misrule. They would remain the worst examples for many post-colonial heads of government.

The Portuguese had begun the slave trade as a crusade, and

the British ended it as another crusade to abolish the sins of the past. Once the London Parliament declared the sale of human beings illegal in 1807, foreigners were not allowed to make money from what Liverpool had to forgo. In the first sixty years of the nineteenth century, the British always kept one or two squadrons of frigates off the west coast of Africa to extirpate the traffic in flesh. These permanent blockaders forced the local chiefs to give up trading in their captives and ruined the West African middlemen, except for those who dealt in the palm oil of the Niger. The British presence in West Africa was reduced to three poor footholds of little importance.

As an investment, the continent was written off. Only South Africa mattered, because of its white colonists and strategic position on the route to India. Even among the reformers, the ending of the slave trade led to a loss of interest in Africa. The Governor of Sierra Leone warned in the very year of 1807: 'To abolish the slave trade is not to abolish the violent passions which now find vent in that particular direction. Were it to cease, the misery of Africa would arise from other causes; but it does not follow that Africa would be less miserable: she might even be less miserable, and yet be savage and uncivilized.'

Paradoxically, the Turkish Sultan, seeking British support in the Crimean War against Russia, agreed to abolish the slave trade in the Ottoman Empire in 1855, before it was even terminated in the United States of America. The rebellious Arabs in the provincial Hījaz around Mecca and Medina used that emancipation as a reason for revolt. The local sheikh issued a fatwa. The ban on the slave trade was opposed to the holy law of Islam. The Turks were heretics. Jihad could now be pronounced against them, and they could be enslaved.

Although the revolt was suppressed, the Ottoman sultans exempted Arabia from its prohibition of the slave trade, which has continued in clandestine forms until this day. Too late, reparations are still sought in the United States for this trade in terror, which mostly ended in the nineteenth century. None can be given. History contains its crimes; it does not excuse them. As a method of trade or government, state terror is only repaid by popular hatred for the past and the hope of a better performance in the future.

14. TERROR AND THE WARRIOR

Panic struck the Trojan hero Hector when Achilles assaulted him outside the walls of his beleaguered city. As Homer sang in the *Iliad*, Hector trembled when he saw the fearsome ash spear of his enemy, whose bronze armour shone as a blazing fire or the rising sun. Hector ran before the avenger, who pursued him as a hawk hunts a she-dove, 'who flies in terror before him':

> Yet he keeps close, screaming at her and lunging
> Time and again, his heart pumping for the kill.

Doomed though he was, Hector turned and was slain and mutilated, regretting his brief attack of fear in front of his watching people.

No lover of lethal heroes, the Medea of Euripides declared that she would rather stand in the battle-line three times than bear a baby once. There was more pain and fright involved in giving birth than seeking death. There was little comfort for fearful men and women, however, in the heroic Norse sagas or the Grail romances. Admittedly, the Danish warriors were terrified in their Great Hall before Beowulf arrived to save them from the night monsters, Grendel and her offspring. Yet in the sagas, the berserker Vikings crushed their enemies by horror at their insane ferocity; they preferred the slaughter of the whole warband to any surrender. In the climactic Battle of Bravellir, where Sigurd Hring destroyed his uncle Harald Wartooth, the encounter was an early Armageddon, according to the twelfth-century *Danish History* of Saxo Grammaticus:

The sky seemed to fall suddenly on the earth, fields and woods sank into the ground. All things were confounded, and old Chaos came again, heaven and earth clashing in one tempestuous turmoil, and the world rushing to universal ruin.

In the Grail romances, too, there was little time for fear. Retribution was so savage that the knights and the squires fought to the last man, fearing torture or decapitation. The word 'crusade' has remained anathema in Islam because of its hidden message of cruelty and oppression. There are few records of the feeling of recruits in wartime before the eighteenth century, when some rules of engagement were followed, so that prisoners might be taken, and the foot soldier might tremble in front of his officers more than the enemy.

Terror certainly enforced discipline in the early British army and navy. By this time, the slitting of the ears or the nose or the branding of the forehead of the disobedient private was forbidden, but he could still be hamstrung or thrust for weeks into a black hole or given up to five hundred lashes, tied to a wheel. Worse penalties were running the gauntlet of whips, or flogging round the fleet, an offender rowed to all the men-of-war to receive two, three, or five hundred or even a thousand lashes. Before his death on the Plains of Abraham before Quebec, Major-General James Wolfe told the 20th Foot in his regimental orders:

A soldier who quits his rank, or offers to flag, is instantly to be put to death by the Officer who commands that platoon, or the Officer or Sergeant in rear of that platoon; a soldier does not deserve to live who will not fight for his King and country.

The soldiers of the republican armies that were to follow were frightened not so much by their commanders as by the conditions of combat and their enemies. During the American revolutionary war, a rebel attack on Quebec, now held by British troops, left the later traitor Benedict Arnold defeated in street fighting. He went on besieging a superior force in the Canadian city with the remnants of his volunteer army. Ravaged by winter, the Americans held on. Their morale was explained by the amazement of a British major, who found that the captured Yankee officers consisted of a blacksmith and a hatter, a butcher and a tanner, a shoe-maker and a tavern-keeper, who all 'pretended to be gentlemen'.

So social mobility and lack of punishment led to Arnold's troops surviving until they had to retreat in 1776, when the snows allowed. Disease killed them as in so many expeditions before. Death pits were dug all the way to Ticonderoga; smallpox and typhus, malaria and dysentery laid low more than British bullets. The same was true in General George Washington's winter camp the following year at Valley Forge, after a series of defeats around occupied New York. The soldiers lived on 'fire-cake and water'. A Dr Waldo could not swallow 'a bowl of beef soup, full of burnt leaves and dirt, sickish enough to make a Hector spew.' The troops were sustained by the iron rules of their Prussian drill-master, Friedrich Wilhelm von Steuben, and their patriotic hatred of the foreign invaders, especially the Hessian mercenaries.

Propaganda against the British also kept them going. As a Pennsylvanian attorney wrote about his belief of the behaviour of the foe, they were 'banditti, headed by that monster of rapine, General Howe ... destroying and burning what they please, pillaging, plundering men and women, stealing boys above ten years old, deflowering virgins, driving into the City for their use droves of cattle, sheep, hogs; poultry, butter, meal, meat, cider, furniture and clothing of all kinds, loaded upon our horses.'

Such a historical process of living off the land was repeated by the most feared of the British commanders, Lieutenant Colonel Banastre Tarleton, the only one to thrash the Americans with his own guerrilla tactics. He took no prisoners in his long marauding rides. He executed Quakers and rebels alike. 'Tarleton's Quarters' meant no mercy. Yet after his defeat at Cowpens, his campaign of terror could not save the army of Lord Cornwallis from its surrender at Yorktown, where the British capitulated to George Washington and the marquis de Lafayette, who then wrote home: 'The play, sir, is over.'

That had been a bloody play, but in this republican war, the prisoners were reasonably treated and eventually returned home after a peace convention was signed. In the French Revolution, however, the levied soldiers turned on internal rebels with horrid ferocity, and they treated foreign invaders with equal barbarity. Although they held themselves to be citizen soldiers under loose discipline with elected officers, they were whipped into a professional army by Napoleon and his generals, who treated their defeated rivals with some respect. All broke down, however, in the terrible retreat from Moscow of 1812, when the French army was reduced to starvation and cannibalism, while the Cossacks exacted the fearsome revenge of mountain cavalry upon the invaders.

While Vice-Admiral Horatio Nelson won the decisive Battle of Trafalgar with a press-ganged and terrorized fleet of bluejackets, Arthur Wellesley, the Duke of Wellington, equally triumphed in the Battle of Waterloo with many of the criminal classes of England in his ranks, who feared him almost as much as he feared them. In the imperial wars of the Victorian age, however, the iron discipline which kept together the thin red lines and squares of the army was sometimes superseded by the fear of a certain horrible end in the case of defeat. If desertion or mutiny nearly always ended in failure and punishment, disembowelling or flaying at the hands of an Afghan or Ashanti or Bini opponent was a worse prospect.

Once at war against a tribal enemy, the only thing which would save a soldier's life was to stick by his comrades and his officers. This was the ultimate boost to morale, the need to cohere in order to survive. And it led to the extraordinary defiance of the British redcoats at their defeat by the Zulus in 1879 at Isandlwana and the amazing defence of Rorke's Drift. These were fights to the final survivor, because any kind of death was cleaner by assegai than by torture after the battle.

There were twin terrors in any armed force. The first was the terror of discipline, which ranged from flogging to breaking on the wheel to a firing squad. The second was fear of the hostile array. Before Isandlwana, the raw soldiers opposing the Zulus at Fort Newdigate panicked and fired into the rustling night, wounding three of their own men: this outpost was then called 'Fort Funk'. The reality of certain death led such recruits to individual courage in the ranks, worthy of the Norse or crusader heroes. That was the paradox of war, the cowardice conquered by comradeship, fear giving way to fury, a harsh regime producing a fighting force capable of resisting ferocious foes.

15. THUGGEE

The East India Company, backed by the British state, ran for too long a mercantile empire in the Asian subcontinent. After the defeat of Napoleon and the French, it was only opposed by some secret societies and cults. The most interesting of these were the Thugs. After Lord Mornington's capture of Seringapatam in 1799, Mysore and several of the neighbouring kingdoms in southern India came under British control. The scattered British soldiers and administrators began to discover that gangs of stranglers infested the roads of southern India in the winter season of travel; about a hundred of these murderers were caught near Bangalore. They also seemed to operate in the north; in 1810, the bodies of thirty travellers, ritually dismembered, were found in wells between the Ganges and the Jumna. Travellers were frequently killed in various parts of the vast subcontinent. Authority was weak, and many bands of robbers lay in wait for villagers or townsmen stupid enough to wander abroad out of their own areas.

There was nothing to prove that these murders were in any way connected until Richard Sherwood, a surgeon at Fort St George in Madras, managed to find informers among the ritual killers who terrorized the Indian roads. His account of the sect eventually led to its investigation and suppression. He entitled his article 'Of The Murderers Called *Phansigars*'.

The *Phansigars*, or stranglers, are thus designated from the Hindustani word *Phansi*, a noose. In the more northern parts of India, these murderers are called *Thugs*, signifying deceivers. The sect was often protected by local rulers, with whom it shared the loot seized from murdered travellers, and its members lived as ordinary peasants. The killers never attacked Europeans, for fear of retribution; and they operated a good hundred miles from their homes against fellow travellers on the roads. *Phansigars* never commit robbery unaccompanied by murder, their practice being first to strangle and then to rifle their victims. It is also a principle with them to allow no one to escape of a party, however numerous, which they assail, that there may be no witness of their atrocities. The only admitted exception to this rule is in the instance of boys of very tender age, who are spared; adopted by the *Phansigars*; and, on attaining the requisite age, initiated into their horrible mysteries.

They operated in gangs of ten to fifty men. They were mainly Muslims, yet they did have Hindus among them, and they worshipped Hindu deities. Their advance intelligence was excellent. They sent ahead scouts to investigate and win the confidence of wealthy travellers. Later, the main body of the Phansigars joined their companions as strangers. Scouts were placed in front and behind the victim or victims, in case these should escape.

Two *Phansigars* are considered to be indispensably necessary to effect the murder of one man, and commonly three are engaged ... While travelling along, one of the *Phansigars* suddenly puts the cloth round the neck of the person they mean to kill, and retains hold of one end, while the other end is seized by an accomplice; the instrument crossed behind the neck is drawn tight, the two *Phansigars* pressing the head forwards; at the same time the third villain, in readiness behind the traveller, seizes his legs and he is thrown forward upon the ground. In this situation he can make little resistance. The man holding the legs of the miserable sufferer, now kicks him in those parts of the body endowed with most sensibility, and he is quickly dispatched.

The murderers' weapon was the *rumal*, or handkerchief, which they wore knotted around their waists. If other travellers came up before the body was buried, the gang would wail over it, as if one of their own number had died, and they would often feast or camp on the grave of their victims to destroy traces of newly dug earth. The bodies of victims were mangled, both to prevent identification and to satisfy the ritual demands of the cult. The legs were disjointed, the face was disfigured, and body was gashed and gutted 'to expedite its dissolution, as well as to prevent its inflation', for jackals might detect and dig up a decomposing corpse (see plate 36). Each band of Phansigars had a special ritual butcher to attend to the deceased.

The sect worshipped Kali or Bhowani, the Hindu goddess of Death (see plate 37). Before a marauding expedition, a sheep was sacrificed in front of an image of the goddess, a black-skinned vampire-like figure, smeared with dried gore. Beside her were images of the lizard and the snake and the emblems of murder – the noose, the knife and the pickaxe, which was so sacred a tool that it was supposed to fly automatically into the hand of its user. Flowers were scattered about; fruit and cakes and spirits were offered to the goddess. 'The head of the sheep being cut off, it is placed, with a burning lamp upon it and the right forefoot in the mouth, before the image . . . and the goddess is entreated to reveal to them whether she approves of the expedition they are meditating. Her consent is supposed to be declared, should certain tremulous or convulsive movements be observed, during the invocation, in the mouth and nostrils, while some fluid is poured upon those parts.'

The religious tradition of the sect believed that in the golden days of mythology Kali helped her followers by devouring the dead bodies of their victims. On one occasion, however, a novice looked back and saw the goddess in the act of eating a corpse; as a punishment, she refused to continue gobbling down the evidence. Yet she liked her devotees well enough to present them with one of her teeth for a pickaxe, a rib for a knife and the hem of her sari for a noose. She ordered her followers in future to cut up and bury their prey, and she also told them that they should favour the colours of yellow and white, even in their nooses.

As do most efficient secret societies, the Phansigars had a vocabulary of secret signs and a secret language. Certain marks on the road showed that a victim had been prepared, and pointed the way taken by the scouts. 'Drawing the back of the hand along the chin, from the throat outwards, implies that caution is requisite – that some stranger is approaching. Putting the open hand over the mouth and drawing it gently down implies that there is no longer cause for alarm.' The phrase 'Sweep the place' meant 'See that no one is near.' 'Bring firewood' meant 'Take up your positions.' 'Eat betel' meant 'Kill him.' 'Look after the straw' meant 'Take care of the corpse, bury it and keep watch.' 'Descendants of Bhowani?' meant 'Are you also Phansigars?' Intermarriage helped to preserve the cult's secrecy. Indian families in their own villages kept very much to themselves, and the Phansigar women knew that any disclosure of the secrets of their menfolk would mean the destruction of them all.

Initiation into the order was by birth, though some captured male children were also initiated. Boys of ten or more were allowed to accompany the murder bands, with a near relative as a tutor. The tutor forced the child to be absolutely obedient and to carry his bundle and his food. Slowly, he taught the boy to understand the mystery of Kali and to be wholly silent to strangers. 'He is instructed to consider his interest as opposed to that of society in general; and to deprive a human being of life, is represented as an act merely analogous and equivalent to that of killing a fowl or a sheep.' At first, the boys were only allowed to watch the murders at a distance; but soon they took part in the operation as scouts, and eventually, after the age of puberty, as murderers themselves. Sometimes the young murderers used hemp and other drugs to nerve themselves for an attack, but most of the older Phansigars used no drugs in their stranglings.

At the height of the sect's activity, tens of thousands of

voyagers were killed annually. One member at his trial claimed to have been a witness to so many ritual murders that he had 'stopped counting when he reached the thousand'. The Phansigars inspired such terror that they had operated for centuries without much retribution, for no one would inform against them. Yet the Indian authorities, when they caught a band, walled each one up alive in a pillar or cut off his hands and nose.

What shocked Dr Sherwood most about the sect was that it murdered without guilt.

> What constitutes the most odious feature in the character of these murderers, is, that prodigal as they are of human life, they can rarely claim the benefit of even the palliating circumstance of strong pecuniary temptation. They are equally strangers to compassion and remorse – they are never restrained from the commission of crimes by commiseration for the unfortunate traveller. '*Phansigari*,' they observe, with cold indifference blended with a degree of surprise, when questioned on this subject, 'is their *business*'; which, with reference to the tenets of fatalism, they conceive themselves to have been pre-ordained to follow.

Fatalism also led them to compare themselves to tigers; for they claimed that just as the tiger fulfilled the designs of nature by preying on other animals, so they simply fulfilled their own destiny in preying on men. Everyone's fate was written on his forehead; the servants of Kali were merely agents of the goddess, not the cause of men's deaths. So ended Dr Sherwood's account of the Phansigars, who were known from then onward by their northern name of Thugs.

One of the first people to read Sherwood's paper was William Sleeman, a young officer in the Bengal Army who already had a strong interest in native affairs and had learned four Indian languages. Sleeman became absorbed in the problem of Thuggee, and he began to investigate Thug activities within his territory. His discoveries there created a sensation because they suggested that the murderous sect was a nationwide organization. In 1830, the governor-general, Lord William Bentinck, officially appointed him to suppress Thuggee over the whole of central India.

Sleeman found a situation of particular difficulty. The Thugs were nearly impossible to distinguish from the dacoits (robbers) and other bandits along the roads. They were protected by villages out of fear, and by local rulers, whom they bribed. As the bodies of dead travellers were rarely found, no one knew whether missing relatives had fled, been eaten by beasts, died of natural causes, or fallen to the marauding armies of the native princes, which extorted plunder from all and sundry. There were no police outside the British possessions in India, and so Sleeman had to found his own force.

The British officer had learned the Thugs' language, Ramasi, from Sherwood's paper, and he was able to build up a network of informers among them. He also mapped out the usual scenes of their crimes, plotted their habits and catalogued their methods of choosing and disposing of their victims. His new body of armed helpers was sent after the Thugs wherever he found them, despite protests from some of the native rulers and the British administrators of some neighbouring states. And in studying his Thugs as carefully as Sherlock Holmes studied Moriarty, Sleeman became their historian.

According to him, the Thugs might originally have been Persian light horsemen from the pastoral tribe of the Sagartii, whom Herodotus had described as fighting with only a dagger and a noose of twisted leather. They came to India, perhaps, with the Muslim invaders. The Thugs themselves boasted that the eighth-century carvings in the caves of Ellora showed Thugs already engaged in ritual murder. 'In one place,' a Thug leader, Feringheea, testified, 'you see men strangling; in another burying the bodies; in another carrying them off to the graves. There is not an operation in Thuggee that is not exhibited in the caves of Ellora.' A Persian historian told of 1,000 Thugs captured at Delhi about 1290 and released, in a mistaken act of clemency, to terrorize Bengal. In the sixteenth century, the Emperor Akbar captured another 500 Thugs, while the French traveller Thevenot remembered the 'cunningest robbers in the world' strangling travellers on the road from Delhi to Agra.

The Thugs themselves explained their origin in terms of the Hindu tradition that a demon had devoured mankind as each human was created. The demon was so large that the depths of the sea covered him only to the waist. Then Kali came to the rescue and cut the demon down; but from every drop of his blood, another demon sprang up. When she killed these new devils, each drop of their blood produced still more demons. While orthodox Hindus maintained that Kali solved the problem of the multiplying demons by licking the blood from their wounds, the Thugs claimed that Kali grew tired and made two men from the sweat on her arms. She gave these two original Thugs handkerchiefs and told them to kill all the demons without shedding a drop of blood. The Thugs immediately obliged and then offered to return the handkerchiefs. But Kali made them keep the handkerchiefs to serve as a memorial and to provide a holy and profitable way of life for them and their descendants. The two men were not only permitted to strangle men like they did demons, but were commanded to do so. A Thug born into the trade could not escape his duty of religious murder.

Between the Thugs and Sleeman there developed a strange kind of understanding. Sleeman felt himself very much the instrument of God and destiny, as did the Thugs. A popular historian of the sect commented that one of their replies to Sleeman might have come from the mouth of an ancient Hebrew defending the record of his conquering and chosen people. 'From the time that the omens have been favourable,' the Thug declared, 'we consider travellers as victims thrown into our hands by the deity to be killed, and that we are the mere instrument in her hands to destroy them.'

Though Sleeman interrogated captured Thugs at length, he failed to discover why, although dedicated to a Hindu deity, they

should include so many Muslims. When he taxed one Muslim
Thug with disloyalty to his religion, he tried to justify his worship of Kali by declaring that she was identical with Fatima,
the daughter of the Prophet Muhammad. Yet Sleeman revealed the
Thugs as a religious cult, whose members had a sense of communion with each other and with their goddess and a dedication
to their way of life which have rarely been equalled in the history
of secret societies.

The symbol of the sacred pickaxe was as important to the
Thugs as that of the skull was to the Templars. It was consecrated
in an elaborate ceremony, being passed through fire seven times
and used as the guarantee of an oath. A perjurer was meant to
die a terrible death within six days of swearing by the pickaxe,
his head gradually turning round until his face stood over his
shoulder. If the sacred pickaxe fell from the hands of its bearer in
the gang, his death or the dissolution of the gang was certain
within a year. 'Do we not worship it,' a Thug said of the pickaxe,
'every seventh day? . . . Is its sound ever heard when digging
the grave by any but a Thug? And can any man even swear to a
falsehood upon it?'

Sleeman wrote a detailed description of the ritual feast or
Tuponee which was given after every murder, sometimes upon
the grave of the victim. The *goor* or coarse sugar took the place
of the Christian communion bread and wine. It was placed on
a blanket or sheet, spread on clean ground. Near it was placed
the consecrated pickaxe and a piece of silver as an offering. The
leader of the gang sat on the cloth, facing west; ranged around
him was an even number of the more distinguished stranglers.
The rest of the cult members of inferior grades sat around the
cloth on the ground. The leading Thug poured a little of the *goor*
into a hole and prayed: 'Great goddess, as you vouchsafed one
lakh and sixty-two thousand rupees to Joora Naig and Koduck
Bunwari in their need, so we pray thee, fulfil our desires.'

Such an honest prayer for gain was rarely uttered, even by a
gambler. The other Thugs repeated the prayer, while the leader

sprinkled holy water on the pit and the pickaxe and put a little *goor* on the hands of the members who sat on the blanket. The signal for a symbolic strangling was given, and the Thugs ate the *goor* from their hands in solemn silence. The remainder of the *goor* was then distributed to the surrounding acolytes. It was eaten only by those who had actually committed a murder. Any *goor* that fell on the ground was buried in the pit. If by chance a novice ate some of the *goor*, he was forced to go out and do his strangling at once. Because of the need for secrecy, curtains were always carried to erect a tent in which the *Tuponee* murder feast could be performed.

Feringheea spoke of the extraordinary impact this ceremony made: 'We all feel pity sometimes, but the *goor* of the *Tuponee* changes our nature. It would change the nature of a horse. Let any man once taste of that *goor*, and he will be a Thug, though he know all the trades and have all the wealth in the world. I never wanted food; my mother's family was opulent, her relations high in office. I have been high in office myself and become so great a favourite wherever I went, that I was sure of promotion. Yet I was always miserable while absent from my gang, and obliged to return to Thuggee. My father made me taste of that fatal *goor* when I was yet a mere boy; and, if I were to live a thousand years, I should never be able to follow any other trade.'

Sleeman declared that among the Thugs he had rarely discovered

> *wanton cruelty*; that is, pain inflicted beyond what was necessary to deprive the person of life – pain either to the mind or body. The murder of women is a violation of their rules to which they attribute much of our success against the system . . . but no Thug was ever known to offer insult either in act or in speech to the woman they were to murder. No gang would ever dare to murder a woman with whom one of its members should be suspected of having had criminal intercourse.

The Thugs were dedicated to killing for Kali; but outside their profession, they were pillars of family morality. One of Sleeman's assistants, indeed, paid the cult member Makeen Lodhi the compliment of being one of the best men he had ever known, to be trusted 'in any relation of life save that between a Thug who has taken the *auspices* and a traveller with something worth taking upon him. They all look upon travellers as a sportsman looks upon hares and pheasants; and they recollect their best sporting grounds, and talk of them, when they can, with the same kind of glee!'

Sleeman's intelligence from Thug informants, called approvers, was so good that he could forecast the movement of Thug gangs in the winter killing season. The government of the British in India printed his genealogical tables of the cult and maps of its crimes. Meanwhile, his European assistants, sepoys, troopers and armed irregulars rounded up the gangs of Thugs, whose pride in their past achievements began to work against them. They had always been proud of being perfect deceivers, capable of gulling any traveller about their true identity; now they fell like pigeons into Sleeman's net. They had been confidence men for so long in order to make friends with prospective victims that they eventually became the victims of overconfidence.

The size of the Thug gangs had grown by Sleeman's time, particularly in the north of India. They now moved about in groups of twenty or thirty and could combine quickly into greater gangs large enough to murder up to thirty travellers at a time. Greed had brought more Thugs out onto the roads, and they had begun to kill indiscriminately for profit, selling off girl children to prostitutes and leaving too many live witnesses and unburied corpses behind them (see plates 36 and 37). When Feringheea himself was caught in 1831, he had just returned from an expedition on which he had been present at the murder of a hundred men and five women. Yet Sleeman did support Feringheea enough to secure a pardon for him, despite the reluctance of the British administration to spare such a notorious killer. And Feringheea, in return, provided valuable information.

Sleeman was helped in his suppression of the Thugs by the kangaroo courts he used to try them. Though many of them were sentenced to death or imprisoned, those who turned into informers were pardoned, and Sleeman actually founded schools to teach their sons another craft. The parents found such an idea degrading; but, in the end, they themselves joined the schools to learn brickmaking, building and weaving. Their carpets became so famous that Queen Victoria, whose agents had eliminated the Thugs as a threat to the Pax Britannica, commissioned one for Windsor Castle.

Thuggee may have been a rigorous cult in its early days before the coming of the British, but when it was exposed, it had already become a degenerate form of a secret society – the Thugs' looting and murder for the sake of religion could hardly be distinguished from plain criminality. Their faith was important to them, but capable of evasion. Throughout the long holy wars between Hindus and Muslims in India, there was complete religious tolerance among the Thugs. Muslim devotees adopted Hindu beliefs and Hindu members did not despise the Qur'ān or the idea of paradise. Most curiously, the Thugs never played the role of a resistance movement to the British. Their compromise on Hindu and Muslim differences allowed them to accept any form of political authority, as long as they could kill for their belief.

If the Thugs had any political effect, it was negative and divisive. In the chaos and anarchy that the British found in India, the British could easily apply their principle of 'divide and rule' and use the troops of one petty state to conquer those of another. The Thugs helped to add to the general feeling of insecurity and terror in the subcontinent, so that the peasants often welcomed the British as their only guarantee of justice. The elimination of the killing cult by Sleeman and his assistants was the most graphic proof which the peasants could have; the villagers saw for the first time in Indian history the possibility of safe travel, guaranteed by troops and police who were not venal. In a society dominated by caste, the addition of another caste of conquerors hardly mattered. What did matter was the establishment of a strong central government, which could end the extortion and murder practised by local rulers and groups of bandits.

So the Thugs wished death upon themselves. Their fatalism and their religion allowed them to act out the urge toward murder and suicide in a way not permitted to civilized men outside the state of war. When they became degenerate, they almost willed their own suppression, as many secret societies do when they are conscious of backsliding. The Ku Klux Klan, for instance, in its third and most corrupt form, was to be as guilty about its tarnished image and as riddled with government spies as the Thugs in their decline. Yet the Klan was always something of a southern resistance movement against the North of the United States, while only in recent times has Thuggee been associated with Indian nationalism.

In an interesting letter, John Masters, who used Thuggee as the theme of his novel *The Deceivers*, told of ten years of strangling in the Gwalior area after Indian independence. 'There was a lot more than kidnapping – there were several murders, with or without robbery at the same time. There was a single Robin Hood type of figure, who was obviously being helped by the villagers, partly through fear and partly through some claim on his behalf, or by him, to be a modern Thug . . . thinking for one thing that it would be a nice patriotic Indian sort of murder/robbery.'

With the rise of nationalism in India, bandits were bound to use the Thugs as a justification for their crimes, although, as Masters pointed out, modern communications prevented a revival of the cult. 'It was essential for Thuggee to flourish that men should set out on six-month journeys through lands infested with cholera, cobras, flooded rivers, and ordinary bandits – so that when the travellers didn't return, no one worried for two years; then it was too late to find out; and the cobras got blamed again.'

The Thugs in India could exist only in chaos and ignorance. The British suppressed them more effectively by the railway and the telegraph than by the noose they used against their enemies. A modern industrial nation cannot tolerate any threat to its tourists or its lines of communication. Efficient modern Thugs, such as the America Mafia or Cosa Nostra, find it more profitable to control some of the lines of communication than to plunder them. After all, it is easier to rob a traveller by making him pay a toll for the service he needs than to strangle him for his wallet. You can only strangle a man once, while you may make him pay taxes all his life.

16. THE SECRET SOCIETIES
OF CHINA

The centralized rule of China began under the Han dynasty in the 200 years before the birth of Christ. The Emperor was absolute. As the Son of Heaven, his duty was to rule in righteousness. If he failed, there was a holy right of resistance. When the usurper Wang Mang took over the throne in AD 9, a bandit secret society, known from their masks as the Red Eyebrows, played a part in his overthrow. They were the forerunners of other mystic insurrectionary groups, known as the Copper Horses and the Iron Shins, who believed in the heretic thinking of Taoism as opposed to the official religion of Confucianism, just as Gnosticism was the antagonist of state Christianity under Byzantine rule.

Taoism was the earliest of the doctrines of sacred subversion. Such manifestos of fatalism rivalled the extreme beliefs of Islamic rebels. 'Do nothing,' was one canon, 'because heaven does all things.' Thus to be passive was allowed, but also allowed was the utmost resistance to tyranny. There were no natural laws to govern human behaviour, because the Way of Heaven was indifferent to what happened upon earth. As the Chinese scholar Lin Tung-chi declared: 'A typical Taoist native becomes a revolutionary as a rule. He does not mix with the people. With his pride as an artist, he stands alone without comrades. He is predestined to foresee a war of one against all and against everything. A more exalted and fraught frame of mind may not be imagined.'

With such a radical philosophy, the last emperor of the Liao dynasty would consign himself and his concubines, his servants and his works of art into a Viking pyre with the declaration: 'Let all things perish with me, the final ruler of my dynasty.' Such a mythical *Götterdämmerung* was the product of a sacred philosophy that denied the rule of human law. Its principles would be worked out in the ultimate bunker of Adolf Hitler.

In China, another secret society called the Yellow Turbans arose to fragment the Han empire. These rebels had a charismatic leader, Chang Chüeh, who subdued much of northern China. He was followed by three other bandit chieftains, who became Robin Hoods, enshrined in folk veneration. Kwan Yu and Liu Pei and Chang Fei were meant to have sworn a blood oath of resistance in a peach orchard. This initiation ceremony became the legendary basis of future Chinese secret societies.

With the breakdown of the Han empire, the Buddhist religion flourished under the succeeding kingdoms. When it was persecuted, it developed its own secret societies, particularly the White Lotus, which resisted the Mongol invasion of the Yuan dynasty. In the fourteenth century, White Lotus leaders in a campaign from the country to the city succeeded in taking over China in the name of the Ming dynasty, which survived until it was taken over by Manchu and Chi'ing successors.

Almost nothing is known about the ultimate agent of destruction, Chang Hsien-chung, who came from north China at the end of the Ming dynasty, and destroyed the rich province of Szechuan, killing many millions of people in the space of a few months. He was twenty-nine when he ordered the deaths of all the scholars of his capital at Chêng Tu because they disputed his title of King of the Great Western Kingdom.

Having destroyed the educated, Chang set about murdering the merchants, then the women, then the officials; finally he gave orders that his own soldiers should slaughter each other. He ordered the feet of his officers' wives to be cut off, and to make a mound of them; on top of the pile he placed the feet of his favourite concubine. He tallied the ears and feet which his bodyguard hacked from the bodies of villagers from the remote districts, and he stated his own reason for annihilation on a stone tablet which he caused to be erected in his memory:

> Heaven brought forth innumerable things to support man.
> Man has not one thing with which to recompense Heaven.
> Kill. Kill. Kill. Kill. Kill. Kill. Kill.

After Chang's death, the tablet was reversed and walled up. It was believed that if it were ever read again, it would herald another time of mass destruction.

Chinese secret societies, including the clandestine Triads, continued to attack the rulers at Peking with a series of peasant insurrections. The most extraordinary of these revolts was led by a scholar from Canton, Hung Hsiu-ch'uan. In 1837, he had a series of divine revelations, which were explained to him when he read a Gospel tract translated into Chinese. The Ten Commandments seemed to Hung to ratify his visions. Even more quickly than the first Apostles, Hung spread his primitive Protestant beliefs among the disaffected peasants of southern China. His Society of God Worshippers, or T'ai P'ings, captured Nanking, the southern capital of the Manchu empire, and they threatened the great European treaty ports as well as northern China beyond the Yangtze River. Hung took the titles of Younger Brother of Jesus and Heavenly King, who had come to install the Great Peaceful Heavenly Dynasty.

Initially, the European powers supported this extraordinary Christianized rebellion. The Anglican Bishop of Victoria, also called Hong Kong, declared that the insurrection of the T'ai P'ings was another crusade. Their troops did not rape or pillage. They forbade the opium trade and the foot-binding of women. Their only acts of destruction were those of early Protestant iconoclasm, the hurling down of Buddhist or Taoist images of the divine. They even distributed the entire Bible, now translated into Chinese (see plate 39). As another Messiah or Muhammad,

Hung Hsiu-ch'uan appeared to be ordained to bring his version of the Gospels to his reactionary homeland.

The European powers, however, were in China more to trade than to pray. They attacked the weakened Manchu government, and in 1860, Peking was taken and ravaged. A Royal Engineer, Captain Charles George Gordon, was one of the destroyers of the magnificent Summer Palace. 'We went out, and, after pillaging it,' he wrote to his mother, 'burned the whole place, destroying in a Vandal-like manner most valuable property . . . It was wretchedly demoralizing work for an army. Everybody was wild for plunder.'

A craven Manchu peace treaty offering a huge indemnity and trade concessions made the European powers switch their sympathies from the T'ai P'ings. Hung Hsiu-ch'uan was now condemned as a false prophet. Christianity must only reach China through European missionaries, not a warlord who claimed a divine revelation in the manner of Moses (see plate 39). Private armies subsidized by the merchants of Shanghai and supported by the British navy were sent out to aid the Manchu forces, first under an American adventurer, Frederick Ward, then under George Gordon, who took over the 3,000 troops of the 'Ever-Victorious Army'. Savagery was now shown by both sides. The rebels carried the heads of Manchu officers stuck on their spears, while hundreds of the T'ai P'ings were beheaded at Tsingpu, until the streets ran with blood. The revolt of Hung ended in horror, as so many other crusades had done.

The last of the Manchus had mortgaged China to the extortion of Western capitalism. Against such foreign control rose the ultimate Chinese rebel society, the Boxers, otherwise known as 'The Fists of Righteous Harmony' (see plates 15, 16 and 40). As with Islam, their influence lay in a belief in fatalism, which meant that all fighters were invulnerable. 'Cannon cannot injure,' they were told, 'water cannot drown.' Their xenophobic slogan was: 'Protect our country, drive out foreigners, and kill Christians.'

The scheming Empress Dowager supported the Boxer siege

The battle over the corpse of Achilles.
om a fifth-century Greek vase.

2. The destruction of Jerusalem.
From the Book of the Maccabees.

3. The Gunderstrup Cauldron,
dating from the first century AD.
In the relief work, a procession of
Nordic warriors move towards
the cauldron of sacrifice and
regeneration.
Courtesy of the National Museum,
Copenhagen.

4. An episode from the Albigensian
Crusade. An attack on a Cathar castle,
showing the naked celebrants of a
heretical rite.
From a bas-relief in the church of
St-Nazaire at Carcassonne.

5. The burning of the Jews as suspect poisoners during the Black Death. From a fifteenth-century woodcut.

6. 'Knock Devil Knock'. The spreader of the pestilence. From a woodcut printed in Cologne, 1508.

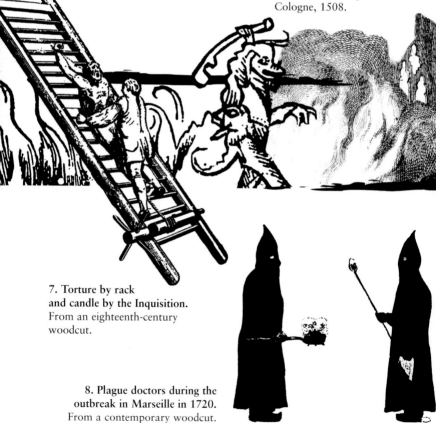

7. Torture by rack and candle by the Inquisition. From an eighteenth-century woodcut.

8. Plague doctors during the outbreak in Marseille in 1720. From a contemporary woodcut.

9. The killing of Jack Cade.
From a fourteenth-century painting.

10. The burning of St John's Monastery near Smithfield by Wat Tyler's men.
From a nineteenth-century engraving.

11. Highwaymen were hanged on gibbets as a dreadful example.
From an eighteenth-century engraving.

12. Max Schreck plays the Transylvanian vampire count in the first film on Dracula, Murnau's *Nosferatu* of 1922.

Hie facht sich an gar ein grausam
liche erschröckenliche hystorien. von dem wilden wü-
trich Dracole weyde Wie er die leüt gespist hot vnd
gepraten vñ mit den haütren yn einē kessel gesotten

13. King Vlad III Dracula impales and mutilates his victims. From a German woodcut, c.1500.

14. The European view of cannibals from the Americas. From German sixteenth- and seventeenth-century woodcuts.

15. A woodcut from *The Water Margin* or *All Men are Brothers*, reflecting popular sympathy for Chinese bandits. Rebels ambush government forces.

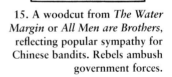

16. A European cartoon of 1900 depicts giant China behind the Great Wall opposed by European forces during the Boxer Uprising.

mit id inbeſſen ſpeculiren, und die Leute ge=
ſchidt rangieren tann; denn davon hängt alles
ab. Jd werde in dieſer Figur mit ihnen operieren.

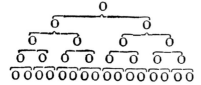

17. *The Cell System of a Conspiratorial Society* drawn by Adam Weishaupt.

ALPHABETS DE SOCIÉTÉS SECRÈTES.

Francs-Maçons.

Illuminés.

Rose Croix, 1º.

Templiers.

18. Transcriptions of the secret alphabets of eighteenth-century Masonic societies.

19. A woodcut of the Republic. From the Musée Carnardet, Paris, 1794.

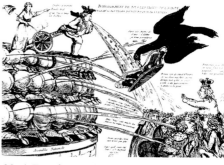

20. A French pamphlet of 1792, 'The Bombardment of All the Thrones of Europe'.

21. From the *Irish Magazine* of 1810, two engravings show scenes in the suppression of the Rebellion of 1798.

22. Members of a North Carolina den of the Ku Klux Klan prepare to hang a local Republican.
From a newspaper illustration of 1871.

24. A warning of the vengeance of the Ku Klux Klan.
From the *Independent Monitor*, Tuscaloosa, 1868.

23. A Black Hand death-note of 1900.

La Brute Sauvage.

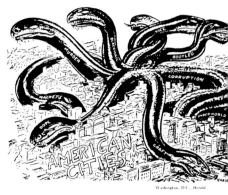

Washington, D.C., *Herald*

25. *La Brute Sauvage.*

26. Cartoon of 1920s corruption.

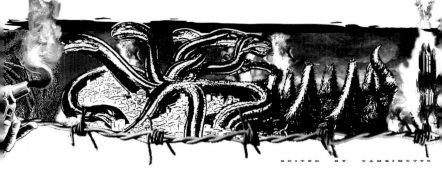

EDITED BY TAMBIMUTTU

Louseous Japanicas

The first serious outbreak of this lice epidemic was officially noted on December 7, 1941, at Honolulu, T. H. To the Marine Corps, especially trained in combating this type of pestilence, was assigned the gigantic task of extermination. Extensive experiments on Guadalcanal, Tarawa, and Saipan have shown that this louse inhabits coral atolls in the South Pacific, particularly pill boxes, palm trees, caves, swamps and jungles.

Poetry LONDON **X**

Flame throwers, mortars, grenades and bayonets have proven to be an effective remedy. But before a complete cure may be effected the origin of the plague, the breeding grounds around the Tokyo area, must be completely annihilated.

27. *Louseous Japanicas.*

28. Cover by Mervyn Peake.

of the Legation Quarter of Peking in 1900, until European expeditionary forces relieved the trapped ambassadors and their staff. The Chi'ing dynasty lingered on until 1911, when it was finished by the Triads and the Republican Party of Sun Yat-sen, who knew, as the American and the French revolutionaries had known, how to use secret movements with widespread cells to overthrow an existing government. He virtually recognized the Triads in China, as the Irish Republic would the IRA, for acting as a propaganda group and a collector of foreign funds.

To European Freemasons, the Triads appeared remarkably similar in their organization as well as in their ritual. Their oaths of initiation of the peach garden resembled those of the Egyptian mysteries, from which the Freemasons claimed a heritage. If the modern Triads developed into European and American protection rackets, they fragmented as the Mafia did overseas. With the Japanese invasion of China in the 1930s, the Triads shifted the reason for their existence from the political to the criminal, particularly with the emigration of large Chinese colonies to the United States and England, where the word 'Triad' meant merely a gangster living on the drug trade or prostitution or worse. His method of survival was to terrorize the Chinatown in which he lived. He prospered by torture and assassination. So a national political movement devolved into a seedy racket.

The Europeans, facing the first threat to their Asian empires from a resurgent Japan, called this danger a 'Yellow Peril'. The Japanese with their own samurai societies under their Emperor defeated the Russian fleets and armies off and on Korea and Manchuria in 1904 and 1905, provoking a revolution by the Bolsheviks at home against the Tsar. This was hardly and terribly put down. The Korean campaign was covered by the socialist American writer Jack London, who wrote back to his wife: 'I have preached the Economic Yellow Peril, henceforth I shall preach the Militant Yellow Peril.' Asia would rebel by all means against the imperialism of Europe.

17. THE ANARCHISTS

After the year of urban revolutions of 1848, the nationalist secret society became more international in its aims. Karl Marx and Friedrich Engels, the German-born authors of the *Communist Manifesto*, preached a class war across national frontiers, though every future Communist insurrection would be carried out within the framework of a single nation. The Bolsheviks imitated the Blanquists in their use of small, close-knit bands of trained revolutionaries, the Carbonari in their appeal to the armed forces, the Irish rebels in their exploitation of agrarian disaffection, and the Paris Communes in their control of the urban mob. Despite their claim to represent the working classes everywhere, the Communist Revolution failed to spread across Europe after the Bolshevik success in Russia because the Bolsheviks were Russians before they were global. The middle-class conspirators of 1848 had given up European solidarity for national squabbling; so the Bolsheviks gave up worldwide revolution for strength in their homeland.

Those who always pursued an exported revolution were the anarchists. They believed in the continual process of direct action in the tradition of Babeuf and Blanqui. As their first objective was the overthrow of governments, they were often forced to work on local lines. The seminal anarchist philosopher Mikhail Bakhunin, however, shared Babeuf's belief that the French Revolution 'was only the forerunner of another revolution, greater and more solemn, which would be the last'. Neither realized that the French experience had loosed nationalism on the world rather than liberty, equality or fraternity.

Bakhunin was a Russian aristocrat who served in the Tsar's army. Seeking some sort of change in the despotic state, he was drawn to the work of the French radical and Freemason Pierre-Joseph Proudhon, whose *Economic Contradictions* was published in 1846 with its slogan, *Destruam et Aedificabo*, 'I will Destroy and I will Build'. When he had his ensuing quarrels with Karl Marx, Bakhunin would say of his French mentor, that Proudhon was a revolutionary by instinct. 'He adored Satan and proclaimed Anarchy. Quite possibly Marx could construct a still more rational system of liberty, but he lacks the instinct of liberty – he remains from head to toe an authoritarian.'

Proudhon had posed the questions which the later Marxists could never answer in their economic exploitation of their terrorized population through the 'dictatorship of the proletariat'. His famous pamphlet, *What Is Property?*, began with these queries: 'If I were asked to answer the following question: "What is slavery?" and I should answer in one word, "It is murder", my meaning would be understood at once . . . To enslave a man is to kill him. Why, then, to this other question: "What is property?" may I not give a similar answer, "It is robbery"?'

Proudhon brought economic arguments for equality into previous utopian protests. For him, the state practised legal theft. This doctrine attracted Bakhunin, who could not accept the Marxist separation of human beings into exclusive classes. 'Class and power and state,' he wrote, 'are three terms. Each presupposes the other two. Yet they can be superseded by the words:– the political subjection and the economic exploitation of the masses.' Bakhunin did not wish to use the old state and imperial principle of divide and rule. He wanted to unite students and workers and peasants in a comradeship, which would combine in an instinctive rebellion for the common good.

During the revolutions of 1848, Bakhunin favoured the struggles of all peoples, Slavs and Magyars and Germans, against their oppressive regimes. In the same period, Marx was condemning the Slavs and peasant revolts and 'the idiocy of rural life'.

Unfortunately, Bakhunin's global vision of revolution was obscured by his backing at this time of national revolts. Put in gaol in Saxony and later extradited to Russia for imprisonment in the harsh Peter and Paul fortress in St Petersburg, he survived to be sent to exile in Siberia. He managed to escape in 1861 and reach the revolutionary centre of all exiles, London. He continued quarrelling with Karl Marx after the foundation of the First International Workingmen's Association, and then he made a disastrous encounter with the Russian revolutionary Nechayev, the godfather of nihilism.

This young charismatic terrorist seduced Bakhunin in 1869 in Geneva into providing funds and subscribing to an imaginary Central Committee of a European Revolutionary Alliance. Together, they produced eight pamphlets; the most extreme of these was the *Revolutionary Catechism*, mainly the work of Nechayev, and the first document to define the ideology and psychology of the political terrorist.

1. The revolutionary is a doomed man. He has no personal interests, no affairs, sentiments, attachments, property, not even a name of his own. Everything in him is absorbed by one exclusive interest, one thought, one passion – the revolution . . .

15. The whole ignoble social system must be divided into several categories. In the first category are those who are condemned to death without delay. The Alliance should draw up a list of persons thus condemned in the order of their relative harmfulness to the success of the cause . . .

22. The Alliance has no aim other than the complete liberation and happiness of the masses, of the people who live by manual labour. But, convinced that this liberation and the achievement of this happiness is possible only through an all-destroying popular revolution, the Alliance will by all its means and all its power further the development and extension of

those evils and those calamities which must at last
exhaust the patience of the people and drive them
to a general uprising . . .

26. To consolidate this work into one invincible, all-
destroying force is the sole object of our organization;
this is our conspiracy, our task.

Nechayev left Switzerland to bring about a revolution in
Russia. He formed a society and a newspaper named *The Retribution of the People*. He organized groups of conspirators on the
principles of the Illuminati – each cell of five members had a chief
who reported to a central committee, which was responsible to
Nechayev alone. Defied for his authoritarianism by Ivanov, a
member of the committee, Nechayev killed him in a park, where
his body was weighted with bricks and thrown into a pond.
Nechayev implicated other revolutionaries in a blood brotherhood of the crime. When the Russian secret police investigated
the murder, Nechayev fled back to Bakhunin in Switzerland. He
was fondly received by the ageing anarchist, who wrote of his
protégé's supposed sufferings and followers:

He has been arrested, was beaten half-dead, then released
and all that only to start all over again. And they are all of
the same calibre. The individual has ceased to count, and his
place has been taken by the legion, invisible, unknown, and
ubiquitous, always at work, daily dying, and daily being
resurrected. They are being arrested by the dozen, but
hundreds come forward to replace them. The individual
disappears, but the legion is immortal and grows in strength
from day to day . . .

Betrayed by a police spy and double agent, Nechayev was
returned to the Peter and Paul fortress to spend the last eleven
years of his life in brutal confinement. Yet so great was his legend
and influence that he managed to correspond with the Narodnaya
Volya, 'The People's Will, or Freedom', an anarchist society led
by Andrei Zhelyabov, who assassinated Tsar Alexander II. After

this murder in 1881, Nechayev was slowly put to death, expiring two years later at the age of thirty-five, the inspiration of count- less terrorists to come.

In spite of Dostoevsky's denials, the murderer Raskolnikov in *Crime and Punishment* was modelled on Nechayev. As the Rus- sian novelist once declared, 'The will is closest to nothing; the most assertive are closest to the most nihilistic.' Such a dream of a destruction leaving few alive and sweeping over Russia inspired Albert Camus in his work *The Plague* after the Second World War.

'In the cities the alarm sounded all day long. Fires broke out, famines came, everyone and everything was coming to an end. The plague grew and swept on further and further. In the whole world only a few men could save themselves – these were the pure and the elect, destined to start a new race and a new life, to renew and purify the earth.'

The Possessed by Dostoevsky dealt with Russian anarchism and nihilism more directly. The conspirators meet and kill the student Shatov, as Nechayev had murdered Ivanov. The murderer describes his crime as an act of will which must result in his suicide, which will invert the death of Christ for mankind and kill God, too. 'Terror is the curse of man, but I will exert my will ... I will kill myself; that is the only thing which will save humanity.' Also stressed is the lesson of the French Revolution, when the terrorist Shigalov declares that his conclusion contra- dicts his original motive: 'Starting from unlimited freedom, I end with unlimited despotism.'

From the Marxist and later Bolshevik perspective on the dialectic of revolution, the anarchism preached by Bakhunin was doomed by the fate of Nechayev. The haphazard use of assassi- nation would never cause an uprising of the workers. Anarchists murdered President Carnot in France in 1894, King Humbert of Italy six years later, and the Empress of Austria and the American President William McKinley in 1901, but the killing of a few powerful rulers would never begin the downfall of capitalism (see plate 41). These victims were all replaceable. The whole structure of society had to be broken and put together again.

European states did not wither away after the assassination of their leaders as Arab kingdoms had done in the days of the Assassins. Before his execution in 1894, one French anarchist, Émile Henry, claimed that his ideology could never be destroyed because 'its roots are too deep: it is born at the heart of a corrupt society which is falling to pieces; it is a violent reaction against the established order.' Yet nationalism proved too strong for the anarchists, despite their fanatical secrecy and terror tactics, and they were eventually destroyed as a political force.

To be successful, a political secret society must seek to control the established order, not to obliterate it. Even the Bolsheviks had to employ the old Tsarist bureaucracy because it was the only group with experience in operating the machinery of a large state. Lenin claimed that housewives could run the government; but when he ran the government, he had to turn back to the old officials.

The theory of conspiracy, as the American historian Richard Hofstadter pointed out, lay at the grass roots of democratic as well as despotic society. The people must always search out villains, real or mythical, to explain their ills. Democracy, by its very nature, could hardly oppress. Conspiracies might be attributed to any secret group, to bankers or armaments manufacturers, Jews or Masons, heretics or anarchists. Once the group was named, it was believed to seek power.

Any identified conspiracy would win the support of those who saw the government itself as a conspiracy against the people. But the plotters had to prove their power by committing acts of terrorism or martyrdom, if they were to gain the publicity necessary for the masses to follow their leadership in a future insurrection. The success of the Bolsheviks, for example, was due to their acceptance as revolutionary leaders by the workers of Moscow and St Petersburg after their exploits in the Revolution of 1905. If the insurrection was successful, the revolutionary secret society became the government. Only the anarchists, who declared all governments to be secret conspiracies against the people, were consistent in remaining a revolutionary secret society, permanently out of power. They could not, by their own declarations, form any national government whatsoever.

'An assassination has never changed the history of the world,' declared Benjamin Disraeli in an effort to quieten the general fear of turmoil after the various anarchist attacks on European rulers. He was a false prophet, because of the Pan-Slavist secret societies, supported by Russia in an effort to extend the influence of the Tsar through the Balkans. The first of these, Omladina or 'Youth', spread down the Danube and could not be suppressed by the Austrian or the Serbian or the Turkish authorities. In 1868, Prince Michael of Serbia was assassinated: in 1903, King Alexander and Queen Draga suffered the same fate. The regicides formed a new terrorist group, the Narodna Odbrana or National Defence Society, which was soon superseded by the Union of Death, commonly called the Black Hand.

Its initiation ceremonies were ghoulish. The insignia was a clenched hand around a skull and crossbones beside a dagger, a bomb and a phial of poison. The oath was not Christian, but 'by the sun which warms me, by the earth which feeds me, by God and by the blood of my ancestors, by my honour and my life.' The cell pattern of the Illuminati and the Omladina was reproduced: each recruit had to enlist five new members. These small groups were known as a 'hand' and were led by a 'thumb', the only one in contact with other groups. All were sworn in across a table covered with a black cloth, which held a candle and a cross, a poniard and a revolver. Death was the instant answer to any treachery.

The spark of the First World War in 1914 was the shooting of the Austrian Archduke Franz Ferdinand and his wife by the terrorist Gavrilo Princip in Sarajevo. With two other Bosnian students, also suffering from tuberculosis, he had decided to cut short his stricken life by provoking an international conflict. At his trial, Princip was matter of fact. 'I went to Belgrade to finish my education,' he said. 'There I was very poor and lived on debts. Then I came here and committed the murders.' But later, when he became a nationalist hero as a student revolutionary, before his obscure death in an Austrian jail, he boasted that he wanted to be nailed on a cross and burnt alive. 'My flaming body will be a torch to light my people on their path to freedom.'

Without the assassination of the Austrian archduke at Sarajevo, the First World War would only have been postponed. The rivalry of Germany against France on land and against Britain on sea, and the incessant conflicts between Austria and Russia in the Balkans, threatened a conflagration year in and year out. None of the nations knew that the struggle would be so bogged down due to modern artillery and machine guns and barbed wire. If the horrors of the First World War had been foreseen, the armies sent to die in it would not have marched. Yet old glory would still be sufficient to delude and muffle the dead from the new destroyers of cordite and steel.

18. THE ANARCHY
OF THE WEST

The savagery seen in the wars of the American colonists against the Indian tribes was passed on to the European pioneers moving towards the Pacific Ocean. To them, the Indians appeared dangerously free and against all government, particularly their own. 'The Indian was indebted to no one but himself,' the French social historian de Tocqueville wrote; 'his virtues, his vices, and his prejudices were his own work; he had grown up in the wild independence of his nature.' That wild independence became the survival techniques of those Europeans, who had to live like Indians to compete with them. The most extreme of these were the trappers known as the 'Mountain Men' of the Rockies. They dressed in skins and lived on raw meat, without law or conscience. To exist in their environment, the Mountain Men slipped back from civilization to the life of lone wolves.

One of them was called 'Cannibal Phil' because he survived the winter by eating his squaw. All of them ate 'anything that walked, swam, wriggled or crawled'. Like beasts they lived between famine and feast, drinking the blood of the buffalo and eating its liver raw, spiced with the gall from its bladder. The time of the annual sale of their beaver pelts was a time of drunkenness and orgy and killing and waste. The rest of the year was an animal life in the mountains that made a man forget that living was more than survival.

While such extreme individualism was not the case for most of the pioneers, who journeyed west in the wagon trains which were temporary towns on wheels, the forests and the red-grass prairies and the hills and the semi-deserts did push them towards a lawless life. As Abe Lincoln's relatives in Illinois confessed, 'We lived the same as the Indians, 'ceptin' we took an interest in politics and religion – when available.' In Canada, the Earl of Selkirk initiated in 1811 the first settlement in the vast region known as Rupert's Land, sending emigrant Scotsmen to the banks of the Red River to create an oasis of law and trade in the wilderness. The bitter rivalry for the fur trade was settled by a merger between the Montreal North-West Company and the British Hudson's Bay Company. Yet Red River remained for decades the only settlement in an immense region – and itself became the focus of a western insurrection.

Before Canada achieved dominion status, there were two rebellions in 1837 in the colonies of Upper and Lower Canada. Both the revolts of the Patriotes led by Louis Papineau and by the supporters of William Lyon Mackenzie ended in the blazing steamer *Caroline* going over the Niagara Falls; the two leaders escaped to America. South of the border, the Mexican War of 1846 was staged, in which the United States acquired the south-west with a bayonet in one hand and a dollar in the other.

The Civil War brought the conflict between American individualism and American government to a head. The Indian warrior tribes were swept into contact with an organized mounted foe, the Texas Rangers and then the US Cavalry, leading to the classic battles famed in the Western film and the actual atrocities and massacres, some of them led by the local militia. 'Colonel Colt's Equaliser' and the Winchester rifle became the conquerors of the buffalo and the Indian, whose relegation to grave or reservation would be complete by 1890, the year the frontier was officially ended in the completed United States.

The Indians always killed more men than they lost, but numbers and weapons and disease beat them. They also had the white pioneers to contend against, the real initiators of the wars, the miners and the buffalo hunters and the cowboys. Mining greed led to the army invasion of the Black Hills despite a treaty, to Red Cloud's victory against the American forces, to Custer's last stand, and to the final subjugation of the Sioux. Buffalo Bill, the first time he served as a scout for the US Army, horrified the officers by taking the scalp of an Indian as a trophy; later he turned himself into his own legend in an unsuccessful showbusiness career. And the cowboys produced the most potent American folk-myth of all – the Western novel and film with the outlaw often the role model for the young.

The horses and cattle of the cowboys, the mustang and the longhorn, were from Spanish Mexico. Yet, as Theodore Roosevelt wrote, 'the rough rider of the plains, the hero of the rope and revolver, is first cousin to the backwoodsman of the Southern Alleghenies, the man of the ax and rifle.' The first 'cowboys' were Tory bandits, raiding American farms during the Revolution, and the first Western cowboys were still bandits, raiding Mexican ranches across the Rio Grande. They were against the law and authority, and thus they became the founders of Texas, when in 1836 Sam Houston led them to victory and independence against Mexico. They served in the Mexican War and in the Southern cavalry in the Civil War. Those who came back became the heroes of the open range in the later days of the Cattle Kingdom of the Great Plains.

The new rebel was the white man – or black. He had been spawned in the Mexican War and the Civil War, and he was the heir to lawlessness and hatred. Many of the Western bandits found themselves outlaws willy-nilly by serving as Southern guerrillas, unofficial soldiers whom the North never pardoned. Jesse James first rode with Quantrill's Raiders, who used Apache tactics to loot and terrorize Kansas, Oklahoma and Texas. When peace came in 1865, Jesse found himself an outlaw, only seventeen years old and trained to ride, shoot, live rough and rob for a living. A teenage veteran, he could not accept the peace. He and his brother Frank and the Youngers and more of Quantrill's Raiders applied guerrilla tactics to the taking of money from the banks and railway trains. No bandit was ever better known or more imitated than Jesse James. He became a folk hero and set the pattern for the 'Code of the West' in the seventeen years between the end of the Civil War and his death at the hands of Bob Ford, 'the dirty little coward', who shot Jesse in the back while his friend was dusting his mother's sampler, embroidered with the legend GOD BLESS OUR HOME.

After Jesse James, many horsemen went riding into town and held up banks. The trade became less popular after the townsmen of Coffeyville wiped out the Dalton gang in Blood Alley. Yet many outlaws knew no other job and continued in business until they were killed. Their excuse for their murders was usually that they could not help their start in crime. Most of the bandits were Southerners; the first notch on their gun was an uppity, carpet-bagging black man, now freed to oppress the South by a vengeful North. As the worst killer in Texas history, Wes Hardin justified his original sin of killing with his Colt a black man armed only with a stick: 'to be tried at that time for the killing of a Negro meant certain death at the hands of a court backed by Northern bayonets ... thus, unwillingly, I became a fugitive not from justice, be it known, but from the injustice and misrule of the people who subjugated the South.'

Another form of resistance to the government was growing in the West. This was frontier justice or mob law. In Rough and Ready Camp in Nevada in 1850, an independent state was declared. Hangings took place in town after a vote by a crowd. Lynch law reached the mining camps as well as the Deep South, where it was used against any black person accused of rape or even aggression. A chronicler of the California mining camps put it: 'We are irresistibly compelled to think of the whole race of American pioneers from the days of Boone and Harrod to the days of Carson and Bridger; heroic forest chivalry, heroic conquerors of the prairies, heroic rulers of the mountain wilderness, ever forcing back the domains of savage and wild beast. Well did one of the most eloquent of American lecturers once exclaim –

"Woe to the felon upon whose track is the American borderer! Woe to the assassin before a self-empanelled jury of American foresters! No lie will help him, no eloquence prevail; no false plea can confuse the clear conceptions or arrest the just judgment of a frontier court."'

The outlaw and the posse and frontier justice seemed to millions of Westerners the assertion of their liberties against the authority of Washington and the agents of the federal government. Although the Civil War produced its own atrocities, particularly in the Northern General Sherman's march through Georgia in a spoiled-earth campaign of burning townships, prisoners of war were generally treated under survival conditions on both sides, even if unchecked disease led to tens of thousands of deaths in the insanitary holding camps. With the surrender of the Southern states, however, the most persistent and terrifying secret movement was spawned from the ashes of defeat, the Ku Klux Klan. For a century and more it brought infamy to the tradition of liberal toleration within American democracy.

19. THE KU KLUX KLAN

The most intriguing and enduring terrorist organization in the history of the United States was the Ku Klux Klan. After the Civil War, it was a resistance movement. After the First World War, it was a political movement. After the Second World War, it became a racist movement, which repeated itself not in horror, but in derision.

> I before the immaculate Judge of Heaven and Earth, and upon the Holy Evangelists of Almighty God, do, of my own free will and accord, subscribe to the following sacred binding obligation:
> 1. We are on the side of justice, humanity and constitutional liberty, as bequeathed to us in its purity by our forefathers.
> 2. We oppose and reject the principles of the radical party.
> 3. We pledge mutual aid to each other in sickness, distress, and pecuniary embarrassment.
> 4. Female friends, widows and their households, shall ever be special objects of our regard and protection.
>
> Any member divulging, or causing to be divulged, any of the foregoing obligations, shall meet the fearful penalty and traitor's doom, which is Death! Death! Death!

This was the oath of initiation that a former member of the Ku Klux Klan disclosed in 1871 to an investigating committee of the United States Senate. The inquiry revealed the extent and viciousness of the terror tactics which the whites of the South were using against their conquerors from the North and their former black slaves, freed at the end of the Civil War. The Ku Klux Klan was a secret organization of white supremacists, who thought that violence was the only answer to the military and corrupt governments imposed on the defeated Southern states. In its beginning, the Klan could claim to be a resistance movement against intolerable oppression, even if it would end as the mere tool of hate, greed, and sadism.

General Nathan Bedford Forrest, who founded and ran the Klan, definitely thought of it as a temporary guerrilla organization that would last only as long as Northern carpetbaggers and illiterate Negroes and Southern renegades, called scalawags, ruled the Southern states. Forrest was tall and black-bearded; he had been a death-and-glory commander in the Confederate cavalry. His maxim for winning cavalry actions had been: 'Get there first with the most.' At one time he had been a slave dealer, but he had bought himself into the plantation aristocracy. He had been accused during the Civil War of the atrocious massacre at Fort Pillow, when captured coloured troops were exterminated. He was not likely to accept the principle of black people representing white people in the legislatures of the South.

Forrest appeared in front of the Senate investigating committee and was questioned about the Klan. He never admitted to being its leader, though he had given interviews to the newspapers telling them of the Klan, and its rise in various Southern states began immediately after his travels. He was, however, absolutely sure of the righteous purposes of the Klan and told the Senate committee of them:

> There was a great deal of insecurity felt by the Southern people. There were a great many Northern men coming down from there, forming leagues all over the country. The Negroes were holding night meetings; were going about; were becoming very insolent; and all the Southern people all over the State were very much alarmed. I think many of the

organizations did not have any name; parties organized themselves so as to be ready in case they were attacked. Ladies were ravished by some of these Negroes, who were tried and put in the penitentiary, but were turned out in a few days afterward. There was a great deal of insecurity in the country, and I think this organization was got up to protect the weak, with no political intention at all.

In his incoherent way, Forrest set out the haphazard social pressures that may lead to the foundation of secret societies – dislocation in a defeated group, the urge to resist tyranny, fear of humiliation at the hands of troops, old servants becoming rulers, the excuse that a league of the enemy needs to be fought by a conspiracy of friends, and the dark sexual imaginings which seek revenge at the rumour of outrage. Forrest also showed that a particular secret society flourishes when little bands of rebels are widespread everywhere and are looking for a uniform and a leader who can cloak a political purpose under the hood of a benevolent society of brothers.

The oath a Klansman had to take on initiation hardly justified Forrest's mild description of the secret society. In fact, the Klan was a group of Democrats who hated freed slaves, Northerners and Republicans. After the Civil War, the defeated men of the South had found, as their devastator General Sherman declared: 'Mourning in every household, desolation written in broad characters across the whole face of the country, cities in ashes and fields laid waste, their commerce gone, their system of labour annihilated and destroyed. Ruin, poverty, and distress everywhere.'

The Southerners tried to seize back the government of their states and reduce the freed slaves to serfdom through new laws which came to be known as 'Black Codes'. The radical Republican Congress retaliated by imposing military rule on the South, after the murder of the moderate Lincoln and the ineffectiveness of his successor, Andrew Johnson. When the Northern

Commander-in-Chief, General Grant, became president in 1868, there was no control over the radical Republicans in Congress. A reign of political corruption run by Northerners and carpetbaggers exploited the ruins of the South.

There was bound to be resistance on the part of the hundreds of Confederate veterans, who had little to do in the economic slump after the war. In 1865, six young men in Pulaski, Tennessee, formed a hooded society of mock ghosts and ghouls; they called it Ku Klux Klan, derived from the Greek word *kuklos* meaning 'circle' and the Scots word 'clan'. Wherever the original Klansmen rode by night in their shrouds on shrouded horses, they found that the blacks, often uneducated and superstitious, were terrified by such sinister visitors, who claimed to be the ghosts of the Confederate dead, pretended to drink a gallon of water at a gulp, and produced a skeleton hand out of their sleeves to grasp a victim's palm.

Forrest saw immediately the possibility of using such practical jokes to terrorize the Southern countryside. He claimed 550,000 hooded riders by 1868 under the name of Klansmen, Palefaces, the White Brotherhood, the White League, or Knights of the White Camellia. Although he was aided by other ex-Confederate officers, he did not have a proper military organization, and could not keep control of his men. He may have intended to be a Robin Hood, as the early Klan oath suggests, and he may have tried to protect the weak against the freebooters working in the name of government. But soon the local Klans degenerated into a horde of gangs, denounced by one of the Klan founders as often composed of 'rash, imprudent, and bad men'.

These gangs rode at night for personal revenge, profit or thrills. Any rogue could put on a hood, whether black or white man; the cloak over the face hid all responsibility. Secrecy, which had been the strength of the early Klan, became its weakness. The mystery of its organized terror forged a licence for the vengeance of anarchic criminals.

The number of murders and outrages committed by the Klan before 1872 is impossible to establish. Every criminal or man who wanted to pursue a vendetta wore a hood. In almost all Southern counties there was sporadic warfare between the armed black Republican militia and Southern veterans. Terror was used by both sides, though undeniably the blacks suffered the worst (see plates 22 and 24). The Senate committee found that in nine counties of South Carolina, over a period of six months, the Klan had lynched and murdered thirty-five men, flogged up to three hundred men and women, and otherwise outraged, shot, mutilated, raped, or burned out another hundred people. During this time, the blacks had killed four men, beaten one man, and committed sixteen other outrages. There was no known case of the rape of a white woman.

White Southerners killed or attacked blacks in nearly all the thousands of murders which took place in the South in the decade after the Civil War. The motive for this broadcast violence was simple; to keep the black man in his place and away from the polls. W. E. Du Bois, one of the great black leaders and historians, summed up the 'significantly varied' reasons for the Klan outrages: 'the victims should suffer in revenge for killing, and for some cases of arson; they were Republicans; they were radical; they had attempted to hold elections; they were carrying arms; they were "niggers"; they were "damn niggers"; they boasted that they would own land. They were whipped for debt, for associating with white women, and for trying to vote.'

The horror inspired by the Klan was due more to its haphazard assaults than to its state-wide organization. Though Forrest was never in control of his Klansmen, he organized the Klan on paper like a Southern army. The whole South was called the Invisible Empire; each state was a Realm, each congressional district a Dominion, each county a Province, and each locality a Den. Forrest was the Grand Wizard, and his staff were the ten Genii; each Realm had a Grand Dragon and eight Hydras, each

Dominion a Grand Titan and six Furies, each Province a Grand Giant and four Goblins, each Den a Grand Cyclops and two Night Hawks.

This demonic hierarchy could have worked if the Klan had not been a hidden organization; but as it was, Forrest could not hold accountable any Den for senseless outrages committed by hooded riders in its area, because local Klansmen could always claim that the guilty hooded riders might have been black men in disguise. Forrest's failure to control his men was shown by the Dens' refusal in 1869 to obey his order to disband. Forrest himself had seen that they had got out of hand and were increasing the disorder of the South instead of putting an end to anarchy.

Once Forrest and the best of the Klan's military leaders had left the organization in disgust for its reckless acts of indiscriminate revenge, the sadism and childishness of local Klansmen had no restraints. The General Orders of the Klan in Tuscaloosa, Alabama were headed:

Hollow Hell, Devil's Den, Horrible Shadows, Ghostly
    Sepulchres.
Head Quarters of the Immortal Ate of the KKK.
Gloomy Month. Bloody Moon. Black Night. Last Hour.

Yet such an infantile fantasy of Halloween gibberish resulted in real murder and the mutilation of blacks and Republicans. While the Senate investigating committee sat, petitions from terrorized black people flooded into Congress. One from Kentucky asked for laws to suppress 'the Ku Klux Klans riding nightly over the country, going from County to County and in the County towns spreading terror wherever they go, by robbing whipping ravishing and killing our people without provocation, compelling Colored people to brake the ice and bathe in the Chilly waters of the Kentucky River.'

President Grant was too much of a military man to support a guerrilla insurrection. In 1870 and 1871, the Ku-Klux Acts were passed to put the federal government in charge of Southern elections; they also gave the President the power to declare martial law in the Southern states and to suspend the writ of habeas corpus. Klansmen were frequently thrown into jail without trial for long periods, because they were usually acquitted by a local jury – except when it happened to be a black jury. Excessive vengeance by lawlessness was now replaced by excessive vengeance by law.

Moderate Southern opinion supported the legal and illegal attack on the Klan. Many Southerners had had enough of anarchy; like one moderate Mississippi minister, they thought 'that Ku Kluxing is unnecessary and foolish, whether engaged in by whites or blacks.' In face of this public disapproval, and because white Democrats were gradually winning back control over state governments in the South, the Klan withered away. The white and red and black hoods were put aside, the ghoulish jokes and outlandish costumes were once more confined to Halloween and to Mardi Gras in New Orleans. By a tacit compromise in 1877, the Democrats were allowed to rule the South in the name of white supremacy in return for allowing the Republicans to rule the North in the name of big business. When the South was allowed by Congress to reduce the freed slaves to voteless sharecroppers, there was little need for the Klan to ride. The carpetbaggers went back North to loot their fellows there. Racism below the Potomac and corruption above lay down quietly side by side.

Southerners love the past, and they love gilding it. In their memory, a patch becomes a plantation and a cowed slave is transformed into a contented mammy. As Malory once turned the feudal robber barons of the Middle Ages into the Arthurian Knights of the Round Table, so white Southern memories transformed the brutal Klansmen into the white knights of chivalry and romance. There was much more Walter Scott in their fond folklore than actual fact. And when the cinema came, a Southern genius called David Wark Griffith could conjure up millions of hooded riders merely by representing the first Ku Klux Klan as a group of chivalric heroes who hunted down a black murderer and rapist. If *Uncle Tom's Cabin* incited the Civil War in the North, *The Birth of a Nation* of 1915 helped to revive the dead body of the Klan in the South and West. Griffith, one Southerner noted, 'made the Ku Klux as noble as Robert E. Lee'.

In the year Griffith's film classic appeared, a racist sniffed the wind of reaction against alien influences and decided to become a second General Forrest for the sake of the Old South. William Joseph Simmons of Alabama, a one-time soldier and minister and salesman of ladies' garters, was a great joiner. He belonged to some fifteen fraternal organizations, including the Masons. 'I believe in fraternal orders and fraternal relationships among men,' he stated, 'in a fraternity of nations.' In the name of the brotherhood of the white Protestant American people against the rising tide of colour and Catholics and Jews and immigrants from southern Europe, Simmons strode to the top of Stone Mountain near Atlanta with fifteen followers in 1915 and burned a fiery cross by night at the side of a rough stone altar, on which lay the American flag, an open Bible, a naked sword, and a canteen of 'holy' river water. There, Simmons declared himself Grand Wizard of the revived Ku Klux Klan and administered the oath of allegiance to his kneeling disciples, who rose as Knights of the new Invisible Empire.

Yet Simmons was a failure as an organizer and as a salesman; the Kaiser in Europe seemed a more important enemy than the alien at home. Simmons nearly ruined himself in attracting a few thousand members to the cause of the revived Klan; but when he was on the point of bankruptcy, he met two more successful merchandisers of hate. Edward Young Clarke and his mistress, Mrs Elizabeth Tyler, ran a public relations and promotional business called the Southern Publicity Association. They raised funds for the Young Men's Christian Association and the Salvation Army; but they decided that the profits of bigotry might exceed the profits of brotherhood. Meeting Simmons in 1920,

Clarke signed a contract by which the Grand Wizard remained the figurehead of the revived Klan, while the Clarke–Tyler combination took recruiting in hand and tapped the pockets of the Knights of the Invisible Empire.

With Klan hoods sold as ruthlessly as American flags during the First World War, the membership of the Klan reached 100,000 by 1921 and about 4,000,000 within another three years. It captured the imaginations of the fearful small towns of the South and West, and even won adherents in the rural North. The very success of the Klan's recruiting, which Clarke and Mrs Tyler had seen merely as a method of bamboozling Babbitts into joining another nonsensical fraternity, changed the purpose of the Klan from a fund-raising racket to a political force inside many states and within the Democratic party. When its members came to be numbered in millions, it was transformed into a nationwide threat to democracy, while the first Klan had only subverted popular government in the South.

The second Klan would have amounted to little, if a politically conscious group of rebels led by a plump Texan dentist, Hiram Wesley Evans, had not seized control of the secret society. Installed by Simmons as national secretary, or Imperial Kligrapp of the order, Evans won enough support among Klan leaders to elevate Simmons to the powerless post of Emperor of the Klan, and to push out Clarke and Mrs Tyler. These two had, anyway, been discovered half-dressed and drunk together, and so were convicted of disorderly conduct. Evans organized the Klan as a political power-group within the Southern Democratic Party. Klan candidates reached the United States Senate and the governorship of several states.

In Indiana, David C. Stephenson, who worshipped Napoleon and wanted to be President, was Grand Dragon of the State. He effectively took over the whole local government, appointing his henchmen to every office. After the great Konklave at Kokomo on 4 July 1923, when Stephenson, clad in a purple robe, arrived in a gilded aeroplane to address the faithful, the Klan virtually ran Indiana. The organization may have called itself secret, but it was never exclusive. It wanted all the members it could get, for both their money and their votes. 'They just throwed the doors open,' a disillusioned Texan Klansman declared, 'and every man that had the money, they took him in to get his vote . . . and if he did not have any money, they took his note payable in the fall.'

Simmons himself turned the gibberish of the old Klan into a new mumbo-jumbo of idiocy. He was besotted with the magic of the letter K. The meeting of a Klan was called a Klonvokation; cases were tried at a Kloncilium. Under the Exalter Cyclops of each local Den, now called a Klavern, sat a Klaliff, a Klokard, a Kludd, a Kligrapp, a Klabee, a Kladd with various Klageros and Klexters and a Klokann. The book of ritual of the new Klan was called the Kloran, a strange title for the bible of a Christian organization. The ritual itself was a hotchpotch of Masonic rites and childish rhetoric put together by Simmons, whose one inspiration was to burn fiery crosses at each Konklave in order to spread terror and to prove faith in Christianity. Yet, in a curious way, the Klan's burning of the Cross was as blasphemous as the supposed spitting on the Cross by the Templars. The merciful nature of Christ would be denied by any such action.

The Klan of the 1920s, indeed, was very different from the first Klan. While the original order had proceeded against blacks and Republicans in the South, its imitator attacked Jews, Catholics, radicals and immoralists as much as it attacked black people. The Negro had seemed the chief political and social threat after the Civil War; by the 1920s, he had been reduced to social insignificance outside the slums of the great cities. 'Our antagonists are the lawbreaker, the prostitute, the Negro, the Jew, the Catholic, the foreigner, and the misguided Protestant,' a Klan clergyman declared in full flower of faith, and then asked his congregation in Ohio to declare which side it supported.

Unless the Klan, despite its clumsy trappings, had appealed as a genuine reform movement and tapped an urge to a better

Christian life, it would never have had the success it did in the Bible Belt of the United States. 'The Ku Klux Klan is sweeping this great nation like a forest fire,' a Klan newspaper declared. 'Nothing of its kind ever has swept America like this wonderful movement for Christianity ... The fiery cross is moving on, spreading its beautiful light everywhere for the betterment of humanity and the triumph of those principles which have made this nation great.'

The second Klan was both more bigoted and more of a revivalist movement than the first. The first Invisible Empire had a visible enemy, carpetbagger rule; the second Empire had an invisible foe, urban change. The new Klan invoked at the simple choice of black and white in the rural Protestant mind. It was also spawned in the age of American fraternal organizations with new, efficient techniques for raising money through membership. Stephenson in Indiana became a millionaire through the Klan, while tens of millions of dollars poured through the treasury in Atlanta.

The attraction of the Klan for the small-town businessman of the 1920s was shown by the most effective of the new Klan's methods, that of economic boycott. Compared with the tens of thousands of outrages committed by the first Klan, the second appeared a comparatively mild affair, even though hundreds of cases of murder, lynching, whipping, tarring and feathering, and running out of town were attributed to it. The new method of economic boycott, however, proved irresistible. The virtue of 'clannishness' taught Klan members to deal only with fellow Klansmen. Signs reading TWK (Trade With Klan) appeared in the shop windows of Klansmen; undesirable shopkeepers were named at Klan meetings and boycotted until they went out of business.

The comparative sophistication of some of the techniques of the later Klan – discrimination, contributions to pro-Klan clergymen, and charity to Klan widows – did not prevent it from committing many horrible deeds. Mass conscription of anyone with ten dollars into Klan ranks gave sadists and criminals the opportunity to flog and torture any victim they chose. Hooded thugs could take the law into their own hands and call it moral justice. The resurgence of the Klan increased the persecution of blacks in the South; there were multiple cases of lynching in the Klan centre of Georgia alone in two years. The Governor declared: 'In some counties the Negro is being driven out as though he were a wild beast. In others he is being sold as a slave. In others no Negroes remain. In only two of the 135 cases cited is the "usual crime" of rape involved.' In fact, the attack on the blacks, as on Catholics or Jews, was now mainly for economic advantage to get their business or land cheaply by forcing them out.

The sporadic anarchy of the Klan in the 1920s was less serious than its political organization as a potential group of American Fascists. Its successes in state politics reached their apogee in 1924 at the Democratic presidential convention. The popular and anti-Prohibitionist Catholic Governor of New York, Alfred E. Smith, wanted the party's nomination for the White House; against him stood the Klan-backed William Gibbs McAdoo, a stern Prohibitionist of good Protestant Anglo-Saxon stock. With the galleries howling for Smith and the Klansmen threatening Southern and Western delegates, the convention deadlocked for 102 ballots, before choosing a compromise candidate. At least as powerful as Mussolini's Fascists before their takeover of the Italian government, the Klan could hope for great things in the future.

Yet American nativist movements, at the moment of their greatest strength, seem to wither suddenly. The Klan was no exception. Its very success led to arrogant and stupid behaviour by its leaders and to a real assault on it by decent democrats and the press. Old-time politicians suddenly realized that a rival for power and patronage was demanding its slice of the pie, and that they would do better to eliminate the Klan than to share office with it. The result was that when D. C. Stephenson mutilated and raped a girl on an express train, and was named by her before her death from taking poison, he was unexpectedly convicted of second-degree murder and sentenced to life imprisonment. The proof of bestial immorality on the part of the leading Klansman of the Midwest turned away the Knights in their millions. In Indiana itself, membership of the Klan dropped by three-quarters in two years. 'We have had some good men in the Klan,' a minister from the Midwest told a Senate investigating committee in 1926. 'They are not staying by it now.'

The lechery and profiteering behind the hoods of the Klan were now exposed. Secrecy, which allows lack of responsibility, allows corruption. Even the new Grand Wizard, Dr Evans, well knew the calibre of the people he attracted to his organization. When he was asked by an Exalted Cyclops in Indiana why he did not let the Klansmen parade with their hoods raised, he replied cynically, 'The morale of the Klan would kill itself.' The same Exalted Cyclops also admitted to the Senate committee the credulity that Evans exploited, by declaring that the Grand Wizard 'could almost convince the average Klansman that we had in the State of Indiana that Jesus Christ was not a Jew.'

The end of the second period of the Klan was as sudden as its rise. Stephenson, brooding on the injustice of not being able to fix his release from jail, turned state's evidence and exposed details of Klan corruption and graft in Indiana. His testimony jailed a Congressman, the Mayor of Indianapolis, the Sheriff of Marion County, and other officials; the Governor was saved only by the statute of limitations. By 1927, when Stephenson's testimony came out, the Klan had dwindled to a mere 350,000 members. The hysteria against aliens that had made it sprout was equalled only by the revulsion against corruption that made it wither.

Many blacks served in the armed forces during the Second World War, or became used to high wages and good jobs in munitions factories. When the conflict ended, the South was faced with a black movement demanding civil rights and equal treatment. The Klan now rose for a third time; its object was similar to that of the first Klan, to keep the black people in an inferior condition. Yet this time the born-again Klan lacked the excuse that white Southerners did not control the government of their states. They pretended that the federal government – and later the Supreme Court – was oppressing the governments of the states and forcing civil rights down the throats of the white majority in the South.

There were no Northern troops to resist the third group of Klansmen. In fact, in the more brutal and backward places of the Deep South, the local sheriffs wore Klan hoods by night. As often as not, policemen in small Southern towns helped Klansmen terrorize local blacks and keep out civil-rights workers. Before American Presidents became aware of the power of the black vote in presidential elections and infiltrated the Klan with agents of the Federal Bureau of Investigation, those who laboured to help civil rights in the Deep South had little hope of protection by law from assault and murder.

The third eruption of the Ku Klux Klan was curiously unrewarding. Briefly, it had an initial success in Georgia politics, after fiery crosses were burned on Stone Mountain again in 1945, and some 50,000 Klansmen enrolled in the order once more. Yet horror at Nazi atrocities against the Jews made the Klan's anti-Semitism stink in the nostrils of the nation, especially as the Klan had been linked with the pro-Nazi Bund before the Second World War. Governments in various states refused to permit the chartering of the Klan. Even Georgia, after flagrant Klan intervention in an election for the governorship, forced the state Klan to surrender its charter. Thus the remnants of the national organization, now banned in its headquarters, writhed on their own, as the tentacles of an octopus chopped off from their parent body.

The local Klans had a new enemy to fight, the Federal Bureau of Investigation. The Lindbergh kidnap case in 1932 had forced the FBI to take over investigations that had been the concern of the state police; its intervention was sanctioned by the Interstate

Commerce Acts, which made the transportation of people across state borders for illegal purposes a federal crime. Political considerations also began to persuade American Presidents that they should proceed against the Klan to satisfy the powerful black vote in the Northern cities. FBI informers broke up the Klan in North Carolina and sent twenty-three Klansmen to jail. The Klan's weakness was that it was filled with poor people who could be bribed. When the federal agents needed information, they could pay the necessary price or slip their own men into the hooded order.

In 1960, when the black 'sit-in' movement with its techniques of passive resistance reached the South, the split Klans held a convention and agreed on a loose federation. Klansmen under the Grand Dragon of Georgia were present at the riots that took place at the University of Georgia when black students were admitted for the first time. Robert Shelton, titular head of the United Klans, held recruiting drives; but these fizzled out, although Shelton's brand of hatred of Jews, blacks, Communists, the Supreme Court, brainwashing through mental health, and fluoridization of water appealed to some of the lunatic fringe of the American right wing. The liberation forces ranged against the Klan and led by the charismatic Martin Luther King, who was himself assassinated, exposed the pitiful and retrograde standards of the last major American racist movement.

The United Klans were a sorry vestige of the first and second Klans. They were fighting a losing battle against the advance of Southern urbanism and industrialization as well as against the progress of black people. Their mumbo-jumbo was out of touch with modern times, a hiccup rather than a roar. Their appeal was only to the frustration of the poor white, who lacked the education necessary to keep up self-respect in the automated society of our day. The reductio ad absurdum of the terrorist group and the Christian military orders, their remnants were a mere bar-room brawl.

20. THE MAFIA

The word *mafia* probably comes from the same word in Arabic, which means 'place of refuge'. During the Arab rule of Sicily, which began in the ninth century, the land was split up into smallholdings; but when the Normans conquered the island two centuries later, feudal overlords seized little properties and ran them in estates as large and despotic as the Roman slave-farms denounced by Cicero. Many dispossessed smallholders ran to a *mafia* in the hills rather than become serfs for the masters who had engorged their fields.

When the Spaniards conquered the island in the fifteenth century, the Inquisition used heresy trials to torture and plunder both rich and poor. Then the mountain outlaws represented the only resistance to despotic government. The bandits of the hill towns, invulnerable while they kept the respect of their local communities, became the champions of the oppressed. Thus the roots of the Mafia, known to Sicilians as the 'Honoured Society', lay in the millennia of misgovernment suffered at the hands of various invaders – Romans, Arabs, Normans, Spaniards, Neapolitan Bourbons, and, to a certain extent, northern Italians. Although the modern Mafia dates only from the nineteenth century, its traditions stretch back to tribal days.

The strength of the Mafia lay in the fact that it was a family society: its discipline grew up because justice for the wrongs suffered by a member of a family could be expected only outside the official government. Where no one trusted the law of the invaders, the writ of family law ran.

This family discipline – similar in many ways to that of the

Scottish clans – went under the name of *omertà*, or 'manliness'. It included the refusal to give any information to the authorities after an act of violence, because revenge was a family's duty, not the state's or God's; the exaction of an eye for an eye and a bullet for a bullet in a quarrel between families, until all the men of one family were dead; the stoic and bland acceptance of insults from the enemy or the oppressor, until the time was ripe for vengeance; the lifelong refusal to forgive or forget an injury; blind obedience to the head of the family, whose will was law; and a love of secrecy, because the official law was always hostile to any small society within a greater society. Such a code produced in the families of the Mafia an extraordinary self-respect and sense of honour and duty; it also produced murders of a barbarity and meanness rarely equalled in modern times.

The transformation of the Mafia families from outlaw bands into the real rulers of Sicily took place in the nineteenth century, when feudal power in the island disintegrated. The landowners, who were becoming less and less interested in working their own soil, began to employ agents called *gabellotti*, who agreed to work the land in return for the payment of a fixed yearly sum. The *gabellotti*, many of whom belonged to Mafia families, sublet the plots to the peasants.

When Garibaldi invaded the island with his Redshirts in 1860, this new Sicilian class of middlemen transferred its support from the Bourbon regime to him; and in the ensuing Republic, it controlled the politics of the island by force and by the intimidation of voters. The *gabellotti* had already hired other members of Mafia families to collect rents from the peasants and to protect the orange groves, the sulphur mines and the property of the landowners; eventually, they bought the estates at low prices from the aristocrats, and they consolidated their control over the town governments. Their rule was as oppressive and savage and unjust as that of the former rulers. Their vengeance was as terrible and even more sure, because they were local people.

The reason why the Mafia and its family code still exist in

Sicily lies in the backwardness of parts of the island. Deep suspicion of the law and the central government, an economy where a man might find work for only about a hundred days a year in times of sowing or harvest, the exclusion of women from social life, overpopulation and fanatical Catholicism all allowed Mafia families to exploit their traditions as champions of the people in order to remain the exploiters of Sicily. The Honoured Society remained the funnel through which many jobs and much patronage and trade had to flow in the name of a secret island power which ruled in some places far more effectively than the official government in Rome. The Mafia also preserved its secrecy by allowing few informers to live.

Although the Mafia was a protection racket that took its percentage on practically every transaction made in the island, it remained a force of law and order – its own law and its own order. Sicilians had to pay a double tax, the first to the government to subsidize the official police and the official judges, the second to the Mafia to maintain its police and judges. For while petty crime might flourish in Sicily without the Mafia, the Honoured Society, which brooked no competition, had almost eliminated the small criminal. Those who did not pay protection had their sheeps' throats cut, their olive trees chopped down, their automobiles bombed, and their homes burned; but those who paid – and that meant nearly the whole population – had their stolen goods restored to them when even the police were ineffective.

The organization of the Mafia depended on a loose form of democracy within certain Sicilian families, but membership might also be conferred on outsiders of great daring and of Sicilian blood. One of the few known confessions of a Sicilian Mafioso, that of Dr Melchiore Allegra, told of an association split up into families, each one headed by an elected chief or *capofamiglia*. The family was made up of men from neighbouring towns and villages who were connected either by blood ties or by their status in the community. The *capofamiglia* was the effective ruler of his area and was independent; but he was expected to cooperate with all the other local chieftains of the Mafia and to obey the elected head of them all, the *capo dei capi*. The association was not confined to Sicily; it had offshoots in Tunisia and Marseille, as well as in North and South America.

Allegra also told of certain passwords and signs by which one Mafioso might know another; these, however, were few, and were confined for the most part to the display and exchange of coloured handkerchiefs. More interesting, perhaps, was Allegra's description of the ceremony by which he was initiated into the society. The tip of his middle finger was pierced by a needle and blood was squeezed from it onto the small paper image of a saint. The paper was burned, and the ashes were put into his hand. He was then made to take this oath: 'I swear to be loyal to my brothers, never to betray them, always to aid them, and if I fail may I burn and be turned to ashes like the ashes of the image.'

Although the Mafia was a family society, internal feuds were common. Its efforts to keep the peace among its members were complicated by the code of the vendetta, which governed members and non-members alike. A Mafia member was bound to avenge not only the death of another Mafia member, but also the death of a blood relation. Frequently, Mafiosi in various parts of Sicily almost eliminated the organization by killing each other in blood feuds. Thus, 153 murders took place in the Mafia stronghold of Corleone within five years. Between 1918 and 1960, nearly one-tenth of the population of the town of Godrano was killed in blood feuds, despite the *capo dei capi*'s efforts to make peace. Such murders were often done in a spirit of resignation and despair. A peaceable farmer suddenly became head of his family and inherited the inescapable obligation to murder several men of an opposing family to satisfy family honour and secure a corpse for a corpse.

Sicily, plundered through the century by invaders, eventually sent its own sons to plunder abroad. The Mafiosi, who controlled most of the land in Sicily, left much of it to waste in order to drive up the prices of their products and to have a permanent pool of cheap labour under their control. From the late nineteenth century, armies of jobless peasants discovered that the only way to feed themselves and their families was to emigrate, preferably to America, and to send money home until their families had enough to join them. More than a million Sicilians reached the United States, finding work as labourers, particularly in the docks.

For the newcomers, there were not many ways of rising fast in the world, though these few opportunities were many more than at home. Undoubtedly one of the routes was through crime, and soon Mafia chieftains were established in all the Little Italies of the big-city slums, where they enjoyed much the same respect as they had in their own communities in Sicily. The American public first became aware of these groups in 1890, when Italian gang warfare broke out in New Orleans. Two brothers from Palermo, called Matranga, had set up a protection racket over all cargo loaded or unloaded in the port. Sicilian dock workers, used to a similar extortion in Palermo and scarcely able to speak the American language, let alone understand American law, accepted the traditional system of paying tribute.

Gang leaders from Naples had also moved into the New Orleans docks: the Provenzano brothers from the rival Camorra, a Neapolitan secret society which was wholly criminal. Soon several murders a week were taking place by revolver and bomb and dagger. The local chief of police, an Irishman called Hennessey, decided to investigate the murders instead of allowing foreign criminals to butcher one another and solve the law's problems outside the law. He learned so much about the organization of the Mafia and the Camorra, which was less rooted in the social fabric of its mother city, that he was shot down a few days before he was due to testify before a grand jury.

Indictments were eventually returned against nineteen Sicilians; but half the jury was intimidated or bribed, and batteries of America's top lawyers were engaged for the defence. The result was that judgement was suspended on three of the defendants, while the rest were declared innocent. The familiar Sicilian pattern of trials of Mafiosi seemed to have been established in America; but in Louisiana the custom of lynch law antedated the custom of Mafia law, and the immigrants had not allowed for the citizens taking the law into their own hands. A mob of several thousand gathered, dragged eleven of the Mafiosi out of the city jail, strung them up in the street, and riddled them with bullets.

The fact that the offenders were not prosecuted led to a break in diplomatic relations between the United States and the home country of the criminals. The Italian Foreign Minister implied that the Americans were barbarians, incapable of enforcing their own laws. The Secretary of State replied that the United States, though a relatively young country, did not have the bandit societies that seemed to flourish in Italy. Nevertheless, diplomatic relations and immigration were resumed, and the American Mafia developed into a brilliant and powerful organization, perfectly adapted to the techniques of American urban crime.

Just as the Irish, in their secret political organizations at home, had developed the family political techniques that made them the bosses and policemen of the sprawling new American cities, so the Italians, and particularly the Mafia, were the natural inheritors and developers of organized crime in the United States. For individual acts of violence, however, the tradition of the American West was just as bloody as anything arriving from the Mediterranean, while the South had its own tradition of family vendettas. The immigrant Mafiosi had only to learn the techniques of bank and train robbery developed by the American outlaws and add them to their own expertise in protection rackets to create a far more profitable heist on American soil than was possible in the homeland.

The American Mafia, however, differed vastly from the Sicilian. The very virtues bred by the social situation in Sicily – the *omertà* caused by poverty, suspicion of the law, and hatred of the courts – were badly affected by the concept of the American melting pot. Slowly, the conspiracy of silence began to crack.

Informers on the Mafia were found with far greater frequency among American citizens and the Mafiosi themselves than had ever been found at home. Moreover, the American Mafia could hardly claim that it was the defender of the people against government oppression. On the contrary, many Mafiosi actually escaped from the electric chair because of legal snarls caused by the conflict between state and federal law.

Imitators in crime were soon bred. In the 1900s, the United States became familiar with the phenomenon of the Black Hand. Demands for protection money were sent out among the Italian community; on each demand was drawn a crude black hand (see plate 23). Fear was the bludgeon. The selected victims were threatened with kidnapping and murder or mutilation of their children if the ransom was not paid. Americans already used a single name for all Italian immigrant gangs: the Italian Society. Now, they leapt to the conclusion that a single gang was behind the Black Hand. But the New York Police Department had an exceptionally persistent detective, Lieutenant Joe Petrosino. As he was of Italian origin, Petrosino could gain information from among the majority of Italian immigrants, who were honest working people. He discovered that there was no central Black Hand organization; any criminal who wished to terrify someone into paying protection used the warning tactics of the Mafia or the publicized symbol of the Black Hand.

Petrosino spent twenty years compiling huge dossiers on Italian criminal groups and secret societies, including the Mafia and the Camorra. Ironically, while disproving the myth of the international conspiracy of the Black Hand, he became the first victim of the Mafia's international conspiracy. In 1909, he visited Italy to establish contact with the local police, so that the New York police could be warned when Italian criminals set sail for the United States. This pioneer in Interpol met his death at the hands of the founders of international crime syndicates. As soon as he landed in Palermo to check on the police records of the

Mafia, he was killed by the *capo dei capi* of all Sicily, Don Vito Cascio Ferro himself.

Don Vito, who was acquitted of twenty murders during his rule of the Mafia, used to boast only of killing the American. He had taken time off from dinner with a Member of Parliament to kill Petrosino with a single pistol shot as he came out of the Palermo docks. Don Vito's comment showed that he clearly recognized the importance of the detective's attempt to set up international police cooperation. 'My action was a disinterested one,' he used to explain, 'and was taken in response to a challenge I could not afford to ignore.' Don Vito was eventually jailed by Mussolini's chief of police on a false charge of smuggling, and died in prison.

The virtue of the Mafia in Sicily had been its extreme clannishness. Yet this quality proved a vice in the context of American crime. The Mafia's efforts were spent on fighting rival gangsters instead of devising new ways to plunder the public. Once Alphonse Capone had established himself as head of the Italian gangster groups in Chicago in the 1920s, he began to demonstrate the virtues of combination. He was to crime and ruthlessness what J. P. Morgan was to Wall Street, the first man to exert national influence over his trade. For all its tight-lipped family base, the Mafia often seemed to take clannishness to the level of paranoia, and to spend more of its time in killing off rivals and suspected traitors than in bringing in the loot. Perhaps because Capone was a Neapolitan among Sicilians, or perhaps because he was an immigrant among native Americans or a businessman among bandits, he preached the virtues of cooperation among rival Italian and Irish and Jewish mobsters. America was the land of opportunity, surely there was enough for all.

Certainly, the legal prohibition of alcohol seemed to have created enough loot for every determined American gangster. The passing of the Eighteenth Amendment to the Constitution – the only one ever to be repealed, after thirteen years of Prohibition –

did more to create a national hatred of the government and its revenue agents than all the rest of the laws put together. Having a drink was held to be the natural right of man. Prohibition also made folk heroes out of urban killers. Now there was no need for hundreds of rival criminals or small gangs to squabble over plunder from a few banks or train robberies, when the whole city of Chicago could be carved up into territories, where Mafia chiefs could organize on a small scale the sort of bootlegging operation that netted Capone $60,000,000 a year from booze alone.

Jesse James and Billy the Kid were hopelessly out of date in the Chicago of Al Capone. He could even call an international gangland convention in 1929 at Atlantic City. There he could parcel out the whole nation among various mobs. Crime under Capone reached its stage of oligopoly and price-fixing agreements, with one man its acknowledged leader. The small-time crook was eliminated in the big city as small businesses were by big business. In this the associated gangs were a positive benefit to society.

Capone's myth was to become more powerful than Jesse James's in the age of urban crime. The new people with the right to kill wore fedora hats and striped suits and black-and-white shoes and diamond rings. Their haunts were nightclubs and speakeasies. Capone could even aspire to culture and say, 'With me grand opera is the berries.' Yet he and his conspiracy of looters were vulnerable through their vanity. He liked publicity; but when he became too much of a scandal, the federal government would not tolerate him and put him in jail for tax evasion, a more exact crime than murder because he was tidy enough to keep books on his rackets. For those who oppose governments, only death and taxes usually bring them down. When the newspapers who had made Capone notorious destroyed him through his celebrity, he realized his mistake too late, saying, 'No brass band for me. There's a lot of grief attached to the limelight.' In 1947, he died in prison.

But while fame had lasted, Capone and his men had been

spectacular. The murder of the Irish gangster Dion O'Banion while he was shaking the hand of one of his killers in his own flower-shop was a baroque masterpiece, particularly as Capone had ordered a wreath from O'Banion for the funeral of one of their criminal mutual friends. The fact that never a gangster was executed for murder when the murder rate ran among the mobs at over a hundred a year in Cook County showed Capone's supreme position above the law. And the finale of vengeance, the St Valentine's Day Massacre in a garage, was as gory as any last scene of Grand Guignol or the guillotine. Humphrey Bogart and George Raft and James Cagney became international film stars and heroes from their imitation of crime culture. Where would the idiom and the opportunity of the gangster movie have been without the bloody brevity of Capone, whose only epitaph on O'Banion was to observe that his rival's 'head got away from his hat'?

Capone might have been tolerated longer in Chicago if he had not tried to become respectable. The prospect that he would use his profits and his methods of murder and torture and threat in the sphere of legitimate big business caused the wealthy of Chicago to turn against him. There was society and there were criminals. Each to his own. 'Yes, it's bootleg while it's on the trucks,' Capone used to complain, 'but when your host at the club, in the locker room, or on the Gold Coast hands it to you on a silver tray, it's hospitality.' To the hundreds of thousands of whiskey-makers in their stills in the Appalachians, Capone was almost another William Wallace, protesting against an unjust prohibition on alcohol and killing revenue agents for their income.

The new era of cooperation among gangsters ushered in by Capone spawned the famous national network of killers called Murder Inc., which included non-Sicilians and which killed for hire as the Assassins at Alamut had done in their later degenerate days. For greed was exalted in the American Mafioso over the discipline of *omertà*, and particularly over the concept of unquestioning obedience to the elder Mafiosi. In their lust for a greater

share of the spoils, the younger American mobs began ousting
the elder generation by elimination. In 1931, led by Charles
'Lucky' Luciano, they began a systematic shredding of the old
Mafiosi and their families, beginning in New York. They killed
off some thirty or forty of their previous chiefs. Their group,
though known as the Unione Siciliana, was an entirely American
criminal gang.

With the destruction of the patriarchal and hereditary
structure of the American Mafia, the social basis of *omertà*
disappeared. The life of rich Sicilian Americans in large cities had
little in common with the life of the small-town Mafiosi in Sicily.
The Americans were dealing with billions of dollars raised from
an alien, industrial nation; the Sicilians were dealing with much
smaller sums raised from a backward and poverty-stricken rural
society. The American Mafia became sophisticated; it learned
how to move into legitimate industry and to work the levers of
capitalism. While it kept those practices of the old Mafia that
were useful for a criminal gang in the United States – vengeance
on informers, the intimidation of juries, and corruption of the
law – it abandoned the traditional philosophy. In Sicily, however, the Mafia remained a way of life as well as a means of
exploitation.

The Sicilian Mafia survived many attacks, the most brutal of
which was undoubtedly the campaign waged against it in the
early 1920s by Cesare Mori, Mussolini's chief of police. After
flogging, maiming, flaying, and castrating hundreds of suspects,
and deporting hundreds more, Mori declared in 1928 that the
Mafia had been wiped out. His account of the campaign, though
vainglorious and inaccurate, contained a few points of interest
about the mind of the criminal terrorist.

'The most salient and perplexing factor in the psychology
of the typical Mafioso,' Mori wrote, 'is his conviction that he
is doing no wrong. As long as he obeys the rules of *omertà* –
whether he extorts, steals, or even murders – he is, to himself, as

well as to his brethren, an honourable man. His conscience is at peace.' The rules of war, by which some societies might allow members of their armed forces to murder and loot, were applied by members of the Mafia in times of peace, because they always felt themselves to be at war with a wider society. Nevertheless, Mori was not the man to moralize against the Mafia's correct view that the Fascist government in Rome was in a state of open and bloody warfare against its very existence.

Mori did not believe that the families of the Mafia elected their chiefs. He claimed that these chiefs chose themselves and imposed themselves. In a way he was right, for a family confirmed as its chief the one who showed most authority among them. Mori also recognized that the Mafia would absorb any talented Sicilian who had the qualifications it thought desirable; but once the Mafia suspected that one of its members might compromise the others, he was murdered or retired by force and threats. Mori emphasized that the Mafia was as much a philosophy as a society. It had little use for passwords and secret signs – the Mafiosi knew one another by a way of speaking, a dignity and reserve of manner, a cold-eyed stare, an intuition. Tullio Vinay, an opposition Protestant pastor, confirmed this view, declaring that in Sicily, 'the ideology of the people *is* the Mafia – to be strong, to be potent, to dominate. That is the first thing, and it is the effect of the history of Sicily, because the people of Sicily *need* to be somebody. And the Mafia is first the desire to dominate. To be the *lord of the situation*.'

In America, too, the Mafia had flourished because it met the immigrants' need for prestige. Yet the nineteenth-century tradition of extortion and robbery was an anachronism in a society where big business had outgrown its brutality and refined its techniques of success. As many Sicilian families grew rich by legitimate means and joined the American middle classes, the old Mafia died; its successor became increasingly hard to differentiate from big business. The new American Mafia owned trucking firms, hotels, casinos, restaurants, whole resorts. It even organized prostitution, a thing unthinkable to the old Sicilian Mafiosi. And with the end of Prohibition, it switched to the trade in narcotics.

The successful American Mafiosi, who had retained links with their homeland, eventually taught new techniques of extortion to the Sicilians. The beginnings of this influence lay in the Allied conquest of Sicily in 1943, when the local Mafia, so adept at picking winners, decided to take the advice of its American branch and allow the island to fall like a ripe plum into the hands of the invaders. For this purpose, the Allies enlisted the aid of 'Lucky' Luciano, who was serving a thirty-year sentence and had already been used to stop Italian-American stevedores from sabotaging Allied ships in New York. The pervasive influence of the jailed head of the Mafia was evident. Hardly any cases of subversion were reported from the docks, and the resistance to Allied armies was negligible in Western and Central Sicily, where the Mafia was most powerful.

So the leaders of American democracy delivered Sicily back into the hands of the Mafia, from which Mussolini had almost delivered it. It was ironical that the Allies should owe one of their cheapest victories in the Second World War to the cooperation of American and Sicilian gangsters. The price of this victory, however, was paid in full. Luciano was paroled from prison and deported to Naples, where he became the acknowledged head of the international Mafia, while the old *capos* again assumed control of most of the small towns of Sicily and took their cut from much of industry and agriculture.

From its experiences under Fascism and in America, the Mafia had learned that the best climate for extortion was capitalism, while the weakest system of law was under democracy. As one notable analyst of Italy, Luigi Barzini, declared, 'The Mafia sides with those in power. The Mafia was with the Bourbon kings before 1860 and immediately shifted its power, its loyalty, to Garibaldi when Garibaldi landed. The Mafia was on the side of the Americans when they landed in Sicily. The Mafia is siding with the Christian Democrats who are running the country now, at the present time.'

The Christian Democrats soon found that the way to gain seats in Sicily and to keep back the Communist vote was to cooperate with the Mafia. This alliance led to the most tragic episode in Sicilian postwar history: the massacre in 1947 of townspeople near Portella della Ginestra. The Christian Democrats had done badly in the Sicilian elections of that year. The townspeople had voted for Popular Front candidates, and the powers that were in Sicily decided that the Reds needed a lesson. The agent of revenge chosen by the Mafia and the few aristocrats still powerful on the island was the successful bandit Salvatore Giuliano, a popular outlaw who had backed the Separatist movement after the war and had even invited the United States to annex Sicily – a solution which would certainly have solved the island's problem of overcrowding and the Mafia's problem of getting its members from one country to the other.

Giuliano was never actually a member of the Mafia. He was promised a safe passage to Brazil with his men if he cooperated in the deterrence of the Reds. He duly opened fire with machine guns on the townsfolk celebrating May Day at Portella della Ginestra, killing eleven of them and wounding fifty-five others. The peasants in Sicily took this lesson to heart. In the next election, the vote for the Christian Democratic candidates climbed. Salvatore Giuliano, being of no further use to the Mafia, was then due to be eliminated. In the new age of international gangster conspiracies, the outlaw folk hero was a rusty tool, to be thrown away after one last use.

Giuliano proved more difficult to destroy than to employ. Warned of a Mafia plot, he tried to kidnap the *capo dei capi*, Don Calò, and also the Archbishop of Monreale. Far from submitting to the Mafia, he was actually trying to overthrow it. But the Mafia won over his lieutenant and cousin Pisciotta, who murdered Giuliano in July 1950. When tried for his part in the massacre at Portella della Ginestra, Pisciotta succinctly explained how the Sicilian Mafia and the police and the bandits cooperated, rendering unto the government what was the government's – the votes – and rendering unto the rest what was theirs – a share of the loot.

'We were a single body,' Pisciotta testified, 'bandits, police and Mafia, like the Father, the Son and the Holy Ghost.' This trinity of power, linked and barely divisible, ruled in Sicily, while the Sicilians who emigrated to the North to work became the staunchest supporters of the Communist Party.

Nicola Gentile, formerly a leading American Mafioso, told in 1963 of the increasing centralization of the Mafia. Although local organizations were still autonomous, modern communications had given much more authority to the Sicilian *capo dei capi* and to the 'king', his counterpart in the United States. The huge profits of international drug-smuggling demanded a far higher measure of cooperation and subordination. Contact with the American Mafia enabled its Sicilian counterpart to exploit the industrialization that was slowly creeping into the island.

Luciano and other expatriated American gangsters advised on fresh techniques of extortion, and then they masterminded them. The result was that new blocks of flats and factories in Palermo were just as much under the control of the Mafia as the old orange groves and sulphur mines. A bandit in a pinstripe suit remains a bandit. When Brecht made Mack the Knife turn from burglary to business and ask his famous question, 'What is robbing a bank compared with founding a bank?', he forecast the path the modern Mafia would take. He could have added as well, 'Why be an outlaw when you are the law?'

In July 1963, the central government in Rome, urged on by influential opinion in the rest of Italy, sent its Anti-Mafia Commission to Palermo. Even the Sicilian police were forced into action. Despite the assassinations of judges and investigators and 2,000 arrests, the Mafia survived the investigation as it had survived many worse enemies. 'It will take a generation to eradicate the Mafia,' said Luigi Barzini, a member of the commission, 'and even then, can we be sure that Sicilians, who have invented this terrific technique of living in a law-abiding state as if the law did not exist, can they forgo it when it offers – even an honourable man – so many advantages?'

The only way to eradicate the Sicilian Mafia was to elevate the poverty and rural morality that had spawned it. Prosperity would bring an end to the old Mafia, because the peasants would no longer need it to find jobs, while the new city Mafiosi would seek the respect of the rich and the urban rather than of their own kind.

In the most famous early exposé of the Mafia in the United States, the hearings before the Kefauver Committee in the Senate in 1951, the Senator found it 'a fearful thing to contemplate how close America has come to the saturation point of criminal and political corruption.' He forgot one thing. When saturation point is reached, the thing that saturates the body politic becomes the body politic. In the end, the American melting pot was working, and the United States was absorbing the Sicilian Mafia, as once it absorbed the Irish Bowery Boys. As the Mafia families became part of big business, so the control of organized crime would slip to other underprivileged groups, working for international terrorists in the global traffic in narcotics.

The Mafia had moved from being rural bandits to bankers in the computer revolution. Their ancient code of honour and theft was medieval in the age of digital robbery. Before his murder, Robert Kennedy as Attorney General had used the FBI and the Department of Justice to pursue the Mafia ruthlessly. Many of the old *capos* were sent away. The young Mafiosi were losing the control of the lucrative drugs trade to machine-gun mobs from Caribbean and Hispanic countries, backed by the rebel cartels of South America. New technologies, however, allowed a third generation of the Mafiosi to move to money laundering from narcotics and casino gambling, and to leave behind direct extortion and pushing drugs on the streets. They were no longer interested in being as old fashioned as their condemned fathers had been.

The aspirations of these new digital bandits had already been summed up by 'Lucky' Luciano, who died in 1962, about to be arrested again on charges of aiding the new billion-dollar business – the global drug traffic. 'If I had my time over again, I'd do the same sort of thing, only I'd do it legal. Too late I learned that you need just as good a brain to make a crooked million as an honest million.'

Crime does pay, as any study of the Mafia shows. But when crime pays really well, criminals become respectable. The first to do so were those who became criminals only to win respect.

21. THE IRISH REBELLION

The most enduring conspirators in the history of terror were the Irish rebels. After the passage of the Act of Union in 1800 and the suppression of the United Irishmen, there was a period of quiet. In 1829, the Catholic Emancipation Act was passed through the pressure of the Irish barrister Daniel O'Connell and his Catholic Association, whose officers had acquired more real power in the south of Ireland than the official administration. Even so, the heirs of the United Irishmen, a radical group who would call themselves the Fenians, still wanted complete independence, an Irish Republic separate from the British Crown. Although Catholic emancipation had removed one popular grievance, the Great Famine gave the Fenians a vast fund of hate to use in their search for recruits.

On the outbreak of the potato blight, *Phytophthora infestans*, in 1845 among the staple crop of Ireland, the British government would not supply proper relief, but it called out the troops against any hunger marchers. The extraordinary thing, as in the Highland Clearances, was the docility of the starving Irish masses. A large mob even knelt in Westport, County Mayo, in front of Lord Sligo, begging him for aid instead of tearing him to pieces. There was also little official effort to cope with an epidemic of 'relapsing fever', or jaundice, and typhus, both carried by the ubiquitous louse.

Malnutrition added to the deadliness of the infections. The immune systems of the hungry were run down. Such government neglect appeared to be a form of genocide, as the Irish have always remembered. A million of them died, while another million emigrated to the United States of America to continue the struggle for independence.

In the words of a contemporary Irish historian, the policy of Anglo-Irish landlords and British governments had led to a system 'by which a beautiful and fertile island, producing noble and superabundant harvests year after year, became gradually poorer and poorer – was reduced to buy its bread – reduced, at length, to utter starvation, and, finally, to cannibalism.' The English commercial system of free trade and the repeal of the Corn Laws in 1846 had further beggared Ireland. The problem had been aggravated by Ireland's enormous increase in population because of the abundance of the potato crop. Even so, it was easy to lay the fault on 'Irish landlordism ... grown so rotten and hideous a thing that only its strict alliance, offensive and defensive, with British oligarchy, saves it from going down to sudden perdition.'

In 1848, some rebel Irish Catholics attempted to organize an armed rising. The government, informed of the plan, deported the leaders; but three of them – John O'Mahony, Michael Doheny and James Stephens – fled to the United States. On the soil of America, where there was cheap land for the asking and no system of rack-renting, they founded the Fenian Brotherhood, also to be called the Irish Republican Brotherhood. They sent funds to Ireland for the formation of an Irish wing. The Fenians were organized on the Continental revolutionary model of cells of ten men, whose members were theoretically unknown to other members. The oath they adopted was frankly revolutionary; it paid no lip service to reform. The Irish version ran:

> I, X, do solemnly swear, in the presence of Almighty God, that I will do my utmost, at any risk, while life lasts, to make Ireland an independent democratic Republic; that I will yield implicit obedience in all things not contrary to the law of God, to the commands of my superior officers; and that I shall preserve inviolable secrecy regarding all the

transactions of this secret society that may be confided to me. So help me God! Amen.

In spite of the form of the oath, the Catholic priesthood in Ireland proved hostile. As early as 1858, a Catholic priest informed on a group of Fenians in Ireland, who were brought to trial. The oath was then amended to exclude the vow of secrecy; it was replaced by a vow of allegiance to the Irish Republic, which stated that the republic was 'already virtually established', and thus turned rebellion into a form of patriotic resistance.

The American Civil War provided the revolutionary Irish-Americans with a training in military tactics and in the use of arms. The conflict also gave the Fenians the hope that the British government's sympathy with the Confederate South would lead to intervention and thus create an opportunity for a successful rebellion in Ireland. The Fenians were able to operate in security on American soil because the Irish vote was an important factor in American politics. Feeling safe from persecution, they dropped most of their efforts at secrecy and held a public convention in 1863 in Chicago. There, they called for the establishment of an Irish Republic; but this was only to be achieved after the invasion of Canada, and the establishment of an independent Canadian Republic.

Three attempts were made by the Fenians to raise a revolt in Canada; on each occasion, they were quickly dispersed. In 1867, they made attempts to take over military supplies held at Chester Castle in England and to start a rebellion in Ireland itself, but the risings were put down with ridiculous ease. The Fenians' activities ceased a few years later. Apart from the murder of a policeman and a few civilians, and the successful engineering of one prison escape, they had achieved nothing.

By operating publicly, the Fenians had lost all the advantages of secrecy. Any expatriate Irish-American who landed on Irish soil was an obvious target for the British police. Both the United

Irishmen and the Fenians recruited indiscriminately and were riddled with British informers, so that the British authorities were warned of most of their planned attempts at insurrection. From the point of view of a successful uprising, a hard core of well-armed, expert revolutionaries, such as the Bolsheviks were to have, would have been more useful than a milling mass of emotional adherents, armed only with loathing and liable to melt away at the first charge of the militia or the police.

Each failure of a nationalist secret society tends to provoke the elimination of its moderate elements by the ruthless, on the grounds that measures have not been extreme enough. On the ashes of the Fenians in America rose the Clan-na-Gael, a secret organization with plans to assassinate Queen Victoria, sink British shipping with submarines, and blow up the House of Commons with nitroglycerine manufactured in a hidden factory near Birmingham. In the 1880s, explosions actually occurred in the House of Commons and the Tower of London and at London Bridge. Yet the terrorists injured nobody except themselves – a fate similar to the attempt in 1894 of the anarchist who aimed to blow up the Greenwich Observatory.

The Clan-na-Gael's use of naked terror in England alienated many English supporters of more Irish independence. Parnell, the Parliamentary leader of the Irish Home Rule party, refused to recognize terrorism, and the more moderate of the old Fenian supporters in Ireland joined him in his campaign for land reform through the Land League. The Irish bloc in the British Parliament helped to secure the disestablishment of the Anglican Church in Ireland and a Land Act to protect tenants. Perhaps every open movement for political freedom needs its hidden militants to terrorize the powers that be, although its leaders must officially condemn the violence of those militants. In the opinion of one Irish historian: 'In the last analysis, it was the Whiteboys and the Ribbonmen and Captain Moonlight who made possible the respectable superstructure above them which condemned them.'

A group of ex-Fenian terrorists called the Invincibles murdered Lord Frederick Cavendish, the Chief Secretary for Ireland, and Thomas Burke, the Under-Secretary, in 1882 in Phoenix Park, Dublin. Their action was particularly embarrassing to the Irish cause, because the Liberal Party in England was then planning to introduce reforms in Ireland, and it seemed that independence might be gained by political means. Only when attempts to pass Home Rule bills for Ireland failed did the impetus again pass to the revolutionaries. An attempt to stem the rising tide of English influence by reviving the national language, Gaelic, culminated in 1905 in the formation of the political revolutionary movement Sinn Féin. In this case, as in the case of so many other nineteenth-century movements, attempts to preserve an eroding culture led to a new revolution.

Arthur Griffith, who resembled Wolfe Tone as a pamphleteer and journalist, turned the Gaelic League into a political move-ment. Sinn Féin meant 'We Ourselves'; it called for Irish independence through action in Ireland by Irishmen. It sought to make the Irish conscious of their own traditions, their own language, their culture and their separateness. The folly of the English House of Lords in delaying the third Home Rule Bill for Ireland in 1912 led to a surge of support for the Irish revolution-aries as against the Irish constitutionalists. The Protestants of Ulster, fearful of future Catholic domination, were also given time to organize and arm. They found a determined leader in Sir Edward Carson, who declared in 1914: 'I am not sorry for the armed drilling of those who are opposed to me in Ireland. I certainly have no right to complain of it; I started that with my own friends.'

On the declaration of the First World War in 1914, the Home Rule Act was suspended for the duration. On Easter Monday 1916, the revived Irish Republican Brotherhood and two other revolutionary groups seized the General Post Office and other strategic points in Dublin, and held them for a week. They issued a proclamation declaring 'the right of the people of

Ireland to the ownership of Ireland, and to the unfettered control of Irish destinies, to be sovereign and indefeasible'. Thus the movement for Irish independence was asserted in blood, confirming the Irish revolutionaries as the leaders of the Irish Catholics and strengthening their claims in the peace settlement after the war. The execution of sixteen of the captured revolutionary leaders provided the movement with martyrs – the last ingredient necessary to end moderation and invoke a full-scale civil war (see plate 38). In a poem entitled 'Sixteen Dead Men', W. B. Yeats wrote:

> O but we talked at large before
> The sixteen men were shot,
> But who can talk of give and take,
> What should be and what not
> While those dead men are loitering there
> To stir the boiling pot?

In the General Election of December 1918, Sinn Féin won 73 of 105 Irish seats, and in January declared an assembly (the Dáil Éireann): that month a guerrilla war broke out in Ireland. This rapidly grew into a full-scale insurrection, for its Catholic leaders had widespread popular support. The propaganda and tactics of the Irish Republican Army were inspired. Its first object was to destroy the Royal Irish Constabulary, whose officers and constables were the forces of law and order, and who had local knowledge and respect. They were mostly drawn from the neighbouring Catholic small farmers, who occupied the land, which was said to be occupied by Britain. Even if they were armed and operated from barracks and posts, they were a recognized part of the community.

The rebel leader Michael Collins saw that his forces could take over the countryside if the Royal Irish Constabulary was frightened and humiliated. An anathema was passed on the police force by the Sinn Féin and its women's arm, the Cumann-na-mBan. At Mass, nobody would sit in a pew occupied by a 'peeler'. A woman who went with a policeman had her hair shaven. One woman had pig's rings put in her buttocks for supplying milk to a police barracks, and a donkey was stabbed in the forehead for carting turf there. No tradesman or farmer dared to supply the barracks. The old weapon of the boycott was enhanced by intermittent intimidation.

One account told of the constable's life spent

in constant apprehension of danger. If he would go out of barracks, he was compelled to do so as one of a party operating in practically an enemy's country. He could never predict the moment when a hail of bullets would burst upon him from a carefully prepared ambush, his assailants being the apparently harmless citizens who surrounded him every day. Every means was employed to tempt him from his allegiance. Letters reached him warning him to resign if he wished to escape the death penalty.

The Cumann-na-mBan cursed the police with the 'Aceldama' or 'Field of Blood':

For money their hands are dipped in the blood of their
    people . . .
They are the eyes and ears of the enemy.
Let those eyes and ears know no friendship.
Let them be outcasts in their own land.
The blood of the martyrs shall be on them and their
    children's children, and they shall curse the mothers
    that bring them forth.

The rebellion began with sporadic assaults on the scattered police barracks, some of which were only stockades held by a dozen men. The attacks spread from the south and west to cover all Ireland. Constables were murdered on duty and off duty, and they began to retire to their fortified district headquarters. By August 1920, a thousand constables had resigned, a tenth of the total force. Meanwhile, in commemoration of the Easter Rising,

Michael Collins ordered the abandoned barracks to be put to the torch, and 182 of them were set ablaze. To this day, outside almost every town and many a village in Ireland stands a ruin of recent date, the quarters of the Royal Irish Constabulary.

The riposte of the British was to recruit auxiliaries for the police. The first of these took the nickname of the 'Black and Tans', later to be known by the regular British army as the 'Blacks and Scum'. They wore the dark jacket of the Royal Irish Constabulary over the khaki trousers of the Tommy, but these colours were also those of the Limerick Hunt, called the Black and Tans. This debris of the First World War treated Ireland as an occupied country to loot and terrify, while all Irishmen were murderers or 'Shinners'.

The ranks of the Black and Tans were supplemented by more disciplined and formidable Auxiliaries, who had been army officers with good records. These recruits were trained in police work at the Curragh and wore a dark green uniform with a tam-o'-shanter and crowned harp badge. Mobile in their armoured cars and tenders, they were intended to answer the flying columns of Michael Collins over the length and breadth of Ireland.

Although the new Commandant of the RIC, Major-General H. H. Tudor, rearmed the force with rifles and machine guns, and also had the barracks fortified with steel shutters, there was a mutiny of the force at Listowel. The constables refused to hand over their quarters to the military and take up dangerous positions in the outlying countryside. Then and there, the war of atrocity was declared official by a one-armed veteran, Colonel Smyth, the Divisional Commander for Munster.

'Now, men,' he announced:

Sinn Féin has had all the sport up to the present, and we are going to have the sport now ... If a police barracks is burned or if the barracks already occupied is not suitable, then the best house in the locality is to be commandeered,

the occupants thrown into the gutter. Let them die there –
the more the merrier. Police and military will patrol the
country at least five nights a week. They are not to confine
themselves to the main roads, but make across the country,
lie in ambush and when civilians are seen approaching,
shout 'Hands up!' Should the order be not immediately
obeyed, shoot and shoot with effect. If the persons
approaching carry their hands in their pockets, or are in
any way suspicious-looking, shoot them down.

Atrocity was now matched by atrocity, ambush by ambush.
Eighty victims had been detailed by Michael Collins to be killed
in Dublin, and a force of Irish Volunteers gathered on Baggot
Street Bridge for this purpose; but only fourteen British officers
were murdered. A seventy-year-old woman, Mrs Lindsay, was
torn to pieces by women of the Cumann-na-mBan for informing
the British forces of an ambush. A resident magistrate was buried up to the neck in sand at low tide to watch the sea water
rising to drown him.

Between April and June 1920, some sixty towns and villages
were 'fired up' or partially wrecked by British soldiers and auxiliaries. At Templemore, the Northamptonshires raided a drink
shop and a draper's, dressed in women's blouses, and burned
and sacked the town. Eventually, Cork itself was put to the
flame in an orgy of destruction. Curiously, the general who had
led the Protestant mutiny at the Curragh before the First World
War, Sir Hubert Gough, warned against government policy:
'I don't think any truthful or sane person can avoid the conclusion that the authorities are deliberately encouraging and, what
is more, actually screening reprisals and "counter murder" by
the armed forces of the Crown.'

Worse than the actual atrocities – for around thirteen hundred people were killed on both sides in the rebellion and
damage to property was assessed at only £5.5 million – were the
rumours and fears of violence. In the words of one witness:

Terrible tales were whispered in those final weeks of the dying year. Tales of frenzied men hunted by bloodhounds. Tales of pitiless ambushes, of police slaughtered to a man, and the bodies hacked to pieces with axes. Tales of savage reprisal followed on shameful deed, of burned shops, of deserted farms, of peasants gone to couch with fox and hare. Tales of new proclamations and new restrictions falling alike on guilty and innocent.

So futile was the attempt to suppress the Irish rebellion that the British Prime Minister, Lloyd George, was forced to recognize the Irish revolutionary cabinet, which held effective control of large areas in southern Ireland. A treaty was signed in December 1921 to give the southern counties the status of a dominion and in 1922 they became the Irish Free State. Ulster was excluded, however, for the Irish guerrilla army had not established its control in the north of the island.

The Irish conspirators were in many ways a reflection of the other nationalist secret societies of the period. They began by pressing for constitutional reform within the laws of the United Kingdom; they ended by taking revolutionary action against the British army. They splintered apart into squabbling groups during the negotiations with Britain and after independence was won. The Sinn Féin leader, de Valéra, refused to recognize the treaty for many years, though he became the Prime Minister of Ireland. And the rebels succeeded in their long-term object – what Arthur Griffith defined as 'making England take one hand away from Ireland's throat and the other out of Ireland's pocket.'

The Irish secret societies, as the Continental nationalist societies, had educated middle-class leaders who capitalized on a tradition of agrarian lawlessness. But there was one important respect in which they did not follow the Continental pattern. They never succeeded in influencing the city mob, which was usually hostile to them, if not in sympathy with the British.

22. STATE TERROR AND THE BOLSHEVIKS

The Tsar Ivan the Terrible invented the system through which the Bolsheviks would kill his heirs and run the Russian state. Brilliant and paranoiac, he established a secret police, the Oprichina, to destroy his warlord rivals, the Boyars, as King Vlad III had done in Wallachia. He then used these murderers to terrify his own population into unquestioning allegiance. A spy informed him in 1569 that the richest city in the land, Novgorod, wanted to secede, with the help of the King of Poland. He surrounded the disaffected city with a stockade to prevent all escape. He then ordered the Oprichina to torture and kill 60,000 citizens, who were roasted or drowned or flogged to death. He showed the few survivors and the city councillors the carpet of corpses and declared: 'God bless Our imperial power, and victory over all open and hidden enemies!'

The following year, a greater vengeance was visited on Moscow by the Khan of the Crimean Tatars, who put the wooden city to the flame. Hundreds of thousands died: a contemporary record spoke of 'people smothered and burned ten thick, one lying upon another'. Their holocaust was followed by the plague, which ravaged the survivors. The worst Ivan the Terrible could do to Novgorod was less than the Tatars then inflicted on Moscow. What the Russian serfs understood was not to oppose arbitrary police or military power.

The later Tsars carried on a system of police terror in order to rule, but not on the scale of ferocity of Ivan the Terrible. The

Bolsheviks would never have risen to take over Russia without the leniency of the secret police, who believed that it was better to penetrate the revolutionary committees than to destroy them immediately. Karl Marx, who inspired Lenin and the Bolsheviks, loathed Russia. He could not see how a nation of peasants could achieve a proletarian revolution of city workers.

Yet his doctrines made for the successful Bolshevik takeover of Russia under the command of Lenin. Marx himself had learned from the Jewish Messianic tradition in Europe. While reacting against religion, he still believed that scientific determinism would ensure a victorious apocalypse. The proletariat, the factory workers, would dissolve the existing world order. The harder they laboured to produce the things owned by the bourgeois middle class and the feudal capitalists, the worse would be their misery. As Marx's collaborator, Engels, put it, a miracle would be created – poverty in the middle of plenty. Even the capitalist had to compete or succumb. Private property was self-destructive. Only the annihilation of the ruling class and a Communist system, which was not communal because it was directed by the state, would produce a fulfilled society.

The problem for Marxism was that this future paradise and utopia on earth promised to all workers could only be produced through tyranny. Watching the failures of the revolutions of 1848, Marx concluded in his 'Address to the Communist League' that social democracy was opposed to the success of a proletarian revolution. 'With us,' he declared, 'it is not a matter of reforming private property, but of abolishing it; not of hushing up class warfare, but of abolishing classes; not of bettering the society we have, but of establishing a new one.'

What Marx aimed to do was to establish 'a secret as well as a legal organization of the working-class party' with independent cells on the model of the Illuminati over the whole of Europe. Apparently allied with the liberal democrats, their clubs would be subverted in the interests of a workers' insurrection. There had to be an ongoing and global revolution which had cells in the army and the police and the munitions factories. Without them, the overthrow of governments could not be achieved.

When Vladimir Ilyich Ulyanov, who would style himself as Lenin, took over the Bolshevik movement and then the Russian state, he was inspired as a student by the execution of his elder brother, Alexander. A friend of the aristocrat Piotr Shevgrev, the founder of a cell of the People's Freedom, Narodnaya Volya, Alexander plotted the murder of Tsar Alexander III, whose father had already died by assassination. He wrote a programme for democratic socialism, which the Tsar himself thought the same 'as the Paris Commune'. This conspirator was hanged in 1887, and his brother Vladimir was persecuted and exiled. When he was met in Switzerland by another Russian radical, Peter Struve, he already saw in Lenin 'an abstract social hatred and a cold political cruelty'.

In the manner of Blanqui and Marx, Lenin became a professional revolutionary. He escaped from Siberia to play a small role in the Russian uprising of 1905. He believed that propaganda was all, if the masses were to join any radical leaders. He had met the charismatic Lev Bronstein, alias Trotsky, and had worked on the socialist newspaper *Iskra*, published in Munich, London and Geneva. He had ruthlessly purged anybody who did not support his programme of personal dictatorship, so that his minority Bolsheviks had to split from the more democratic Mensheviks. And there lay the success and the failure of the coming revolution in Russia.

The anarchist Bakhunin had always opposed the Marxist doctrine of the revolutionary state with its control by a privileged few. He could not accept 'the ruling of the majority by the minority in the name of the alleged stupidity of the first and the alleged superior intelligence of the second.' The state would always remain an institution of domination and exploitation. There was no other way of emancipating the people economically and politically and providing liberty, 'but to abolish the state, all states, and once and for all do away with that which until now has been called politics.'

If Marx or his disciple Lenin were to succeed, there would be the same sorry result, 'the rule of great masses of people by a small privileged minority'. If the people were uneducated, as in Russia, they would be 'regimented into one common herd of governed people'. This could hardly be emancipation. Although the Marxists claimed that their dictatorship of the proletariat would wither away and lead to a socialist paradise, this would not happen. The Communist Party would always remain in control. If dictatorship was the means to free the masses, they would remain in slavery. Only anarchist leaders would destroy the state for ever, 'the everlasting prison for the toiling masses'.

Bakhunin was absolutely correct on the Bolshevik programme for the future of Russia, which led to the deaths of tens of millions from the collectivization of the land and the elimination of so-called subversives in the Gulags of Siberia. In the revolt of 1905 as well as the coup of 1917, the Bolsheviks showed that they had learned all the tactics of state terror from the Opritchina. They also learned from the new secret police, the Okhrana, under Sergei Zubatov, its inspired Moscow chief.

Conspiracy may be contained by penetrating the conspirators, or even misleading them, as Zubatov tried to do. Seeing the discontent of the exploited Russian factory workers, Zubatov set up in the major cities of the Tsar's realm many Societies for the Mutual Aid of Workingmen in the Mechanical Industries. With the assassination of the Minister of the Interior Sipyagin in 1902, the new appointee Plehve put Zubatov in charge at St Petersburg. He recruited as his organizer the brilliant preacher Father Gapon, whose Assembly of Workers rapidly superseded the nascent police-led unions in a national network. A conflict with management at the Putilov plant, which manufactured guns and railway carriages, was followed by a strike at the vast Nevsky Machine and Shipbuilding Works and other plants. Unused to industrial action, Gapon led 200,000 protesters in a petition to the Tsar, who retired from St Petersburg to his Winter Palace outside the city. Panicking Cossacks and riflemen killed and wounded some thousand people on a Bloody Sunday. This was the necessary martyrdom for the insurrection to come.

Assassination was still the preferred method of the rebels. Plehve was killed by another bomb, and then the Tsar's uncle and commandant in Moscow, the Grand Duke Sergei, was dispatched by Kaliayev, a dedicated anarchist. He displayed a compassion that later suicide bombers would not: in a previous attempt he had failed to throw his explosive because the Grand Duke was sitting in his carriage with his young niece and nephew on the way to the opera. Kaliayev could not kill children, although he blew the Grand Duke to bloody fragments shortly afterwards. When the Tsar's sister visited him in his condemned cell, he told her that her family had declared war on the people, and that the challenge had been accepted. At his trial before his hanging, he would not accept the authority of the courts, declaring that they were the death throes of tyranny. 'The judgement of history is upon you.' As a revolutionary, he hurled his hatred into the faces of the enemy 'with a single battle-cry: I accuse!'

With the losing of the war against Japan, strikes began to be declared across Russia, particularly in Odessa, an outbreak which the film genius of the Russian Revolution, Sergei Eisenstein, converted into the early masterpiece of state propaganda, *Battleship Potemkin*. Indeed, the sailors on the Black Sea cruiser did revolt, but there was no massacre on the steps of Odessa, because there were no steps. The Tsar's secret police, however, changed their tactics, recruiting counter-revolutionary groups known as the Black Hundreds, as the British would recruit the notorious Black and Tans. While effective at the beginning, these Russian paramilitaries were caught out by major strikes in Moscow and St Petersburg. Trotsky and a few other Bolsheviks did wonders in organizing the workers, particularly on the railways, while Lenin overcame his fear and returned to Russia to try to take over the St Petersburg Society, which held power for fifty days with deputies elected by factory workers.

Lenin struggled against the Mensheviks to control the strike newspaper *Izvestia*, later the name of a Communist publication. Although the Tsar had to allow elections in a succession of Dumas, Lenin called this limited democracy 'parliamentary cretinism'. The Cossacks and the Black Hundreds put down a peasant revolt by hanging, flogging and arson. Trotsky led a workers' uprising, but as the rebels only had eighty rifles, they were slaughtered and mutilated. Thousands were killed in the repression; tens of thousands were sent to Siberia as a lesson to the Bolsheviks of how to rule by terror. Forced into exile in Finland, Lenin's conclusion on the failure of the coup was to deny Marx and seek 'a democratic revolutionary dictatorship of workers and peasants' – of course, under his sole control.

No dictatorship could be democratic, but Lenin used language merely to advance his party. He now took to bank robbery and banditry to finance the Bolshevik machine. He himself had Kalmuk Asiatic ancestors, who derived from the Mongol horde, while his Georgian lieutenant, born Iosif Dzhugashvili, later known as Stalin, and trained as a priest in a seminary, was aided by two other comrades, Kamo and Krasin, to buy arms, manufacture explosives, counterfeit rouble notes, run terrorist training camps, assassinate enemies, and carry out 'expropriations' to bring in money for the cause. The state bank in Tblisi was robbed in 1907 of 350,000 roubles, while the fortune of Nikolai Shmit, a young Bolshevik killed in prison, was manipulated from his relations into Lenin's coffers. This outlawry offended the Mensheviks, as did the fact that one of Lenin's close advisers, Malinovsky, was an Okhrana agent, whom Lenin could not dismiss. Mistakenly, the Okhrana would rather penetrate the Bolsheviks than eliminate them, as they had Nechayev and the Nihilists: Stalin was condemned three times to Siberia, but allowed to escape. By 1914, with the outbreak of the First World

War, Lenin's small faction appeared to be doomed to obscure failure. Its leader retired to exile and depression in Switzerland.

Pushed backward by the German armies on the war fronts, the generals of the Tsar had adopted the old tactics used against Napoleon, the form of terror called a scorched-earth policy. Yet if the advancing Germans found no supplies, the ravaged Russian peasants had to flee back towards the Urals and the Baltic to find food and security. These refugee masses reached the discontented cities. A February workers' revolution in 1917 in St Petersburg, then called Petrograd, was surprisingly successful. Although there was a garrison of 160,000 troops, the insurgents called on these conscripts to join them, and whole regiments switched their allegiance. The Tsar abdicated in favour of his sick son. A new Duma and a Soviet was led by the moderate Socialist Alexander Kerensky, who formed a Provisional Government. There was a fissure in Russian affairs, which was the opportunity of the Bolsheviks to take over the mechanics of state terror.

German intelligence organized the return of Lenin in a sealed train with his Bolshevik comrades to their native land, in order to destabilize their opponents still more. Greeted by crowds at the Finland Station in Petrograd, Lenin declared: 'Any day now the whole of European capitalism may crash. Long live the worldwide Socialist revolution!' He immediately began plotting the overthrow of the Kerensky government and his own takeover of the urban Soviet. Through the revolutionary organ *Pravda* and the guerrilla genius of Trotsky, who helped to organize committees in munitions factories and the disintegrating army, Lenin could mount a coup against the First Congress of elected Soviets – only one in eight of them were Bolsheviks.

Although Kerensky opposed Lenin, telling him that he wanted to imitate the failed French Terror which resulted in the dictatorship of Napoleon, Lenin put together a putsch from some soldiers and workers. The first attempt failed, and Lenin fled again to hide in Finland, clean-shaven and wearing a blond wig. With the Bolsheviks gaining strength through their commissars and cells in the barracks and the factories and whatever political committees there were, Lenin agreed with Trotsky to launch an armed rebellion to seize power through a Military Revolutionary Committee.

The coup took place in October, when Bolshevik forces took over Petrograd. They still had to ravage the base of the Provincial Government in the Winter Palace, which was easily accomplished with the usual incidence of rape and murder. Lenin had won an extraordinary victory by assimilating the past mistakes of previous terrorists. In his pamphlet *What Is to Be Done?* he had insisted on revolutionary violence and armed struggle, followed by the dictatorship of the proletariat. The state must be destroyed and replaced. A new Constituent Assembly was dispersed by troops led by Bolshevik commissars; a Central Executive Committee ruled: democracy was dead. Afterwards, a new state would be set up to rule by terror in the name of the people, who would export a world revolution.

A shameful peace had to be concluded with the victorious German armies, giving away at Brest-Litovsk much of Poland and Finland and the Baltic countries, while independence was granted to the Ukraine. More important for Lenin was to consolidate his grip against an inevitable Tsarist reaction, backed by the capitalist powers and named the 'White Terror'. The Okhrana was replaced by the Cheka, a commission set up to fight counter-revolution and sabotage and speculation. Within one year, the new Soviet secret police had 30,000 employees, some of them recruited from the previous Tsarist force because of its expertise. Trotsky became the Commissar of War and showed his formidable powers in forming a political Red Army, again employing many officers from the previous regime.

The following year, with White and peasant armies seizing much of Siberia and the Caucasus, aided by British, French and Japanese expeditions, the Bolsheviks seemed ready to crumble. Enforcing campaigns of requisition to feed the Revolution, Lenin used force to subdue and starve the Ukraine, particularly the peasants with property, called kulaks. His instructions were precise: to hang publicly a hundred bloodsuckers, to remove all their supplies, to take hostages. Such state terror was unprecedented in modern Europe. All land was seized, and the peasants herded into collective farms, where they would be worked to death.

A Red Terror followed, including the liquidation of the Russian imperial family. As Lenin ordered, 'Exterminate all the Romanovs, a good hundred of them.' This decree began a campaign of horror which was extended by Lenin's successor Stalin over the whole of Russia, once the White insurgents had been crushed. Worse than Ivan the Terrible, Stalin had modern communications at his disposal. After the purges of the 1930s, he set the pattern for the new barbarism of the twentieth century, which slowly killed innocent people in their tens of millions, where old times had merely been able to slaughter tens of thousands of victims.

23. THE REVOLT OF LABOUR

Karl Marx believed that the workers' explosion would begin from William Blake's 'dark Satanic mills' in England. The toiling masses of the Industrial Revolution would throw their masters into the furnaces. Marx should have seen that religion was not the opium of the masses; the drug was an elected government.

Since the French Revolution there had been various organizations of rebels, the Corresponding Societies, the Hampden Clubs, the National Union of Working Classes, and the Chartists. These secret and travelling committees were vulnerable to infiltration and betrayal. The Luddites had some successes in their machine-breaking, but their instigation of the unarmed uprising in Manchester in 1819, was easily put down by the local Yeomanry, helped by the Hussars. Repression by hanging and the gagging of the free press followed. 'I have never known a period,' the contemporary historian Henry Cockburn wrote, 'at which the people's hatred of the Government was so general and so fierce.'

No workers' revolution happened in Britain because the masses were led by bourgeois leaders, who believed in democracy and Parliamentary reform. Furthermore, there was no popular push for a revolution on the French model, which was abhorred as a foreign bad example. Because of lack of education, with most job opportunities in the factory, national sentiment remained patriotic, given the expanding markets and opportunities of the Empire. Indeed, malcontents could be exported as far as Australia to help to rule elsewhere. At home, riots were local and easily suppressed. And the huge Chartist demonstration in the summer of 1848 was put down by many tens of thousands of special constables, policemen and regular soldiers. Loyal and numerous instruments of repression held out no hope for any workers' movement in Victorian times.

In the United States there was labour insurgency, which disconcerted even the White House. Particularly interesting were the Molly Maguires of the 1870s, who founded American industrial action. The Irish have always had too much of a sense of history and grievance. They do not forgive or forget, but they recollect and demand vengeance for past wrongs, even in other nations. As immigrants to the coalfields of Pennsylvania, the Irish miners found that they had not left oppression behind them. The coal-owners and the foremen were all Protestants. As in the Great Famine, the Irish workers still had to live in one-room shacks on rotten food bought from an exploiting company. So the old tactics of rural violence were revived against the mineowners.

The Molly Maguires began as a group of Irish drinkers, who sallied out to defend a priest from being insulted by a gang of Protestants. Rapidly, ambitious and bitter miners with all the Irish talent for politics and organization set up a confederation of gangs which spread over most of the Pennsylvania coalfields. The leader of the Molly Maguires was Jack Kehoe. He saw himself, as so many bandits and criminal leaders have, as 'a kind of Robin Hood'. In the reported words of Detective McParlan, who penetrated and betrayed the Mollies: 'Maybe if things had been different, he could have been a leader of a decent group of miners fighting for their rights instead of heading a pack of night killers.'

The Mollies were never more than a gang of terrorists, who avenged insults to their own members by murder, and who used pistols and dynamite to assert their power. Perhaps the brutal behaviour of the Pennsylvania Coal and Iron Police – the owners' private army – encouraged the despairing Irish to join illegal gangs of their own. Perhaps the failure of the nascent miners' union in the long strike after 1874 and the complete victory of their enemies seemed to prove that only the violence of the Mollies made any impression on the bosses. Eventually, the gangs were totally destroyed and their leaders hanged. With the priests and the majority of the God-fearing Irish against them, they were doomed, once the power of the mineowners was shown to be greater than theirs. Their terror tactics appeared to be worse than those of their employers.

The government, however, was permitting the recruitment of private armies or security forces against organized labour. The weapons had to be in the hands of the industrialists, not the workers. Here rural populism forged a rare alliance with urban protest. During the Pullman strike, for instance, the Governor of Colorado told a Populist rally, 'This strike can never succeed because the entire armed forces of the United States are against the success of the laboring man ... The United States government is using all its military power to build up monopoly.'

Only two 'armies' ever marched on Washington as Jack Cade and Wat Tyler had on London. Coxey's army of the unemployed produced in 1894 on Pennsylvania Avenue a larger crowd than for the President's inauguration. Yet it was unarmed and easily dispersed by the mounted police, while Coxey himself was arrested for trampling on the grass. Far more serious was the camp for the Bonus Marchers – war veterans as Shays' had been – who threatened in 1932 the Congress and the White House. They were cleared from their shacks at Anacostia by four troops of cavalry and six tanks and a column of infantry with fixed bayonets, under the command of a future President, Major Dwight D. Eisenhower. The orders for the clearance were given by General Douglas MacArthur, who considered that the mob was animated by 'the essence of revolution' and was about to seize control of the government.

After these early labour movements arose the superlative and only union of migrant labourers, the Industrial Workers of the World, also called the 'Wobblies'. American capitalism could not have succeeded in the west without travelling labourers, footless and wandering, the hobos. A million of them used the railroads to become seasonal workers, who followed shifting trades. An anarchist fantasy led to an effort to organize them into One Big Union in Chicago in 1905, where all the railways met, and where modern communications might turn this impossible dream into truth.

On revolutionary principles, the IWW was collated by industries, particularly in mining and forestry and agriculture. 'Locals' would report to 'departments' and then to union headquarters. Some hundred thousand members were recruited by 1912, although many were scattered 'on the road or riding the rods'. The Wobbly leader, Big Bill Hayward, was acquitted in Boise for the assassination of the Governor of Idaho, although the troubadour of the movement, Joe Hill, was shot in Salt Lake City with the apocryphal dying words: 'Don't mourn for me – organize.'

The IWW used intimidation to recruit members. Unless a red card was carried, migrant workers were thrown off freight trains or refused casual jobs in the west. Such tactics led to the opposition of the established craft unions of the east, who wanted less trouble. The American Federation of Labor, led by Samuel Gompers, rejected independent political struggle and class contradictions. The unions in the Federation were also basically against migrant and immigrant workers, who might threaten basic American jobs.

By the tenets of Marxism, the hobos and the Wobblies were doomed by the factory system. They were homeless and voteless and disorganized, although they were militant. They were the skirmishers of the proletariat, but hardly its victors. During the First World War, followed by a 'Red Scare', Big Bill Hayward served two years in federal prison before his deportation to Moscow. His ashes were buried by the walls of the Kremlin: his legacy to the Communists was useless.

In his trilogy and masterpiece *USA*, John Dos Passos gave the reasons for the failure of a workers' revolution in his country. The rise of the trusts and an urban capitalist economy destroyed any chance of an agrarian revolt. What was the fate of the radical wanderer after the First World War?

> The punch in the jaw, the slam on the head with a nightstick, the wrist grabbed and twisted behind the back, the big knee brought up sharp into the crotch, the walk out of town with sore feet to stand and wait at the edge of the hissing speeding string of cars . . .

The prosperity of the United States in the 1920s eliminated any thought of a proletarian revolution, as it had in the United Kingdom. Neither would the Great Depression change the general belief in the government of either country. The two major London riots, the Pall Mall affair of 1866 and 'Bloody Sunday' of 1887, had shown that ranks of constables backed by the Life and Grenadier Guards could contain and put to flight any mob in the West End. Engels despaired of the first rioters, calling them a 'stray rabble rather than unemployed workmen [who] had brought further discredit upon socialists.'

As for the labour demonstration in Trafalgar Square on 'Bloody Sunday', Irish Nationalists showed more resistance, as they would on another 'Bloody Sunday' in Londonderry nearly a century later. Wearing red and green armbands and chanting the 'Marseillaise' and 'Starving for Old England', they fought the police at Westminster Bridge: twenty-six injured people ended up in St Thomas's Hospital. The tens of thousands of protesters who reached Trafalgar Square were soon dispersed by the hoofs and bayonets of the Guards. 'You should have seen that high-hearted host run,' George Bernard Shaw wrote. 'Running hardly expresses our collective action. We skedaddled, and never drew rein until we were safe on Hampstead Heath or thereabouts . . . it was the most abjectly disgraceful defeat ever suffered by a band of heroes outnumbering their foes a thousand to one.'

In the affray, two hundred were wounded, and two died. The socialist leader John Burns was sentenced to six months in Pentonville prison for provoking an armed assault on the police, although the mob only had sticks as weapons. When he was released, Burns gave a speech on Bastille Day, saying he was ashamed and disgusted with the working classes. They were not educated as they ought to be, and that was due mostly to their own apathy and indifference. The radical reformer William Morris also complained that political agitators could not strike a spark out of the bulk of the people on any subject whatsoever, although his utopian novel *News from Nowhere* forecast a socialist millennium, heralded by a massacre of workers in Trafalgar Square, leading to a General Strike and the collapse of the government, a wrong prophecy of events to come.

The first elected Labour leader, Keir Hardie, deplored in 1903 'the fatalistic patience' of the unemployed in London. To him, 'these crowds of helpless atoms' had no fight left in them. In the words of the popular music-hall ditty, they would do nothing but 'wait till the work comes round'. And even in the actual General Strike of 1926, they proved themselves more collaborators with capitalism than combatants against its evils.

24. THE PSYCHOLOGY OF
WORLD WAR

In the twentieth century there were two world wars and forty-one other conflicts between many nations. In four out of five struggles, Europe played a part. These encounters caused 85,000,000 direct deaths between the combatants, while indirect casualties through wounds and disease and famine and working prisoners to death in camps led half a billion people to expire before their time. The scale of slaughter and terror was increased exponentially by the machinery available to carry out the fantasies of tyrants and political philosophies, which almost seemed to desire an Apocalypse or an Armageddon. A new language of global annihilation was invented – 'bioterror' or 'meltdown' or 'total war', mouthing the end of civilization.

To confront this insanity lay the developing science of psychiatry. The fear of the enemy, whoever they might be, could be mitigated by understanding them. They were not brutes to be treated bestially, but fellow humans. As far back as the early Hindu saga, the *Mahabharata*, the great battle of the Bharatas was fought between the justified milk-white Pandus and the notorious black Kurus. Yet the Pandus were advised by the Lord Krishna to triumph by villainy, while the Kurus were counselled by Satyavati, the daughter of truth. Absolute good and evil were illusory. Even though the Hindus believed in their conquest of other regions to save pagan countries from moral anarchy, there was no right or wrong way to take over other lands. This should be done by the minimum use of force.

The more the sense of the enemy as a demon, the greater the horrors of the struggle (see plate 25). The propaganda machines of the First World War were fortunate in trying to make devils of the troops on the far side of no-man's-land, because conditions on the Western Front had deteriorated by 1915 to something like Dante's *Inferno*. The millions of Boches and *poilus* and Tommies in their sandbagged sewers and dugouts lived in a state of fright and frightfulness in the front line. Swamped and overrun by rats and lice and the stench of rotting flesh, forced to die in hundreds of thousands on barbed wire and by machine guns, on mines and by poison gas, they were terrorized before their likely deaths. The brave poet Robert Graves wrote that 'everyone who had served in the trenches for as much as five months, or who had been under two or three rolling artillery barrages, was an invalid.' Many survivors suffered from shell shock, with alternate moods of apathy and high excitement, due to noise and fears: those who did not have a quick nervous breakdown collapsed badly a few years later from their nightmares.

Henri Barbusse was put in hospital four times because of his sickening experiences at the front. His documentary novel of 1916, *Under Fire: The Story of a Squad*, demonstrated the horror inflicted on 'the thirty million slaves, hurled upon one another in the mud of war by guilt and error.' Continual bombardment reduced all the squad to cower in their funk-holes.

> All the time, in a monotony of madness, the avalanche of fire and iron falls on; shrapnel with its whistling explosion and overcharged heart of furious metal, and the great percussion shells ... The air is now glutted and obscure, it is crossed and recrossed by heavy blasts, and the murder of the earth continues everywhere, deeply and more deeply, to the limit of fullness.

The slaughter of half the squad, particularly in the assault on the International Trench held by the Germans, provokes a killing rage in Barbusse's comrades, although previously their enemies were thought to be just another lot of poor sods caught in a quagmire of desolation.

> They carry the luck of their survival as if it were glory; they are implacable, uncontrolled, intoxicated ... We trample soft bodies underfoot, some of them moving and slowly altering their position, crying out in trickles of blood. Like posts and heaps of rubbish, corpses are piled anyhow on the wounded, and press them down, suffocate them, strangle them ... In the cataclysm of earth and of massive wreckage blown up and blown out, above the hordes of wounded and dead that stir together, above the moving forest of smoke implanted in the trench and all about it, every face is inflamed, blood-red with sweat, eyes on fire. Some groups seem to be dancing as they brandish their bayonets. They are elated, immensely confident, ferocious.
>
> The battle dies down imperceptibly. A soldier says, 'Well, what's to be done now?'

In the opposed trenches across no-man's-land, Erich Maria Remarque described in 1929 in *All Quiet on the Western Front* a dark mirror image of the horrific life of the French. The German soldiers particularly hated the bioterror of the poison-gas projectiles, bursting upon them. 'The gas still creeps over the ground and sinks into all hollows. Like a big soft jelly-fish it floats into our shell-hole and lolls there obscenely ... It is better to crawl out and lie on top than to stay where the gas collects most. But we don't get as far as that; a second bombardment begins. It is no longer as though shells roared; it is the earth itself raging.' As it happened, 90,000 soldiers died from chemical weapons in the world war, twenty times fewer than from shell or bullet or bomb.

Remarque illumined fear and shell shock under the continual bombardment of the French before an attack. 'We are deadened by the strain – a deadly tension that scrapes along one's spine like a gapped knife. Our legs refuse to move, our hands tremble, our bodies are a thin skin stretched painfully over repressed madness.' Yet when the French assault with smooth distorted faces under their helmets, the terror of the Germans turns to rage, as Barbusse had described for his squad.

> We have become wild beasts. We do not fight, we defend ourselves against annihilation. It is not against men that we fling our bombs, what do we know of men in this moment when Death is hunting us down ... overwhelmed by this wave that bears us along, that fills us with ferocity, turns us into thugs, into murderers, into God only knows what devils; this wave that multiplies our strength with fear and madness and greed of life, seeking and fighting for nothing but our deliverance.

Unlike *Under Fire*, *All Quiet on the Western Front* was not published until eleven years after the end of hostilities. To Remarque, the brutalities and the traumas had been compounded by a double betrayal, the futility of the peace for the young. Talking behind the front line of the future, one character was made to declare, 'The war has ruined us for everything.' The author commented:

> He is right. We are not youth any longer. We don't want to take the world by storm. We are fleeing. We fly from ourselves. From our life. We were eighteen and had begun to love life and the world; and we had to shoot it to pieces. The first bomb, the first explosion, burst in our hearts. We are cut off from activity, from striving, from progress. We believe in such things no longer, we believe in war.

The mercy of the First World War, if there was any grace in it at all, was that so many officers and men broke down that only a few were shot for cowardice, while most of these mental casualties were returned to be doctored before being sent back like Barbusse to another carnage on Flanders fields. The appalling conditions of the fighting also made hatred of the enemy more relative, because soldiers usually loathed their own generals

more than any foe. The Kaiser was successfully turned into a comic
Satan, and the Germans were castigated for torching French
cathedrals, but as the Central Powers treated the Allied wounded
and prisoners no worse than the Allies did their captives, there
was a certain understanding between most of the soldiers consigned to the mud and the blood, the shit and the shells, which
they all endured in common, a liberty to die daily, an equality of
horror, a fraternity against the appalling High Command. Only
in the blood lust of an assault was killing a delight.

As in the *Mahabharata*, the original fight between good
democracy and evil imperial powers ended in a general relativity
and a fear of any more massacres by modern techniques of mass
murder. This sensibility was increased by a new pestilence and
the disillusioned armies returning with poison in their pens. After
the Armistice of 1918, an epidemic of Spanish or septic influenza
killed 27,000,000 people, twice as many as died in the Great
War. The Germans blamed their half-million new deaths on the
naval blockade, which had weakened their resistance and immune
systems. Nearly 9,000,000 died in India alone, where the scourge
was again seen as a form of imperial contamination spread by
the British Empire. And with the continuing civil wars in Ireland
and Russia against Green and Red revolutionaries, the demobil-
ized armies went home, sick from the war and sick of any other
war to come.

Of the generation of 1914, many of the best were said to be
dead. Those bright ones, such as the philosopher Bertrand Russell, who had avoided fighting, were convinced of the virtue of
their pacifism. They had stayed alive and so had the final say.
Those who survived often felt guilty. 'Nobody, nothing, will shift
me from the belief, which I shall take to the grave,' the author
J. B. Priestley, a lieutenant in the war, wrote, 'that the generation
to which I belong, destroyed between 1914 and 1918, was a
great generation, marvellous in its promise. This is not self-praise,
because those of us who are left know that we are the runts.'

The myth of the missing generation grew not because of the

horrors of combat, but because of the disillusion afterwards, particularly among the disabled. More than 120,000 ex-service-men were still receiving pensions for psychiatric traumas at the outbreak of the next world war. John Maynard Keynes was the chief representative of the British Treasury at the postwar nego-tiations in Paris, and he denounced the terms reached at Versailles in a polemic called *The Economic Consequences of the Peace*. It condemned the punitive reparations exacted from Germany and the self-interested land exchanges of the victorious powers. He foresaw that the consequences would be the financial ruin of Europe and another world war. 'Vengeance,' he predicted, 'will not limp.' Nothing would delay a final civil war between the forces of reaction and revolution. In that conflict, the horrors of the late assault on Germany would fade into nothing. It would destroy 'whoever is the victor, the civilization and the progress of our generation.'

This became the governing attitude of many of the leading intellectuals. Members of the generation of 1914 which had gone to war so readily were discomfited by the peace. Their feeling of betrayal by the old men governing them led to revolutions in Europe, suppressed outside Soviet Russia, and to the rise of Fascist movements, particularly in Italy. Extreme solutions advo-cating social change of the left or of the right promised a catharsis as violent as the recent European conflict. The leader of the British Fascist movement, Sir Oswald Mosley, had served in the war, which was his vital experience. The peace was the disillu-sion; the old values and the old men who had failed in both processes needed replacement. As Mosley wrote of the Armistice Day celebrations:

> Smooth, smug people, who had never fought or suffered, seemed to the eyes of youth – at that moment age-old with sadness, weariness and bitterness – to be eating, drinking, laughing on the graves of our companions. I stood aside from the delirious throng; silent and alone, ravaged by

memory. Driving purpose had begun; there must be no more war. I dedicated myself to politics.

He declared war himself against the old men, 'who muddled my generation into the crisis of 1914, who muddled us into the crisis of 1931 – the old men who have laid waste the power and the glory of the land.'

The legend of the lost generation sacrificed by the ancient who muddled the war and the peace became a cult of the dead that accounted for the failures of the present. The best young minds were said to be killed, although hardly anyone counted the future Labour leaders among them. In fact, Clement Attlee survived the fighting, but many other leading young Socialists did not. They were not alive to oppose the false old men with the wrong values. The inadequate were rising to take their places.

Two French writers of genius had survived the terrible combat to inform their generation of what all that suffering really signified. Henri de Montherlant had 'loved life at the front, the bath in the elemental, the annihilation of the intelligence and the heart'. He felt his peers were betrayed on their return to Paris, and so he became 'the knight of nothingness'. His contemporary Drieu la Rochelle led a bayonet charge at Charleroi in an excess of courage, yet he had broken under the German bombardment at Verdun and had pissed in his trousers and screamed with terror under the remorseless steel rain.

In his volume of war poems, *Interrogation*, Drieu la Rochelle confessed to crying no to pain at Verdun. Yet it had returned him to the anarchist principle that human destruction was necessary for renewal. He joined the Italian Futurists in their cult of violent movement and regeneration by extreme change. 'Everything that is new is good. Beyond the new, there is no good living. Humanity can only endure by reforging itself all the time, by killing within years its old age . . . When peace comes, the unease will not be over.'

The most extreme revolts against the horrors of war were a

reversion to nihilism. Dadaism and early Surrealism denied patriotism and glory and medals by claiming 'Dada' was everything and nothing, while *pissoirs* were works of art. This rage against past values served as a rehearsal for the youth revolution of 1968 across the world. Ineffectual though it was, Surrealism did make many question what was happening between the two world wars.

In Italy, as at the time of Machiavelli, a regime of state terror was being born. In 1914, the founder of Futurism, Filippo Marinetti, had issued a manifesto to students. Only conflict knew how to spur on the young. A new generation was born with a new spirit, which would lead to a new revolution. As the influential Renato Serra wrote, this was an apocalyptic transition, 'the hour of renewal: of death and life laced together in a knot of bloody intoxication'.

The heir of this mishmash of anarchism and nihilism was Benito Mussolini, the founder of Fascism. He was a conspirator of great talent, who could gauge the mood of the masses. He was wounded and discharged after serving in the elite regiment of the Bersaglieri. Beginning as a socialist nationalist, he directed his newspaper *Popolo d'Italia* at the discontented postwar army officers, who were said to be the 'authors of victory'. The soldiers were the stupid masses. If given the right direction, they would transform Italian life and recreate the ancient empire of Rome. 'Everything must be changed in the modern city,' he declared. 'It is possible to destroy in order to create anew in a form more beautiful and great.'

Mussolini founded groups of thugs in the Squadrismo, who attacked socialist cooperatives, peasant leagues and labour unions. In the first six months of 1921, they destroyed seventeen newspapers and printing plants, and hundreds of the headquarters of the left-wing parties in Tuscany and Emilia and the Po Valley. With the support of military cadres, as Lenin had in the Russian Revolution, Mussolini then stage-managed a bloodless veterans' march on Rome, which toppled the democratic government. Once designated as the Prime Minister by the King,

Mussolini began to create a flexible cult of youth. His slogan was the myth that he was always right. Faith in him would lead to the triumph of Italy in the world. This illusion was backed by a formidable and vicious secret police, formed from the previous Fascist militias, the Squadristi, under officers called 'consuls' and 'centurions', responsible only to Mussolini, who now declared himself Il Duce, ready to terrify and convince most of the population into belief in his crude vision of a rosy dawn.

In Germany, defeat led to civil war and extreme experiments. The Kaiser had given way to a weak Weimar republic, which used the embittered and jobless army officers to form Freikorps and put down Communist attempts at revolution. These same Freikorps resisted the Polish invasion in the east and the French occupation of the Rhineland. Some, like Ernst Röhm, joined Hitler's National Socialist Party, while most approved of his Beer Hall putsch of 1923 in Munich. They wanted to establish a strong state, dependent on them. As the leader of the military league, the Stahlhelm, declared: 'We must fight to get the men into power who will depend for support on those who fought at the front – men who will call on us to smash once and for all these damned revolutionary rats and choke them by sticking their heads into their own shit.'

Hitler converted elements of the Freikorps into his first storm troopers. He knew the value and the use of terror as a path to power. He despised the lack of discrimination of the Bolsheviks, who had killed off most of the former ruling class. That was the ancient classic method recommended by Machiavelli. 'I go further,' he said. 'I make use of members of the old ruling class itself. I keep them in fear and dependence.' He could have no more willing helpers. And if they turned against him, he could always return to the ancient classic method of elimination.

In early street-fighting, Hitler told his storm troopers to use frightful methods to attract fear and obedience and publicity. But too much frightfulness might deter. There was a balance in terrorism, which must be deployed skilfully to cow the masses, who secretly were longing for strong government. As *Mein Kampf* stated:

> The importance of physical terror against the individual and the masses also became clarified in my mind, and here too an exact calculation of the psychological effect is possible.
>
> The terror in the workshops, in the factory, in the assembly hall and on occasions of mass demonstrations will always be accompanied by success as long as it is not met by an equally great force of terror.

If the Roman and the British empires had followed the maxim of 'divide and rule', Hitler came upon the brilliant device of splitting his terror squads and ruling them by an oath of loyalty to himself. In the notorious case of 1934, when he had Ernst Röhm and 700 of his Brownshirts destroyed by rival Blackshirt thugs, he claimed that they were the nihilists, who wanted to destroy Germany. In fact, they threatened his supreme power, and he now terrorized his terrorists, who had sworn their lives to him. Inside the feared SS was a group of political watchers, the SD, and in the army were watchdogs like Russian commissars, the Waffen-SS. And overlooking all the secret police was the most brutal group, the Gestapo. Yet the venomous heads of this Medusa of terror were all linked in the head of state, the Führer, whose will was law. He took the science of terror to its apotheosis in the Final Solution of the concentration camps.

In Britain and the United States, the disaffected officer classes were absorbed back into the economy, and the disillusion with the war was often replaced by the pursuit of delight. Neither Communism nor Fascism made the people afraid enough to follow them. As Ludwig Wittgenstein pointed out in his *Philosophical Investigations*, 'We should distinguish between the object of fear and the cause of fear.' The cause of fear is often not its cause, but its target. Its existence, however negligible, makes it the victim of the fears of others. The British Communist Party and Bolshevik intelligence and propaganda in the 1920s were only targets. Yet the fear of them brought down the first Labour administration of Ramsay MacDonald, a Scots Socialist.

The government had decided not to prosecute the editor of the *Workers' Weekly* for an article urging soldiers to drop their weapons in a class or military war. Before the next election in 1924, the publication of the Zinoviev Letter – allegedly some instructions from the Third International based in Moscow to British Communists on the subversion of the state – also seemed to damn the Labour Party as a Communist front. Ramsay MacDonald had been brilliant in making Labour appear a democratic and rational party, not, as he wrote, 'a "Red Terror" to the minds of large masses of people who knew little about it.' Now the apparent waving of the Soviet flag lost political control.

Engels had once told Marx that the British proletariat was bourgeois, not revolutionary. That was proved by the General Strike of 1926, which began with a protracted miners' strike and was followed by a resolution of the Trades Union Congress to bring out all unionists. The workers' revolution was, however, only a nine days' wonder. Its failure effectively destroyed the idea of the militant overthrow of the government by the workers and put the trade union movement into moderate Labour hands until the millennium.

In the booming United States of the 1920s, the chief preoccupation of the intellectuals was the futility of the prohibition of the liquor trade, which had transferred $2 billion a year from decent brewers to mainly Italian gangsters (see plate 26). H. L. Mencken warned against 'the massive delusion which is our national disease'. Many of the writers fled to Paris and followed the creed of Ernest Hemingway's Lieutenant Frederick Henry, 'I was not made to think. I was made to eat. My God, yes. Eat and drink and sleep with Catherine.' The trinity of good food and liquor and sex, the directness of action and thought and word, which was the last refuge of sophistication, the search for the simple life and the American Adam, which had once been the mythological right of the frontiersman and the Indian – these were what that Lost Generation sought in the Select and the Ritz Bar. They sought a distance from the Puritan morality which they could never escape.

In their flight, they created masterpieces such as *The Great Gatsby*, in which crime had subverted the values of Old Glory. They thought their works sprang from nihilism and Dada, but these really sprang from their dream of the ignored youth of a great nation, now corrupted in their minds by the materialism of easy money and the caricature of idiotic reforms. They could not follow Tristan Tzara, who invented Dadaism only to end as a Communist, in declaring 'no more anarchists, no more Socialists, no more Bolsheviks, no more proletariat, no more democrats, no more bourgeois, no more aristocrats, no more weapons, no more police, no more countries, enough of all these imbecilities, no more of anything, *nothing, nothing, nothing.*'

That was going too far. Nor would they join the brooding Naphta of Thomas Mann's *The Magic Mountain*: 'No, liberation and development of the individual are not the key to our age, they are not what our age demands. What it needs, what it wrestles after, what it will create is – Terror.' Not until the Great Depression of the next decade would the voluntary American exiles turn to the preoccupation of the Europe they were misunderstanding – a workers' state run by a strong tyranny, which might replace and renew a feeble democracy.

25. THE ROAD TO BARCELONA

The Anarchists and the Syndicalists achieved a brief power in Spain at last. By 1874, there were 50,000 members of the Spanish International, which in spite of proscription, had remained powerful in the north-east of the country, Catalonia, and the south in Granada. Occasional peasant rebellions had disturbed the state, while organized groups of workers bided their time in industrial Barcelona. As in France and Germany, intellectuals such as Miguel de Unamuno and the younger José Ortega y Gasset developed a philosophy of regeneration from the tired old regime through action and will power. 'What a beautiful sight,' Unamuno wrote, 'to see a new man emerge from the ruins of a civilization!'

After the First World War, Spain might have gone the way of Tsarist Russia. For five years, strikers and terrorist attacks rocked the country. As the Catalan historian Jaime Vicens Vives testified, 'Syndicalists, theoretical anarchists, professional terrorists and hired gunmen mingled in one of the most explosive, destructive moments' in the years of unrest after 1918. They wanted to annihilate the state in one great revolution and initiate a life for all in agrarian communes and free municipalities. 'An enervated utopia, with no possible counterpart in the world, it was purely the reaction of an illiterate peasant transformed into the mechanized worker of an urban enterprise.'

A weak dictatorship of General Miguel Primo de Rivera was replaced in 1931 by a republic, which abolished the monarchy in a bloodless coup. Ortega formed a Group in the Service of the Republic and was elected to office, but he was soon disillusioned.

He wrote his most influential book, *The Revolt of the Masses*, complaining that the elites of Europe were failing to provide ideals and leadership for the struggling workers in the Great Depression. When the Spanish Civil War broke out in 1936, he was forced to flee into exile.

Ortega did not see as a solution the Fascist tyrannies of Mussolini and Hitler or the dictatorship of the proletariat of Stalin. Mussolini had reverted to the imperial dreams of the lesser Roman emperors. Although he had been anti-imperialist in his youth, denouncing the Italian occupation of Libya, now he sent severe Fascist governors to Libya and Eritrea and Somalia, where Cesare de Vecchi instituted a reign of terror, riding on horseback into mosques, burning down rebel villages and shooting prisoners in their thousands.

The plan was the expropriation of Ethiopia, the ultimate assault on the last independent major African state. Half a million Italian soldiers were exported to East Africa, the largest colonial expedition ever mounted. Mussolini intended to terrorize the population into submission through bombing from the heavens, the first major European air assault against an African or Asian population, which foreshadowed the American skyborne assaults on Vietnam and Iraq and Afghanistan. Even mustard gas was used as well as a scorched-earth policy. When the capital Addis Ababa was captured, all prominent Ethiopians were executed to eliminate any possible resistance, while every Italian death was followed by the murder of ten Ethiopian hostages. Up to 500,000 of the enemy died against only 5,000 Italians with their superior weaponry.

Mussolini was also a pioneer in running terrorist training camps for the Croat minority against the Serb majority in the Balkans. The Croats, led by the butcher Ante Pavelic, who was later to massacre over 500,000 Serbs in the Balkans, aimed to assassinate King Alexander of Yugoslavia; in 1934, the murder was achieved, and Pavelic was given asylum in Italy. The killing was blamed on the 'Jewish International'.

In Germany, Hitler was proving the weakness of France and Britain by retaking the Rhineland from French occupation without provoking a war. He now pushed forward plans to absorb Austria in another bloodless Anschluss. He expanded his bodies of secret policemen and set up the first few of his concentration camps, mainly for political prisoners and those who were called degenerates, Freemasons and homosexuals and gypsies. He was learning his lessons from the master of modern mass imprisonment, Joseph Stalin, who had decided to turn Russian agriculture from the family to the collective farm.

The richer peasants called kulaks were deported and starved and worked to death in Siberia. About 1,000,000 of them were killed by the secret police, the NKVD, while 9,000,000 died slowly in the Gulags of the frozen lands east of the Urals, where gold and other minerals were found. Famine also struck the fertile fields of the Ukraine and the Volga, because the produce was requisitioned for the factory workers and the cities, while 30,000,000 farmers were left with little to eat. This draconian extermination of all rural opposition was extended to purges of the Communist Party itself: four in five of the leading delegates and members of the Central Committee were shot. Then the army was decimated by the killing of eight marshals and the murder or imprisonment of 40,000 officers. In 1940 the refugee Trotsky was assassinated in Mexico by an ice pick driven through his skull. With modern methods of mass communication, Stalin had proved himself even more paranoiac and murderous than Ivan the Terrible. The numbers of the dead approached the ravages of the Black Death.

So Fascism and Communism were expanding the use of state terror extravagantly by the time of the outbreak of the Spanish Civil War. Yet their villainies were hidden: their collaborators in other European countries would not believe in the purges and the mass atrocities. In France, the right wing organized itself on the Italian and German models for the overthrow of the Third Republic, although this had the support of a majority of Frenchmen. The classic pattern of the nationalist secret society in the twentieth century was used to attract support from traditionalists of all classes, who feared an international conspiracy, whether of Jewish capitalists or of proletarian Communists.

The chief propaganda organ of the right was Léon Daudet's *L'Action Française*. From 1908 to 1944, this newspaper concentrated on smearing republican or left-wing politicians and officials in order to sap the French people's faith in democracy as a system. In his columns, Daudet denounced government ministers as self-confessed sex maniacs, debauchees of the lowest order, tearful pansies, drawing-room hermaphrodites, syphilitics, prostitutes and bits of brothel refuse. He accused the police and the civil service of conspiring with politicians to suppress his supporters. In 1935, under the filthy smoke screen of Daudet's propaganda against what he called 'democrashit', dissident members of *L'Action Française* formed a paramilitary group called the Secret Organization of National Revolutionary Action. This organization was popularly known as the Cagoule ('Hood') because in some of its provincial branches members wore hoods like Klansmen to conceal their identity.

The Cagoule, which drew much of its support from existing nationalist conspiracies, had its own oath of secrecy and was structured on military lines. It aimed to recruit 120,000 members – about the strength of the Bolsheviks in the Russian Revolution. It had execution squads for dealing with traitors and enemies; its intelligence branch was told that 'the sense of duty and the realization of the circumstances must be so exalted that every man must consider himself free of every moral and social obligation when engaged in the execution of a mission. He must give himself up to his job without reserve, any idea of pardon for a failure must be ruled out, for a man who enters such a team does not leave it.'

The Cagoule imported arms, including machine guns and dynamite, from Germany, Belgium, Spain, and Italy. In September 1937, it engineered two explosions in the offices of the

industrial employers' associations in the Étoile district of Paris, in
the hope of inducing big business to support the cause. But the
arrest of the Cagoule's leader, Eugène Deloncle, in October, led
to the discovery of its arms dumps and the confiscation of its
weapons and munitions.

The right wing, now effectively disarmed, had to wait until
the outbreak of the Second World War to spread defeatism in the
French army, to welcome Hitler and Mussolini, also Pétain with
his Vichy government. The rightists, of course, were a power in
both northern France and Vichy during the war years, though it
was curious that a nationalist group such as the Cagoule should
have accepted the German domination of their homeland. As a
satirist commented in *Le Canard Enchaîné* in 1936: 'There are
people who are astonished to hear our supernationalists who
want, so they say, France for the French, howling: "Long live
Mussolini! Long live Hitler!" This attitude is, however, traditional. The ultra-patriots, for the last century and a half, have
always preferred foreign governments to their own.'

Other conspiracy theories were flourishing in France. Perhaps
the most interesting and modern of these, which displaced the
forged 'Protocols of the Elders of Zion' and the theory of the
international conspiracy of Jewish bankers, was the theory that a
number of politicians in power belonged to a secret society called
the Synarchie, which aimed to take control of France and the
world by manipulating bureaucratic and technocratic levers. The
conspiracy was meant to have begun in 1931, when an official
called Jean Coutrot formed a group called 'X-Crise', in order to
bring about a 'synarchic' order.

In this new regime, a perfect collective life could be achieved
by the smooth exercise of power – a sort of pacific national
socialism based on hierarchy and the specialization of function.
The supposed conspirators were dubbed 'technocrats' because,
like Coutrot, all were distinguished ex-students of the École
Polytechnique in Paris. This theory appealed to the popular fear
of faceless bureaucrats, who seemed to many to be even more

sinister than any Red or Black conspiracy against the democratic
state, for the hidden technocrats ran everything for everyone
behind a blanket of silence.

The Spanish Civil War seemed to most radicals to be the
prelude of a Second World War, in which the Fascist powers
would attack Communist Russia, which might not be aided by
the champions of non-intervention, France and the United Kingdom. As the Labour politician Sir Charles Trevelyan said: 'When
the war that is looming comes and Japan and Germany crash in
to destroy Soviet Russia, I hope the Labour Party will have some
other policy to offer than sympathy, accompanied by bandages
and cigarettes.' That was not to be in the event of General
Franco's attack on the Republican government of Spain.

As for England, in the opinion of Robert Graves, there had
never been a foreign question since the French Revolution that
so divided intelligent British opinion as the Spanish Civil War.
'It could be seen in so many ways: as Fascism versus Communism, or Totalitarianism versus Democracy, or Italy and Germany
versus England and France, or Force versus Liberty, or Rebels
versus Constitutional Government, or Barbarism versus Culture,
or Catholicism versus Atheism, or the Upper Classes versus the
Lower, or Order versus Anarchy – however one's mind worked.'
For George Orwell, however, who actually fought in Spain,
unlike many other British Marxist poets and intellectuals, the
experience turned him into the most devastating modern critic of
the tactics of terror, the literary scourge of the Soviet Union.

Without assistance from Mussolini, Franco's coup would
probably have failed, as had an abortive royalist coup four years
before. The Italian Duce ended by committing 100,000 troops to
the Spanish war, as well as developing the blitz techniques of air
raids, aided by Hitler's technicians and dive-bombers. The lacer-
ating picture by Picasso of the assault on Guernica remains the
most devastating indictment of the new terror from heaven.
Mussolini also used forty of his submarines to sink neutral
shipping, especially cargoes from Russia intended to resupply

the Republican forces. He wanted to prove to the feeble British government that the Mediterranean was once again a Roman sea, although the Royal Navy, based at Gibraltar and Malta and Cyprus, was far superior to the zigzag paint on the Fascist fleet.

Without question, the Republicans had begun the atrocities in the Civil War, particularly against the Catholic Church with the destruction of hundreds of ecclesiastical establishments and many outrages against nuns and priests and aristocrats. The colonial troops brought by Franco from Morocco proved even more ferocious in terms of mutilation and murder and rape, a violence hardly seen in Spain since the expulsion by Ferdinand and Isabella of the Moors, now allowed to return and wreak their vengeance in support of the Catholic faith.

Wounded in the throat in the northern campaign, Orwell survived to write his *Homage to Catalonia*, excoriated at the time by the left wing. He had not served in the Marxist International Brigade, but in the Catalan Anarchist and Syndicalist militia. He gave his reasons.

> The Anarchists were the opposite of the majority of so-called revolutionaries in so much that though their principles were rather vague their hatred of privilege and injustice was perfectly genuine. Philosophically, Communism and Anarchism are poles apart ... The Communist's emphasis is always on centralism and efficiency, the Anarchist's on liberty and equality. Anarchism is deeply rooted in Spain and is likely to outlive Communism when the Russian influence is withdrawn. During the first two months of the war it was the Anarchists more than anyone else who had saved the situation, and much later than this the Anarchist militia, in spite of their indiscipline, were notoriously the best fighters among the purely Spanish forces.

With the supply of Russian weapons and foreign advisers to the Republican government, the Spanish Communist Party assumed more control over affairs. A sort of civil war in Barcelona led to an Anarchist attack on the Communists after Republican forces had seized the telephone exchange and demanded that the Anarchists surrender their arms. Street-fighting was followed by a Communist putsch against the Syndicalists and Anarchists, who were accused of being Trotskyites or Fascists in disguise. Just as the Bolsheviks had eliminated the Mensheviks, the Communists now suppressed their socialist opponents, and Orwell had to flee for his life.

Franco's eventual victory in Spain in 1939 led to hundreds of thousands of Republican refugees struggling over the border into southern France, where they were interned in primitive concentration camps guarded by Senegalese troops. Franco was recognized by France and the United Kingdom as the ruler of Spain, adding a third dictatorship to confront the two chief remaining European democracies. Hitler now felt free to intervene in Czechoslovakia and Mussolini in Albania: these rapes of territory were again accepted in the terms of Prime Minister Chamberlain's famous fudge, that he had agreed with the Führer, 'Peace in our time'.

As battle lines were being drawn for the next world war, the competition was beginning for the new device of mass destruction, which would serve as the ultimate weapon of terror or deterrence until the next millennium. By 1938, Niels Bohr in his research institute in Copenhagen had informed Western physicists that Otto Hahn had successfully performed nuclear fission on the uranium atom in his Berlin laboratory. Equally, the Cambridge-trained Russian Peter Kapitsa had been detained by Stalin to work on a Soviet nuclear programme. A month before the outbreak of the Second World War, Winston Churchill informed the British Air Minister that an atomic weapon could be manufactured within several years. He doubted, however, if Hitler would commit enough resources to make a nuclear bomb sooner. 'There is no immediate danger, although undoubtedly the human race is crawling nearer to the point where it will be able to destroy itself completely.'

There was little moral debate on the development of this ultimate weapon of obliteration. C. P. Snow, a historian as well as a scientist, summed up the situation just before the declaration of another world war. It was no secret that laboratories in the United States, Germany, France and England had been working feverishly on atomic fission for several months. If the manufacture of a bomb was practicable, physics would have altered the scope of warfare. Scientists were losing hope. Even the invention of flight had been perverted to bomb human beings. As Snow declared:

> We cannot delude ourselves that this new invention will be better used. Yet it must be made, if it really is a physical possibility. If it is not made in America this year, it may be next year in Germany. There is no ethical problem; if the invention is not prevented by physical laws, it will certainly be carried out somewhere in the world. It is better, at any rate, that America should have six months' start.
>
> But again, we must not pretend. Such an invention will never be kept secret; the physical principles are too obvious, and within a year every big laboratory on earth would have come to the same result. For a short time, perhaps, the US Government may have this power entrusted to it; but soon after it will be in less civilized hands.

26. THE FAILED
AMERICAN REVOLUTION

During the Great Depression, a second American Revolution did not happen, in spite of mass discontent and unemployment. The conditions were different elsewhere. The Russian Revolution had been made possible by the arming of many Bolsheviks and their sympathizers during the First World War, and their recruiting of armaments workers. The Chinese Revolution had as its focus a guerrilla army, which fought and made propaganda for twenty years before its victory. In America, except among the farmers, there were few weapons to oppose national and local forces of order, and there was no armed guerrilla nucleus to attract malcontents to its side.

Yet in America, there was a radical tradition and a history of ferocity. The United States had been born in a bloody revolution and in Civil War; frontier conditions and the urban jungles had kept violence as a part of everyday life. This heritage of protest, however, was individual rather than collective. Jesse James was the folk hero, a bandit rather than an organizer. From Shays' Rebellion down to the farmers' revolts in Iowa in 1932, Americans attacked present injustices in an immediate way. And the rebels were rural property owners wanting preservation of what they had, not redistribution of land under a new social system.

The second failure of the American revolutionaries among the many intellectuals who swung left in the early 1930s was their lack of success in attracting a mass following. They did not persuade the workers that they were men of the people with labour's interests at heart. The essayist Edmund Wilson, who voted Communist in 1932, noted that in a curious way the depression touched the living standards of the intellectuals hardly at all. There were no Big Bill Haywards or Jack Londons to attract the workers to the cause of Socialism or Communism. Although Upton Sinclair nearly won the Governorship of California for the Socialists, he was a rare case of a thinker who managed to attract a mass following, and even he had to work within the framework of the traditional parties.

Revolution on the whole also comes less from temporary misery than from groups in society with a rising standard of living who feel themselves deprived of political power. While there were many groups in America who felt that political action was useless and that some form of dictatorship might be necessary, few felt themselves totally deprived of all influence. They did have votes, except for blacks in the Southern states. Paradoxically, the moment for a social revolution had already passed. That was in 1912, when there had been a progressive majority in the country, a million voting for the Socialists who believed in class war, and a militant army of Wobblies, who, although weaponless, believed in violent strike action. A radical social change could have been brought about if the First World War had not encouraged repression of all dissent, and if the Russian Revolution had not scared off the progressives from any form of social change that smacked of socialism.

Even so, if a personality as persuasive as Franklin D. Roosevelt had not become President of the United States in 1932, with his offers of hope and persistent bold experimentation, the outbreaks of sporadic violence in the farm belt and in the cities would have grown and grown, until there could well have been widespread anarchy. As in the Spanish Civil War, there could have been scattered and local risings, which used state or provincial patriotism as levers to power, as Huey Long did in Louisiana. These broadcast revolts in a time of national emergency might have spread across the continent, if faith in the man in the White House had not left some coherence in the political programme.

Franklin Roosevelt appeared at the right time. In this, capitalism in America was most fortunate. He had enough of a national mandate to introduce a modified socialism; with little protest, he could have nationalized the banks and the railroads, but he did not do so. He saved private ownership from bankruptcy and put through adequate measures of social welfare to bring the United States into line with contemporary Europe, although unemployment would finally only be resolved by rearmament for the Second World War. Another American Revolution was prevented by the election of Roosevelt, whom the rich thought had destroyed capitalism and the poor found had saved it.

The labour unions had long cooperated with the employers. The leadership of the most powerful union, the American Federation of Labor, was imbued with the spirit of Samuel Gompers, who had built it up to a membership of nearly 5,000,000 workers. He repudiated the theory of class antagonism, although the preamble to his constitution declared that 'a struggle is going on in all nations of the civilized world, a struggle between the capitalist and the labourer, which grows in intensity from year to year . . .' Although Gompers did use the strike weapon against employers, he denied that unionism had any political end. He said that Engels's dictum 'A struggle between two great classes of society necessarily becomes a political struggle' was wrong in the United States. Unionism should merely achieve the limited economic advance of the workers, despite the savagery of such strikes as those of Homestead and Ludlow, and the Pullman and the Pittsburgh ones.

By not holding to the doctrine of class and the brotherhood of all workers, Gompers split the labour movement, especially the skilled old-American stock workers from the new immigrant unskilled labourers. Ethnic divisions and conflicts of interest kept the craft unions under conservative leaders from the large

unions with their unskilled labour, such as John L. Lewis and his
United Mine Workers. Moreover, all the labour leaders in the
1920s shared the capitalist myth that any hard worker could
become a factory owner himself, and that every labourer carried
Andrew Mellon's millions in the strength of his arm and his
brain. Thus they opposed any 'socialist' theories in the unions,
saying that these were already under attack from the employers,
and that they must become respectable at all costs. By distinguishing themselves from the Wobblies, the American unions
extinguished what revolutionary tendencies they had in them.

Moreover, the conflict between the skilled and the semi-skilled
and unskilled workers weakened the working class. Jealous of
their positions in the craft unions, sensing the levelling process
of increasing industrialization which removed the need for tech-
nical efficiency from much of labour, the craft groups restricted
membership and accented the separation between themselves and
the unskilled. Organized labour created its own aristocracy,
which discouraged a united front against the employers. In the
national and international unions, the officers accepted the ideas
of American business methods. Labour went into business for
itself and its officers acted as owners of a corporation rather than
administrators of a strike fund. The goal of most unions was
financial solvency, and their large treasuries usually became a
reason to resist strikes, not support them.

Gompers was succeeded in 1924 by the conciliatory and
second-rate William Green, who preferred to keep peace with big
business at all costs. As late as 1935, he was still saying, 'The
majority of employers sincerely and honestly wish to maintain
decent wage standards and humane conditions of employment.
They neither seek the exploitation of labour nor the exploitation
of the consuming public. They are inspired by a keen sense of
justice and are influenced in all their business dealings by a spirit
of fair-dealing and fair-play.' Indeed, Green went so far as to say,
'The right to strike involves so many considerations that it ought

to be utilized only as a last resort.' Thus the weapon of a General Strike, the precondition of a social revolution, was never used.

Under Green's uninspiring leadership, the AFOL lost more than half its members, until by the critical year of 1933 it numbered 2,000,000 card-carriers. Wildcat strikes broke out sporadically everywhere despite the leadership; but Green's answer to the depression was the repeal of Prohibition. Beer would, in his words, 'exhilarate industry and lift us out of the depression just as the automobile took us out of the bad times of 1921.' Although Green did once warn that hunger could produce revolution, and that the AFOL might use force if it did not get a six-hour day and five-day week, he explained that he meant by force only economic force, picketing and boycott.

He cooperated with Roosevelt to reduce trades union militancy. He denounced strikes as 'illegal', and he refused to protest against the killing of workers by police and vigilantes, and the terror tactics used in the Southern states against unions. He was so conciliatory and weak that John L. Lewis broke with him and formed the Committee for Industrial Organization, to unionize the unskilled labourers and to provoke more militant action. Yet Lewis was no revolutionary himself: he was also a conciliator, not a supporter of barricades.

The labour movement, despite its weak and conservative leaders, was rotten within itself. Prohibition had begun the penetration of the unions by racketeers, especially the communications unions such as the Teamsters, who trucked in the bootleg booze. There was frequently an unholy alliance between unions and ward politicians to deliver blocks of votes in return for bribes or jobs. In addition, as a study of labour spies showed in 1937, American big business was spending $80,000,000 a year on secret agents, who reported on the activities of the workers, had themselves elected to high posts in the unions to break them up, and had militant unionists sacked by the companies.

At least 40,000 men were infiltrated into the union locals by the detective agencies of the country such as Pinkertons and the Burns Agency, which masqueraded as 'industrial consultants'. These men did their best to wreck and inform, and they made united union action very difficult. Moreover, the rise of 'company unions' in the 1920s had left a distrust of all unions in the minds of many workers, especially when they noticed that the companies laid off first the troublemakers and so-called 'reds' in the works.

In fact, the American unions, in their search for respectability, had adopted the shibboleths of the people, who employed them. The class-consciousness of the American worker consisted in his wanting to join the middle class of his country. Detailed studies of this phenomenon, such as in *Middletown in Transition*, have shown this again and again. As the Lynds discovered, 'to most people . . . of whatever group, "class differences" and "class consciousness" are vague, unfamiliar, and, if recognized, unpleasant and sinister terms'. By identifying radical social change with either Communism or Fascism, and by failing to distinguish between socialism and Communism, and by excluding supporters of both these doctrines, American unions linked their fates to the existing economy.

When capitalism fell, the union leaders looked for its rise again, not its replacement. Thus, as the anti-trust reformer Thurman Arnold noted in 1937, nearly everyone, even those who would benefit from the change, opposed many alterations for fear of their supposed implications.

> The holy war between Capitalism, Communism, and Fascism is one of the greatest obstacles to practical treatment of the actual day-to-day needs of the American people . . . Every practical scheme for social betterment had to be tested for tendencies leading to one or to the other of these systems. If it led to Communism or Fascism, it was thought better to humiliate the unemployed or to waste natural resources rather than take steps which would change the capitalist system.

Three parties could have led a revolution in the 1930s, the Communist Party, the Socialist Party, and the Farm parties of the Midwest. Individually, certain people could have begun a revolution, such as the inadequate Waters of the Bonus Marchers. But the extraordinary lack of radical leadership outside the organized parties and the failure within them was less for lack of opportunity than for the missing men. There were no Lenins or Mao Zedongs in America.

The Communist Party never exploited its opportunity in the Depression. Its failure lay in Stalin's and Trotsky's struggle for power in Russia. The leaders of American Communism were called to Moscow after Stalin's victory, when the Trotskyites were purged. Earl Browder, a Stalinite zealot, was given control of the Party, and William Z. Foster, a militant and competent candidate, was put up for the Presidency; but the comrades were split and disintegrated at the time of the Great Crash. Although its strength of card-carrying members rose to 12,000 in 1932, the party failed to penetrate the American unions, and its efforts to set up rival groups earned undying hostility. Not until 1935, when the Comintern switched policy, did the American Communists get the go-ahead to collaborate with the official labour unions and to infiltrate into positions of power. By then, it was too late.

Although the Communists tried to exploit some of the extreme strikes, they could never break the workers' suspicion of them as being under 'foreign' orders. And yet, the majority of the unskilled labour in the United States was immigrant 'foreign' labour. The wish of the newcomers, however, was to become Americanized as soon as possible. They accepted the reigning ethic as the right ethic; they wanted to be accepted. Except among the intellectuals of America, and certain class-conscious workers and bitter blacks, the Communists made hardly any progress. In the election of 1932, they received little more than 100,000 official votes. The party failed, as it had few arms and practically no following among the munitions workers or army sergeants with which to start an uprising.

The Socialists did better, but badly. They polled 1,000,000 votes – perhaps 2,000,000 if political conditions had allowed an equitable counting of the polls. Their attraction – and their fatal weakness – was their candidate for the presidency, Norman Thomas. He was a product of the Social Gospel, a Christian and a gentleman. He had none of the fire and fury of Eugene V. Debs, who had polled 1,000,000 votes way back in 1912 and had really seemed a threat to the established order in a time of comparative prosperity. He could never say, as Debs had said: 'While there is a lower class I am of it, while there is a criminal class I am of it, while there is a soul in prison, I am not free.'

The leading American humorist of the time, Will Rogers, had always expressed scepticism of farm leaders. 'I was raised on a farm, we had farm hands, farm hired girls, farm horses, farm mortgages (not many), but I never saw a farm that raised farm leaders.' In fact, he was right. The farm movements were not led by farmers. On the other hand, the leaders in 1932, Ed O'Neal of the Farm Bureau, John A. Simpson of the Farmers' Union who believed capitalism was doomed, and Milo Reno of Iowa with his Farmers' Holiday Association, all promised action. In Iowa, farmers for a time controlled the state with their pickets, while Reno said that the situation was out of control and could no longer be stopped any more than the Revolution of 1776 had been stopped. But the divisive tendencies of American farmers, the distances and the tradition of individualism made it difficult to organize the most dangerous radical groups in the country.

Among the personal leaders, none of the crypto-Fascists, such as Father Coughlin with his immense radio following, or Huey Long, had yet made enough of an impact to present a serious alternative to either of the major parties. A careful survey showed that nearly one in four of the jobless, although only one in sixteen among the employed, agreed that 'a revolution might be a very good thing for this country'. Yet nearly all of them reacted strongly against such terms as 'Communism' and 'alien radicals' and said that 'a man should be willing to fight for his country'.

Fascism was not yet powerful enough in Europe, as Communism was in Russia, to seem a possible alternative government, although many rich people cast longing eyes at Mussolini in Italy and called for a temporary dictatorship in America.

As Richard Neustadt declared in his penetrating book *Presidential Power*, 'Because he cannot control happenings, a President must do his best with hopes.' Unlike Mussolini or Hitler, Roosevelt's charisma was that of the common touch and the sympathetic voice. While Hitler in his broadcasts could both bully and cajole, Roosevelt appeared as the family friend and kind uncle in his radio Fireside Chats, explaining weekly his measures to help the nation out of its misery.

Without questioning the general belief in the virtues of a changed capitalism, Roosevelt suggested enough to make the Democrats a class party, opposed to the rich and big businessmen. His mention of the forgotten man and his attack on 'economic royalists' changed the basis of Democratic strength from an ethnic and religious and Southern bias to a national one. He seemed to promise economic reform without disturbing too much. He stole the Communist and Socialist thunder, as the progressives had stolen the Wobblies' lightning, by promising an altered system of government, not a new one.

The mainstream radical tradition in the United States had always stood by capitalism in a streamlined form. There was no accepted alternative to the system; thus it survived, due to the charisma of a man who seemed to change things a great deal while changing them very little. He did his best with hopes, but he failed to control happenings. When a friend told him that if he succeeded he would be thought the greatest American President, and if he failed he would be thought the worst, he is said to have replied: 'If I fail, I shall be the last one.'

Roosevelt succeeded, because the American people wished to preserve the ways which had made them rich before and might make them rich again. As the humorist Mr Dooley had forecast accurately in 1906: 'What we call this here counthry iv ours pretinds to want to thry new experiments, but a sudden change gives it a chill. It's been to th' circus an' bought railroad tickets in a hurry so often that it thinks quick change is short change.' Slow change in America, done with the vocabulary of the old catchwords, was the limit of the evolution that most people would accept, even in a Great Depression.

The extraordinary thing in 1932 was the weakness of the regular American military. Actually, the strength of the irregular armed forces and private company armies discouraged the sporadic outbreaks of violence from growing into an open revolution. In the reaction against militarism after the First World War, the regular army had been cut to 119,000 men by 1927, and after the Great Crash, more cuts were proposed to save government money. This policy was opposed by the President Herbert Hoover. His reason was explicit enough. Fewer American ground forces would 'lessen our means of maintaining domestic peace and order'. Again, in 1932, when the Senate proposed a pay cut for all government employees, Hoover sent a secret message to ask exemption for the armed forces, as he did not want them disgruntled in case of internal trouble. His fear was echoed across the country. For the first time in its history, Lloyd's of London sold much 'riot and civil commotion' insurance to American clients.

Outside these small regular forces, the defence of the country was left in the hands of the National Guard. Its numbers were low at this time, probably not more than 300,000 men. On the other hand, these forces of ex-veterans were powerful and well-armed. They and the state troopers could gather in a matter of hours a formidable battalion to oppose a strike or local trouble. Watching the shocked reactions of picketing farmers in upper New York State when they were clubbed and tear-gassed by state troopers, Edmund Wilson commented on 'that ominous phenomenon, the military policeman, who has come to play such a role in American life since the war'. The increasing dependence of state governments on troopers and National Guardsmen, who were drawn from the ranks of believers in fundamental American-ism, kept local strikers in awe and prevented the spread of any serious uprising.

A third tradition kept violence in country districts under control and prevented the success of unions there. The tradition of vigilantes, and of the calling on special deputies by the sheriff in time of trouble, gave the business classes of the town an excuse to arm and attack any troublemakers or riot leaders who appeared. The killing, lynching, and beating up of the Wobbly organizers before the First World War, the cursing of the pro-Germans during the war, the assaults on the radicals in the postwar 'Red Scare', and the violent activities of the Ku Klux Klan in the early 1920s, all showed the existence of large and dangerous groups of men in every community who could always be guaranteed to offer themselves as a posse or a mob to assault any subversive in opinion or skin or religion. The tradition of lynch law in the rural districts gave those who appointed them-selves the keepers of local morality the excuse to attack the deviants or the foreign element in that society. According to the Tuskagee Institute, in the fifty years before the close of the Second World War, some 3,400 blacks and 1,300 whites were mobbed and tortured to death.

Although the regular army was weak, local and state forces on the side of conservatism were fairly strong. Weapons such as rifles were chiefly in the hands of the state arsenals or business-men – the only exception to this rule, and the only dangerous element of insurrection, were the farmers, who usually owned weapons. At the sign of a widespread rising among them, such as took place from Pennsylvania to Nebraska during 1932, mort-gage companies and banks and even state policemen beat a retreat.

Due to the particular tradition of the West, the farmers were the most dangerous radical element at this time, armed and ready to fight. But they were, as the union leaders were, a democracy of expectant capitalists practically to a man. Although the president of the National Farmers' Union could denounce the wealthy as 'cannibals that eat each other and who live on the labour of the workers', and although there was talk of revolution almost everywhere, nobody knew who and what to follow. The farmers wanted a new American Revolution like that of 1776 – and the old one had not been a social one. They wanted to restore a golden age, not forge a new world.

Wilbur J. Cash, in his marvel of a psychological study, *The Mind of the South*, probably gave the best picture of the feeling in country areas:

> Everybody was either ruined beyond his wildest previous fears or stood in peril of such ruin. And the general psychological reaction? First a universal bewilderment and terror, which perhaps went beyond that of the nation at large by the measure of the South's lack of training in analysis, and particularly social analysis. Men everywhere walked in a kind of daze. They clustered, at first to assure one another that all would shortly be well; then, with the passage of time, to ask questions in the pleading hope of thus being assured; but in the end they fled before the thought in one another's eyes . . .
>
> And in the last days before the coming of Roosevelt, some of them, despairing of making sense of it, were falling into the impatient mood natural to simple men when confronted with what defies their understanding and wishing that they might sweep it all aside and start again with a more readily comprehensible world; they were using the word 'revolution'. Very cloudy was their wishing, very far were they from the will to action, very greatly did they fall short of being the majority as yet, and very unclear was every one of them as to precisely whom and what it was he meant to rebel against. Nevertheless, there the word was, marching about in the open . . .
>
> At the summit of the matter, indeed, some of them were

actually – not embracing the notion of revolution, certainly, but at the last, viewing it with the apathetic eyes of men who have looked so long on terror that they no longer feel much of anything. They were talking of it in quiet voices as something which was sure to come soon or late, unless there was a great change, unless there was a great change.

And so it fell out that no section of the country greeted Franklin Roosevelt and the New Deal with more intense and unfeigned enthusiasm than did the South.

Even so, there were farm and small-town riots in plenty. The fact that they came to nothing was due to the vastness of the continent and the impossibility of communications between turbulence and troublespot. If serious riots had broken out in the large cities to act as a focus of discontent for the country, something might have developed. But the cities were extraordinarily spineless. The urban mobs of unemployed in the Hoovervilles and shanty towns that grew up near rubbish dumps did not rebel. With 13,000,000 jobless in 1932, there were few major disturbances, other than the slaughter of Hunger Marchers outside the Ford plant at Dearborn.

The reasons for urban apathy were diverse. The first was that the city businessmen and the Churches, fearful of discontent and starvation, made huge attempts to dole out private charity in soup kitchens. Few people officially died of starvation, although there were sporadic hunger riots throughout the United States until the election of 1932 and Roosevelt's victory. New leaders promised new events.

Most sinister was the inability of the jobless to find weapons to use against the forces arrayed against them. Henry Ford alone employed 8,000 ex-criminals in his largest factory; the Ford Service Department of secret policemen was 2,000 strong. It was tied up with the underworld in a mutual deal which gave gangsters pickings in concessions at the plants in return for their help against labour organizers and reds. Similar deals were done in all large cities, especially Detroit. By murder, looting, shooting, bombing, arson and derailing trains, striking Pennsylvania miners were twice defeated by the 3,000 auxiliaries of the Coal and Iron Police.

Union organizers and revolutionaries had to contend against federal and state forces, the police and the vigilantes, the gangsters and the detective agencies, allied with the private company armies. As these forces had a practical monopoly of weapons, they were difficult to attack, and the fear of criminal and company enforcers had become prevalent during the 1920s. People were afraid to risk their lives and jobs to bring about a revolution, which also offended their deep-rooted beliefs in the virtues of American capitalism and patriotism.

In one of the few dangerous moments for the government in Washington, when the Bonus Marchers were waiting outside the Senate for the result of the vote on their bonus, they formed up in ranks and sang 'America' instead of attacking Congress when the bonus was turned down. Fifteen thousand veterans had paraded weaponless to Washington, not to overthrow the government, but to get a money handout for past patriotism to tide them through present bad times. Although no action was taken against the Bonus Marchers for several months, they were driven out in the end by troops and tanks under General Douglas MacArthur's command. They were still unarmed and had resisted all attempts by Communists to convert them to violent insurrection, even though their leader Waters was beginning to flirt with a Fascist solution.

Indeed the converts to Communism and socialism at the time were the intellectuals, not the masses. With the collapse of the old system, they turned to the possibility of a fresh start. But the intelligentsia and the rest of America have never got on too well with each other. And the left wing never threw up a leader or organizer to match the political expertise of Franklin Roosevelt. As a poem in the conservative *Atlantic Monthly* entitled 'Bread Line' stated:

It needs but one to make a star,
Or light a Russian samovar.
One to start a funeral pyre,
One to cleanse a world by fire.
What if our bread line should be
The long slow-match of destiny?

27. THE SHAME OF JAPAN

Bad as the Mongol attack on China was, in the Second World War the Japanese matched their brutalities. Nothing seemed to have been learned in civilized behaviour since the Middle Ages. And in spite of the Tokyo War Crimes Tribunal of 1946, after which only seven imperial officers were hanged and the Emperor left on his throne, little was explained of the most unprecedented barbarity of modern times. R. J. Rummel, who coined the term 'democide' to include both genocide and mass murder by government policy, came up with the aphorism: 'Power kills, and absolute power kills absolutely.'

With the infamous Rape of Nanking of 1937, more atrocities were proven at the War Crimes trial. Biological warfare was used against the Chinese people, with whole cities and regions targeted. As in Nazi Germany, in Unit Ei 1644 in Nanking, medical experiments were carried out on prisoners, who were injected with varied snake venoms, arsenic and cyanide. Ten or more victims died weekly and were incinerated. Nurtured in the infamous biological warfare centres in Manchuria run by the Japanese army Unit 731, which killed another 10,000 prisoners of war in its medical experiments, cartons of bubonic plague lice, cholera and typhus bomblets and anthrax spores were dropped throughout China, followed by scientists, who dissected the corpses to check the results of the horrors falling from the air. A policy of democide was carried out in the north to cleanse the land by the 'Three-all' policy: 'Loot all, kill all, burn all'. Within nine years, the population was reduced from 44,000,000 to 25,000,000 people, mainly through starvation and epidemic.

The deliberate use of terror tactics was further documented at the War Crimes trial. There was the Bataan Death March, where the prisoners were killed as they dropped out, unable to totter forwards; the appalling conditions during the building by Allied prisoners of the Siam–Burmese Railway, the floggings and the water and electric tortures, the starvation and the untreated diseases; the beheading and the disembowelling of captives, and even cannibalism. While the Nazis only killed one in twenty-five of their American prisoners of war, the Japanese killed one in three.

The Rape of Nanking set the standard in the Japanese tactics of domination, which were designed to terrorize all their enemies. Under orders to execute their prisoners, the Japanese armies shot or beheaded at least 200,000 captives. There were even samurai contests between Japanese lieutenants; how many serial heads could be severed at one stroke from the sword. The orgy of rape and mutilation and torture inflicted on the civilians in the capital of China was abominable. The Japanese officers referred to the Chinese as pigs or dogs, and so the victims were treated as beasts or worse. Women were violated and spitted, as though King Vlad III was again on the rampage. In the declaration of one witness, now a healing doctor at home,

> few know that soldiers impaled babies on bayonets and tossed them still alive into pots of boiling water. They gang-raped women from the ages of twelve to eighty and then killed them when they could no longer satisfy their sexual demands. I beheaded people, starved them to death, burned them, and buried them alive, over two hundred in all. It is terrible that I could turn into an animal and do these things. There are really no words to explain what I was doing. I was truly a devil.

The question was why the Japanese military, known for their politeness and obedience, loosed such violence on their enemies. The first answer was the repression of the soldier, his degradation and humiliation by his officers until he became a mindless killing machine. He was beaten and slapped and tortured until he obeyed by instinct. He was passing on his own pain to other victims. He was ordered to use prisoners as bayonet or target practice and throw them alive into pits to be burned with kerosene. He was taught the total contempt of fellow Asians and effete Westerners. The Shinto cult of the divine Emperor instructed him that the Japanese were a superior race, who should dominate the world. As an American chaplain told the War Crimes Tribunal, he had interviewed many surviving veterans, who believed 'that any enemy of the Emperor could not be right, so the more brutally they treated their prisoners, the more loyal they were being.'

In the words of a professor who had studied in the Kaiser's Germany, Uesugi Shinkichi: 'Subjects have no mind apart from the will of the Emperor. Their individual selves are merged with the Emperor. If they act according to the mind of the Emperor, they can realize their true nature and attain the moral ideal.' That ideal was discipline and self-sacrifice and complete obedience and worship of the divine structure of command. *The Cardinal Principles of National Policy*, issued in 1937 by the Ministry of Education, made the declaration that the Japanese were different from materialistic and enfeebled Europe. Their spirit was pure and unclouded and sacred, while the influence of the West led to the corruption of the mind and the spirit.

The ultimate self-sacrifice was that of the kamikaze pilots at the end of the war. They had been indoctrinated as successfully as Hassan al-Sabah had brainwashed his youthful Assassins into dying for his cause. Imbued by Shinto rhetoric, the kamikaze airmen believed that they would attain the highest honour of a samurai in the service of their Emperor by crashing their fighters into an American aircraft carrier, as would the al-Qaeda hijackers into the twin towers of Manhattan. What was notable about these teenage suicide bombers was their extreme youth, as it would be for the carriers of death of the Hamas and other terrorist groups. Immolation worked best among those who had not even begun to live their lives, nor knew what they had to lose.

Yet if the Emperor inspired the military forces of Japan, why was he held unaccountable? Hirohito certainly knew of the barbarity of his forces at Nanking. But the terms of the Japanese surrender after the two atomic bomb attacks exempted him and all members of the imperial family from judgement (see plate 27). In an act of realpolitik worthy of Machiavelli, Hirohito was allowed to remain on the throne to reassure his people during the American occupation of Japan under General MacArthur after the war was over. Once Mao Zedong and his Red Army had conquered China, the United States needed a stable Japan under its military control to face down a Communist East Asia in the Cold War. The imperial bureaucracy was left largely untouched, and an imprisoned war criminal became in 1957 the Prime Minister of his country, now called a democracy. There was little retribution for the slaughter of some 25,000,000 people by barbaric techniques in the nine years of war, when Japan tried to establish an Asian hegemony, which it called a new age of Great Harmony.

28. FEAR, STRANGE MERCY AND ANNIHILATION

Outside the ideological killing of the Japanese warriors, and the German SS and the Russian NKVD on the Eastern front, there was a curious understanding and a sort of decency among the soldiers in the Western theatres of operations. After the teachings of Freud and Jung had spread, the combatant was more self-conscious. In Britain, indeed, there was a renaissance of the arts, provoked by the horrors of the Second World War, as there had been in ancient Athens and the Renaissance Italian cities during their internecine struggles. The worldwide Great Depression had given the masses across the globe a certain common sympathy, while the coming of the war was a solace to those who had found themselves inadequate to deal with the successive crises of the 1930s. As Edward Higham made his marginal hero *William Medium* declare:

> Here, at last, after years of sultry oppression which precedes the storm, came the lightning, the thunder, the rain; and, like millions of others, while outwardly grave, I welcomed the storm. For what had the peace meant to so many? It had meant semi-starvation on a grudged dole. Or hard work, at uncongenial labour, for a bare living wage, without any security. These facts are notorious. But there are others; no young man or woman, of whatever class, could say that, when he or she left school, there would be interesting and remunerative work to do. But what would happen now that the war had come? There would be a sense of purpose and

community of interest. The youth, leaving school, would face not misery, not boredom, but dangerous adventure, which is congenial to a young man, if he be sufficiently fed . . .

As for the poet David Gascoyne, who walked a tightrope between sanity and forbidden homosexuality, he was struck by the horror of actuality. 'At the same moment the mental and spiritual war which had been going on inside me for weeks and months – perhaps years? – beforehand, suddenly reached its final cataclysm, and I knew that it had to come to an end, had in fact already ended. *Zero is over*. Now I have some sort of assurance and strength which I never had before.'

In the next great war, Liam O'Flaherty thought before its declaration, pilots would seize power. There would be flying barons, an aristocracy of the air instead of the earth. They would quarrel among themselves, until all cities lay in ruins and civilization had disappeared. After 1939, most people believed with O'Flaherty that Nazi bombers would destroy all British cities, although the raiders failed to do so. The fighter pilots who defended the urban sprawls did become aerial knights, each a Galahad in his Spitfire or Hurricane, the first of the Few. But they seemed a marked aristocracy, bound to die. They thought they were doomed and usually achieved their fate. In proportion to the rest of the armed forces, airmen were suicide squads. Death fell from the sky, and brightness from the air.

A contrary wind blew when defence changed to attack. British fighters left home ground to fly over France, while thousand-bomber raids destroyed the old civilization of Germany as well as the factories filled with Nazi slave labour. There was a change of atmosphere. The pilot was no longer sentry and sacrifice. He was abstraction and avenger. He did not guard homes, he savaged abroad. William Blake's Invisible Worm, who flew in the night and the howling storm, now destroyed the dark secret heart of the Third Reich.

In that terrible retribution, the vision of the fliers altered towards a common pity, a mutual mercy. Those about to die in the air also broadcast death upon the earth. Revenge was not sweet, but apt. The joyride was over, and it was a damned unnatural sort of war. The pilots in the clouds might be sure of their values, but they could not even see the people beneath they were to destroy. They were themselves murderers, who were also murdered in the air. This irony was particularly clear to the American airmen, when they joined the war, for America had not even been bombed. Randall Jarrell saw himself and the lethal Eighth Air Force as part of the general 'Losses':

> In bombers named for girls, we burned
> The cities we had learned about in school –
> Till our lives wore out; our bodies lay among
> The people we had killed and never seen.
> When we lasted long enough they gave us medals;
> When we died they said, 'Our casualties were low.'
> They said, 'Here are the maps'; we burned the cities.

Yet it was a just war that burned the cities. The guardians of the air above Britain had become the executioners, but their aim was right. The problem was O'Flaherty's main point: the retribution from the air on the cities of Europe did destroy civilization, particularly by the chemical warfare of incendiaries. 'I cannot look at any more maps,' Elias Canetti wrote in 1943. 'The names of cities reek of burnt flesh.' The destruction by firestorm of more than 100,000 civilians in Dresden as a blood sacrifice to Stalin's advancing Red Army was the worst atrocity committed by Winston Churchill during the hostilities.

The later theme of the common victim and the common dead also surfaced in the war at sea. At first, it was the convoys which suffered from submarine attack. Ships loaded with refugees were sunk as well as troop transports. G. S. Fraser mourned the children lost on the SS *City of Benares*, the blood of the innocent smearing the sky, while Roy Campbell evoked the soaring headlands of the Cape as the monument of a troopship that went down:

> Where, packed as tight as space can fit them
> The soldiers retch, and snore, and stink.
> It was no bunch of flowers that hit them
> And woke them up, that night, to drink.

Many worried about becoming justified murderers. Their duty, if not their right, was to kill the enemy. To be killed was an evasion or dereliction. As Denis Saunders wrote in 'Almendro':

> Today I killed a man. God forgive me!
> Tomorrow I shall sow another political corpse,
> Or be dead myself. And strangely
> I am satisfied to be applauded killer.
> Holy Mary plead my dutied sin's legality . . .

The resolution of righteous murder was best expressed in the *Iliad* of the campaign against Rommel in North Africa. In his *Elegies For the Dead in Cyrenaica*, Hamish Henderson recognized that among the fallen, 'there were our own, there were the others'. The point was to remember the great words of Glencoe's son, 'we should not disfigure ourselves / With villainy of hatred'. Yet the horrors of the sick ideologies of the 1930s had to be defeated. Here Henderson recalled Kirkpatrick's words, when Robert the Bruce did not know whether or not he had stabbed the Red Comyn to death: 'Aweel, I'll mak siccar.' ('I'll make sure'):

> Meaning that many
> German Fascists will not be going home
> meaning that many
> will die, doomed in their false dream
>
> We'll mak siccar!
> Against the bashing cudgel
> against the contemptuous triumphs of the big battalions

mak siccar against the monkish adepts
of total war against the oppressed oppressors
mak siccar against the leaching lies
against the worked out systems of sick perversion
mak siccar
        against the executioner
against the tyrannous myth and real terror
mak siccar

The scale of the atrocities stilled all understanding and description of them. The first intolerable horror was the discovery of the Nazi concentration camps, the second was the dropping of the atomic bombs on Hiroshima and Nagasaki. During the war, the British had suffered only a quarter of their casualties in the First World War, although the blitz had killed some 50,000 civilians. Thus when the obscene murder machines of Hitler's diseased Final Solution were discovered with their many millions of victims and emaciated survivors, they were too terrible to take in. One British artist and writer, Mervyn Peake, was sent to Belsen to prepare a series of drawings (see plate 28). He was also illustrating Coleridge's 'The Rime of the Ancient Mariner', and he found the Nightmare Life-in-Death was Belsen incarnate. When he returned from the camp, his wife found that he looked inward, 'as if he had lost, during that month in Germany, his confidence in life itself.'

The supreme artist of his age, Francis Bacon, admitted to the direct influence of newsreels, which showed the Belsen camp, but only through 'an intense, active unconsciousness. I see the violence of existence. We must recall it.' This he did in the gaping mouths of his figures in torment, the white streaks enclosing them as torture cages, the distorted bodies swollen by death or greed. His most disturbing and profound picture, *Painting, 1946*, now hanging in the Museum of Modern Art in New York, recalled Fascist tyranny as well as Belsen and the atomic bomb (see plate 44). The work of art was redolent of decay and bleeding flesh under a mushroom cloud, here represented by a black open umbrella. In his 'armchair of meat' sat a repulsive black figure with a red-fanged face taken from war photographs of Himmler or Mussolini or even T. S. Eliot's Apeneck Sweeney, with the 'oval O cropped out with teeth' of his murderous mouth.

At the beginning of the atomic age of deterrence, the events of the war which ended with the surrender of Japan seemed too horrible to most people to imagine. In his own reaction from his memory of tossing his 'bricks' of fire and annihilating all living things on a Proustian beach and watching the destruction of his fellow rocket-ships off Walcheren, William Golding later wrote a full assertion about the impossibility of bearing witness:

> The experiences of Hamburg and Belsen, Hiroshima and Dachau cannot be imagined. We have gone to war and beggared description all over again. These experiences are like the black holes in space. Nothing can get out to let us know what it was like inside. It was like what it was like and on the other hand it was like nothing else whatsoever. We stand before a gap in history. We have discovered a limit to literature.

29. THE FINAL SOLUTION

'This war is not the Second World War,' the Nazi Air Marshal Hermann Goering declared. 'This is the great racial war. In the final analysis it is about whether the German and Aryan prevails here, or whether the Jew rules the world, and that is what we are fighting for out there.' As the Japanese had considered the Chinese as dogs and pigs, so the chief of propaganda, Joseph Goebbels, thought of the Jews after visiting the ghetto in the Polish textile city of Łódź. 'These aren't human beings any more, these are animals. This is therefore not a humanitarian, but rather a surgical task.' The solution was to make 'really radical cuts', the operation of the death camps.

In his systematic campaign of horror on the Eastern Front, Hitler first eliminated the elites of occupied countries such as Poland; this was followed by Stalin in the infamous massacre of 15,000 Polish officers and officials at Katyn. But until Hitler's attack on Russia in the summer of 1941, the Nazi–Soviet Pact of opposed ideologies had agreed on one principle, the maximum use of state terror, which would result in the systems of the concentration camps and the Gulags in Siberia. This was the appalling collaboration of two monsters, each bent on cleansing any named pollution from the pure body politic, which should only be Aryan or proletarian, whatever these two shibboleths were meant to mean.

As slow methods of killing had led to the invention of the guillotine by the Revolutionary Tribunal in Paris during the 'Terror', so the gas wagon and the gas chamber had reached the first German concentration camps before the invasion of

Russia. By 1942, when the extermination of the Jews had become official policy, Heinrich Himmler, the SS leader, stated that 'in accord with the will of the Führer, a simple decision had been made, and the decision is that the Jew must die in agony.' Those in Poland were herded into ghettos and then sent in railway vans, often coated with quicklime and shunted into sidings, so that they were dead on arrival at the camps, where other methods of slow torture unto a mass grave awaited any survivors.

After Hitler's successful incursion into western Russia, his racial madness prevented his decisive victory. The ravages of Stalin's commissars in the Ukraine with the removal of millions of kulaks to Siberia enabled the Germans to recruit six divisions of troops there. Yet their treatment of the Slav population was even worse than had been suffered under the Communist regime. One of Hitler's preferred generals, Field Marshal Keitel, was quoted at the Nuremberg Trials as giving the order: 'It should be remembered that human life in unsettled countries counts for nothing and a deterrent effect can be obtained by unusual severity.' According to him, the killing of prisoners was useful for the fertility of the earth. One order even authorized his troops 'to take any measures without restriction, even against women and children, in order to achieve success.'

Hitler was no longer using the tactics of terror with precision. His determination to annihilate the Jews appeared to extend to the destruction of the 36,000,000 Slavs between Germany and the Ural mountains. Instead of conciliating anti-Bolshevik elements, the Nazi officials aimed to turn the Ukrainians into slave labour under worse conditions than on the collective farms. All major factories and modern machinery were to be transferred back to the Third Reich. What the Russian population had to expect was a low standard of living and terrible reprisals in the event of any resistance. As the SS chief in Prague, Reinhard Heydrich, outlined the policy, a German military elite would rule like the Spartans a mass of Slav 'helots'. The Jews would be exterminated, and the Poles and the Slavs cleared toward Siberia, while German agriculture would push towards the east; each farmer would hold a spade in one hand and a rifle in the other. Leningrad and Moscow would be razed to the ground, as the Mongols had initially wished to destroy all Chinese cities to make pasture for their horses.

Millions of Russian prisoners and civilians were deported back to Germany to labour in squalor in the factories supplying the Nazi war machine. And the ruthless extermination of the Jews and the defectives and the disabled went on. These mass murders were not only done by the SS and the Waffen-SS, but by Fascist squads recruited all across east and central Europe from Croatia up to Lithuania. Romanian death squads killed some 150,000 Jews in Bessarabia and North Bukovina. One of their commanders found an excuse for mercilessness and 'ethnic purification'. 'I do not mind if history judges us barbarians. The Roman Empire performed a series of barbarous acts against its contemporaries, and yet it was the greatest political power.'

By the time the tide turned against the Nazi armies at Stalingrad, their racial policies and harsh reprisals had made all the occupied countries loathe them. And even their most horrible atrocity, the Holocaust of the Jews, impeded their fighting machine, which lost resources in wood and iron, chemicals and transport and manpower. The concentration camps from Treblinka to Auschwitz had to be organized, as had the ferrying of millions of Jews to torture and their slow and foul and degrading ordeal before their planned end. One of the camp survivors, David Rousset, tried to explain the inflicted humiliation:

> It is not necessary that a Jew or a Pole should have taken part in the fight against National Socialism. They were by birth predestined heretics, who could never be assimilated and were therefore dedicated to apocalyptic fire. Death was an insufficient punishment for them. Only expiation satisfied the demands of their lords. The concentration camps, therefore, assumed the shape of engines of expiation,

extraordinary and complex machines, which ground out death slowly, and with calculated abandon in order that the moral and physical fall from grace should take place only by degrees, making the victims conscious of being damned, expressions of the evil principle rather than humans.

For the first time, the Nazis introduced the factory methods of the conveyor belt to the murder of the condemned masses, who were branded with numbers as if they were industrial products. The ledgers of their murders were like a census, which logged a serial number and name, date and place of birth, profession and last address, grounds for execution and its date, and any comments. The weight of gold taken from their extracted teeth, of hair shaven from the women, the catalogue of stripped clothes, the time-sheets of the guards and the quantity of the pitiful supplies, all were recorded as if running a government department. This was the invention of the bureaucracy of terror, and it led to the enduring crime of the twentieth century, the effort to eliminate efficiently a whole people. In Auschwitz alone, 4,000,000 people were terminated in two years; the total deaths in the camps exceeded 10,000,000; over half of these were Jews.

The industrial expert Albert Speer thought that this Final Solution was not a productive policy and hampered the war effort, which should be supported by more slave labour. Although by 1943, some of the concentration camp inmates were transferred to work in the factories, Speer failed to win his argument, later saying, 'We could have employed uncounted millions of people, but we – that is, Hitler and Goebbels – could never be convinced.'

That was the tragedy of the unspeakable times. Modern accountancy and machinery made possible the elimination of more people more quickly than at any time in history. The human being was reduced to a statistic on a death register. The perpetrators of the crimes such as Adolf Eichmann, the chief of the Jewish department of the Gestapo, were no more than petty

officials, although he was finally condemned in Israel for his
pitiless disassociation, his rubber stamp on mass murder.

While the Russian armies approached Berlin and the British
and American forces crossed the Rhine, Hitler saw himself as
a Wagnerian hero, who would die with his whole people in
the *Götterdämmerung* of his creation. As in the Ring cycle, his
delusion was that he was both the creator and destroyer of the
Third Reich, whose people were finally not worthy of the destiny
he had given them. He gave orders to Eichmann from his Berlin
bunker that all the concentration camps must be destroyed in a
Wolkenbrand of cloud and fire, the arsenic poisoning of the
inmates followed by their immolation. The evidence of the programme of annihilation must be annihilated.

Yet the bureaucracy had ground down. The concentration
camps yielded up to their appalled liberators the survivors of this
conspiracy of genocide, largely concealed until that time. With
his mistress, Hitler himself committed suicide by poison and
bullet and fire. He had declared that he would not surrender: 'We
may be destroyed, but if we are, we shall drag a world down
with us – a world in flames.' He only destroyed the Third Reich
with him, not the German people, although another 10,000,000
of them died as well in his dream of Germanic glory. Few indeed
returned of the millions of prisoners captured by the Red Army
and sent to the Gulags of Siberia, where Stalin was already
imitating Hitler in decimating his own people.

Although the Allied powers won against the Axis, and
although Nazi war criminals were tried at Nuremberg by the
principles of law, the technology of the Western powers had won
the World War, not their principles. The Nazis had achieved the
rocket-propelled V-bombs too late and not the atom bomb, while
neither side had dared to use biological warfare on each other for
fear of retaliation. Hitler left no legacy to Germany, except the
downfall of his people. His evil inheritance was his example of
the effective use of state terror. He was also another prophet
of the never-ending revolution, which must destroy before it may

create. He could have echoed the words of his hero Richard Wagner, writing on the 1848 revolts:

> The old world is in ruins from which a new world will arise; for the sublime goddess REVOLUTION comes rushing and roaring on the wings of storm; destroying and blessing she sweeps across the earth; before her pipes the storm; it shakes so violently all man's handiwork that vast clouds of dust darken the air, and where her mighty foot treads, all that has been built for ages past in idle whim crashes in ruins, and the hem of her robe sweeps the last remains of it away.

30. AFRICAN SECRET SOCIETIES

The perfect example of a nationalist secret society taking over the reins of government by legal means and putting its programme into action was supplied by the Afrikaner-Broederbond. This society grew up among Afrikaners of Dutch descent after they had lost their independence in the Boer War, which ended in 1902, and then in 1910 became part of a united South Africa. They were a minority of the white population; but they believed they might be a majority in the future. The Broederbond was founded in 1918 as an Afrikaans cultural society, and by 1934 it had become a nationalist splinter group within the ruling elite. It aimed to break away from the English-speaking South Africans and the Commonwealth. Its declared solution for the country's ills was 'that the Afrikaner-Broederbond should rule South Africa'. Nevertheless, under the leadership of the ex-Boer General Jan Smuts, who was determined to have peace between the English-speaking whites and the Afrikaners, South Africa remained a dominion within the British Commonwealth and fought for Britain in both world wars.

In 1938, the Broederbond was a driving force behind the centenary of the symbolic re-enactment of the Great Trek, by which Cape Afrikaners had moved north and escaped British rule. This celebration inflamed the forces of Afrikaner nationalism, which began to identify themselves with Nazi racism. Dr Malan, a founder-member of the Broederbond and Prime Minister from 1948 to 1954, was pushed by the Bond into raising a new paramilitary Afrikaner organization called the Ossewabrandwag, which claimed as many as 400,000 adherents – more than the total strength of the South African armed forces.

In 1940, when the Nazis appeared to have won the war in Europe, and Britain and its Commonwealth stood alone, the Afrikaner nationalists threatened to rebel with their Ossewa-brandwag. But with the entry of the United States into the war against the Axis powers and the German defeats in Russia and North Africa, where two South African divisions had earlier yielded the defence of Tobruk, the Broederbond turned against its paramilitary organization. It was canny enough to see that its chances of taking over democratically, as a nationalist party from the ageing Smuts, were far better than its chances of leading a successful pro-Nazi putsch.

The motives of the Bond were well analysed by the novelist Alan Paton.

> What was the Broederbond? A clique seeking power? Agitators playing on grievances? Afrikaner zealots with one overriding and patriotic purpose? Undoubtedly it was all these. Whatever else it may have been, it drew much of its power from the resentments of the 'Century of the Wrong'. Its relation to Afrikaner Nationalism was vital, yet obscure. Not every member of the nationalist Party was a member of the Broederbond, and some Nationalists . . . condemned it root and branch. Of course both the Broederbond and the Nationalist Party kept wounds open and played on grievances of the past, but who can doubt that the grievances were there?

Smuts thought the Broederbond so subversive that in 1944 he forbade civil servants to join it. He feared its tactics of infiltration and saw that it might well take over the levers of government, both secretly within the bureaucracy and overtly through the Nationalist party at the polls. Smuts' ban, however, did not halt the gradually increasing power of the Bond, and in 1948, when the Nationalist Party came to power through the polls with

a seemingly permanent majority in favour of its policy of apartheid, the conspiracy achieved its object. As a leading Bond
member, J. G. Strijdom, who would become Prime Minister, once
declared: 'German nationalist socialism strives for race purity.
That philosophy is most certainly the nearest to our national-
Christian philosophy in South Africa.'

A one-man commission appointed by the South African
government in 1964 to enquire into secret organizations found
the Bond 'not guilty of any conduct mentioned in the Commission's terms of reference'; these included attempts to dominate
the Prime Minister, treason, nepotism, and subversion of the state
and of morals. The commission's report, which put the Bond's
membership at 6,768, described its organization as having 473
local divisions, each of which had between five and fifty members.
It found that membership was restricted to white Afrikaans-
speaking Protestant males over the age of twenty-five; men who
were Freemasons were not eligible. At a 'simple but dignified'
initiation ceremony, the candidate pledged not to divulge his
membership or that of others, and not to disclose anything he
might learn from the Bond's documents, discussions, decisions,
and activities. He was told that the members of the Bond were
'mission-conscious Afrikaners who desire to represent and serve
the best that is in our nation'.

In fact, the Afrikaners led by the Broederbond represented
one of the most fiercely anti-egalitarian secret societies of all time.
Their slogan might well have been Repression, Inequality and
Apartheid. While the rest of Africa was casting off its colonial
shackles, the Pretoria administrations were enforcing a colour bar
worse even than in the American Southern states after the Civil
War. The dispossessed black majority found leaders in the
Marxist African National Congress, which made little progress
for several decades in subverting the powerful leaders of South
Africa, which even developed nuclear weapons (along with Israel)
to defend its concept of racial supremacy. The terrorist crimes
committed by the ANC, indeed, were distinguished by their

limitation, which added to the worldwide veneration of their imprisoned chief, Nelson Mandela, the future leader of his country.

In complete contrast was the Kenyan secret society of resistance to white colonial rule, the Mau Mau. The Kikuyu tribe of 1,250,000 people had been cleared from their lands by white occupying farmers. After 1950, a conspiracy of 12,000 militants was organized to eliminate European settlers and any opponents. Fronted by an inspirational politician, Jomo Kenyatta, through his Kenyan African Union, the Mau Mau was formed on the model of the early Masonic lodges. The initiate must pass through a plaited arch, have his head circled seven times with raw goat's meat, and take an oath of unity, with the vow that he would fight for:

> The lands which were taken by the Europeans
> And if I fail to do this
> May this oath kill me,
> May this seven kill me,
> May this meat kill me.

More primitive oaths were later sworn, to murder anybody on command for the soil, to burn and slay without question, to accept any punishment if any secret were betrayed. A system of terror in Kikuyu villages forced most of the males to join the movement with the promise that they would inherit the land. A campaign of arson and assassination began. In 1952, a State of Emergency was declared, and a Home Guard or militia of ten thousand men from other tribes was enlisted to back up the recently introduced battalion of Lancashire Fusiliers. A Mau Mau massacre with tribal mutilation at Lari shocked world opinion as badly as the Nazi obliteration of Lidice.

Mau Mau defectors now joined British intelligence forces, including a self-styled 'General China'. More than 77,000 Kikuyu were put into detention camps, the old practice of the British Empire during the Boer War. Military drives through the Aberdare mountains were failures. In fact, the turning of Kikuyu sentiment against the Mau Mau was due to its psychopath of a commander, Dedan Kimathi, the forerunner of many African resistance leaders, who would turn into bloody tyrants.

Kimathi proclaimed himself 'by God Knight Commander of the African Empire'. He hacked and mutilated and strangled all his rivals and opponents. His followers reverted to a bestial life in the forests, as they lost all urban support. He was hunted down by his former allies for blood money. More than 10,500 of the Mau Mau were killed, but only 32 European civilians and 63 European servicemen. The whole uprising was a senseless brutality. In 1963, Jomo Kenyatta was proclaimed the Prime Minister of Kenya, and all the remnants of the Mau Mau were pardoned. So independence was gained without the need for another insurrection.

The resistance to the German occupation of France, which was followed by the Algerians' resistance to the French colonization of their country, provoked a new understanding of terror as well as the commencement of many a jihad by Islamic warriors against the West. Albert Camus was brought up in Algiers, but fought in the French Maquis and became the editor of *Combat*, an influential postwar newspaper. His masterpiece, *The Plague*, first published in 1947, talked of oppression as bioterror. The pestilence which strikes the city of Oran causes a moral contagion among a terrified population. The only answer is not to be a victim, but 'to reject everything that, directly or indirectly, makes people die or justifies others in making them die'.

Faced by any epidemic of cruelty or disease, the decent man must resist. 'On this earth there are pestilences and there are victims – and as far as possible one must refuse to be on the side of the pestilence.' Camus saw that the problem of evil and terrorism would be the greater problems of the postwar decades. This was already evident in Algeria. 'The plague bacillus never dies or vanishes entirely ... the day will come when for the instruction or ill fortune of humanity, the plague will rouse its rats and send them to die in some complacent city.'

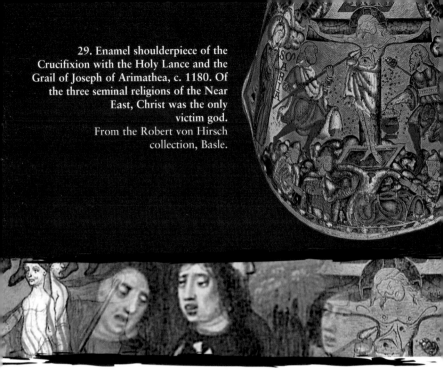

29. Enamel shoulderpiece of the Crucifixion with the Holy Lance and the Grail of Joseph of Arimathea, c. 1180. Of the three seminal religions of the Near East, Christ was the only victim god.
From the Robert von Hirsch collection, Basle.

30. Philip IV of France watches the execution of Jacques de Molay, the Grandmaster of the Templars, in 1314.
From *Les Chroniques de France*, c. 1388.

31. The Old Man of the Mountains distributes wine laced with hashish in his stronghold backed by the Garden of Paradise.

32. Hulagu besieges the Assassin castle of Alamut in 1256. From fourteenth-century French illustrations for *The Travels of Marco Polo*.

33. (right) *Europe a Prophecy*. William Blake.

34. *The Assassination of Spanish Guerrillas by the French Army on the Third of May, 1808, at Madrid.* Francisco de Goya.

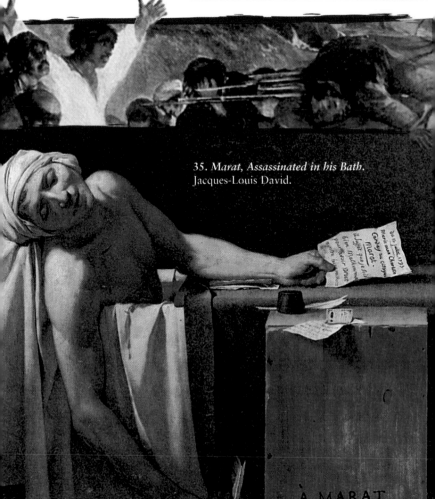

35. *Marat, Assassinated in his Bath.* Jacques-Louis David.

À MARAT

36. & 37. Kali, the Indian goddess of death, while Thuggees immolate their victims in her name.

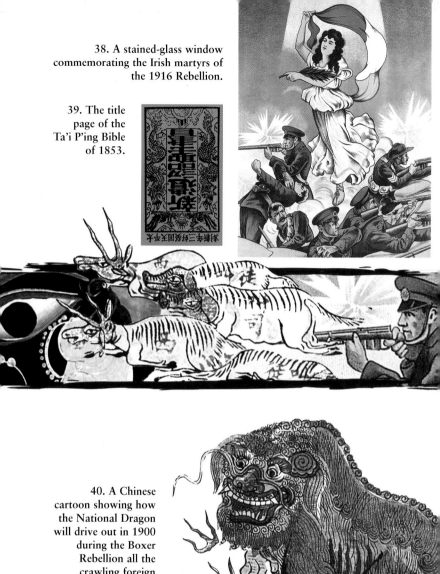

38. A stained-glass window commemorating the Irish martyrs of the 1916 Rebellion.

39. The title page of the Ta'i P'ing Bible of 1853.

40. A Chinese cartoon showing how the National Dragon will drive out in 1900 during the Boxer Rebellion all the crawling foreign invaders.

41. The anarchist Ravachol preparing to dynamite the home of the President of the French Court of Assizes, which had condemned his comrade and would have him executed, 1892.
Illustration by Flavio Constantini from *Ravachol et ses compagnons* (Editions du Chêne, Paris, 1976).

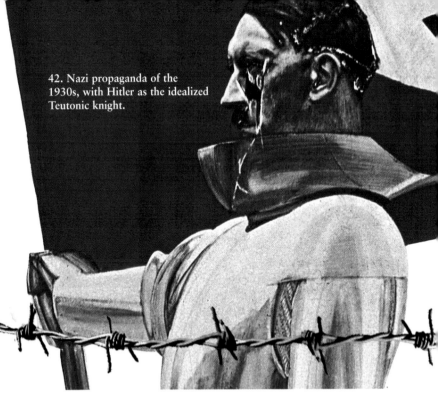

42. Nazi propaganda of the 1930s, with Hitler as the idealized Teutonic knight.

43. Hitler Youth marches on.

44. *Painting, 1946.*
Francis Bacon. Courtesy of the Museum of Modern Art, New York.

In Algeria, indeed, the seeds of the militant Islamic attack on Western values sprouted in the revolt of the 1950s, which ended in 1962 with the withdrawal of the French administration after more than a century of occupation. The rebels were called mujahedin or holy warriors; their slogan was 'Algérie Musulmane'. The war was brutal. Some 2,000,000 people were displaced, while 300,000 Algerians were killed and as many tortured. 24,000 French soldiers and 40,000 Muslim *harki* auxiliaries were atrociously put to death. As General Aussaresses said at the time, 'Yes, torture was necessary. Without it, we would have lost Algeria.' They still lost. A socialist and authoritarian state took over, which used Islamic schools to counterbalance Marxist elements, which might seek to oust the FLN leaders. Unfortunately, these 'wild' mosques spawned a whole movement of fundamentalist anti-French Arabic-speaking pupils. From them sprang the Islamic Salvation Front or FIS, which would win the general elections of early 1992, only to be removed by a military coup.

A civil war began with worse atrocities than in the struggle against the French. Ten thousand FIS supporters were detained in concentration camps in the Sahara desert. The mosques and resources of the banned religious party were seized. An expanded secret police used elaborate torture tactics to extract confessions. Algerian mujahedin, returning from fighting Soviet forces in Afghanistan, attacked army barracks and police stations and prisons and any government official. Whole villages were butchered, as the 300 men and women and children in Sidi Rais. Terrorism was matched by terrorism, either from the religious rebels or from factions within the security forces.

The French Revolution had exported both tactics of the 'Terror' and nationalism to North and Central and South Africa. Fuel was added to these fires by racism and religion, which sought in patriotism any excuse for the maltreatment of whatever enemy, whose skin or faith were held to be at fault. Tolerance was in short supply south and east of the Mediterranean Sea.

31. THE GULAG LIES

Two writers of genius exposed and condemned the Nazi and Soviet systems of terror, until their infamy stank in the nostrils of all the world. In his parable *Animal Farm* and then in his realistic and futurist novel *Nineteen Eighty-Four*, George Orwell indicted the Communist lies he had met in Catalonia and then the propaganda he had to contest while working in the British Broadcasting Corporation during the Second World War. In his short novel about beasts as humans, Orwell began with old Major, the prize boar, telling the other animals on Manor Farm that Man was the only creature who consumed without producing. 'Man is the only real enemy we have. Remove Man from the scene, and the root cause of hunger and overwork is abolished for ever.'

Instead of Jews or kulaks, the bourgeoisie or the capitalists, Man was indicted as the cause of the distress of the animal kingdom, an ominous foretaste of later Animal Rights terror campaigns against people. At Manor Farm, the beasts win a revolution for their freedom. The pigs take over with an SS squad of killer dogs. Liberty is replaced by tyranny, and other animals work harder for less, until in the end the pigs do a deal and give a feast for the human farmers around them. 'No question, now, what had happened to the faces of the pigs. The creatures outside looked from pig to man, and from man to pig, and from pig to man again; but already it was impossible to say which was which.'

So revolution turned to reaction, and the techniques of control in postwar Russia became the perversion of manner and language. In his later masterpiece, *Nineteen Eighty-Four*, Orwell gave a modern gloss to the old Jesuit techniques of the double logic. In his society to be, the world was split into three groups officially at war; Oceania was led from Britain. Run by the semi-divine dictator Big Brother and his Thought Police, the official language of Newspeak ground words into pap, until all meant the opposite of what it had meant before. The rationing agency was called the Ministry of Plenty. Bread was dark, tea was rare, coffee tasted filthy, cigarettes fell apart, and nothing was plentiful except synthetic gin, as bad vodka always was in Russia. In Newspeak, there was no word for 'science', which was a method of inquiry, because the state ruled thought through Doublethink. This had been called 'reality control': it now signified the power of holding two contradictory beliefs simultaneously, and accepting both of them. What was true was known to the Thought Police; what the people were told to believe, they had to believe. Apparently continually at war with the two rival blocs, there were never any victories for Oceania because the oppressed population might question why it always lived in such dreadful conditions. 'Efficiency, even military efficiency, is no longer needed. Nothing is efficient in Oceania except the Thought Police.'

In each variety of Socialism that had appeared, the goals of establishing liberty and equality were more openly abandoned. The three power blocs of *Nineteen Eighty-Four* 'had the conscious aim of perpetuating *un*freedom and *in*equality. These new movements, of course, grew out of the old ones and tended to keep their names and pay lip-service to their ideology. But the *purpose* of all of them was to arrest progress and freeze history at a chosen moment.' The New Class of rulers would only be replaced by their sons, as would happen in certain dictatorships in the Middle East and North Korea in the later decades of the century.

The heirs of the English and the American and the French Revolutions had believed in their words about the rights of man and freedom of speech, equality before the law and some welfare in the state. But human progress towards an earthly paradise had become discredited at the time when technology and machinery had made it viable. The beginnings of globalization and modern communications were leading to more means for repression. The truth of Stalin's Gulags was largely suppressed by misleading propaganda. Every new political theory now led back to hierarchy and regimentation.

> And in the general hardening of outlook that set in round about 1930, practices which had been long abandoned, in some cases for hundreds of years – imprisonment without trial, the use of war prisoners as slaves, public executions, torture to extract confessions, the use of hostages and the deportation of whole populations – not only became common again, but were tolerated and even defended by people who considered themselves enlightened and progressive.

As Orwell noted, the invention of print had made manipulating public opinion easier, further quickened by films and wireless broadcasts. And with the development of television, 'private life came to an end'. Every citizen could be kept continually under the surveillance of the police while being made to listen to official propaganda and nothing else. 'The possibility of enforcing not only complete obedience to the will of the State, but complete uniformity of opinion on all subjects, now existed for the first time.'

Published in 1949, Orwell's novel was too pessimistic a prophecy. While correct in viewing television and other communications during the computer revolution to come as means of more state terror, he did not foresee the failure of Communist Russia and China and other tyrannies to close down foreign channels, which showed alternative ways and standards of life. In the end, the demonstrations of how other peoples lived well under capitalism were the trumpets that brought the Communist walls of Jericho tumbling down. The truth of how alternative nations lived and worked could no longer be suppressed in digital times, until even the Internet might have to be policed as too accessible a means for the worldwide dissemination of guerrilla tactics and the methods of international terror. Future communications destroyed old regimes, but they also continually threatened the new ones in a permanent revolution.

The weak rebel hero of *Nineteen Eighty-Four*, called Winston after Churchill, was finally interrogated by a terrorist expert of the Thought Police named O'Brien. He would not destroy Winston, because the methods of the persecutors of the past were no longer necessary. The heretic would become the believer. He would be reshaped before he was killed. 'Even the victim of the Russian purges could carry rebellion locked up in his skull as he walked down the passage waiting for the bullet,' O'Brien said. 'But we make the brain perfect before we blow it out. The command of the old despotisms was "Thou shalt not". The command of the totalitarians was "Thou shalt". Our command is *"Thou art"*.' All would be brainwashed clean.

Finally, Winston was terrified by rats which might be loosed into a face-mask to eat out his eyes, a common punishment in Imperial China. As O'Brien noted, the worst horror varied from individual to individual. It might be the punishment of being buried alive or death by fire or drowning or impalement or fifty other ways to go. But faced with the rodents at his eyes, Winston collapsed. He denounced his lover, he wrote that 'FREEDOM IS SLAVERY' and 'TWO AND TWO MAKE FIVE'. He was purged and cleansed, at last.

In Newspeak, forced labour camps were called 'joycamps' and the propaganda organization was the Ministry of Truth. So Aleksandr Solzhenitsyn actually experienced in the Stalinist methods of the Gulags. In his collected work on the sufferings of his people, *The Gulag Archipelago*, he confirmed what Orwell had suspected and predicted. As O'Brien broke Winston, so the NKVD and other Soviet security organs broke the will of the prisoners without leaving any scars. They did not want to appear to be torturers, as the Inquisition had been. They desired a willing recantation, a total conversion.

They began with psychological breakdown, then led to more demanding tortures. Interrogation at night, sleep deprivation and permanent bright light, threats alternated with promises, varieties of humiliation and intimidation to induce confusion, menaces to all lovers and family, the outright lie and the high-pitched sound, tickling the nose and beating the body, the solitary sweat box or the packed prison pit, standing for days in ice or shit, infestation by lice or rats, starvation and fifty-two kinds of beating, flaying and electric prodding, pouring water down throats until the stomach wall burst, tearing out fingernails and slow death by intestinal poisoning, these were some of the methods used to achieve a useless confession of errors. For there was no mercy or forgiveness in the Gulag system. The least 'crime' meant ten years' forced labour in Siberia without remission.

Solzhenitsyn quoted a statistical estimate that, from the Bolshevik October Revolution until 1959, some 66,000,000 lives were lost by internal repression. Yet these figures were unverifiable in this vast and uncatalogued slow massacre, which was used to colonize the cold eastern steppes. Who were these victims? The first were the millions of the enemies of the people, selected by Lenin and Trotsky and the commissars. The second were the 15,000,000 peasants removed as kulaks to the tundra. The third wave of the exiled were ethnically cleansed by Stalin, the Crimean Tartars and the Kalmuks and the Chechens, whose survivors would return to the Caucasus to haunt future Russian administrations.

After 1945, there were tens of millions of German and Japanese war prisoners to send away, also Russian prisonersp or émigrés taken and returned by the Allies, and Polish and Romanian and Hungarian and Balkan nationalists, who would oppose Communist governments in their own countries. The Finns in occupied Karelia were removed, also hundreds of thousands of the bourgeoisie from the Baltic territories. This was the largest and most brutal movement of population in recorded history.

The conditions in the labour camps of the far north-east were run on the Japanese rather than the Nazi model. The aim was to extract as much work as possible from the inmates before they died from malnutrition or disease or random cruelty. Gold had been discovered in the Kolyma area; the price of mining a tonne of the metal was some thousand dead; so each prisoner was worth a kilogram of the yellow stuff.

Timber was another product, although three weeks of logging was called by the starving sufferers a 'dry execution'. Hardly nourished or clothed, tens of millions simply froze to death. In the railway camp of Pechorlag, during the winter of 1941, four-fifths of the 50,000 prisoners died. And until one prisoner emerged, who could condemn the horror and the thirty-year massacre? All that was known of Stalin's terror was the admission, as in Newspeak, that 'certain errors were committed'.

32. THE FORCED REFUGEES

Just as Stalin and his successors hid the evidence of the Gulags for decades, so the first two examples of appalling ethnic cleansing in the twentieth century have been swept under the blanket of oblivion. The young Turkish nation eventually forged by Kemal Atatürk was responsible for both atrocities, the massacre by forced march of more than a million Christian Armenians – a ghastly reprise of the crusades – and the rape of Smyrna, now called İzmir. Because of the long necessity of keeping Turkey on the side of Western Europe against Russian expansion to the Mediterranean, the survivors of these hordes of refugees were ignored and almost forgotten.

In 1913, a Young Turk party led by a triumvirate pushed aside the last Ottoman sultan and declared a policy of extreme nationalism. An alliance with the Axis powers on the outbreak of the First World War allowed the Young Turks to devour the Christian pocket of Armenia in an advance on the Muslim Caucasus, then under Russian control. This revenge of Islam was cabinet policy. As one historian commented, 'The victims of twentieth-century premeditated genocide – the Jews, the gypsies, the Armenians – were murdered in order to fulfil the state's design for a new order.' The condition of war was used 'to transform the nation to correspond to the ruling elite's formula by eliminating the groups conceived as alien, enemies by definition.'

In an echo of the St Bartholomew's Day massacre in Renaissance Paris, hundreds of Armenian leaders in the Turkish capital were arrested on 23 April 1915, and put to death. Then the population of Armenia was commanded to be removed from the Black Sea to the Syrian desert.

> The whole of Asia Minor was put in motion. Armenians serving in the Ottoman armies had already been segregated into unarmed labour battalions and were now taken out in batches and murdered. Of the remaining population, the adult and teenage males were, as a pattern, swiftly separated from the deportation caravans and killed outright under the direction of Young Turk officials and agents, the gendarmerie, and bandit and nomadic groups prepared for the operation. The greatest torment was reserved for the women and children, who were driven for weeks over mountains and deserts, often dehumanized by being stripped naked and repeatedly preyed upon and abused. Many took their own lives and their children's lives by flinging themselves from cliffs and into rivers rather than prolonging their humiliation and torment. In this manner an entire nation melted away, and the Armenian people was effectively eliminated from its homeland of nearly three thousand years.

The German Embassy in Constantinople estimated that nearly 1,000,000 Armenians died; a third of the 845,000 survivors were forcibly converted to Islam. In another Young Turk invasion some 100,000 Armenians were killed, and more died in desert concentration camps. To the shame of Western diplomacy before the surrender of Turkey, nothing was done to preserve the remnants of this Christian and independent nation, in spite of the words of Lord Curzon:

> The Armenians, the most unhappy people in the world, have been broken by persecution, destroyed by massacre, almost battered out of existence, with only a few fragments remaining. The Imperial War Cabinet must realize the fact that a victory of the Germans and Turks in the region means, in all probability, the final extinction of that unhappy people. We

are bound by every tradition of our policy, and every pro-
nouncement of our leaders, to do what we can on their
behalf.

Although there were postwar proposals for a British occupation of Baku with its oil supplies, the collapse of the White Army
of General Denikin in 1920 and the triumph in the north-east of
Turkey by Kemal Atatürk and the revived Nationalist army led
to the Allied abandonment of the cause of an independent
Armenia. An agreement to partition the country produced a
temporary Turco-Russian pact in the Caucasus. In return for
arms supplies, Atatürk declared: 'Victory is to be accomplished
through the Bolsheviks.' An alliance between Islam and Communism crushed the last bastion of Christianity in the Near East,
outside the French protectorate of Lebanon. The Western powers
had not intervened in the expectation of detaching Atatürk from
any future alliance with the Kremlin. This cynical policy and the
barbarity of the Armenian democide were worse than any crusading horror practised in Asia Minor in early medieval times. The
scale of terror tactics had further increased.

Again, the Western powers provoked another atrocity at the
hands of the renascent Turks, who had lost their whole empire in
the Near East and were now threatened in their own homeland.
Both Italian and French warships had taken control of two ports
in western Turkey, while the British held the Dardanelles and had
battleships in the Bosphorus and the harbour of Smyrna. The
Greeks were encouraged in 1919 to take back Asia Minor, which
they had not held since the collapse of Byzantine Constantinople
five centuries before.

Quickly successful against the Turkish forces, the Greeks
pushed into Central Turkey and seized their old lands of Eastern
Thrace. A counterattack, however, by the Turkish Nationalist
armies drove the Greeks back on Smyrna two years later. And
as the power of Kemal Atatürk increased, so Greece found itself
abandoned by other European governments, now seeking to

ingratiate themselves with Atatürk, who even signed a Franco-British deal to exploit oil resources.

In their advance, the Turks repeated their strategy of horror against any Armenians or Greeks who were met on their way forward. Reports of massacres from the humanitarian Near East Relief Organization provoked indignation as far as New York, but no Western nation was prepared to fire a gun to defend the persecuted Christians. The ineffectual President of the United States, Warren G. Harding, mused: 'I am wondering whether the possible manifestation of our impotence would not be more humiliating than our non-participation is distressing.' All that was done was to send a couple of American warships into the bay of Smyrna, where a whole European multinational force lay at anchor.

The Turkish forces entered the city in battle formation as the Greek army fled, seeking evacuation. Before the looting and the burning began, particularly of the Armenian Quarter still in existence, the Greek Archbishop Chrysostomos had his eyes gouged out and his beard torn off, then his ears and nose and hands amputated. As he bled to death, French marines, standing by, failed to intervene.

The rape and burning of Smyrna now began, and except for the rundown Turkish Quarter, this city was totally ruined. One American witness thought that only the Roman destruction of Carthage could compare to the horror of this sight of cruelty and flame. 'Yet there was no fleet of Christian battleships at Carthage looking on at a situation for which their governments were responsible.' The Turks had been told that the European powers would not prevent them from doing their worst.

More indifference was to come. Except for the American destroyers, the Allied battle fleet refused to rescue the tens of thousands of refugees blocking the quays. Even a visit by Atatürk himself failed to stop the looting. Eventually, a truce for a fortnight was granted. British and Greek ships now began to evacuate the deportees. Nearly a quarter of a million people were taken off, mostly from Smyrna. A successful purge of the Greeks from northern Turkey and recaptured Eastern Thrace added to the misery. In makeshift camps, now housing over 1,000,000 people, the old epidemics of typhus and smallpox broke out to compound the general starvation.

After a final international settlement in late 1923, some 2,000,000 displaced persons were forced to migrate. Some 400,000 Muslims left Greece for Turkey, while the remainder including 100,000 Armenian survivors were returned to Greece, increasing its population by a third. Although these atrocities would never be forgotten by the two cleared peoples, the rest of the world laid aside these examples of race hatred in order to conciliate Turkey. Only Hitler profited from the lesson, declaring soon after the outbreak of the Second World War in 1939 to his High Command: 'Who, after all, speaks today of the annihilation of the Armenians? The world believes in success alone.'

Such an international silence also descended on the dreadful consequences of the partition of India. Paradoxically, as in Palestine under their mandate, the British occupation of India had prevented both separation and the outbreak of religious wars. Although imperial policy was always accused of dividing in order to rule, it was not responsible for the Muslim and Hindu and Sikh riots that broke out in the autumn of 1947 a year before independence was granted. As its arranger, Lord Mountbatten, reported on his arrival as the last Viceroy: 'The whole country is in a most unsettled state.' There were riots in the Punjab and the North-West Frontier Province, Bihar and Uttar Pradesh, Amritsar and Calcutta, Bombay and Benares 'and even here in Delhi'.

While civil disorder was breaking out, the British army and its supporting Indian Army regiments were the ultimate force of law and order. Yet as the Muslim leader, M. A. Jinnah, pressed for an independent Islamic state against the wishes of Pandit J. Nehru, who wanted a single secular India, even if dominated by a Hindu majority, the problem for Lord Mountbatten was to split the national regular forces along religious lines without provoking a civil war. Communal conflicts broke out, particularly in the Punjab, where rival Muslim and Hindu groups burned villages over fifty square miles, while the Sikhs inflicted a terrible vengeance on all their enemies. Troops were hardly sent in to quell the violence. The militant politician Sardar Patel observed that the British, however, had little difficulty in putting down Indian freedom movements.

A Punjab Boundary Force was formed from Indian Army regiments under a British major-general, T. W. Rees; but although it numbered 55,000 men in this early peace-keeping operation, it could do little to stop the mass migration of millions of the villagers into sympathetic religious areas. The local policemen were themselves split in the holy wars. As T. W. Rees reported:

> Communal bitterness was at a peak, and the masses were egged on and inflamed by shock-troops of resolute and well-armed men determined to fight ... Throughout, the killing was pre-medieval in its ferocity. Neither age nor sex was spared; mothers with babies in their arms were cut down, speared or shot. Both sides were equally merciless.

The civil terror before independence was granted now forced the partition of the subcontinent into Muslim Pakistan and modern India, which still retained a large Muslim population. With millions of refugees on the march, the greater slaughter took place on the rail carriages, packed with refugees, or the crawling road convoys of desperate people. The Punjab Boundary Force ceased to exist among the anarchy, although it had prevented many an atrocity. There was no counting of the casualties: later figures suggested between 200,000 and 1,000,000 men, women and children dead.

Sacred wars always release the worst in human revenge. The partition of a nation also induces the use of terror to frighten whole populations of heretics to flee across the new frontiers into a safe haven. In this division, however, as in Palestine, the unsettled boundaries of the largely Muslim Kashmir caused endless confrontations between the two emergent nations. The Maharajah of that state had ceded it to India, when a group of 5,000 tribal Muslim raiders invaded to take over Srinagar and the administration. Enough Indian troops were sent out to secure the city and its airport, and the battle lines were drawn for yet another partition, which would never be forgiven or forgotten.

33. THE PROBLEM OF
PALESTINE

In the foundation of Israel, terrorism was always a two-edged sword. Two of its future leaders had been terrorist leaders, and they would always have to speak with forked tongues when Palestinian and Islamic terrorist tactics were used against the new state. The paradox of the creation of Israel by the Balfour Declaration of 1917 from the ruins of the Ottoman Empire was that British policy would allow the free migration of dispossessed European Jews to their homeland under the mandate granted to the British Empire after the First World War. All the surrounding Islamic states were fabricated without regard to tribal boundaries, particularly Jordan, Syria and Lebanon, then under a French mandate, and Iraq and Iran. This splintering of Islam was a situation which had met the crusaders, when they first occupied the Holy Land, now being given back to the returning Jews, who would themselves cause a mass exodus of frightened refugees.

To plan a state is never to run a state. However much the British tried under their mandate for Palestine to reconcile Zionist and moderate Jewish opinion with Arab nationalism and the needs of the Muslims, there was no way to pacify the irreconcilable. Ruling ended friendship, administration bred enmity. As the military governor of Jerusalem, Ronald Storrs, declared, he was not wholly either for the Jews or the Arabs, but for both. 'Two hours of Arab grievances drive me to the synagogue,' he wrote, 'while after an intensive course of Zionist propaganda I am prepared to embrace Islam.'

The refusal of the British authorities immediately to allow a provisional Jewish government in Palestine led to the formation of the Hashomer, a clandestine defence force, arranged by Vladimir Jabotinsky, who had inspired the recruitment of the three battalions of the 'Jewish Legion', which had helped the British in the war to recapture the Holy Land. His campaign was aided by Arab raids against the Jewish settlements of Tel Hai and Metullah in Upper Galilee, where the pioneer farmer Trumpeldor was killed, followed by a riot against the Jews in Jerusalem. Nine Jews and Arabs were murdered, two hundred injured, synagogues burned. Jabotinsky tried to intervene during the riots with a hundred armed volunteers, but he was turned away and arrested and sentenced to penal servitude. On his release he resolved to form Haganah, a Jewish army ready to fight for a forthcoming state of Israel. He also organized with the young Menachem Begin the Polish youth movement Betar, in which the militants were drilled and learned to shoot.

The Arabs were also preparing for a future holy war. A secret group of militants named al-Fatah, or the 'Young Arabs', was started in Paris in 1911 and was transferred with French backing to Damascus to pursue its struggle against the British mandate and Zionism. This group later developed into an Arab National Congress. As in the crusades, the Christian powers were divided in their policies over the Holy Land. Alongside Jabotinsky was amnestied Haj Amin al-Husseini, who was fiercely opposed to both the British and the presence of the Jews in Palestine.

He was allowed to become Grand Mufti of Jerusalem, a position which he used to foment riots in the cause of Arab independence, especially when he and his associates took over a Supreme Muslim Council set up by the British administration. The Grand Mufti also headed the Muslim religious courts and controlled the Wakf, extensive religious endowments given by the faithful for the Islamic cause, whether peaceful or aggressive. He was an instigator of various attacks on the immigrants to Palestine. Forty-three Jews were murdered in 1921 in Jaffa, one hundred and fifty in another assault eight years later. The Grand Mufti eventually became a supporter of Hitler and his 'Final Solution'.

The riots provoked a British policy of stopping or slowing Jewish immigration, which was chiefly from Poland at that time. The High Commissioner declared that Britain could not have a second Ireland on its hands, another religious war of Catholics against Protestant immigrants. This policy turned the Zionists against the British, who had helped them so effectively back to their homeland. The Ashkenazi majority of the settlers from Europe was also anti-imperialist and loathed the British mandate; its ideology was chiefly socialist and the common languages were German and Yiddish with a future commitment to Hebrew.

Numbers on the soil and in the cities were essential, if the Jews wished to reduce the large Arab preponderance. Fortunately for them, Winston Churchill was appointed Colonial Secretary in 1921 and issued a White Paper the following year, defending British aims. His Majesty's government did not intend to create a wholly Jewish Palestine, which would become 'as Jewish as England is English'. The whole of the country would not be converted into a Jewish National Home, but 'such a home should be founded *in* Palestine'. The existing Jewish community should be developed where it was 'as of right and not on sufferance'. Churchill's wording seemed to imply a later partition of the Holy Land, for Jewish settlement was forbidden in Transjordan.

He did lift immigration restrictions; but the response was disappointing to the Zionists until the Great Depression and the rise of Fascism in Europe. In the twelve years after 1920 during a third and fourth wave of settlers, the average annual inflow into Palestine was 10,000 Jews, until they numbered one-sixth of the population; three-quarters lived in the cities and one-quarter on the land, where the socialist experiments in cooperative farming aided by a Labour Brigade were developing.

In the summer of 1929, the young Jews of the Betar organized a demonstration at the Western Wall, demanding free access and worship, and hoisting a Zionist flag. A week later, the Muslim crowds at prayer on Mount Moriah were told of a Jewish plot to destroy the al-Aqsa mosque and the Dome of the Rock in order to rebuild the Temple of Solomon. An orchestrated riot began with pogroms carried out by young Arabs in the Jewish Quarter in Jerusalem, in Hebron and in Safed and other towns; 140 Jews were killed, many more wounded. The only retaliation was in Jaffa, where an imam was killed by Betar members from Tel Aviv along with six more Arabs. British forces were sent into action and the riots were put down with the loss of more than 100 further Arab lives. Yet the mandate could not rule or bridge the religious divide.

The rise to power of Hitler in Germany and the beginning of the worst persecution of the Jews in history led to the floodgates opening for immigration. In the three years after 1932, 150,000 Jews entered Palestine; the following year, they numbered three in ten of the population. Arab opinion could easily be inflamed at such a sudden increase. Nazareth became the centre, not of worship of the birth of Christ, but of an underground movement led by a Syrian, Izzed Din al-Qassem, which sabotaged rail tracks and oil pipelines.

Equally, Haganah was being developed as a Jewish defence force, responsible for organizing illegal immigration and acquiring weapons for a future conflict. It was advised by an extraordinary young British officer, Orde Wingate; he put together 'night squads' for quick response and came to be called the Lawrence of Judaea. The Betar followed the path of al-Fatah and formed a group of militant secret cadres known as the Irgun Zvai Leumi, or the National Military Organization. The fuse and the powder were laid for a conflagration that only needed a spark.

Fresh anti-Jewish riots occurred in 1936 with the formation of the Arab Higher Committee under the leadership of the Grand Mufti, who called a general strike until Jewish immigration was suspended and a National Arab Government was instituted. The British sent in another division of troops; 1,000 Arabs fell in the subsequent civil strife, and 100 Jews. An investigating commission recognized the implacable hostility between the Zionists and the Arab nationalists, saying that 'neither community believes in its heart that it will be safe unless it is master in its home'. It recommended what Churchill had implied, the partition of Palestine into three parts, Jewish and Arab and a British mandate responsible to the League of Nations with a proposed jurisdiction similar to that of the last Kingdom of Jerusalem – an enclave including the Holy City and Bethlehem and Nazareth and stretching to the sea. A Pan-Arab Congress in Syria wholly rejected the proposal, which appeared to give 'the richest land to the Jews, the holiest to the English, the most barren to the Arabs'.

Before the outbreak of the Second World War in Europe, both religious groups in Palestine were preparing for a holy, as well as a civil, war. Jabotinsky kept on splitting the Zionists into revisionist or New Zionists. 'Zionism is a colonizing adventure,' he declared, 'and it therefore stands or falls by the question of armed force. It is important to build, it is important to speak Hebrew, but unfortunately, it is even more important to be able to shoot.' Such principles had inspired Joshua and the tribes of Israel. They must be revived. Judaea had fallen in blood and fire, according to Jabotinsky, and in fire and blood it would rise again.

After the outbreak of the Second World War, the Jews in Palestine were demoralized by the Nazi–Soviet non-aggression pact. Stalin was conducting purges of the Jews, particularly after Trotsky had been forced into exile. Many of the Ashkenazi immigrants, however, were nostalgic for the early socialism of their homeland before it was tainted by the horror of the Gulag, a civil genocide that was to exceed the Holocaust in the numbers of the dead. The alliance of the Communists with the Fascists to partition Poland was too cynical to excuse, while the consequences of that conspiracy were too dreadful to contemplate. The Ashkenazim were also imbued with German culture, and its perversion by the Nazis was another slow death to body and soul. Yet these European betrayals of the ideals of socialism and civilization were fuel to the Zionist fire in creating a new Israel, where the Jews could forge their own identity and community in the Levant.

With belligerent Europe even more dependent on their oil supplies, the Arabs saw their opportunity as well as their disability. Although Turkey was deterred from supporting Germany again, it exercised a benevolent neutrality, while certain nationalist Arabs such as the Grand Mufti and some politicians in Iran and Iraq saw the Italian and German advance on the Nile through North Africa as a chance of overthrowing the hated Anglo-French hegemony in the Middle East, as well as the artificial national boundaries imposed on the Near East.

Moreover, the Palestinian Arabs considered that they were suffering from Europe's sins against the Jews, whom Islam had generally treated with tolerance. The Germans were responsible for genocide, not them. The concentration camps and the policy of extermination, which was initiated by a cultured and officially Protestant power, carried the pogroms of the crusades into the nightmares of mass murder, far worse and more deliberate than the massacre perpetrated at the fall of Jerusalem. Yet this was the sin of Christianity against Judaism. Islam had nothing to do with it. Why then should Europe encourage the institution of a state of Israel in Palestine, where the Arabs had dwelt for more than a thousand years and still held a large majority? Europe appeared to be another Pilate, washing its hands of the murder of Christ's people by exporting its collective guilt into the Muslim world.

The first offer of forming a Jewish Brigade for the British forces in Egypt was refused. The situation, however, was ambiguous, because by the end of 1940 there were 15,000 armed Jews who were officially forming the Jewish Settlement Police, but also unofficially members of Haganah. Yet the underground movements, the Irgun and the more extreme Stern Gang (Lohamey Heruth Israel, or Fighters for the Freedom of Israel), were beginning reprisals against the Arabs and attacks on British military bases. Although Jewish commandos were used in an attempt to quell rebellion in Iraq, the raid failed. Eventually the British did recruit 26,000 Palestinian Jews and 9,000 Palestinian Arabs into their armed forces.

The Grand Mufti, now deposed, was also recruiting from his headquarters in Berlin. Although Lord Moyne was assassinated in Cairo by Zionist terrorists in 1944, under American pressure Churchill accepted a plan that the serving Jews should be able to sew the Star of David on their tunics. Their religious fight against Fascism was recognized by that symbolic action, and in the closing months of the world war, a Jewish Brigade of 5,000 men was formed at last.

Hitler had tried to exterminate all the Jews in Europe in the Holocaust. Nearly 1,500,000 survivors, some from the concentration camps of Auschwitz and Belsen and Buchenwald and Treblinka, had only one sure refuge left in a murderous continent. Outside the safe havens of America and Britain, they had suffered unspeakably in Christian Europe, usually handed over to Nazi annihilation. When the emerging Jewish leader, David Ben-Gurion, was asked by a United Nations special committee why the Haganah was encouraging illegal immigration into Palestine, he pointed to what the British had done at Dunkirk. They had saved their expeditionary force in small boats, turning a military disaster into a moral triumph. 'We suffered a greater disaster in Europe than the British army,' Ben-Gurion said. 'Not a few thousands, not tens of thousands, but millions – six million were put to death. Can anybody realize what that means to us?'

The Jews had expected the Labour government, after its mammoth triumph against Winston Churchill in 1945, to be even more sympathetic to the formation of a state of Israel than the great British war leader had been. They were cruelly deceived. The Foreign Secretary, Ernest Bevin, had been a union chief, but he was no Zionist. Relationships with America and Russia and the Arab oil states were more important to him than with the Jews, whom he bluntly said were not at the head of the queue. Old hulks crammed with Jewish refugees from Europe were turned back by the Royal Navy; the passengers once again ended up in camps in West Germany, now under Allied military occupation. With this rejection, the Zionists won their Dunkirk. The refugee odyssey gave them a moral victory that could no longer prevent free immigration to Palestine, which was rapidly descending into chaos and civil strife and becoming what Arthur Koestler called 'John Bull's other Ireland'.

As the British dragged their feet over creating a Jewish homeland, Ben-Gurion swung into action in Palestine. The Palmach, the commando wing of the Haganah, cooperated with the terrorist Irgun in a series of attacks on British air force bases, military camps, port installations, and even the Tel Aviv radio station. As Jewish militance increased, so did British repression. Twenty-seven hundred Jewish leaders were interned for some months after a massive snatch by British intelligence. The reprisal was the Irgun's bomb explosion at the King David Hotel in Jerusalem, where ninety-one lives were lost, Jews and Arabs among the British. The revulsion from this atrocity polarized the enmity between the Zionists and the Labour government in London, which now had less stomach for supporting a disintegrating situation without much strategic importance. There were no oil wells in the Promised Land. Bevin announced in the House of Commons that the problem would be submitted to the United Nations, which would give its decision.

On 31 August 1947, a Special Committee on Palestine published its report, recommending that the British mandate should be ended within a year, that Palestine should be partitioned into sovereign Arab and Jewish democratic states, that the rights and interests of all minorities should be protected, that the two independent bodies should unite economically, and that the city of Jerusalem itself should become a demilitarized and neutral zone, while both new states guaranteed the protection of all holy places and freedom of conscience and worship. The Jewish state was to include western Galilee, the coastal plain, and the Negev down to the Red Sea, while Arab Palestine would incorporate the rest of the country outside international Jerusalem. In spite of Arab opposition, the report of the Special Committee was passed by the United Nations to create the State of Israel.

The Arab states, however, would have nothing to do with the partition proposals. They would only accept a plebiscite in a single Palestine, which would lead to an Arab majority governing a Jewish minority. And as for the Jews, they had lost their primary reason for coming home to Israel – Jerusalem, which was to be administered by an international trustee who was neither an Arab nor a Jew.

The British government did not approve of the United Nations' resolution, but it declared that it would evacuate Palestine in due time. The interim of the mandate became a vacuum with the British forces hardly able to enforce their authority and staying out of the crossfire between the emergent Jewish and Arab armed groups, preparing for the inevitable battle for the land. 'If troubles begin,' the last British High Commissioner told Ben-Gurion, 'I fear that we shall not be able to help you. We shall not be able to defend you.' The Haganah could protect the coastal strip around Tel Aviv, but it was difficult to assist the majority Jewish population of Jerusalem, particularly those in the Old City.

Here the outrages started, two explosions which destroyed the *Palestine Post* building and the commercial centre of the New City, Ben Yehuda Street, with the loss of fifty-three lives. The Zionists accused the British of responsibility, denied by them and the Arabs. The Irgun and the Stern Gang then executed ten British soldiers, followed by the horrific slaughter of the Arab village of Deir Yassin beside the Jaffa road. Two hundred and fifty men and women and children were killed and mutilated in a ghastly reprise of what the Nazis had done to the Jews at Lidice and other European villages. This calculated massacre was a deliberate instrument of terror, aimed at making the Palestinian

Arabs flee from Jaffa and Judaea, although they hoped to return behind the advancing Arab regular armies from the south and the east.

In the end, 650,000 Palestinian Arabs became refugees; only a quarter of that number stayed where they were. Deir Yassin was the worst atrocity of the struggle for Palestine, and it provided the Arabs with propaganda for decades to come, especially when the terrorist leaders Menachem Begin and Yitzhak Shamir became Prime Ministers of Israel. The Irgun and the Stern Gang, however, seemed to most moderate Jews, such as the later military governor of Jerusalem, Dov Joseph, 'dagger men who believed in "the holy lie" and "the holy murder".'

The former Grand Mufti had now reached Cairo and still preached jihad for the recovery of Jerusalem. Yet what would save the nascent state of Israel was what had saved the Kingdom of Jerusalem for two centuries, the divisions among the Islamic countries. The Arab Legion of King Abdullah of Transjordan, with its British officers, was certainly the most efficient fighting force ranged against the Haganah, and the King intended to expand his influence into Palestine and Jerusalem. This policy put him at odds with the former Grand Mufti, who was supported by Egypt and Syria, and whose family was a powerful clan in Jerusalem, probably responsible for the retaliatory attack known as the Hadassah massacre, when seventy-seven doctors and university teachers, nurses and patients were killed in a convoy from the Hebrew University and hospital on Mount Scopus.

Abdullah was responsible for no atrocities with his well-disciplined forces, although he did declare to his troops: 'It is our duty to join in the holy war, a war in which the neighbouring Arab states will participate.' In fact, only Iraq and Lebanon joined Egypt and Syria in the fighting: Saudi Arabia sent one company of soldiers. Yet such were the potential numerical odds against Israel that the British Field Marshal Montgomery said that the Arabs would 'hit the Jews for six' and push them into the Mediterranean.

The reverse was the truth. The Haganah prevailed everywhere, especially on the old crusader battlegrounds. Haifa was taken, along with Safed and Jaffa and Acre. The road was opened to Tiberias and eastern Galilee. The exception was the Old City of Jerusalem, which proved indefensible after the intervention of the Arab Legion. The Jewish garrison had to surrender to the Jordanian troops, on the pledge of a safe conduct for the whole Jewish population to the new Jerusalem of the western city suburbs, still held by the Haganah.

The terms were scrupulously observed by the Muslim troops, and none of the Jews was harmed in the evacuation. The Holy City passed back under Muslim control. King Abdullah was its effective ruler along with the areas west of the Jordan River occupied by his soldiers. After the breakdown of the first truce between the opposing Jewish and Arab forces, the troops in the Haganah secured the corridor from Jerusalem to the sea, as the crusaders had once done. They took Lydda and Ramleh and Nazareth, where the Israeli soldiers were strictly ordered to refrain from doing any damage to the Christian holy places. They eventually advanced to Beersheba, incorporating four-fifths of the area of the previous Palestine.

They failed to recapture the Old City, although the Haganah twice broke through the Jaffa Gate and established a bridgehead at the New Gate, but there was no dislodging of the Arab Legion from its control of the rest of Jerusalem before a final ceasefire and armistice with the five hostile Arab nations, which still refused to end their declared state of holy war. They and the Arab League, however, did give up supporting the former Grand Mufti with his shadow government of Palestine, and they recognized the result of the fighting. The territories which Jordan had annexed, including the Old City of Jerusalem, were to remain 'a trust in its hands until the Palestine case is finally solved in the interests of its inhabitants'.

The mediator for the United Nations, Count Folke Bernadotte, had his own plans for the partition of Palestine, later

posthumously published in his book, *To Jerusalem*. He asked the
French Foreign Minister, Georges Bidault, whether his country
would agree to Jerusalem as an Arab centre. Bidault replied that
such an action would make the whole Christian world join in a
new crusade. A similar suggestion to the provisional government
of the state of Israel provoked another sharp response to such a
'disastrous' scheme which ignored the past.

Faced with this implacable opposition, Bernadotte returned
to old proposals for the whole of Jerusalem to be placed 'under
effective United Nations control, with maximum feasible local
autonomy for its Arab and Jewish communities and safeguards
for access to the Holy Places'. The Stern Gang demonstrated
against the Swedish count's presence with posters declaring,
Stockholm Is Yours; Jerusalem Is Ours. Then he was assassinated
in the Holy City, and the mediation came to an end. His killers
were never brought to book. What had been won by the gun in
Jerusalem remained in the hands of the victors, with the Holy
City partitioned between Jew and Muslim, as Berlin and Vienna
were divided between the occupying Allied powers. Any lasting
peace was murdered with Bernadotte.

So the creation of the new Israel began with murder and
terrorism, and ended with assassination. None of the lessons of
the crusades had been learned. Surrounded by Arab kingdoms
partitioned by European diplomacy, Israel would continue to use
the strategy of the Christian kingdom of Jerusalem, so vastly
outnumbered by the forces of Islam. Such tactics were reprisals
and sudden attacks by the new military knights in armour, the
tank brigades, also cross-border raids and killings carried out
by various secret and intelligence services. These had always
been the necessary weapons of the few against the many. Small
wonder that their frequent use would provoke a continuing jihad
against the very existence of Israel, which intended to endure for
longer than the old and lost Christian foothold in the Near East.

34. THE KILLING FIELDS
OF ASIA

'The poor want to remake their lives. The old system is dying. Chicken feathers really are flying up to heaven. In the Soviet Union they have already got there. In China they have started their flight.' So Mao Zedong announced in 1955 the beginning of his revolution in China, after his defeat of the Kuomintang, who were thereafter confined to Taiwan. As the first total metamorphosis since the Mongols, who had fought from the steppes to the cities, Mao had won with the support of the peasants as well as the Chinese workers. He used land redistribution to eliminate the old proprietors and warlords. Marxist cadres were established in their hundreds of thousands to empower the peasants; some 100,000,000 rural workers were given smallholdings in land they had never owned. What Chairman Mao did not tell them was that they were part of a continuous process, which would end in Stalin's collective farms, now to be called rural communes.

As well as being a guerrilla of genius, Mao was something of a poet and an intellectual, who had read Western history and philosophy, although he preferred Napoleon to Robespierre. He had been taught the values of the never-ending revolution, in order to keep one's own house clean. In a dictatorship of the proletariat when he was the sole dictator, he would brook no rivals any more than Cesare Borgia or Hitler. As he declared in 1968: 'It is not that the social struggle is a reflection of the Party Central Committee. Rather the struggle within the Party Central Committee is a reflection of the social struggle.'

Mao went on to comment that the task of the revolution was never completed, as it was not yet determined 'who, in the end, will overthrow whom'. When he unleashed his tens of millions of young Red Guards on China, their task was as much to cow all opposition to Mao within the Party as to collectivize Chinese agriculture through forced labour. Mao thought that only men bestowed rights on other men. The rights of the Party were given by the people, mainly the workers and poor peasants.

In more defiance of French doctrine, Mao declared that liberty was the understanding of the necessity of obeying his orders, which expressed the People's Will, which should replace the word 'fear' with the word 'dare'. 'Either the East Wind prevails over the West Wind or the West Wind prevails over the East Wind, and there is absolutely no such thing as equality.'

The loosing of the Red Guards was calculated to purge all the opponents of the tyrant who ruled China. In 1965, Mao had made his intentions most clear in a poem:

> Seize the day, seize the hour! . . .
> Away with all pests!
> Our force is irresistible.

He had refused his generals' wish to support the Vietnamese in their struggle against what was seen as American imperialism after French colonialism. In a tacit understanding with the United States, the knowledge that Mao would not aid the Vietcong – and indeed might have a border war with Vietnam – made large-scale American intervention possible. There would be no repetition of the American-led invasion of North Korea, when the Red Chinese armies had poured across the borders of Manchuria. So Mao was free to cleanse China along with his youthful revolutionaries.

Mao denounced his opponents in the Party, whom he said were conducting a 'White Terror'. As the Party magazine, the *Red Flag*, said of his teenage storm troopers, they were using Mao's thought to condemn and reform the country, 'to wipe out completely the old ideologies, culture, customs and habits accumulated over thousands of years'. They wanted to turn the old world upside down and to build a new world. 'Is this fanaticism? No, it is not. It is earth-shaking revolutionary ambition.'

In the early stages of the Cultural Revolution, the various bands of the Red Guards arrested and looted and tortured and humiliated some 40,000 'reactionaries', whom they thought represented the Old Guard of the Party. In his New Year's Day proclamation of 1967, Mao incited further violence against 'monsters and demons anywhere in society', not only in offices and schools, but in factories and mines and the rural areas. The result was national chaos along with civil and economic disruption.

Out of control, millions of Red Guard bands even began fighting the regular Red Army. In a battle in the Yunnan provincial capital of Kunming, there were 1,300 casualties. The British legation in Beijing was burned to the ground, while Red Guards even occupied the Chinese Foreign Ministry. This was the beginning of the end of the internal revolution, which had removed tens of millions of urban officials and their families to forced labour on the slow killing fields of the rural communes. The Red Guards had acted according to Mao's principle: 'If cadres do not participate in labour, they inevitably must become divorced from the labouring masses and revisionism must inevitably arise.' Actually, Mao was repeating the 'Terror' of Robespierre and the Jacobins, who had revelled in the humiliation of the educated and the comfortable.

Mao was now forced by his Red Army to purge the forces he had unleashed, and to make them the scapegoats for his Cultural Revolution. They were accused of crimes against the state. They had used Mao as their figurehead, and they were harshly condemned for their errors. The army supported Lin Piao, now declared Mao's successor, and he explained the turn-around as the failure of the Red Guards, who had represented the Chairman's 'revolutionary successors', but had become a 'reactionary evil wind', blowing out of control. Thus Mao had to return to the true support of the working class to arouse the masses and strike down the bad people who had gone wild.

In the classic pattern of atrocity and radical violence, the ageing Mao had called up the forces of vengeance and then destroyed them in order to prove that he still held all the reins of power. Paradoxically, his Machiavellian use of tyranny was the inspiration for the freedom revolts of 1968 across the cities of most of the world. The apparent official complicity in Chinese youth attacking their elders and betters was cocaine to the restless students in the United States and Britain and Europe, so that governments trembled at their onslaught. *The Little Red Book* of Mao, indeed, was a bestseller among the insurrectionaries of the West.

The failure of the urban revolts of Europe made the new Left look to the example of Mao and Castro and currently the Vietcong. Régis Debray, imprisoned during Che Guevara's campaign in Bolivia, had come out in 1967 in his *Revolution in the Revolution?* with the *foco* theory, using Cuba particularly as an example. The establishment and uninterrupted development of a guerrilla *foco* in the countryside was the key to the revolutionary process. First, it attracted peasants to the cause; secondly, it defeated scattered government forces; thirdly, it drew support from the towns; finally, it took over the capital by infiltration as well as attack.

The book was written before Guevara's disastrous attempt to create a *foco* in Bolivia. Yet the successful Cuban example under Castro and the struggle of the Vietcong from the jungle towards Saigon were magnets for these radical activists. They were moving more and more towards guerrilla acts of sporadic violence from motivated cells or groupuscules set against the power of the capitalist state.

For the United States with its disastrous intervention in Vietnam, television defeated involvement. The rise of the pervasive media in a democracy, which enshrined the right to free speech, demonstrated to an appalled public the terror tactics needed to win a jungle war. A photograph of a naked little girl, running along a road and stripped by the blast from the bombardment of a village, shocked America. Then the reports of Lieutenant William L. Calley's massacre of the population of the hamlet of My Lai recalled Lidice and Nazi atrocity. Scalping and spitting stomachs, rape and sodomy, had been part of Charlie Company's slaughter of the 500 old men and women, children and babies. In his memoir, *Body Count*, Calley showed no more remorse than had the militia attackers of the nineteenth century on Red Indian villages:

> Our mission in My Lai wasn't perverted, though. It was simply 'Go and destroy it'. Remember the Bible: The Amalikites? God said to Saul, 'Now go . . . and utterly destroy all that they have, and spare them not; but slay both man and woman, infant and suckling, ox and sheep, camel and ass'.

At their later trials, the perpetrators of the horror of My Lai claimed that they were only obeying orders, as Eichmann had at his trial in Israel. Calley was sentenced to life imprisonment, but he was paroled after seven years, three under house arrest. A country-and-western song about him as a wronged hero, set to the tune of 'The Battle Hymn of the Republic', sold a million records within a week. Reprisal had its appeal in the Southern states.

The ideological conclusion of the violence and terror inflicted by Mao in his country, and the Vietcong and the Americans during the Vietnam War would be carried to its ultimate dreadful conclusion by Pol Pot in Cambodia, the Kurtz of Conrad's nightmare. Indeed, the film of the atrocious madness in Vietnam, *Apocalypse Now*, would culminate in Marlon Brando pronouncing the words, 'The horror! The horror!' So it was in the conquest of Cambodia by the Khmer Rouge, also pushing from the jungle towards their capital city of Phnom Penh, which in 1975 was occupied. So began the genocide of urban dwellers by radical peasants, copied from Robespierre's Terror, also from the frenzies of Stalin and Mao. Pol Pot's regime took to the extreme the rule of fear and torment. A fanatical Marxist, he denied his teacher's contempt for 'the idiocy of rural life' by driving out 2,000,000 citizens from Phnom Penh to be worked and beaten to death in the killing fields of rice production. Only half of these forced labourers survived the next three years, until an invasion from Vietnam sent Pol Pot's movement, the Khmer Rouge, fleeing to jungle guerrilla warfare on the borders of Thailand.

There were only seven survivors of the 20,000 victims consigned to the confessional torture school, S21, in the evacuated capital. No such pyramids of skulls had been heaped up in human history since the assaults of Genghis Khan and the Mongols on the cities of Central Asia. Picturing himself as kind and caring, Pol Pot was an atavistic monster in the name of the leading materialist cult of the modern age. The Vietnamese incursion, leading to a quasi-democratic regime in Cambodia, revealed the weakness of terrorism and mass murder. The fearful survivors in Cambodia wanted no more of the Khmer Rouge. There was a rebellion against them by the frightened people, who would rather lead their own peaceful lives than suffer any more for ideological dreams. Terror is its own indictment. As Mao had said, 'The relationship between the party and the masses is comparable to that between fish and water.' In this case, the sea rejected the sharks.

35. GUEVARA:
SWIMMING IN A DRY SEA

In the South American guerrilla wars, Mao would be proved right: if one was a rebel or a piranha, one needed an Amazon of sympathy to swim in. The peasants had to be won over, not terrified, or they would provide no support. The icon of the freedom fighters, as they came to be known, was Che Guevara. His success and his failure redefined the strategy of revolt.

After an initial disaster on landing with eighty-two rebels from the yacht *Granma* in 1956 on the Cuban coast, Fidel Castro's guerrillas were reduced to a dozen men. Che Guevara fled with seven other comrades to the Sierra Maestra mountains. They were totally dependent on the local people, for they had committed no atrocities, unlike the dictator Batista's armed forces. A few peasants joined the rebellion, although most of the rural population was sitting on the fence, waiting for success. As Che Guevara wrote in his classic *Guerrilla Warfare*, 'In that period, it was very difficult to enlarge our group; a few men came, but others left; the physical conditions of the struggle were very harsh, but the problems of morale even more so.'

The months in the Sierra Maestra taught the guerrillas that their dependence on peasant support was based as much on calculation as idealism. Che's memoirs of the Cuban War are full of accounts of executions of rural informers, denounced by other peasants. The rebel force would protect its friends and neutrals and treat them fairly, but it was ruthless towards anyone who aided Batista's men. In many areas of the Sierra Maestra, it was eventually more dangerous to help the government than to help the rebels, in contrast to the later war in Bolivia, when Che was perpetually betrayed by Indians whom he could not control or terrorize into silence.

In the Cuban War, however, Che noted of the peasants: 'denouncing us did violence to their own conscience and, in any case, put them in danger, since revolutionary justice was speedy.' He discovered a cold ruthlessness in his nature. Spilling blood was necessary for the cause. Within two years he had ordered the death of several hundred Batista partisans at La Cabaña, one of the mass killings of the Cuban revolution. And after the failed Bay of Pigs invasion, all the captured Cuban exile leaders were shot.

Such contact with the peasants profoundly affected Che's whole theory of revolutionary strategy. Direct and personal experience in the Sierra Maestra informed the fundamental statements with which he began *Guerrilla Warfare*. 'In the under-developed countries of the Americas, rural areas are the best battlefields for revolution.' Moreover, he insisted that 'the guerrilla makes agrarian reform his banner.' Che and his fellow Cuban revolutionaries emphasized later that they were not indebted to Mao Zedong's theories on peasant warfare, stressing they had not even read his writings or others of the same kind. Direct experience was always Che's best teacher.

One other lesson was learned in the early days of the war. Castro insisted on his troops behaving as humanely as possible towards wounded enemy soldiers, prisoners, civilians and peas-ants who did not collaborate with the enemy. The result was that the reputation of the guerrillas grew in contrast to the general brutalities practised by Batista's men, whose cruelty in putting down a student plot in Havana brought new and essential help to the thirty men of the guerrilla force. A campaign of terror by the army in the Sierra Maestra had begun to shake the sympathy of the peasants, but now fifty new recruits from the cities joined the guerrillas.

The rebel band had begun a period of continuous growth, which created new problems with food and supplies. The second phase of the Cuban War had started, with the guerrillas settled in semi-permanent encampments. There they formed service and supply sections, becoming a government in miniature. Small industries, radio stations and hospitals were established, laws were decreed, justice was administered through courts and an intensive campaign of indoctrination was set in motion. Castro's forces had, to all intents and purposes, converted themselves into something approaching a regular army bivouacking in friendly territory. They were fish swimming in a welcoming sea.

Che's own 'long march' through the island at the end of Castro's winning campaign, which cut the island in two, confirmed his prejudices against the value of urban action. For he liberated the towns from the mountains. He cut off communications between the cities, and thus isolated and finally seized Santa Clara and an armoured train. His own experience was of setting up a rural base, of expanding until towns fell into his hands, of isolating cities until they also fell. To Che, the country had to liberate the city.

Urban centres had to be conquered from without, not from within. The Sierra campaign and the defeatist attitude of the Cuban Communist Party gave Che a strong bias against the Marxist-Leninist dogma of a rising led by the urban proletariat through a series of strikes, through sabotage and through a final revolt. The armed peasants could conquer the countryside until the cities tumbled like rotten bananas into their laps. This was the experience which was to lead Che into geographical isolation and death in Bolivia.

By the time that Fidel Castro's provisional government took over from Batista in January 1959, Che was a proven guerrilla fighter of great courage, power and ability. Now one of the leading figures in the new Cuba, he would soon be looked upon as the most important theorist of the revolution. His job was to put together 'in a systematic and coherent fashion' an ideology from the multitude of contradictory theories proliferating in Cuba in the wake of Castro's victory.

The Cuban War forged Che politically and ideologically. His contact with the peasants turned him into an 'agrarian revolutionary'. The near unanimity of the opposition to Batista's tyranny in the later stages of the struggle made him think in terms of a 'people's war'. The part played by the United States, which aided and supported Batista during most of the struggle, confirmed Che's hatred of 'Yankee imperialism'. From his own experience of guerrilla combat, Che applied maxims to cover most military strategy and the possibility of world revolution. Two recurrent themes in his *Episodes of the Cuban Revolutionary War* were the basis for all his future thinking.

First, actual combat was the best way of learning to be a guerrilla fighter. No amount of theory could make a good fighter. Only the experience of a revolutionary war itself could sort out the true *guerrillero* from the dreamer or latent traitor. Secondly, actual combat forged a believer as well as a fighter. A man might join the guerrilla group totally ignorant of ideology. His social conscience as a revolutionary must develop hand in hand with his military skill, as combat experience alone would never carry him through the hardships of a guerrilla war. Logically, therefore, the best fighter was also the most political man, and he was more fit than anyone else to become a leader after the war was won, being more realistic and revolutionary than anyone who had not fought.

Che's writings on guerrilla warfare were truly revolutionary. They outlined how a rising by a few men might win against the forces of modern armies and technology. Minimal resources, little initial popular support and poor communications were no reason not to begin an insurrection, which could pin down a regular army while gaining new recruits every day. Atom bombs were little use in putting down jungle guerrillas; tanks could not operate in forests and mountains. The success of the Cuban attempt inflamed many others; its influence was global. From

Vietnam to Afghanistan, Che's theories on guerrilla warfare held or defeated modern armies which were equipped to crush anything except this form of fighting.

The fact that the Cuban revolutionaries won without the support of the Cuban Communist Party, and the fact that they won long before they themselves turned to Communism as an ideology, accounted for the chief unorthodoxy of Che's writings. Even the Chinese had never dared to put forward such a heresy. For Che's Cuban experience made him preach the autonomy of the guerrilla group *outside* the central control of the monolithic Communist parties, usually based in the cities. The leaders of the Communist Party of Cuba had not risked everything, nor had the political exiles, nor the democratic groups which opposed Batista. Therefore, they did not deserve to lead the new Cuba. They only deserved to serve under those who had actually won the victory with their blood and sweat and sacrifice.

What made Che's *Guerrilla Warfare* extraordinary was his moral position against the tactics of terror, which only should be used when necessary and must fall short of atrocity for fear of antagonizing the people. If the rebels were too ferocious, they would lose the sea in which they were swimming. The collectivization of the land into rural communes as in China must come after the seizure of power, which Castro accomplished in 1959 by capturing Havana, the island capital.

Indeed, the first measure of the new administration was a law for Agrarian Reform, nationalizing the land for state farms and collectives, although the small farmers, whom Stalin had called kulaks, were still left in charge of their properties, to be dealt with later. This change ushered in the concept of a class struggle, dividing Cuba into two camps. On the one side were the landowners; on the other side were the landless peasants, now supported by the urban workers, who had little property themselves.

Che Guevara now switched his support from the peasants to the city workers as the vanguard of the proletariat. His altered emphasis as the new Minister of Industry seemed cynical. When he had needed the support of the peasants, he had called for their self-denial and backed agrarian reform. But when he needed the urban workers more than the peasants, he called for their self-denial in the name of industrial growth. During the first stage, hatred of the landowners forged a bond between the guerrillas and the peasants; during the second stage, the bourgeoisie was attacked in order to appease the workers. In both cases, the theory and the ideology seemed to be justifications of realpolitik; the success of the revolutionary dictatorship under Castro was paramount.

Che Guevara gradually became disgusted by his role in Cuba, where he appeared as the Trotsky supporting world revolution against Castro's Stalin. Now 15,000 subversives were contained within concentration camps, while hundreds of thousands of exiles fled to the United States. Their failed return at the disaster of the US-backed Bay of Pigs expedition merely increased the atmosphere of terror and repression. Che's vision of an artistic and democratic renaissance was doomed. He left Cuba in 1965 to become a permanent wandering freedom fighter, preoccupied with extending the war against imperialism to Latin America and the whole planet.

Some thousand Cubans were killed in the ten years after their victory against Batista, while they were engaged in revolutions abroad. Che led several of his old comrades from the Sierra Maestra to fight in the savage wars of the Congo. After the killing of Patrice Lumumba in 1961, there had been sporadic rebellions there to seize power from the European mining interests which controlled the new governments. These finally resulted in the dictatorship of Sese Seko Mobutu. Secession failed in Katanga, and the revolution was continued by groups in the east operating from Rwanda and Burundi under a Committee of National Liberation – one of its members, Laurent Kabila, used that same base for a successful conquest of the Congo thirty years later.

In the west, Pierre Mulele was fighting: he had been Lumumba's Minister of Education and ended in pieces, fed to the crocodiles of the River Congo. By the time Che arrived, Belgian and South African mercenary units had already defeated and contained both the eastern and western independence movements. They had been squashing their enemies like lice, unforgivable in their brutality, even executing their black prisoners for the benefit of an Italian camera crew.

Che could hardly see the futility of his chosen guerrilla role in Africa, although President Gamal Abdel Nasser in Egypt had told him that his efforts to command African troops would make him look like Tarzan. In March 1965, with 130 black Cuban troops and pilots, Che disappeared for a year from Havana on his secret expedition to Central Africa. Working with Kabila's forces in Rwanda and the Congo, he taught them some military skills and medicine, only to find that they believed in *dawa*, a magic potion blessed by witchdoctors that deflected bullets. They also ate their enemies from time to time, in order to increase their courage.

Che realized that he was trying to swim in a witches' cauldron and not a warm sea. He knew he could contribute little to the African liberation movements, noting in his journal, 'The main defect of the Congolese is that they don't know how to shoot.' His own Cuban followers also fell ill and were badly disciplined. Under assaults from the South African mercenaries, Che's Congolese troops ran away, and the morale of his Cuban special force was shattered. In November 1965, he was forced to retreat on an evacuation fleet of small boats across Lake Tanganyika. He emerged, as he wrote, believing more than ever in guerrilla warfare; 'but we failed'.

His lack of success did not make Che Guevara learn his lesson. Whatever his ideology, he appeared to the African tribal warriors as just another mercenary, as the 'Arabs' in al-Qaeda seemed to be foreign invaders later in Afghanistan instead of Islamic revolutionaries. Che was not wanted; the Congo was no tepid bath. Yet he himself soon left for Bolivia to begin a war that he hoped would liberate Argentina and the whole of his continent from the rule of imperialism. He wanted to be the new

Bolívar and be even more successful than the Great Liberator had been. Not only would he expel the power of imperialism, but he would also unite Latin America in a socialist bloc.

While he was still preparing his last rebellion, Che sent back to Cuba a summary of a philosophy gained by spending so long in fighting for the poor peoples of the earth. He began by asking if there really had been twenty-one years of relative peace after the end of the Second World War. The struggle in Vietnam, for instance, had been continuing for nearly thirty years, while the people there had fought three imperialist powers in turn – Japan, France and the United States. The Vietnamese were still suffering the bombing and escalation of the war by the Americans, who were guilty of aggression.

What could the Third World countries do, if the threat of an atomic world war caused a stalemate between the advanced Communist and capitalist countries, and permitted the genocide in Vietnam? Che's answer was that the threat should be ignored. 'Since imperialists blackmail humanity by threatening it with war, the wise reaction is not to fear war.' Latin America, Africa and Asia must liberate themselves at any price. In Asia and Africa, a continental revolution was delayed; but in Latin America it had already begun from its focal points in the guerrilla groups operating in Guatemala, Colombia, Venezuela, Peru and Bolivia.

If these focal points were to become real battle-grounds, then the United States would be forced to intervene with modern weapons and to commit its regular troops. This was the way to help the Vietnamese struggle and to humble the United States.

It is the road of Vietnam; it is the road that should be followed by the people; it is the road that will be followed in Our America. The Cuban Revolution will today have the job of creating a Second or the Third Vietnam of the world.

These battles shall not be mere street fights with stones against tear-gas bombs, or pacific general strikes; neither shall the battle be that of a furious people destroying in two

or three days the repressive scaffolds of the ruling oligar-
chies; the struggle shall be long and harsh, and its front shall
be in the guerrillas' hide-out, in the cities, in the homes of
the fighters . . . in the massacred rural population, in the
villages and cities destroyed by the bombardments of the
enemy.

The only way to help Vietnam was to wage total war on the
North Americans. No Yankee soldier should feel safe in his
quarters, in the cinema, on the town. He had to be made to feel
like a cornered beast, and, as he behaved more and more like a
beast, so his decadence would provoke his own downfall. Such
would be the creed of the al-Qaeda terrorists.

All must fight together in a true proletarian internationalism.
To die under the flag of Vietnam or Venezuela or Guinea or
Bolivia would be 'equally glorious and desirable for an American,
an Asian, an African or even a European'. By fighting and dying
to liberate another's country, each man was helping to liberate
his own. Che's fate as a martyr in Bolivia, where he failed his
own tests of a successful insurrection, elevated him to the status
of an icon as well as a quasi-saint. With thirty guerrillas, only a
few of them local Indians, he was bound to die.

Che and the other group leaders were Cubans, while revolution in Latin America had always had a strong nationalistic
streak. There was friction within the guerrillas between the
Cubans and their Bolivian comrades, while the Indians not only
distrusted the Cubans as foreigners, but also as another lot of
lying white men. Bolivia had already had a land reform during its
previous left-wing regime. The Bolivian Indians might be miser-
ably poor, but they did own their own barren soil for the first
time in 300 years, and an acre in the hand was worth any utopia
in the bush.

Che's total failure to recruit one single peasant to the cause
during his eleven months of preparation and fighting was the
basic cause of his defeat. As he had stated in *Guerrilla Warfare*,

the fundamental reason for the success in Cuba had been the aid of the peasants in the Sierra Maestra. 'To try and carry out this kind of war without the support of the population is the prelude to inevitable disaster.'

Other factors doomed the guerrillas' campaign. Isolation was the worst blow. The middle-class sympathizers in the large cities were soon betrayed by three of the weaker guerrillas, who defected. Parallel risings in Peru and other Latin American countries fizzled out, through a failure of nerve and communications. Che could not now bring himself to be ruthless enough to kill potential traitors both inside and outside of the guerrilla force. As a result, his base camp fell into enemy hands. Then he split his own small force into two parts, which were hunted down and destroyed separately. A certain resignation and lack of aggression in Che as a commander also began to show itself, as he grew physically sick and weak. His heroism lay in his unceasing struggle against the sight of his own and his group's decomposition. As long as he could stand, he would fight on. After the surprising rebel attack on Sumaipata in July 1967, when Che's few guerrillas captured a whole town and its garrison, the Bolivian government tottered. The legend of Guevara's guerrillas briefly caused both Argentina and Peru to close their frontiers and to mobilize their troops. Apparently, Bolivia was becoming the focus for a continental revolution, particularly as there had been a spontaneous rising in June in the Bolivian mines, which the national army had suppressed with great brutality.

By October, after the disastrous ambush at the Yuro Ravine, Che was wounded and captured, while his surviving guerrilla group was dispersed. The care that the Bolivian army authorities took to assassinate Che showed the fear that the military governments of Latin America felt about his dream of uniting the continent through armed struggle. They knew that his cause would not die with his body. They might inter his corpse, but they could not bury his ideal. He was executed in a schoolhouse by six shots to the body and his remains were flown by helicopter to Vallegrande, where they were washed, photographed and displayed to prove that the legendary guerrilla commander was really dead. Yet, as in the film of *Viva Zapata!*, the general might look down on the riddled corpse of the dead guerrilla leader and say, 'Sometimes a dead man can be a terrible enemy.'

Che's death was the prelude to the full fury of the Red Guard movement in Mao's China and the Tet Offensive of the Vietcong in South Vietnam. With him as their personal symbol and the Red Guards as their general model, many of the students of the world revolted in 1968 during that turbulent summer. The events of that year were curiously similar to those of 1848, when a wave of insurrection had swept through most of the capital cities of Europe and ended in the victory of the powers that were.

Both Che and the Red Guards were inspired by the concept of a rural revolt that would sweep out of the countryside to purge the corruption of the cities. The middle-class students who fought in the streets of Paris during the May Revolution, or in Chicago during the Democratic Convention, or in Berlin or London or Buenos Aires or Tokyo or Mexico City or twenty other cities during the year after Che's death came from an urban or sub-urban setting. They did not want to know of their misconception of Che's and Mao's thought. Yet Mao would remind them, when he sent 20,000,000 of the Red Guards back to labour in the countryside. And Che's end, too, had been the result of a middle-class doctor and guerrilla failing to win over the poor farmers and miners of Bolivia.

In 1968, the governments of the world won. In Communist and capitalist countries, in developed and in underdeveloped countries, the protest of the young was defeated by the power of the old. In Latin America nearly all the guerrilla risings were suppressed. Harsher measures were taken in Kenya as well as in Czechoslovakia, in Mexico as well as in France, in China as well as in the United States. This was a global reaction against an international revolt partially inspired by Che's death. But just as Bolívar failed five times before succeeding in Latin America, and

Che himself failed twice in the Congo and Bolivia for his one success in Cuba, so crushing the rebellions did not mean the end of them. For Che's most explosive idea was that the revolution was successive and that the revolution created itself.

The insurrections continued for decades in Nicaragua and Colombia and Peru with the Sendero Luminoso, or guerrillas of the Shining Path. In Nicaragua, the Sandinistas fought the government with its death squads, backed by the United States, to a standstill, and their leader led a new government, only to be thrown out at a general election. For once, democracy triumphed over state and rebel terrorism: the Sandinistas had alienated the peasants.

In Colombia, the two terrorist and socialist groups, the FARC and the ELN, used the huge profits generated by the drug cartels to finance their brutal campaign against the jungle and mountain communities, who were frightened into support. Kidnapping and banditry complemented the trade in narcotics. 'Cocaine and liberty, long live the revolutionary struggle' was one slogan. The worst moment in the strategy of the Irish Republican Army was to have three of its operatives captured in Colombia as late as 2001, while teaching the Colombian rebels the use of various explosive devices. This idiocy would have condemned them to be banned as a terrorist organization across the globe after the aerial attack on the Twin Towers and the Pentagon, if they had not already been engaged in the Good Friday agreement to terminate the civil war in Northern Ireland.

In Peru, however, the Sendero Luminoso had a charismatic leader, Abimael Guzmán, who would end his days shackled in a prison cage as a latterday conquered Persian king by a corrupt leader called Fujimori, taking the place of Tamerlane. Guzmán had put together an odd mixture of Maoism and apocalyptic beliefs, which included ancient Inca rituals. In the beginning, this strange doctrine had widespread support in the Andes, where the people dreamed of a revival of the Inca empire. They and an allied Indian movement, Tupac Amaru, flourished for a while, until they turned on the snowy mountain villages, which supported them. Their suspicion led them to retribution against any informer. They killed 20,000 of their supporters, but only 2,500 of the soldiers and the police sent against them.

Half a million frightened people were driven from the highlands to the hopeless slums of Lima and other cities. Peru could not be taken from the countryside without another urban revolution. In spite of a guerrilla attack on the Japanese Embassy in 1997, no progress was made, and all the attackers were executed. Some 100,000 people were also killed in a Thirty Years War in Guatemala that achieved nothing.

In spite of all these insurrections by terrorist groups, whose atrocities were matched by those of clandestine official death squads, outside Cuba there was not much change among the regimes of Latin America. Perhaps because of the brooding presence of the United States, there was little possibility for insurrection. One fine revolution in Cuba did not make a summer of successful discontent. Che Guevara had proved his point. He was gaffed, gasping on dry land. The rebel had to have the support of a lake, if not a sea, to survive. And this involved paddling with the people, and not throwing sand in their eyes.

36. THE BROADCAST HORROR

Three forms of terror haunted all the peoples of the earth. One was the old horror of the plague induced by human hands. The others were the spread of terror by the media, and the copycat crimes which they induced.

Vaccination against smallpox and typhus, measles and influenza made most Europeans in the later twentieth century forgetful of the dangers of various epidemics still rife in the rest of the world. They could emulate Daniel Defoe's Merry Piper, who would play his tunes from the plague carts and ask: 'Am I dead or am I not?' They expected to survive as long as they did not live in the Third World. They would emulate Max Augustin, when he found himself waking from a drunken stupor in a plague pit outside Vienna. His ballad about his experience is still sung in the great city of the Danube, now prosperous and full of hospitals:

> Every day a feast we had,
> Now the plague is rife and bad,
> Only corpses to be had,
> Oh dear, how sad!
>
> O Augustin, my dear,
> Lie down upon your bier.
> Alas! Vienna dear,
> All gone, I fear.

What had almost gone in modern Europe was any fear of a new plague. The last serious epidemic, Aids, had been contained to a small percentage of the population, although it was killing tens of millions across Africa. There, some left-wingers accused the CIA of spreading the disease, as if the American Secret Service was still sending out blankets infected with smallpox to unsuspecting natives, or the Jews were poisoning the waters of the Congo and the Zambezi instead of the wells of the Middle Ages. Contagions always seek for scapegoats.

Only the Japanese had used bioterror during the Second World War, although the incendiary bomb was technically a chemical weapon, and some 350,000 civilians died because of its use. More effective in saving the lives of American soldiers on the Pacific front, who were incapacitated eight times as much with malaria as by Japanese bullets, was the spraying with DDT of mosquitoes in the swamps by B-25 bombers, who were escorted by P-38 fighters to convince the troops below that they were not being gassed by their own side. To them, however, the Japanese seemed little more than pests. After three weeks of bloodshed on Iwo Jima, *Time* magazine reported that 'the Pacific's nastiest exterminating job was done'.

There was much production of toxins and nerve gas and napalm during both the Second World War and the Cold War. Although little was used in conflict until Vietnam, huge stockpiles of chemical weapons were built up in the laboratories and arsenals of all the major powers. Cornelius Ryan, who wrote *A Bridge Too Far*, estimated that the cost of eradicating people and buildings in one square mile by conventional means was up to $35,000,000, while 'nerve gas could do the same job for one twentieth the amount and leave the buildings and industrial plants intact for an occupying force to take over'. By 1954, the Rocky Mountain Arsenal of the US Chemical Corps was manufacturing nerve gas, mainly sarin, day and night for cluster bombs and shells and warheads. These missiles could be distributed from the air just as DDT was, in order to kill off the enemy as if they were cockroaches or lice.

Not until the publication of Rachel Carson's *Silent Spring* in

1962 did the general public become aware of the connection between pesticides, which destroyed nature, and chemical weapons and nuclear fallout, which might destroy all humanity. Man-made poisons threatened to eradicate all life on the planet. Carson described the aerial spraying of crops across the globe as chemical warfare against people as well as insects. There was no distinction between man and mosquito under this 'amazing rain of death'.

When the Americans became involved in the war in Vietnam, they used three chemical weapons extensively, napalm bombs, DDT and a herbicide mixture called Agent Orange to defoliate the forests that provided the enemy Vietcong and North Vietnamese with cover. This Operation Ranch Hand, in the opinion of the philosopher Bertrand Russell, 'constitutes and results in atrocities, and points to the fact that this is a war of annihilation'. The deaths and deformations from DDT and the herbicides were never counted, although DDT was eventually banned, because of its deleterious effect on the food chain. President Nixon, who ended the war in Vietnam, gave up the first use of chemical weapons and the manufacture of biological weapons. 'Mankind,' he declared, 'already carries in its own hands too many of the seeds of its own destruction.'

Ironically, although 15 per cent of the area of the Rocky Mountain Arsenal was too contaminated for human use, the rest of the land became a wildlife refuge, rather as the no-man's-land between the battlelines dividing North and South Korea. Although the United States and Britain had renounced the use of bioterror, other powers had not, particularly in Islam. The dictator Saddam Hussein of Iraq used chemical agents against the Kurdish opposition in the north of his country, while the Pentagon reckoned that American troops may have been exposed to sarin gas when an Iraqi chemical depot was blown up. In 1995, the release by a religious cult of sarin in the Tokyo underground railway system killed twelve people and affected 5,000 more commuters.

Yet not until the mailing of anthrax spores to Congressional leaders in 2001 during the American assault on the al-Qaeda movement did the fear of bioterror become prevalent. Measures were taken in the United States and Britain to contain the threat of smallpox or anthrax assassins, who would infect themselves to spread the deadly virus across the West. Entire cities might be put under quarantine to fence off this induced plague. Vaccines were stockpiled, emergency plans were prepared and put on hold. Bioterror had become the cheap weapon of the rebel, prepared to martyr himself on his mission to reach paradise.

The jewel in American democracy has always been the right of free speech by the press, backed by the rule of law. During the war in Vietnam, television coverage caused mass revulsion. The horrific means used by the American forces to subdue the Vietcong caused public outrage, which culminated in a film of genius, *Apocalypse Now*, which traded heavily on Conrad's *Heart of Darkness*. The United States appeared to have descended into a war of modern bestiality, which threatened all the Christian values on which the nation was founded.

Because of all the media coverage, the Asian conflict led to more anti-government feeling than at any previous time in American history. In Vietnam, some 50,000 US combatants were killed, while 35,000 more were retired to psychiatric wards. The national draft of young people to fight in a hated foreign war coincided with the withdrawal from society of many millions into a pop and drug culture that set itself against all authority. This spreading protest of a whole generation culminated in 1968 in the student riots in most of the cities of the Western world. The Ohio National Guard fired on the demonstrators at Kent State University, killing four students and wounding nine. So violent were the protests in Chicago outside the Democratic Convention that mounted police were used to clear the streets.

Yet the radical Hippies and the Yippies were unarmed. This was not the case with overt revolutionary groups such as the Black Panthers and the Weathermen, who set the example of using bombs to create urban terror. In 1969 and 1970, seven major companies were bombed in New York, including Mobil and IBM, and forty-three people died from the blasts. It was a prophecy of what could come from the enemy within, as opposed to the enemy without, who were to blast the World Trade Center. Another reaction from the rebellious decade of youth and black power was the retreat to the backwoods. And when the agents and the forces of the states and the federal government suppressed or contained most of the protest movements, the remnants of these retired to a simpler life, imbued with a hatred of authority and the law.

The draft had trained tens of millions of Americans in the techniques of killing. This training was not wasted on a people with the constitutional right to bear arms. A belief in the argument that a gun in the hand ensured liberty in the house was set against any regulation by the government. Even the assassination of the President John F. Kennedy must not disarm the nation. Patriotism was equated with owning the means of personal defence. Every cowboy film since *Shane* had held the same message. The lone rider came into town to dispatch the regime of terror and the corrupt powers, which ruled the land.

The violent streak in American politics was fuelled by millennial and Manichean views of the evil of governments, which must be overthrown before the apocalypse and the reign of Christ on earth. The religious fanatics at Waco in Texas were armed, and so they were able to kill four federal agents before their own mass self-destruction. The revenge taken two years later by the bombing of the federal offices in Oklahoma City was a perversion of the old American revolutionary spirit of the Minutemen fighting the tyranny of the British crown. Timothy McVeigh and his fellow conspirators saw themselves as patriots in defence of their liberties, while the President accused them of being 'promoters of paranoia'. To them, the death of many innocents was irrelevant in the fight against the wickedness of government. To the bombers and bearers of guns, to fight for freedom always was an honour, never a crime.

Again, these images of terrorist attacks against governments were broadcast across the world, showing the possibility of revenge assaults on American power to everyone who could watch a television set. Other documentaries from America showed the serial killing of schoolchildren by their fellows and other deranged gunmen. At Port Arthur in Tasmania, another devotee of violence killed thirty-five people in a gun rampage, which confused the right to carry weapons with wanton murder in the false name of free expression. Both of these extreme murders did, however, lead to legislation against the private possession of handguns and rifles.

If there was one condition common to these events, it was the tragic unfitness for the modern world that the perpetrators exhibited. There lay the most painful recognition, reaching far beyond the legislator's remit. Perhaps these were sicknesses for which there was no cure. The studies proliferated, examining the degeneration of feeling, the collapse of community, the growth of loneliness, the exaltation of acquisitive individualism and the rest. How violence legitimized itself, through television and other images available twenty-four hours a day, was another subject of study, which a liberal age found difficult to pursue.

Onanistic solitude, lived out in a fantasy world ruled by terror and thrilled by incessant gunfire, posed a lethal threat. Media moguls, vastly enriched by promoting these fantasies, denied that any part of society's degradation could be blamed upon them. Society, they said, demanded the pictures. Yet that excuse exposed an awesome possibility which was hard to face. Whom the gods advanced to full modernity, they then made mad. As societies apparently progressed, they left ever more people behind, creating conditions with which they could not cope. At the same time, most governments were drastically reducing care for the mentally ill, which was all that stood between these trends and social disaster.

Moreover, in an age where sadomasochism was recognized as a clinical aberration, the connection between the terrorist and the tortured was often depicted in the media. In the case of the kidnapped heiress Patty Hearst, she was converted to the rebel cause through her sufferings, before being caught on camera while robbing a bank. In some films such as *The Night Porter*, the Nazi exploitation of women in concentration camps became a doomed love affair. In the play *Death and the Maiden*, the vindictive secret policeman serving the cruel Pinochet regime established an unspeakable bond with his female victim. Torment began to be excused in the name of understanding.

The bad temper of the times was high on sporadic violence. The killings of John and Robert Kennedy and of Martin Luther King, all widely viewed on television, appeared to be the apogee of the reign of personal terror instead of political persuasion. The rules of the game were reversed. Bullets and not ballots, assassinations and not armies, were the preferred instruments of change. Paradoxically, the killing of the younger Kennedy, as he was running successfully for the White House in an effort to unseat Lyndon Johnson, defused the rising revolt against the Vietnam War, particularly when Johnson himself refused to run again.

The shooting down of both of the Kennedy brothers showed that nobody was safer in Dallas or San Francisco than in Hanoi or Saigon. When you met murder on the way, it did not wear the mask of LBJ, but of an anonymous gunman, famous only for a brutal and almost pointless act. Its only purpose was to make a celebrity out of obscurity. 'Guns are neat little things, aren't they?' the would-be assassin of the former actor and President, Ronald Reagan, would say. 'They can kill extraordinary people with very little effort.'

In an article called 'Assassination: The Ultimate Public Theatre', reprinted in the programme for Stephen Sondheim's brilliant and ineluctable musical *Assassins*, Robert Jay Lifton affirmed that the pistol or rifle was the appropriate technology 'for annihilating king, leader and father, for becoming immortal by absorbing the power of all three. The "equalizer" presides over a grotesque caricature of American Egalitarianism.'

When targeted by an anarchist at a political meeting, the ex-President Theodore Roosevelt had shown exemplary courage in continuing a public speech while pouring with blood after being shot in the chest and only saved by his spectacle case. He reckoned that assassination was 'a trade risk, which every prominent public man ought to accept as a matter of course'. Yet the problem was whether political assassination had ever been justified by its outcome. In my past words:

> The questions posed at the murder of Thomas à Becket or of Guevara have never been solved. Does the safety of the state demand that a rebel should be butchered in cold blood, even if he happens to be a brave man halfway to sainthood? And if that sort of state exists, which can use murder as a weapon, then does not each man have the right to pick up a gun and assassinate the agents of the government in order to create a better one?
>
> In a police state which denies human rights, who is the political assassin – the tyrannical policeman who murders the innocent citizen, or the armed citizen who murders the soldier obeying orders? The answer is brutal in history. All assassinations which succeeded in changing governments for long periods of time are accepted by their societies, and thus justified. All political assassinations which fail are condemned as treason. As in many walks of life, so in the murder of the great, success is justification.

The assassination of Martin Luther King in Memphis, however, was conspicuous by its failure. It killed the man, but it won his cause, where it was not delivered by the white murderer into the hands of the advocates of black power. There were riots in the ghettos of 110 American cities, the National Guard was called to quell the disturbances, and 25,000 people were killed or injured. Yet this was not a political explosion, but an orgy of arson and looting and aimless counter-violence, hardly what the leaders of the Black Muslims and the Black Panthers had threatened – a race war in the streets unless all the demands for black emancipation and equality were immediately granted.

This was the explosion of mass outrage at the death of a hero. The radical leader H. Rap Brown was wrong in hailing the widespread ghetto riots as 'a rehearsal for revolution', and Tom Hayden in seeing them as an American form of slum guerrilla warfare. They represented an enraged process of the deprived laying hands on what they could not get and destroying what they could not possess.

Ironically, the virtue of free speech and the worldwide dissemination of historical pictures encouraged the growth of the evils of terrorism. The revived Fascist movements of the Western world in the late twentieth century fed on the propaganda films of the Third Reich and the military documentaries of its destruction. In imitation of these viewed atrocities, the Ordino Nero bombed the Rome–Munich express train near Bologna in August 1974, killing or wounding sixty passengers. Its declaration was: 'The Nazi flag did not die in Berlin in 1945. It still lives . . . for the salvation of a renaissance Italy.'

This was the resurrection of Mussolini, who had substituted for the French Revolutionary slogan, 'Liberty, equality, fraternity,' the catchwords, 'Believe, obey, and fight!' The neo-Nazi movements of the end of the century fed on the discontents of a jobless proletariat and the images of a brutalist and beaten regime, shown triumphantly on television. The collapse, however, of the neo-Fascist military dictatorships in Greece and Portugal and Spain in 1974 put an end to any serious threat to democracy in Europe.

More insidious than anthrax and sarin, and far more effective, were the slow toxins of the airwaves. They disseminated terrorism in the name of free speech. To the neo-Fascists, they repeated the emblems of racial hatred of Nazi parades. In action movies, they predicted the paradigm of the explosion of skyscrapers under an aerial attack; these repeated images were to be followed by the Twin Towers disaster in Manhattan. Indeed, one poor deluded teenage pilot, who knew nothing about it, would crash, in the name of bin Laden, a light plane into a high-rise building in Florida, causing little damage except to himself. He had seen the disaster of 11 September 2001 on television; he wished to repeat the experience as a misguided youth, intent on death as fame.

That was the horror of the age, ruled by instant images. Easily available were recipes for making atomic bombs, if the materials were available; for spreading actual epidemics with toxins, which any small laboratory might procure; for forming terrorist groups and the procuring of weapons. As the Internet spread a wonderful community across the globe, so it laid itself open to the fearsome teaching of terrorist techniques. As in old societies, it was penetrated by secret cells of revolutionary groups. And as in the French Revolution, the pursuit of liberty might lead to a future of tyranny. This great and lethal game would have no end.

37. THE UNUSED DETERRENCE

After exploding an atomic bomb, it took the Americans four years to make a hydrogen bomb. It took the Russians four and a half years. The British and the French took a little longer. In Britain's case, the decision to produce the hydrogen bomb was seen by Churchill's Conservative cabinet as reducing the risk of war, for it was feared that the United States might still intervene with nuclear weapons in Asia or make a pre-emptive attack on Russia. Britain's best chance of preventing this was to be the third nuclear power with thermonuclear weapons. 'In so far as any moral principle was involved,' a Cabinet minute read, 'it had already been breached by the decision of the Labour government to make the atomic bomb.'

So advances in weapons systems encouraged competitive governments to blame past decisions for present imperatives. Because one political party began a military programme, another party continued it. Because one power possessed an atomic bomb, another power felt obliged to acquire it. Britain and France refused to consider themselves lesser powers and proceeded to manufacture their independent nuclear weapons.

Yet the Russians were far in advance of the British in spite of the contributions of scientists in England to the Manhattan Project. When the Russians exploded their effective nuclear bomb in 1949, Sir Henry Tizard, now the chief scientific adviser to the Ministry of Defence, gave pragmatic reasons for stopping the national nuclear programme. 'We are not a Great Power and never will be again,' he wrote. 'Let us take warning from the fate of the Great Powers of the past and not burst ourselves with pride (see Aesop's fable of the frog).'

His doubts were not heard by Labour or Conservative administrations. Britain pressed ahead with its nuclear programme. As the Cold War between the Western democracies and the Communist powers intensified after the fall of China to Mao's armies, the pressure on scientists to aid their country's defence programme without moral queasiness grew greater. The unique possession by the United States of atomic weapons for four years after 1945 did not prevent the fall of the world's largest population in China to Communist forces or the spread of Marxism across Eastern Europe. Ideology followed the Red Army, not the mushroom cloud.

If the Russians had possessed the atomic bomb at the end of the Second World War, they would certainly have dropped it on Berlin, but they would hardly have used it thereafter. After letting atomic bombs fall on Hiroshima and Nagasaki, no American President authorized the use of the atomic or the hydrogen bomb, when the United States was their sole owner. Before there was a balance of nuclear deterrence between America and Russia, atomic weapons were rarely used as direct threats, blackmail or bargaining counters, except perhaps during the later Cuban missile crisis and the Korean and Vietnam Wars.

These were the political facts of the postwar years, when Russia and America, Britain and France were still officially allies. Arguably, it was the manufacture of nuclear weapons by Russia that led to the Cold War. The Western nations no longer felt complacent because of their devastating explosive devices. At a meeting between Harold Macmillan and President John F. Kennedy, the British Prime Minister asked his nuclear expert, Sir William Penney, how many hydrogen bombs would be needed to finish off Britain. 'Five, I should think, Prime Minister,' Penney said, then added: 'Just to be on the safe side, let's say eight.'

This safety factor allowed for a narrow margin of error in British foreign policy. A reliance on atomic weapons was an illusion. Although a balance of nuclear deterrence created a common interest between the United States of America and Soviet Russia because they would be the chief victims of a total war, minor powers with a nuclear strike capacity only held wild cards in the international great game. The independent atomic weapons of Britain and France were classified as additions to the American arsenal by the Russians, while Chinese atomic weapons represented a threat which the Russians thought was directed against themselves after their split with the various Beijing regimes.

By the 1980s, many minor nations possessed or would have the capacity to make nuclear weapons, led by Israel and followed by India and Pakistan. Proliferation was the danger to world peace, a minor power or a terrorist organization using a nuclear weapon in a local war. The atomic fission started in Cambridge fifty years before had split open a box of mass destruction. Its last hope of control lay in the imposition by both superpowers of a stalemate on their own deployment of the weapons and in their laying an embargo on the production of nuclear materials and weaponry elsewhere, even by their allies. Dual possession of the final solution by Russia and America might prevent the outbreak of a Third World War as it had for forty years, but it was a game that only two should play. The 'Big Five' powers that officially had atomic weapons were already three too many in the diplomacy of nuclear deterrence.

As Richard Holmes pointed out in his remarkable work, *Nuclear Warriors*, the strategy of atomic weapons in the late twentieth century was what theology was to the Middle Ages. 'We have felt ourselves to be living on the eve of Armageddon, just as our medieval ancestors believed that the Second Coming was at hand: the flash of the nuclear explosion has replaced the flames of hell in our imagination.' The world population no longer expected a self-inflicted aerial Black Death to winnow their numbers by the hundreds of millions. In fact, so aggressive were modern societies, that although the amount of human beings on the planet had increased by over four times since the beginning of the nineteenth century, the casualties of war had risen by some twenty-four times in the twentieth century alone, leaving 80,000,000 victims to die. And what for? When, as the ballad went, would we ever learn?

Of course, the increase of the dead was the result of the new weaponry and of state power. Where previous combat had killed in its tens of thousands, now slaughter ranged in the millions. The very fact that the detonation of a small atomic bomb would wipe out any metropolis anywhere stopped its drop. As the American Secretary of Defense, Robert S. Macnamara, wrote after the Cuban crisis, nuclear weapons served no satisfactory purpose whatsoever. 'They are totally useless – except only to deter one's opponent from using them.' Indeed, when it was realized that a major atomic war would change the climate into long months of radioactive dust and deplete the ozone layer beyond redemption, the United States and Russia stepped back from such a catastrophe.

Outside the nuclear arsenals of the 'Big Five' powers, proliferation remained the chief concern, particularly after the meltdown at the nuclear reactor at Chernobyl. This accident spread contamination as far as Wales, and showed that such power plants were vulnerable to terrorist attacks. The methods of making a low-grade atomic weapon also became available to most American physics students. The only problem was to acquire three kilos of plutonium, which became more facile with the collapse of the Communist Soviet Union, leaving hordes of unpaid scientists with access to nuclear materials and devices.

In 1973 in Argentina, in 1976 in Brittany in France, and in 1979 near Bilbao in the Basque country of Spain, terrorist groups tried to sabotage atomic power stations, as did the militant wing of the African National Congress, which damaged in 1982 two nuclear reactors in South Africa. None of these acts of sabotage produced a critical explosion on the scale of Chernobyl.

During the Chechen struggle against the Russian government, the rebels threatened in 1996 to devastate Moscow by radioactivity. The police there were directed to a hidden source of caesium-137, a fissile material, although no further activity took place. Not until the discovery of nuclear manuals in the camps and caves of the al-Qaeda terrorists did the threat of atomic explosions in major Western cities from bombs packed into suitcases send a fresh frisson of fear around the West, while the acquisition of nuclear warheads by India and Pakistan threatened to make their unresolved conflict over Kashmir go ballistic.

More sinister and more threatening was the spread of cyber-terrorism with the digital revolution. Most of the weapons systems of the world, particularly guided missiles, depended on their electronic links. A brilliant hacker could penetrate secret systems, even at the Pentagon, and direct rockets at the wrong targets. The Director of the CIA stated that an 'electronic Pearl Harbor' was now possible, and that terrorists in the Middle East were being sold the necessary instructions. An infected computer could spread its virus faster than an epidemic to nullify all energy and transport systems from power grids to air and rail traffic. With the global blanket of digital technology and information, all modern systems of communication became vulnerable to a plague no bigger than a mouse.

The cheap computer age put the means of disturbance into the hands of the disturbed. Where the anarchist only had a knife to commit a single assassination, now a youthful radical had a laptop which might disrupt a worldwide organization and destroy its records. What was a smoking bomb exploding compared to downloading a digital germ that could damage the economy a thousand times more?

Cyberterror lacked sleuths. It could occur almost anywhere from anyone, who had a real or imaginary grievance against society. The hacker in his lonely room had a greater power of disruption than any Al Capone. No security service could completely develop a fail-safe programme. The price of cyberspace, as the price of liberty, became eternal vigilance against invisible enemies too numerous to be spotted or counted.

38. ETHNIC TERROR

Africa is a place where terror like a newborn babe reaches out its bloody hands. When the colonial European powers left the continent, they returned it to tribal wars and ethnic cleansing, unfortunately with modern weapons. Once, dozens of European mercenaries could conquer hundreds of their enemies in the Congo and Biafra, as the British had finally been able to defeat the assegais of the Zulus with the Maxim machine gun. Yet in the end, Russia and China gave sophisticated weapons to soi-disant rebels, while China presented modern armaments to the appalling Simbas, who still believed in witchcraft and flaying their enemies alive and the blessing of the urine of their leader Mulele to make them bullet-proof. Parts of Africa were left to the possibility of limitless atrocity in internecine wars, without the benefit of much education.

The wars in the Congo were another *Heart of Darkness*. These last efforts of primitive imperialism were pitted against the failure of the Marxist guerrilla doctrine of a permanent global revolution. The secessionist province of Katanga was the battleground, because of its enormous mining riches, still controlled by the old colonial power Belgium, which was prepared to send in paratroopers to protect its citizens abroad as well as its financial interests. Yet after the deaths of the radical Congolese President Patrice Lumumba and the United Nations Secretary-General Dag Hammarskjöld, that successor to the League of Nations sent in some 20,000 troops to avenge the mercenary occupation of Katanga. Eventually, the serial secessionist leader Tshombe was kidnapped on the day the United Nations forces departed, and was left to die in an Algerian jail.

The corrupt and cruel dictator of the Congo, the self-styled Marshal Sese Seko Mobutu, was backed by the Western powers and allowed to exploit his unhappy land, now called Zaire, for three decades in the manner of King Leopold of the Belgians, who had financed much of Antwerp on the rubber and slave trade. In the Ibo revolt in Biafra, though, the civil war which began in Nigeria in 1967 was a training ground for international intervention. The unorthodox humanitarian measures and the white mercenaries kept the conflict going beyond its due time, even if on the battlefield the Saladin armoured cars and Ferret scout cars supplied by the British to the Federal Government rolled over the opposition. Ancient DCs and Constellations supported the Ibo fighting men by flying in supplies. With a hodge-podge air force, the Swedish Count Eric von Rosen led raids on the oilfields, which were the European prizes of the war, and he landed materials for CARE and the Red Cross. As he said of his combination of combat and humanitarian relief, 'I went all out to try and stop this terrible killing of innocent women and children.'

For the United Nations observers trying to bring in food and hygiene supplies for the survivors, a fearsome problem was posed. Did the airlift of life-giving things prolong the horror of the war, or was it saving the Biafran peoples from genocide? By 1970, when the war was won, the Nigerian leader proved merciful, and there was little more persecution among the Ibos for a while, until Western rapacity for the oil supplies provoked the usual mechanics of state terrorism.

The failure of the Western world to intervene in the slaughter practised by the Hutus against the Tutsis in Rwanda in 1994 was an indictment against European indifference only paralleled by the Turkish massacre of the Armenians more than seventy years before. The French government, indeed, in its post-colonial meddlings in Africa, even armed the perpetrators of the atrocities.

The minority Tutsi tribe had long dominated the Hutus, who seized power after independence under a totalitarian dictator. Rebel Tutsi exiles invaded Rwanda from Uganda, starting a civil war in which the Hutu forces were aided by hundreds of French paratroopers. A brokered truce led to 5,000 peacekeepers from the United Nations being put on demand. A Tutsi coup in neighbouring Burundi, however, provoked more inter-tribal killing, and 350,000 Hutu refugees poured over the border.

An underground Hutu Power movement was preparing to eliminate all the Tutsis in the land. The moment came with the assassination of both the presidents of Burundi and Rwanda by a missile, as they were landing at the airport of Kigali, the capital of Rwanda. There was no outbreak of horror in Burundi, but only the unleashing of the Hutu Power gangs in the next country against all moderates and foreign forces. Ten Belgian soldiers were caught and tortured and cut to pieces. Most of the elite in the capital were butchered, on the model of the Jacobins in the Terror or Pol Pot's Khmer Rouge in Cambodia.

Now the ethnic cleansing of the Tutsis became a national killing game of 'cockroaches'. They were hacked apart by machetes, incinerated in missionary churches, buried alive or drowned in cesspools, mutilated with their parts stuffed into the mouths of their slain families. The small United Nations forces merely evacuated other Europeans and themselves from this orgy of murder. Nearly 1,000,000 innocent civilians perished in this abomination.

The remnants of the Tutsis were saved by the invasion of the rebel Rwanda Patriotic Front, which was determined not to let all its fellow people die. With too many of their forces engaged in genocide, the Hutu army fell back on Kigali and lost the capital. The French government sent in 2,500 troops, officially to save the few remaining Tutsis, but actually to protect the millions of Hutu refugees pulling out to Burundi and Tanzania and Zaire. The Hutu Power leaders were practising a scorched-earth policy, burning the villages of their own people and forcing them to become exiles, and the nuclei for counterattacks from the neighbouring African states. As a United Nations relief leader noted, 'The genuine refugee population is hostage of forces of doom, and so are we.'

Over the borders, the Hutu extremists built up guerrilla groups among the 2,000,000 and more refugees, now living in primitive camps, fed by the United Nations, which had refused to stop the carnage of the Tutsis, the cause of the mass flight. This huge humanitarian effort was the consequence of the failure of Western intervention against unprecedented terrorism. It was estimated that the Hutus had killed the Tutsis at a rate of five times a day more than the Nazis had killed the Jews in all the concentration camps. And now the inability of the aid workers to prevent Hutu Power from controlling the refugee exodus threw Zaire into turmoil again, partially because the triumphant Tutsis wanted to remove the guerrilla threats from across the frontier.

The Tutsi victory in Rwanda was accompanied by the return of 800,000 of their refugees, who largely took over the property of another 1,000,000 dispossessed Hutus, who were now held in 'displaced persons' camps in Rwanda. These mass movements destabilized all of Central Africa and led to its 'Great War', in which fourteen countries participated, squabbling as the European nations had for the mineral riches of corrupt Zaire. As the United Nations debated whether to send in more peacekeeping forces to the deteriorating situation, Uganda and Rwanda struck back against the Hutu guerrillas by backing a Congolese rebel, Laurent Kabila, to bring down President Mobutu and his regime.

With the Hutu militants driven out of the border camps, most of the exiles were no longer scared off from returning to Rwanda. Those who fled with the Hutu leaders were massacred by Kabila's ferocious rebel armies, which took no prisoners. Hunted through the jungle, another 200,000 and more refugees died in appalling ways through malnutrition or murder. As he advanced on Kinshasa, the capital of Zaire, Kabila turned on the

Tutsis and invoked the aid of Zimbabwe and Angola and other African countries, interested in mineral concessions.

When Mobutu fled, Kabila found a wilderness and called it more war. He himself did not rule long: in spite of a ceasefire in 1999, the huge country along the Congo River was condemned to a tribal breakdown with hundreds of primitive and squalid petty wars, backed by other African countries, which were exchanging weapons for precious metals and gems. By 2002, a rough estimate counted 3,000,000 dead in this orgy of interstate terror and plunder. In the words of a UN officer, 'Congo is so green, you don't even see the graves.'

Children, crazed with drugs, were now being given AK-47 assault rifles by local warlords to terrorize whole communities. Amputation of hands and feet, lips and noses was the price of any resistance. This new obscenity was also the fate of Liberia, founded by the United States for those of its Christian black people who wished to return to Africa, and the horror in the older British colony of Sierra Leone, rich in diamonds and bauxite and titanium dioxide.

There the Pied Piper of Terror, who led boys on a war dance into an insane anarchy, was Charles Taylor, an amoral pirate who seized sections of Liberia in the late 1980s, and then sent his warped assassins to aid Foday Sankoh with his Revolutionary United Front. He was bent on seizing the diamond mines of Sierra Leone from another corrupt African government, which soon fell. Some Nigerian and Ghanaian troops and a group of South African mercenaries named Executive Outcomes turned back the rebels without a cause on the outskirts of the capital, ironically called Freetown, and these government forces swept away the RUF from the mineral resources, which were their paymasters.

Pressure from Britain and the United States resulted in an election in 1996; it was disfigured by factional fighting and outrage, but did result in a majority for the exiled Admad Tejan Kabbah, who was soon deposed in a coup, when the South

African mercenaries were disengaged. Helped now by British mercenaries as well as the Nigerians and an interior tribe, the Kamajors, Kabbah returned to Freetown and received emergency aid from the World Bank, usually more choosy in giving out its bounty. Unable to defeat the RUF, Kabbah signed a peace agreement with Sankoh, which gave his rival the control of the diamond mines and a general amnesty for past atrocities.

This unholy alliance could not last. The rebel soldiers went berserk in Freetown at Christmas 1998, killing some 2,000 civilians on a rampage and kidnapping 4,000 more children to serve as soldiers or sex slaves in their rabid ranks. Chaos again descended on Sierra Leone, as it did on Liberia, with the warlords losing control of their own ragtag troops. With the backing of the United Nations, the former colonial power Britain intervened to help Kabbah and the Nigerians to restore some sort of order in the country, to train an effective national army, and to contain the rebels near the Liberian frontier. Some rehabilitation schools for child warriors were set up, also a few relief facilities for the mutilated and the maimed and the maltreated.

Yet all this Western effort was too little and too late. Although now the Cold War was over China and Russia were hardly supplying weapons to Africa, there were enough minerals and gems in rebel hands to get what they wanted from smaller rogue states and greedy arms dealers. And the United Nations and the European Union were fully committed to a problem of ethnic terror on ground nearer home in Kosovo, where again the wrong sort of intervention would be too late to avert massacre and forced flight. In Rwanda and Zaire, the people were merely Africans, although many were Christians and Muslims, while Kosovo was white and closer to home.

The breakup of Yugoslavia with the secession of Croatia and Slovenia was largely the fault of European diplomacy, which seemed to want to pit Roman Catholic countries against Greek Orthodox states. And when revived Serbian nationalism in the wars against the two rival Christian new nations provoked a battleground in the other Yugoslav provinces of Bosnia and Kosovo, many horrors began to be perpetrated by all sides, particularly around Srebrenica. Such frightfulness had hardly been known since the Nazi occupation in the Second World War. The Bosnian conflict provoked reprisals from Catholic Croats and Orthodox Serbians against the resident Muslims, who had coalesced to dominate the official armed forces and the civil service. Assaulted in Bosnia as later in Kosovo, the Muslims saw themselves as the victims of genocide in the last Western crusade in Europe. They even called in Islamic holy warriors from Afghanistan for their defence.

With the intervention of monitors and neutral troops from the United Nations and later from NATO, the thwarted Serbian nationalists under the implacable Slobodan Milošević decided to culminate their crusade in Kosovo, the heartland of their past, even though it now had a large Muslim majority. Attacked from Islamic Albania by a guerrilla force named the Kosovo Liberation Army, Milošević and his supporters set up terror squads modelled on the old Black Hundreds, which murdered 2,500 Muslims in order to induce them to flee the land. Another 250,000 Muslims were rendered homeless in burned villages, while 200,000 crossed over the mountains in utter poverty into Albanian insecurity.

Such harshness provoked the United States and the European powers to decide on another use of their successful bombing campaign against Iraq in the recent Gulf War, now intended to terrify Serbia into submission. Surgical air strikes had already helped to cobble together a solution of sorts in Bosnia, which would not last once the peacekeeping forces were to be withdrawn. Hopefully, continuous aerial assault would put Milošević under the yoke of surrender and an eventual war crimes trial at the new international tribunal at The Hague.

The Serbs could not understand this fellow Christian barrage from the heavens. 'How can our allies in the world war,' Vuk Drašković, the Deputy President of Yugoslavia, shouted, 'join with the Germans to bomb us?' So passionate were the Serbs about myth and history, they might well ask. To them, the attack of Western Europe would appear as another Fourth Crusade.

In 1204, the diplomacy of Rome had sent the crusaders to sack Constantinople instead of retaking Jerusalem. The enemy was not Islam, but the Greek Orthodox Church, which was also fighting Islam. The two great Christian faiths were then divided. Friends had become foes. It should never happen again. Greece and Russia and Serbia were the heirs of the Second Rome of Byzantium and its rituals. They remained tied together by creed as well as the past. The Serbs were still fighting a medieval war of faith. In 1389, Prince Lazar and his troops suffered a heroic defeat at Kosovo Polje before the country was overthrown by the Turks, who imposed Islamic rule for centuries. As he declared, 'It is better to die in battle than to live in shame.' And that had been the belief of the Serbian forces since they achieved independence at the beginning of the twentieth century.

Even when split by ideology, Communism against capitalism, Serbia had always depended on its basic early Christian and Greek faith in defence of its independence. In their recent wars against the Roman Catholic countries of Croatia and Slovenia, the Serbs still considered they were defending their different holy rite. So ingrained were the myths of the past that Serbian atrocities against the Islamic Albanians appeared no worse than the knights of the First Crusade slaughtering all the Muslims and the Jews when they took Jerusalem. For their world war allies to attack them on a modern crusade against the infidels was a betrayal of faith as well as of old alliances. Kosovo was the heartland of Serbian freedom.

That was why the strategy of bombing the Serbs into submission was such an error and so great a tragedy. From the Romans through the Byzantines and the Frankish crusaders and the Venetians until the Turks, no imperial land attack had ever done well in the Balkans for long, in spite of any temporary occupation. Even sophisticated German armour and artillery did badly there. Smart bombs and military peacekeepers on recall could never alter millennia of military failure.

The NATO politicians and generals ignored two thousand years of the history of the clash of religions in Yugoslavia and the idiocy of sending in the legions and the bombers and the tank squadrons against some of the most enduring fighters in the world, who conceived the defence of their land as a sacred duty. The excuse that the attack on the infrastructure of Serbia was a humanitarian mission was political hypocrisy, covering a cruel strategy. A policy of some mercy might have been more adequate. The carpet bombing merely increased the brutality: now 10,000 Muslims were murdered by the black squads, and another 1,000,000 forced over the Albanian mountains, doomed to return to the total devastation of their homes, which might only be rebuilt painfully after the delayed receipt of billions of dollars of foreign aid.

Some of the refugees, indeed, had been killed in their ramshackle convoys by misguided American bombs. In such conflicts, the innocent were hardly divided from the guilty. Jesus Christ had already given good advice on how to resist an occupying tyranny. Render unto Caesar what is Caesar's. Render unto God what is God's. In the name of God and humanity, the NATO powers rendered too much to Caesar, very little to their Christian faith. Even under international law, NATO had no right to assault or invade a sovereign nation engaged in a civil war on its recognized territory, however terrible its policies were.

After seventy-two days of bombing, Milošević collapsed, unable to contain a future civilian revolt. Yet what was the price of this hollow victory? Two wastelands in Kosovo and Serbia; another 350,000 Serbian refugees to balance the Kosovars who came home; half a dozen war criminals put on trial including Milošović, in exchange for some of the international bribery needed to repair the vast damage, even if under a new unstable democratic government. The previous sage of American foreign policy serving President Nixon, Henry Kissinger, issued a warning. The doctrine of foreign intervention for competing truths and faiths had devastated Europe in the Thirty Years War of the seventeenth century. The Western powers ran the risk of 'entering a world in which, in G. K. Chesterton's phrase, virtue runs amok'.

Both non-intervention in Africa and wrong intervention in Kosovo had produced multiple atrocities and the mass and pitiful migration of many millions of refugees, made to flee by terror tactics. The humanitarian aid sent by the United Nations and the Red Cross and other agencies could only patch up the wounds of these errors, and even prolong the agonies of the sufferers. The horrors were multiplied because of the modern technology of war and the bountiful and cheap spread of weapons, so that children and fanatics could become mindless or misdirected killing machines. This was most unfortunate when, as in the Balkans, fundamental beliefs could propel the three seminal faiths of the Near East into a new age of violent actions, so easily come to hand.

39. RETURN TO HOLY WAR

Religion is the trigger of the fanatic. The bullets are fired by the rising fundamentalist movements in the United States and Israel and Islam. Elements in all of them seem to return to medieval extremes of belief. Crimes across the globe are still being committed in the name of God, through the perversion of the various holy texts about the divine.

The object of these sacred acts of violence is to terrify. The Latin word *terrere* originally meant 'to make tremble', both governments and whole peoples, rather as a minor earthquake. The publicity attached to such horrors calls attention to a just cause or a losing cause or an excluded minority. Terrorism is, in the novelist Don DeLillo's words, 'the language of being noticed'.

In the early 1980s, the American State Department included hardly a religious group among its list of international terrorist organizations. By 1998, however, more than half of the thirty most dangerous groups in the world were connected to religious sects. These self-designated holy warriors were attacking what they believed was the state terror practised by governments, particularly in the United States and Israel. They were the fists of the Almighty, once again David taking on Goliath, but with aeroplanes and bombs as their slingshots against the giant of oppression.

Between 1969 and 1996, twenty-two airliners were blown up across the world The most publicized was the explosion over Lockerbie of Pan-Am 103, which eventually led to the conviction in an international court of a Libyan intelligence agent. The most appalling prophecy was the Bojinka plot of Ramzi Ahmed

Yousef, which was intended to destroy eleven trans-Pacific passenger flights on one day in 1995, at the instigation of Osama bin Laden, then little known for what he saw as the holy duty of his financing of terrorism. Yousef had left a nitroglycerine container with a timer beneath his seat, before leaving the aeroplane to continue towards its destination.

Yousef was also convicted with other conspirators of a more chilling forecast of future attacks on what revolutionary Islam called 'the Great Satan'. In 1993, a rented Ford van packed with explosive was parked and detonated below the World Trade Center. Several floors collapsed, six people were killed and many injured; but the structure remained intact. The Central Intelligence Agency and the Federal Bureau of Investigation rounded up and convicted thirteen more revolutionaries, including the blind Sheikh Omar Abdul Rahman, already implicated in the assassination of the Egyptian President Anwar Sadat, who had made peace with Israel. The failure of the American security bodies was not to see that these events were preludes for worse to come.

Attention was drawn, indeed, from terror abroad to internal subversion. The unpopular war in Vietnam had trained young American men in the techniques of killing. An upsurge of fundamentalist Christian and evangelical sects was paralleled by the growth of rural 'militias', which believed that a gun in the hand ensured liberty in the house against any regulation or draft or tax by the federal government. The paranoid streak in American politics was fuelled by millennial and Manichean views of the evil of all authority, which should be overthrown before the Apocalypse and the reign of Christ on earth.

The most extreme cults led to mass suicide by bullet or poison or fire; more than 900 disciples of an insane Californian preacher Jim Jones were immolated in Guyana at the Jonestown People's Temple; another 76 men and women and children of the Branch Dravidians were killed by shot and flame at their Mount Carmel sanctuary at Waco, Texas. Its leader, who styled himself David

Koresh, had already dispatched four federal
trying to storm his outpost. When the army tank
Koresh set ablaze the whole edifice, as if erecti
around his Eden.

Such apparent martyrdom in resistance to Wa
the inspiration for the worst bombing atrocity yet pe   ated in
the United States, the explosion in 1995 at the Federal Building
in Oklahoma City. The structure was wrecked, killing 168 people
and injuring three times as many, including scores of children at
a day care centre. The conspirators, Timothy McVeigh and Terry
Nichols, were veterans and militiamen. Their method was copied
from the previous Islamic revolutionary attack on the World
Trade Center; a van was packed with ammonium nitrate fertilizer
and diesel fuel, and then ignited. The two arsonists saw themselves as patriots in defence of their liberties, while the American
President accused them of being 'promoters of paranoia'. To
them, the death of many innocents was irrelevant in the fight
against the sinfulness of government. As with the Unabomber,
who also terrified the nation over many years with his mailed
explosives, to kill for liberty was a blessing, not a crime.

The new nation of Israel lived in the permanent fear of
guerrilla attacks. The second war against its dominant Arab
neighbours at the time of the British and French fiasco at the Suez
Canal left a UN expeditionary force on the Gaza Strip to prevent
more fedayeen attacks from Egypt. Yet in pulling out of its brief
occupation of Sinai, the Jewish army had destroyed everything
which was material except for the old crusader monastery of
St Katherine of Alexandria. 'God had scorched the Sinai earth,'
the UN General E. L. M. Burns noted, 'and His chosen people
removed whatever stood above it.' An escalation of hostilities by
both Israel and Egypt led to a third war in 1967, into which Syria
and Jordan were drawn.

This was Israel's opportunity to inflict, after a blitzkrieg of
only six days, the worst defeat suffered by combined Muslim
forces in the Near East since the invasions by the Mongols. The

raelis seized the rest of Jerusalem, which was annexed. They also held the West Bank of the Jordan River, the Gaza Strip and the Golan Heights leading to Damascus, while all of Sinai was taken once more. They had put together a resurrected empire of Solomon. They had also sown again the dragon's teeth of more wars and incessant terror tactics, springing from their fractured and enfeebled enemies.

A conflict of attrition across the Suez Canal followed for the next six years. Another 1,000,000 refugees were forced to leave the Egyptian port cities. As well as fighting across the canal from its Bar-Lev fortified line, Israel faced sporadic raids from Lebanon and particularly from Jordan, where Palestinian guerrillas took over large areas of the country. After an attempt to assassinate King Hussein, like his grandfather, in the al-Aqsa mosque, and after the hijacking of four passenger aircraft belonging to the Western powers, the Palestinian fedayeen were expelled by the King of Jordan in spite of Syrian military intervention, which was halted by the threat of Israel's menaces during the crisis.

The new Egyptian President, Anwar Sadat, now plotted with the Syrian President, Hafez al-Assad, to make a surprise attack in 1973 in order to recover their lost territories. Too much had been taken. Retrieval was essential, and the cause of a fourth war. An unusual failure by Israeli military intelligence allowed for a surprise assault across the Suez Canal on the afternoon of the celebration of Yom Kippur. Some 90,000 Egyptian soldiers and 12,000 tanks and other military vehicles crossed the waterway and destroyed the Israeli fortifications, pressing on to the Sinai passes. The operation was named Badr, after the Prophet Muhammad's first victory against his enemies in Mecca, and the troops shouted the holy call, 'Allah Akhbah!'

Simultaneously, two Syrian armoured columns of 500 tanks each, supported by missiles, broke through the defences of the Golan Heights and threatened to descend to attack Galilee. Jordan was mobilizing its forces, as was Iraq, to come to the aid of Syria. The situation was the most serious yet faced by Israel, which reacted quicker than a striking viper. Damascus and other cities were bombed. The Syrian armour was destroyed by expensive air attacks. The ground lost on the Golan Heights was recaptured. Then the Israeli tank commander found a gap between the Egyptian Second and Third Armies in Sinai, thrust between them to the canal and crossed it, encircling the Third Army and opening the way to Cairo itself.

While the United Nations was split on the terms for a ceasefire, Israel agreed one with Egypt and another with Syria. All three countries had their forces in dangerous and extended positions and were short of munitions and supplies. None could claim victory, only stalemate. But Israel had finally begun to learn the bitter lesson of the crusading Kingdom of Jerusalem: how vulnerable it was to a sudden combined pincer attack from the Arab countries surrounding it; how the victories of its far-flung mobile columns did not ensure a lasting enemy defeat; and how it was impossible to hold occupied territory with a hostile population of a hostile faith.

The logjam was broken by the remarkable Anwar Sadat, who chose to ignore the Islamic world and opt for direct negotiations between Egypt and Israel and its backer, the United States; these culminated in 1979 in the Camp David accords. So was set a framework for a peace treaty between Egypt and Israel, which would withdraw from Sinai over three years, if the Suez Canal and the Gulf of Aqaba became international waterways open to all shipping.

On the legitimate rights of the Palestinian people and the status of Jerusalem, there could be no meeting of minds. The Israeli delegation, now led by the former terrorist leader Menachem Begin, nearly went home when it heard that the United States intended to issue an open letter opposing the illegal annexation of the Old City and East Jerusalem. At the end of the day, President Carter only sent a private letter to Sadat saying that there had been no change in the American position on Jerusalem as declared before the United Nations. As a devout Southern

Baptist, he declared his fundamental belief and bias at that time: 'Israel is a return at last to the Bible land from which the Jews were driven so many hundred years ago, the establishment of the nation in Israel is the fulfilment of Biblical prophecies and the very sense of fulfilment.'

In failing to insist on a firm agreement on Palestinian rights as well as the Holy City, Sadat knew that he had condemned himself with the rest of Islam. By making a separate peace, Egypt found itself suspended from membership of the Arab League, which transferred its headquarters from Cairo to Tunis. As with so many radical Arab leaders before him, Sadat fell before the rising forces of Muslim fundamentalism and the assassins' grenades and bullets. His killers called their sect Al-Jihad, the Holy War. His dealings with the West seemed blasphemy to many Muslims as well as treachery to the United Arab cause. His efforts for peace were his death warrant.

In their obduracy over dealing with the rights of the Palestinian refugees and Jerusalem, the Israelis condemned themselves to twenty more years of border warfare, exacerbated by their invasion of southern Lebanon. This overreach provoked a new Shi'ite jihad against them, including suicide-bombing missions, which set an example for a terrible future, as had the first attack on the World Trade Center in New York. In 1983, a youth of twenty drove a green Chevrolet truck into the headquarters of the Israeli Defence Force in Tyre, the ancient Phoenician port. The explosion reduced the building to rubble, killing twenty-nine Israeli soldiers and thirty-two of the Palestinian and Lebanese prisoners under interrogation. The death toll was larger than achieved in five years by the sporadic attacks of the Palestinian Liberation Organization, led by Yasser Arafat, the reverse Moses of his wandering people, trying to return to their promised land.

The response of the outnumbered Israelis facing Muslim outrages was always more than biblical – ten eyes for an eye, a jaw for a tooth. They miscalculated the fervour and spread of Muslim fundamentalism, which found a revolutionary base in

Iran after the mullahs overthrew the Shah in the same year of the Camp David accords. Initially welcomed by the Russians, this radical recall of jihad against infidel influences would make the Soviet Empire lose its colonial war to the mujahedin in Afghanistan before the unexpected and sudden collapse of Marxism and the Union of Soviet Socialist Republics. If Egypt and Israel had correctly selected the victor of the Cold War, their reliance on the United States put them even more at odds with radical Islam, reverting to the concept of a holy struggle against Western materialism.

Equally, many of the Muslims underestimated the power of Christian orthodoxy and fundamentalism. They had not done so in the days of the Kingdom of Jerusalem defended by the knights of the military orders. The crusades stuck in popular memory as the primary invasion by the West. When the Turkish fanatic Mehmet Ali Agca tried to murder the Pope in 1981, he wrote: 'I have decided to kill John Paul the Second, supreme commander of the Crusades.' Curiously enough, many Catholics ascribed the beginning of the downfall of Russia and its Eastern European empire to this Polish Pope, whose support allied Catholicism with resistance in Eastern Europe and a form of people's crusade against the godless materialism of the Soviets.

Although backed by the Western Christian powers, the Shah of Persia was ousted in 1979 by Ayatollah Khomeini and his fundamentalist mullahs. Their purpose was not only to establish an extreme Islamic government with its revolutionary guards enforcing belief as brutally as Orwell's Thought Police; but the goal was also to recreate the Prophet's Umma by jihad, a community of all Islamic believers through diplomacy or war. With the Shi'ite tradition of radical martyrdom, Khomeini had at his command ten thousand times more young men than Hassan Ibn al-Sabbah had recruited to his cult of the Assassins. Seen by many as the messenger of the twelfth Imam, who would bring about a heavenly kingdom, Khomeini allowed Iran to become the leading sponsor and teacher of international Islamic terrorism.

Against Israel, the Iranians backed the two most effective terrorist groups, the Hezbollah in Lebanon and the Hamas among the Palestinian refugees, as well as Kurdish and Afghan Shi'ite resistance movements. More than sixty prominent exiles were assassinated in the old tradition. Yet Israel was preserved as the crusader Kingdom of Jerusalem had been by the divided Muslim powers falling out with each other. The Iranians were already backing a Shi'ite terrorist group, Dawa'a, within Iraq before the declaration of their fearsome war, so reminiscent of conditions on the Western Front seventy years before, with the use of mass frontal attacks, artillery and chemical weapons.

This eight-year struggle was more nationalist than religious, fought along the questionable boundaries drawn by the long-gone European powers. Iran presented itself as the blessed rescuer of the Shi'ite majority in Iraq, ruled by a Sunni minority through the cruel tyranny of Saddam Hussein. During the war, 1,000,000 Iranian martyrs in a youthful army died, charging in the name of Allah the well-armed forces of Iraq, which lost 400,000 dead. The result was a stalemate, which halted Saddam's intentions toward the south. He also planned to seize oil-rich and indefensible Kuwait, perhaps as a preliminary to striking at Saudi Arabia and taking over the custodianship of Mecca and Medina, the core of the Muslim faith. Already, radical Islamic fundamentalists had stormed the Great Mosque at Mecca in protest at the pro-Western regime.

In *The Clash of Civilisations*, Samuel P. Huntington stressed that the majority of wars in the late twentieth century had been religious conflicts. Since the revolution in Iran, when the Ayatollahs declared a holy war against America, four other Islamic states had pursued a jihad against Western targets, Iraq and Syria, Libya and Sudan. Libya was deterred by an unsuccessful desert war against Chad and an oil embargo, also an American bombing raid on the dictator's headquarters, while Sudan had a suspected chemical-warfare plant taken out by aerial attack, as it became embroiled in an endless civil war against the Christian south of the country. In all, the United States launched seventeen military operations in the Near East after 1980, culminating in the Gulf War, all against Muslim countries. The West succeeded through air power, while the only response of Islam could be through the surprise use of violence, the strategy of the Have-Nots against the Haves.

The poor in Arabic countries were the majority. They saw themselves as the victims of the corrupt West and of Israel, supported by America as an outpost of its corroding civilization. Their only possible defence and armoury was terror, which was murder on the cheap. A new Old Man of the Mountains had become their hero, Osama bin Laden. He would strike back, not only at the United States, but at the rich and reactionary Arab regimes in Saudi Arabia and the Gulf States, supported by all the wealthy nations, which depended on oil.

The new technology would be an Aladdin's Cave to bin Laden. He could deploy dedicated believers and small means to topple the mighty. How much thrust did a dagger have, set against a jet liner? What was smallpox on a blanket compared to anthrax in a ventilator? And what even was the killing by Saladin of the crusading Knights Templars after his victory before Jerusalem, put beside the final toppling of the Twin Towers of the World Trade Center, and all the infidels within it?

40. REVENGE OF ISLAM

As a national socialist secret society, the Ba'ath or Resurrection Party was extremely successful. Two of its leaders, Hafez al-Assad and Saddam Hussein, managed to seize power, in Syria and Iraq. Both profited from the overthrow of previous ancient regimes and maintained themselves by terror and a fearsome secret police. On one occasion, Assad had 25,000 opponents massacred in the city of Homs, while Hussein decimated the Kurds in the north of his country and the Marsh Arabs in the south. Both of them did succeed, however, in remaining in control of their countries for many decades, thus proving the couplet of Sir John Harington:

> Treason doth never prosper, what's the reason?
> For if it prosper, none dare call it Treason.

While Assad was always too cautious to commit his country to a frontal attack against Israel without support, he did occupy half of war-torn Lebanon. He differed from Saddam, who was vainglorious and took over the role of the spearpoint of Islam. After the conclusion of the war with Iran, he decided to take on Western materialism by seizing the Gulf states and even pushing on to Arabia. The Kuwait and Saudi dynasties were forced to call upon the former imperialist powers to protect their religious role as well as the oil fields vital to the world economy.

Thus, in his aggression, Saddam could claim that he represented radical Islam in its jihad against Israel, the creation of the infidel West. His rape of Kuwait was presented as a necessary advance in a holy war, while Jordan's heavy reliance on Iraq's economy made that strategic state a covert ally, however much King Hussein wished to remain a friend of the United States. Yet survival proved more important for Jordan than the support of any spurious sacred conflict.

During the American buildup of its force in the Persian Gulf, along with contingents chiefly from Britain and France, Saddam pre-empted massive bombing and missile attacks by launching his Scud missiles at Tel Aviv and Israel, which was restrained by the United States from riposting as it had in a previous sortie against Iraq's nuclear programme. For the Americans feared to offend the susceptibilities of their Arab allies, Arabia and Egypt and Turkey, which would hardly tolerate the Jews joining the struggle against a Muslim enemy.

The 'mother of all battles' ended for Saddam in total defeat with another 250,000 casualties. Western technology with its laser-guided shells and smart bombs destroyed the superior Iraqi numbers and capacity to fight, leaving Saddam with a Kurdish rebellion in the north and a Shi'ite revolt in the south. The Iraqi dictator, however, claimed victory in the face of catastrophe. When he announced the forced withdrawal of his troops from Kuwait, he declared:

> Everybody will remember that the gates of Constantinople were not opened to Muslims from the first attempt and that the cause of dear Palestine which has been neglected by the international community is now again knocking at the closed doors to force them to solve it . . . O Iraqis, you have fought thirty countries, and all the evil and the largest machine of war and destruction in the world that surrounds them. The soldiers of faith have triumphed over the soldiers of wrong, O stalwart men. Your God is the One who granted your victory.

While Richard Cheney, then the American Secretary of Defense, pointed out that 'the mother of all battles turned into the mother of all retreats', he was careful not to follow the path of the Assassins. 'The last thing we want to do is to turn Saddam into a martyr.' And yet, the immense victory was not to be the finish of the interminable jihads and crusades. 'It is the war of the next five hundred years,' a citizen of Baghdad said in 1992. 'It is to say what everybody in the Third World will say – I am independent.' But as the Kuwaiti roving Ambassador said after Saddam's destruction of his homeland, 'They saw a paradise next to them, and they cannibalized that paradise. They destroyed the peace of that land of their dreams.'

Yet the split in the Arab states appeared to be significant, now that they were no longer united against Western threats to their independence, something which Saddam had hardly guaranteed to Kuwait. Even radical Syria had joined conservative Saudi Arabia against Iraq, while King Hussein was forced to change tack and beat a course back towards the American stars. A new chance for a permanent peace was born, because the United States had demonstrated that it was the only superpower left that could destroy all opposition, while Israel was frightened into some sort of accommodation by the proof of its vulnerability to Arab missiles, even though it had already acquired a nuclear capacity of its own.

The first cession was to be minimal, but the basis of a sovereign state for the Palestinian Arabs. They would receive the Gaza Strip and an enclave around Jericho as a taster to the West Bank, the areas which were becoming ungovernable because of a continuing uprising, called the intifada, incited by the extremist Hamas and Islamic jihad groups. That little effort of a state, to be run by Yasser Arafat and his police, would have to prove it was a competent government and could prevent the attacks of fedayeen on Israel over the border. Then more land might be conceded, once Israel was assured of its security. 'In general,' the Israeli leader, Yitzhak Rabin, declared, 'peace is not made with your friends. Peace is made with enemies.'

What stood against this compromise were the Jewish settlements in the occupied territories, declared by religious extremists such as the Gush Emunim to be the inalienable parts of biblical Judaea and Samaria, and the annexation of Jerusalem. As the Kibbutz Dati, representing the religious communities, addressed God in its prayer on Independence Day: 'Extend the boundaries of Your land, just as You have promised our forefathers, from the river Euphrates to the river of Egypt. Build Your holy city Jerusalem, capital of Israel; and there may Your Temple be established as in the days of Solomon.' Gush Emunim had already tried to blow up the Dome of the Rock and the al-Aqsa Mosque so that a Third Temple might be built, after a terrible Arab war of fire and blood, leading to the advent of the Messiah. Fortunately, in 1984 the Israeli intelligence services thwarted this attempt to provoke a Third World War.

The radical religious movements of the Jews and the Muslims were very much the same. Ancient Israel was the focus of the Hebrew militants as the land promised exclusively to the Jews, where they would create an ideal society, while the Islamic believers who preached jihad also wished to create a just community in their traditional places of settlement for more than a thousand years after the coming of the Prophet of Allah. The extremists of the two religions wanted to replace secular with religious law and policy, the Jews with the Torah, the Muslims with the sharia. Both feared Western materialism because it obscured the Will of God, and both had millennial visions that the reign of justice upon earth was imminent after the coming of the Messiah or the last Imam. A fervour for the total destruction of their enemies was a common factor among these zealots. It almost seemed a Christian crusading legacy.

When the Arab-hating Rabbi Meier Kahane, whose followers were rabid opponents of any land concessions to the Palestinian Arabs, was assassinated in New York, his disciple Baruch Goldstein did his best to wreck the peace negotiations by massacring twenty-nine Arabs at prayer in the Hebron mosque. This was followed by Hamas attacks, which killed and wounded more than 250 Israeli citizens. In spite of this retaliation Baruch failed, the peace process continued. 'You are a foreign import,' Yitzhak Rabin said of Kahane's followers. 'You are an errant weed. Sensible Judaism spits you out.' Then he was spat out by the blast of a fanatic Jewish murderer, because of his efforts to make peace.

The ferocity increased in the religious struggles between Christian and Muslim and Jew. The paradox was that while the United States could impose a kind of peace, with Israel accepting a minimal Palestinian state in the Gaza Strip and parts of the West Bank, its global superiority in power and economics after the collapse of Communism in Russia provoked an upsurge of Muslim resistance, particularly in old colonial countries which had remained somewhat friendly with the West.

After a coup, Sudan became ruled by the sharia and pursued the rebel Christian south with a vengeance, while the outlawed Muslim Brotherhood became the alternative power in the land of Egypt. Extreme religious groups were banned in Algeria by the ruling revolutionary party after apparently winning an election there. The underground attacks of the Armed Islamic Group on French aid workers and European businessmen threatened jihad in North Africa, which would engulf the conservative regimes in neighbouring Morocco and Tunisia.

A further paradox of the dissolution of the Soviet Union was that the jihad it had encouraged against Israel was now imported into the newly dependent Asian republics with Muslim majorities. Its failed war in Afghanistan persuaded the guerrillas there to export their religious influence over the borders. In Azerbaijan and Turkmenistan, Uzbekistan and Kyrgyzstan, Kazakhstan and Tajikistan, orthodox Sunni Islamic diplomacy backed by Turkey and Saudi Arabia and Pakistan rivalled radical Shi'ite overtures from Iran to capture the hearts and minds of the 50,000,000 Muslims of Central Asia, now ready to be whipped into religious reprisals against the godless Russian minorities, which had been installed among them by the Tsars and the Bolsheviks. They also had the capacity to smuggle some nuclear weapons to radical Islam.

In the summer of 1994, the leader of the breakaway republic of Chechnya in the Caucasus did threaten jihad against Moscow, which would make the war in Afghanistan pale into insignificance. The Russian government had learned nothing. It began a costly and debilitating struggle in the Caucasus mountains, which would only increase Muslim hostility. The losing war in Afghanistan had already changed the Pakistani city of Peshawar into a capital of militant Islam, ready to export terror and violence not only towards Kabul, but also towards Kashmir, where another jihad was declared against India's occupation of part of that divided province.

The success of the mujahedin volunteers, who had flocked from most Islamic countries to fight the Russians, led to the training in warfare of battalions of young men, rather as American youths had been drafted into violence by their experience in the jungles of Vietnam. Once the Soviet state was beaten, these Arab guerrilla fighters proved the perfect stalkers of American imperialism.

The United States had already been warned in 1983 of the dangers of intervention, when a suicide bomber had put an end to 250 Marines at their barracks outside Beirut in Lebanon. This had led to a certain caution in engagement overseas. Yet Islamic terrorists struck back at home with the first detonation of the World Trade Center, followed by truck bombings of American forces in Riyadh in Saudi Arabia and the Khobar Towers in Dhahran there. A disastrous attempt to end the civil war in Somalia resulted in eighteen American dead paratroopers; some of their corpses were dragged through the streets as Hector was behind the chariot of Achilles.

Even European tourism had become a target of Islamic fanatics, who objected to any Western presence in their lands. At Luxor in Egypt in 1997, fifty-eight sightseers were murdered at that marvel of temples and tombs, which still display the frescos of the Pharaohs putting to death their Nubian slaves. This atrocity was followed by further assaults on the American Embassies in Kenya and Tanzania, in which 257 people were killed and more than 5,000 injured. The rising statistics of the dead provoked an American reaction to what was evidently an international conspiracy.

The named villain was Osama bin Laden, a wealthy son among many from a billionaire family in Saudi Arabia. After an early life as a Western playboy, he had a conversion as dramatic as St Paul on the road to Damascus. Himself a Sunni Muslim, he was expelled from Saudi Arabia for his dangerous activities, and so he took on the role of Husain, the Shi'ite martyr and hero of victim cultures. For him, the Arab crescent of countries had long been the target of killings, destruction and atrocities.

He and his al-Qaeda organization were only defending their holy lands from foreign attackers, so similar to the crusaders. Following the path of Husain, who had opposed the corrupt caliphs who had controlled Mecca after the death of the Prophet Muhammad, bin Laden no longer considered Saudi Arabia an Islamic country. 'Israeli forces occupy our land and American troops are on our territory. We have no other option but to launch jihad.'

Osama bin Laden wanted the American people to rise against their government as they had during the war in Vietnam. 'If we do not get security, the Americans also would not get security.' Thus he aimed to justify any massacre made possible by new technologies in the name of the ancient conflicts between Christians and Jews and Muslims, which had been fought with periods of truce for more than thirteen centuries. His differences from his Prophet lay in the fact that he was not a conquering and generally tolerant war leader, as Muhammad had been, the inspiration of the extraordinary Islamic conquest of North Africa and the Near East within a few decades of his death.

Bin Laden was a wealthy terrorist, who chose to live in well-equipped caves, as the bandits and outlaws used to do. Although he could recruit worldwide sleeper cells and guerrilla fighters on the scale of the anarchists in the late nineteenth century, he failed to incite the masses of poor Muslims to rise against their rulers, who were mostly tyrants who ruled by terror themselves. Their secret policemen far outnumbered the thousands of al-Qaeda members, and their brutality often exceeded even the torture and mutilation, which would be practised by bin Laden's 'Arabs' and his Taliban allies against fellow tribesmen and intrusive infidels. Islamic national security forces, particularly in Saudi Arabia, proved far stronger than the exiled terrorists. However provoked, home revolts in other Islamic countries simmered and spluttered out.

Ironically, Saudi funds and American weapons had created bin Laden's camps and Arab fighting forces in Afghanistan in the war against the Russian invaders. Channelled through the Pakistani intelligence services, the al-Qaeda resistance warriors were supplied and financed, until 60,000 of them were trained at a time in a housing development and 'university' near Peshawar. The Pakistanis used some of these insurgents in their own secret war against India in Kashmir, while the responsibility for the bombings of the business district of Bombay in March 1993, in which 300 citizens were killed, was also laid at their door.

Other Afghan-trained mujahedin, including the notorious Ramzi Ahmed Yousef, had attempted to assassinate the Pope on his visit to the Philippines, before founding in the south on the island of Basilan a Muslim guerrilla movement, Abu Sayyaf, which specialized in kidnapping and threatening to behead tourists. As Yousef said at his trial in America, before being sentenced to many terms of life imprisonment in solitary confinement as a spreader of 'plague and pestilence throughout the world': 'I support terrorism as long as it is used against the United States and Israel . . . You are more than terrorists. You are butchers, liars and hypocrites.'

This was the counter-terror proclaimed by some of the Afghan war veterans, whom America had armed and Pakistan had trained. They were following a most revealing fatwa issued by bin Laden and four leaders of other jihad groups from Egypt and Pakistan and Bangladesh. The language was almost from the Qur'ān:

> The Arabian Peninsula has never, since Allah made it flat, created its desert, and encircled it with seas, been stormed with any forces like the crusader armies spreading in it like locusts, eating its riches and wiping out its plantations. All this is happening at a time in which nations are attacking Muslims like people fighting over a plate of food . . .

The fatwa went on to claim that a 'Crusader–Zionist alliance' had killed over a million Muslims in Iraq and had tried to fragment Saudi Arabia and Egypt and Sudan into 'paper states through their disunity and weakness to guarantee Israel's survival and the brutal crusade occupation of the Peninsula'. All these crimes and sins committed by the Americans were 'a clear declaration of war on Allah, His Messenger and Muslims'.

> On that basis, and in compliance with God's order, we issue the following fatwa to all Muslims:
>   The ruling to kill the Americans and their allies is an individual duty for every Muslim who can do it in any country in which it is possible to do it, in order to liberate the al-Aqsa Mosque and the Holy Mosque (Mecca) from their grip, and in order for their armies to move out of all the lands of Islam, defeated and unable to threaten any Muslim. This is in accordance with the words of Allah, 'and fight the pagans all together as they fight you all together', and 'fight them until there is no more tumult or oppression, and there prevail justice and faith in Allah'.

In response to this declaration of war and the early al-Qaeda attacks, the Americans launched twenty Tomahawk cruise missiles, so effective in the Gulf War against Baghdad, at a presumed chemical warfare plant in Khartoum in the Sudan, and at three terrorist training camps at Khost in Afghanistan, near the border with Pakistan. Bin Laden was not put out of action by this preliminary strike, nor was his organization, now broadcast across the world, ready to be activated.

In this manner, the United States began the pursuit of the most charismatic outlaw for his people since Robin Hood was for the English and Jesse James was in the American West. Terrorism was still the shroud woven by Penelope, the abandoned wife of Odysseus, a web undone nightly throughout history. Tyrants went on weaving it to control their abject subjects. Conspirators frightened people into accepting their takeover by a new illegitimate authority. Fanatics misused sacred texts to justify their crimes in the name of their beliefs. Yet the first international coalition in history, dedicated to eliminate the sources of terrorism, soon arose. Its mission was impossible, because of all the misery and divergent faiths in the world.

41. COUNTDOWN TO KABUL

The Persian word Taliban derives from 'religious students'. The tradition dated back to the eighth century, the Hanafite legal system, one of the four main Sunni schools of religious law. Its emphasis was on the Shi'ite martyr Husain; the claim was that the human mind could clarify and interpret the revelations of the Prophet Muhammad. The doctrine was to the conservative Sunni faith in Arabia what Calvinism was to the Roman Catholic Church, a puritan reform doctrine against false ritual and images. In the eighteenth century, the al-Saud family backed the prophetic Muhammad ibn Abd al Wahhab against the worship of sacred tombs and stones and sacrifices. This puritanical jihad was put down by the Ottoman Turks, but it was revived by the Saudi royal family, when they came to power, as the pillar of the state.

In their teaching schools, or madrasas, the Wahhabis emphasized a strict conformity to Islamic codes of worship, also an oath of obedience to the ruler as long as he led the community according to the laws of God. So the Saudi royal family gave most of the schools of Arabia to these purists of a pre-medieval faith, in return for preaching that none could be saved except by following the divine authority of Allah's representative on earth. The essential oneness of God enveloped all in a single holy community.

This creed became immensely influential in Pakistan, where the madrasas funded from Arabia became fundamental in the 1990s by backing the dictatorship of General Zia ul-Haq. Through them, the Pakistanis were able to train tens of thousands of fanatical religious warriors to set against the Russian occupa-

346

tion of Afghanistan, and then against the various warlords, who tried to run the country after the ignominious departure of the Soviet Red Army. Their internecine squabbles and general brutality, particularly that of Gulbuddin Hekmatyar, who bombarded Kabul with frequent rocket attacks, so weakened successive administrations that there was little will to resist the onslaught of the Taliban.

However cruel the warlords of the later Northern Alliance were and remained, the Taliban with its Arab mercenaries or Afghan holy warriors proved even crueller. They owed allegiance to the one-eyed, ill-educated Mullah Muhammad Omar, representing authority in anarchy and vengeance. After the fall of Kabul, some 5,000 Shi'ite Hazeras, descended from the Mongol invaders, were shot or had their throats cut or perished by suffocation in trailer trucks. Another 3,000 Taliban prisoners were tortured and executed after Mazar-e-Sharif was taken in the north.

Sentenced by sharia law, hands and feet were amputated for theft, adulterers were stoned to death or flogged, a woman had her thumb cut off for applying nail varnish. 'When we cut the hand off a thief,' said the head of the Taliban religious court in Kabul, 'we had observed human rights ... If these types of heavenly orders are not enforced, then corruption will increase.' Most of the Afghan art dating back to Alexander the Great, also immense statues of the Buddha, was broken or blown up.

The real and loathed power in Afghanistan was Osama bin Laden with his Foreign Legion. He had fought with many of them in the battles of Jalalabad against the Russians, but his chief adviser was an Egyptian doctor, Ayman al-Zawahiri, the brains behind the campaign of the 5,000 foreign fighters, bolstering the attack on the surviving warlords in the Northern Alliance. In spite of the brilliant resistance of Ahmed Shah Massoud, the Tajik Lion of the Panjshir Valley, the Taliban took over nine-tenths of the country, with Pakistan giving it logistical support. Massoud was assassinated by a pair of suicide bombers claiming to be journalists, just before Osama bin Laden's greatest triumph and disaster, the aerial attacks on 11 September 2001, on the World Trade Center and the Pentagon, the ultimate symbols of American imperialism.

The success of the total destruction of the Twin Towers and part of the Pentagon by civilian jet liners, hijacked with pen-knives and boxcutters, changed the nature of terrorism for the future. The body count was intolerable: some 5,000 victims, later reduced to 3,000, were killed. The mass murder had happened in the heartland of American business. The calculated method of destruction was American aircraft. The technology of the most advanced civilization on earth had been used as daggers in its own back. While the loss of hundreds of American soldiers and sailors abroad from earlier al-Qaeda attacks was negotiable, this outrage upon the innocent was not.

The new Republican President, George W. Bush, who had achieved the White House by a few chads and a whisker, spoke the language of the American West. Cleverly advised by his Secretary for Defense, Colin Powell, who had beaten Saddam Hussein through a superb bombing campaign, an international coalition was formed in a ring fence around Afghanistan, except for Iran, which remained neutral. Russia and its former Cauca-sian republics joined with Pakistan, where the extraordinary dictator General Musharraf calculated his advantage and changed sides, supporting the United States in return for promises of massive foreign aid. As Anwar Sadat had done in Egypt, he dismissed or imprisoned the extremist leaders in his army and intelligence system, and after a fanatic Muslim attempt to attack the Indian Parliament he detained a further 1,900 terrorists to avert a fourth war over Kashmir. He wanted to move from Zia ul-Haq's theocracy to a modern secular Islamic state with elec-tions for a National Assembly. He also granted the Americans the use of three airfields in his country, risking a fundamentalist revolution.

As it was, the Russian supply of weapons to the Northern

Alliance, and the fearsome American bombing campaign with its 'daisy-cutters', which could even shatter bin Laden's bunkers and deep hide-outs, destroyed by the winter of 2001 the Taliban militia and the al-Qaeda Foreign Legion. Using Texan language, George W. Bush promised to smoke out and catch bin Laden as another Wild West outlaw. A price was put on his head of $25,000,000, the highest in history, for the bounty hunter who took him, dead or alive.

The American President was actually following in the steps of Alexander the Great, the first and last Western conqueror of Afghanistan. When the defeated King Darius of Persia was stabbed to death by the faithless Bactrian satrap Bessus, rather as Jesse James was shot in the back by another outlaw looking for a reward, Alexander pursued the assassin from the south of Afghanistan to Central Asia, seizing and founding cities on his chase. The spiritual base of the Taliban, Kandahar, was probably a corruption of the Greek conqueror's name.

Bessus was abandoned by his allies to his fate, although Osama bin Laden was still rich enough not to be sold. Chained, stripped naked and scourged, Bessus was put in a cage and sentenced to a punishment even worse than the Taliban had inflicted on their enemies during ritual amputations in the football stadium of Kabul. He had his nose and ears cut off and died on the cross. Alexander could not forgive him for assassinating the noble and royal Darius. Mutilation was the right retribution for regicide rather than heresy.

In sorting through the Taliban computer discs and papers in Kabul and Kandahar, manuals were found on making most of the deadly weapons from atomic bombs to poison vapours. The use of sarin gas on Japanese commuters in the Tokyo under-ground system by the 'Armageddon cult' of Aum, led by its insane leader Shoko Asahara, had already shown how toxins as well as nuclear warheads could put capital cities under threat from fundamentalist or millennial groups. The mailing of anthrax spores to leading American senators seemed to be another al-Qaeda outrage, but was downgraded to an attack by a native fanatic, as the Unabomber had been. What it proved was the vulnerability of all sophisticated communities to the ancient and elementary assaults of plague as well as weaponry.

A paradox of terrorism is that the revolution it aims to provoke usually leads to a stronger state. Seeking a global alliance against militant secret societies, most of which miscalled themselves freedom fighters, democratic America had to drop its crusade for human rights and tacitly support China in its suppression of the Uzbek and Tibetan resistance; Russia against the Chechens; Turkey and even Syria versus the Kurds; and Israel in its frequent assassinations of Hamas leaders, who continued to send in suicide bombers to blow apart Jewish civilians. More ironic was the withdrawal of American financial support from the Irish Republican Army and Sinn Féin, after three of their members were arrested and charged with manufacturing deadly napalm bombs with the narco-terrorist Revolutionary Armed Forces of Colombia. Faced with international proscription, the Irish rebels were forced into decommissioning some of their weapons.

The burning of the Twin Towers of Mammon and the Pentagon of Moloch seemed to imply a lasting peace in Éire after many centuries of holy war between Catholics and Protestants in that divided land. Two former IRA officers, Gerry Adams and Martin McGuiness, had been elected to the British Houses of Parliament and were now given accommodation there, in spite of refusing to take the Oath of Allegiance to the crown. Even the erstwhile conspiracy to bomb the whole cabinet at the Conservative Conference at Brighton was forgiven in the hope of a desperate solution to an apparently interminable war.

Thomas Fuller once prophesied the difference between ancient and modern strategies of terror. 'Rebellion must be managed by many swords; treason to his prince's person may be with one knife.' From the lone assassin to the skyscraper obliterator, the crime is equally repugnant. Yet there is a Richter scale of victims.

Too many of the dead provoke a global reach of response, as in the war in Afghanistan. From this far stretch, as when President Thomas Jefferson sent the infant American navy to smoke out the Barbary pirates, the outlaw may have no refuge. His massacre by stealth has no sanctuary. In the words of Periander, 'If you are terrible to many, beware the many.' They will be terrible to you.

In the Jewish and Sunni faiths, Joshua and the Prophet Muhammad had been leaders in holy wars. Even in the Christian faith, the victim Jesus and his disciples had fomented a change in the Roman Empire, which had led to priestly power over the state in Byzantium. What is now ignored by most Western commentators is that Husain, the grandson of the Prophet, played the role of Christ the martyr for the Shi'ites in Islam. He remained the role model for the Assassins and the later suicide troops of Osama bin Laden. Self-sacrifice in jihad was a recognition of the inner truth of Islam, as well as a denial of the corruption of Western capitalism. As an al-Qaeda spokesman, Sulaiman Abu Gaith, declared: 'There are thousands of young people who are as keen about death as Americans are about life.' So it had been with the Christian martyrs in the Roman circuses. So it is for the followers of Husain, as the suicide bombers of Hamas, who imagine that their immolation is a passport to paradise.

For the mullahs with their many interpretations of their sacred text, the Qur'ān speaks with two tongues on the tactics of terrorism. The Prophet preached a doctrine of protection against the infidels. The fundamentalist interpretation believes that the Jewish occupation of Jerusalem, from where the prophet rode to the seventh heaven, and the presence of American military forces on the Arabian peninsula entitle Islam to retaliate worldwide against the Great Satan, which has polluted its holy ground. The use of terror may kill the infidels wherever they may be found. Equally, moderate Muslim clerics do not so interpret the Qur'ān, nor do they declare jihad against the pervasive corruption of the Western world. No more do most of the peoples of the Western world follow Jewish or Christian fundamentalism, demanding the reconstruction of the Third Temple in a Greater Israel and the conversion of Islam itself.

Unfortunately, given the modern media, it is by extremes that we are reported. Any selected text from the Torah or the Bible or the Qur'ān may seem to justify the persecution of people of other faiths, even unto death.

42. THE FUTURE OF TERROR

Modern politics bows to economics, not to history. The lessons of the past are oblivion, the mistakes a daily repetition. Yet this is not true of the Near East. Among the Jews, ancient Israel is today and tomorrow and for ever. Among the Muslims, the Prophet who stepped into heaven in Jerusalem from the Rock, now under its Dome, lives everlastingly. Only the Christians of the West have ignored much of their heritage in the pursuit of a higher standard of living rather than being. Their new Jerusalem lies as much in the supermarket as in the heart. But for the final contenders for the Holy Land on earth, few of the acts of 3,000 years have been forgiven, and none forgotten.

The search for a new and positive identity was crucial in the ideology of sacred wars. So was the concern for social justice and equality. The Shi'ite Iranians, who were indifferent to Marxist analyses of the situation in their country under the Shah, could understand exactly why he was a bad ruler when the principles of Abu Bakr or the Imam Ali were applied to that regime. They had been unmoved by a nationalist explanation of why they should throw off the shackles of the United States and take control of their own destinies. Yet the call to action was deeply embedded in the Islamic tradition. When the Ayatollah Khomeini said in 1996 that 'faith consists of this form of belief that impels men to action', they could understand exactly what he meant.

Islam had always championed the cause of the poor and had encouraged them to stand up for their own rights. Neither the United States nor the Soviet Union had been a real friend to the poor, Khomeini argued. There was no reason why there should be abject poverty in Iran, which was an oil-rich country; the imperial powers had simply exploited this resource so that the people had never benefited from it themselves. Filled with an apocalyptic vision that had inspired other holy wars, Khomeini argued that the poor must take their destiny into their own hands and initiate change by declaring war against the ruling classes. Muslims must lead the way and be a vanguard for all the deprived people of the world who had been damaged by the imperialism of the superpowers. The Islamic revolutionary jihad would bring about a new world order.

The leadership of the Christian world had, however, passed from Europe to the United States. America's approach towards the Arabs and the Jews was bound to be different. Many of the old crusading attitudes had reached America together with the immigrants from Europe. Yet from the days of the *Mayflower*, the Americans had identified with the Jews and had given their new Canaan a biblical identity, before the arrival of the millions of Jews who fled persecution in Europe. A threat to Israel could be seen as a threat to the identity of America itself and as a wound to her integrity.

Crusading Christianity had developed as a response to a long period of withdrawal during the Dark Ages. It was a radical departure, having nothing whatever to do with the pacifist religion of Jesus; but it provided the people of Europe with an ideology that restored their self-respect. The Iranian revolution, with its theme of hatred of the Western world, was born of the humiliation and impotence of the colonial period, when Britain and America were felt to have exploited the people of Iran and to have supported the tyrannical regime of the Shah. Similar to crusading in some ways, the Iranian experience was a radical departure from established Muslim tradition.

The endless holy wars have continued. Because of the medieval blood-libel of the Jews, 6,000,000 were exterminated by the retrograde Nazis in the Final Solution, more horribly than when they were burned alive in their synagogues after the First Crusade took Jerusalem in blood and fire. In the 1980s, a Polish pope unleashed a crusade in Eastern Europe against materialism and Marxism, and he triumphed. The anti-Christian Marxist regimes collapsed with surprising ease. The eighteenth-century Age of Reason had given way to a strong and fundamentalist resurgence of Christianity in the nineteenth century. The secularism of modern times also gave way to a renewed religious passion in many faiths. In Judaism and Christianity and Islam, which all insisted that their myths were historically true, people rediscovered a religious geography which gave them a sense of their place in the world and a connection with the unseen and the hereafter.

In an important article, 'The Dream of Co-existence', the Mediterranean historian Bernard Lewis stressed the common heritage of the three great Levantine religions from the ancient Middle East, from Graeco-Roman antiquity, and from Jewish revelation and prophecy. While the Jews kept to Judaism, they were not exclusive, for anyone might join them, and other monotheists were not excluded from paradise. Traditional Christianity and Islam, however, claimed to possess both universal and exclusive truths. There was no salvation outside their particular creeds, although conversion to the true faith was possible. Missionary activities were encouraged across the world.

The chief danger of a final holy war in the Middle East lay in Muslim fundamentalists taking over a state armed with Western technology, missiles and nuclear weapons. As Lewis pointed out, the Muslim radicals and militants were fighting the enemy within as well as the enemy without.

Sometimes he is the Jew or Zionist – the terms are more or less interchangeable; sometimes the Christian or missionary or crusader, again more or less interchangeable; sometimes the western imperialist, nowadays redefined as the United States; occasionally – though not much of late – the Soviet Communist. The primary enemy and immediate object of attack among many of these groups are the native secularizers, those who have tried to weaken and modify the Islamic base of the state by introducing secular schools and universities, secular laws and courts, and thus excluding Islam, and so also the professional exponents of Islam, from two major areas which they had previously dominated, education and justice.

This was hardly true in Saudi Arabia or Afghanistan under the Taliban, the countries of the madrasas, which also acted as welfare centres, and the sharia law. Yet elsewhere in the world, the secular state had by the second millennium already triumphed over the religious state. Orthodox Islam was fighting in the last ditch. A brilliant Jewish examination of idolatry after the age of Freud equated it with ideology, a form of collective illusion which became an absolute devotion, an attitude that transferred a feeling into a divine being, named 'nation' or 'class' or 'race' or 'blood and iron' or 'earth'. These were idols in an age of apparent materialism. Absolute value could now be conferred upon many things and causes, particularly money, along with 'institutions such as the state, persons, goals, ideologies, and even a football team'. These objects of worship were given a transcendental goal, a form of earthly success hailed as a divine mission or a heavenly victory.

These gross crusades were perversions of the holy wars and jihads that depended on religious zeal. Such abiding and aggressive faith is still an element in Judaism and Christianity and Islam, however much their secular rulers wish to rule it out of their diplomatic considerations. All slaughter in the name of God is a perversion of a sacred text. The most interesting development of the use of terrorism, indeed, has been the kidnapping of religion to disguise nationalist movements, as in Israel and its Islamic neighbours.

Many of the techniques of terror of the political secret society had been formed in the French Revolution, which loosed nationalism on the old imperial powers. To Stefan Zweig, 'the very plague was nationalism, which poisoned the flower of European culture.' Today, it continues to sweep through the countries of the world, and fuel is added to its fires by the dead wood of racism. Wherever any minority rules a majority of another race or creed, a nationalist secret society representing that majority plots to gain power. Its means are legal or illegal, depending on the chances of revolution. Thus in 1964 the Africans in Zanzibar succeeded in ousting their Arab rulers in a nationalist and racist massacre by the majority, sparked off by cells trained in revolutionary techniques.

Whenever a minority fears the oppression of a majority within a given country, it also may plot for independence through secession or partition; the Tamils of Sri Lanka and the Kurds of Iraq and of Turkey and the Basques of Spain, for example, are led by terrorist organizations in their respective fights for independence. There is no limit to the demands of any group for self-rule, once it considers itself to be a nation. And any group can be persuaded that it is a nation, separate and indivisible, by the propaganda of a small political group prepared to lead it to independence. As the Croatian writer Mirko Mirković said, 'Nationalism begins with violence against the human rights of people belonging to another ethnic community and ends with violating the human rights of its own people. It is a land-mine which, blowing up, will destroy both foe and friend.'

In a world split into rival areas of influence – American, Russian, Chinese, and, to a lesser extent, European – would-be conspirators have little difficulty in obtaining supplies of money and arms from a foreign power. Mass disaffection in a particular area or group can be exploited by trained agitators to produce a revolt, and to enable them to seize control. Nationalism is still the cry that rallies the mass of the people to the side of the plotters. Until its fires are spent, subversion by terror will remain a major instrument of change. Even the temporary world alliance against terrorism cobbled together in 2001 cannot endure too long a campaign, which involves the attempts of the CIA to track down the tens of thousands of al-Qaeda trainees, now scattered across the globe, many in sympathetic Muslim states. Most probably, President George W. Bush's threatened attack on the 'axis of evil' of Iraq and Iran and North Korea for trying to acquire nuclear and chemical weapons will be mounted by the United States alone, with some support from Britain.

The terror tactics of religious fanatics and misguided patriots cannot be terminated, yet they may be contained in the east from Kabul to Baghdad, from Khartoum to Benghazi. Adjustment to the political and financial balance between Israel and the West on the one scale and the Muslim countries on the other is the only solution in the long term. But terror will remain warfare by extreme means and the necessary tactic of the victim against the oppressor. Only a strategy of limitation will lessen the count of the dead among the shaken rich nations. For as Edmund Burke said, 'Early and provident fear is the mother of safety.'

In former ages, every civilization used a strategy of terror from time to time. The essential for the modern age is that it is consigned to the dustbins of history, where that foul instrument belongs. No religion may justify its use now, whatever an old sacred text may declare. If we have not progressed from barbarism to some humanity, we are beyond redemption.

Most inadequately, as in its initial campaign against international terrorism, the United States Department of Defense described terrorism as 'the unlawful use, or threatened use, of force or violence against individuals or property to coerce and intimidate governments or societies, often to achieve political, religious, or ideological motives.' This narrow definition excluded the sufferings of the terrorized, particularly under the state brutality practised from the Roman Empire through slavery to the genocides of Hitler and Stalin and Pol Pot. At its worst, terrorism is a deadly statistic, a cataract of murder by horrible means in a climate of fear. Although we call ourselves more civilized than our ancestors, we have been able to terrorize to death at least 100,000,000 people in the twentieth century, a scale of genocide made possible by the modern technology, which is our pride and joy.

Terror has no limits and lacks a comprehensive definition. It is a human state of induced fear, even when the state induces that fear. It is what makes us all tremble, even without the unprecedented mass slow massacres of modern times. These previous illustrations of the use of terror in history have tried to bring out ten principles or general conclusions.

Terror is warfare by extreme means. The Romans and Saints Augustine and Aquinas tried to distinguish between just wars with rules, and combats against outlaws without restraint. Aquinas suggested three necessities for a righteous war: the authority of the prince; an attack only on those who deserved it; and the attackers' belief that they would do good and prevent evil. In such conflicts between sovereign powers, Christianity required a fair treatment of the foe. Yet in illegitimate bandit or guerrilla warfare, every atrocity was permissible. Until the Nuremberg trials of Nazi officials, no war crimes were punishable under international law. The US military also designated al-Qaeda prisoners as 'unlawful combatants', deserving all the maltreatment they might receive.

Terror is the lifeblood of tyranny. By not resisting terrorist politicians early, we have allowed the Hitlers and the Hirohitos, the Stalins and the Maos and the Pol Pots to kill many tens of millions of people, often their own. Had the Nazis been stopped at the Rhineland or the Anschluss with Austria, or the Japanese been deterred after the Rape of Nanking, how many lives would have been saved? Whatever the cost, terror tactics must be fought on a daily basis; otherwise they may become the mass-murder machine of a rogue state or group in a technological age.

Terror is the weapon of the outlaw against the oppressor. As long as there is misery and repression in the world, the celebrated criminal will appeal, even with his cruelty. The hero of millions in the exploited north-east of Brazil in the depressed 1930s, Captain Lampião, was a bandit who tortured old women and slaughtered farm labourers as well as policemen, while enforcing a strict sexual morality which involved castrating seducers. By kidnap and bank robbery, he financed his band. Fright was his chief weapon, yet he seemed a deliverer to the many, whose landlords exploited them by frightfulness. He inspired love and ballads, as did the noble Antonio Silvino and the other robber barons of the *sertão*, the dry scrubland:

> His darling was the dagger,
> His gift was the gun . . .
> He left the rich as beggars,
> The brave fell at his feet,
> While others fled the land.

Terror is murder on the cheap. A second-hand screwdriver costing ten pence killed Elisabeth, the Empress of Austria, at the hands of an assassin. The cost of the seizure of the three jet liners that caused the tragedies at the World Trade Center and the Pentagon has been estimated at $100 a head for the journey of the hijackers. In the land of mass consumption, never did so many suffer so much from so little spent by so few.

Terror is the lash on the back of the refugee. From the forced marches of the Armenians through the Crimean Tartars sent to Siberia to be killed by nuclear pollution and on to the citizens of Phnom Penh, from the induced flight of the Greeks from Turkey and the Arabs from Palestine and the Hutus from Rwanda, atrocity or the fear of it has shifted tens of millions refugees into makeshift camps during the twentieth century, many without hope of return to their homeland.

Terror is victory by stealth for the few. From the Jacobins to the Bolsheviks to the Fascists to the Ba'ath Party, revolutionary conspiracies have occasionally succeeded in taking over great nations. The successful plotters have always used atrocity and deterrence in measured doses, so as not to alienate the masses before they could be controlled by a vicious secret police, in the service of the new state.

Terror is defeat by cowardice for the crowd. Even successful tyrants such as Mussolini and Hitler were amazed at the lack of resistance by their peoples. They despised the supine mob. As Lenin believed, the proletariat needed a dictatorship. While all societies have recognized with Pascal that 'justice without force is a myth', the masses of the world have generally failed to depose early their rulers, who use excessive force against them.

If we are terrorized, we may become terrible to those who make us fear. In the Second World War, the Western democracies defeated the Fascist powers by their superior technology, not their morality. Even so, the morale of the citizen soldiers was fuelled by hatred of Nazi brutality. From the peasant revolts of the Middle Ages to the Peninsular War against the Napoleonic armies and on to modern guerrilla movements as in Cuba, once oppression became intolerable, even the cowed population began to fight back until the government fell.

Terror is measured by the scale of its victims, not the merit of its cause. Modern technology has made us able to murder in our tens of millions rather than tens of thousands. Only the amount of unaccustomed casualties in its heartland provoked the United States into a war in Afghanistan and the first international campaign against terrorism. As we have decided to continue to produce machines and chemicals of mass destruction, both nuclear and biological, and as we cannot control their proliferation, the price of freedom from terror will remain eternal vigilance.

Tolerance of terrorism is no virtue. The cliché that today's terrorist is tomorrow's freedom fighter has no merit. Doomed causes, such as the terrorist fight for an independent Kurdistan or a Basque homeland, are murder without any hope of victory.

Other enduring rebel groups such as the Irish Republican Army bomb and maim hundreds and merely achieve the cemetery, never a United Ireland, which will only come through diplomacy.

Terror will for ever be with us, because there will always be the unjust gap between the rich and the poor nations. There will remain the greedy grasp of globalization on the small starved economies. Yet now there are no just wars to fight. The Prime Minister of Israel, Ariel Sharon, rightly said: 'There is no good terrorism or bad terrorism. There is only terrorism.' The thing is to oppose it, but not to use it.

ENVOI

The war on terror is never-ending. That was forecast at the opening of *The Iliad*, when European armies first attacked Troy. Then Apollo with his silver bow rained down his arrows on the Greeks for nine days, killing thousands with the plague. The funeral pyres of the dead burned day and night, until this divine bioterror was placated by the antidote of sacrifice and the conflict continued. And so the American President George W. Bush pledged in a fiery speech to a thousand graduates at the military academy at West Point that the war against terror would be taken to sixty countries covering a third of the globe in order to keep weapons of mass destruction from tyrannical or bandit hands. 'We must take that battle to the enemy, disrupt his plans and confront the worst threats before they emerge ... In the world we have entered, the only path to safety is the path of action. And this nation will act.'

Yet the problem was whether the sole superpower left in the modern world could act effectively. It had failed to intervene in frightful wars of massacre after the fall of the Soviet Union. More extreme than bin Laden, the leader of the Tamil Tigers had resurrected the ideology of the suicide mission. Velupillai Prabhakaran had conducted a terrorist and guerrilla campaign in Sri Lanka for fifteen years, which killed 64,000 people. His struggle to establish an independent Tamil state in the north of the island was characterized by assassination and the kidnapping of child soldiers.

Such suicide bombers probably murdered the Indian Prime Minister Rajiv Gandhi in 1991, and certainly their own country's Prime Minister two years later, while attacking the World Trade

Centre in Colombo with a truck bomb in 1997 and the international airport in 2001, leaving hundreds of casualties. More than 1,500 died in ten years in many mass-murder attempts. If the bomber survived the explosion, he or she bit a cyanide capsule worn round the neck to avoid capture. More than 200 self-sacrificial killers were dispatched by Prabhakaran, some no older than twelve.

Fanaticism, indeed, is easy to spoon-feed to the young. A little learning is the nipple of the militant, when the mother's milk is hatred and revenge. The child bombers of the Tamil Tigers would be imitated by those of the Palestinian independence movement Hamas. Both organizations would confuse what they called a fight for freedom with the exploitation of the ignorant and the innocent, who were too young to know any better. Indeed, the discovery of the photograph of a baby dressed as a suicide bomber in the Gaza Strip enraged the Israelis, proving to them that indoctrination began in the cradle.

As the predominant power in the modern world, the United States was reproached for failing to prevent genocide in many countries while professing a humanitarian foreign policy. A strong indictment, *A Problem from Hell*, perceived the American refusal to intervene as a kind of tacit consent to mass murders in faraway places. Without public protests at home, as during the war in Vietnam, the Washington establishment demonstrated flabbiness and the evasion of any responsibility. 'The inertia of the governed cannot be disentangled from the indifference of the government.' Yet the disintegration of the World Trade Center in New York had changed the terms of the equation. To earn a death sentence in the twentieth century, it had been enough 'to be an Armenian, a Jew, or a Tutsi. On September 11, it was enough to be an American.'

The global war on terror declared by George W. Bush had its limitations. Without spreading military forces to put out every bush fire, only economic sanctions against rogue regimes, the seizure of their foreign assets, and the jamming of their communications systems were appropriate. Even the American President's intention of following the war in Afghanistan by another campaign against Iraq was delayed by the bellicose policy of the Jewish leader, Ariel Sharon. He had refused to define terrorism as good or bad. Now he categorized a spate of suicide bombings in Israel in 2002 as the state terrorism of Yasser Arafat of Palestine.

In launching reprisal raids against the Arab authorities, Sharon inflicted worse state terrorism against civilians in the refugee camp at Jenin and Ramallah and the Gaza Strip than Israel had suffered in its clubs and shopping malls. Terror only begets more terror and precludes peace. Sharon's blundering retributions merely produced no solution and another generation of martyrs. Furthermore, they denied the United States any support from Muslim nations against a rogue Islamic state such as Iraq until there was a settlement between the Jews and the Palestinians.

This lack of will by the Americans to impose a treaty by economic and military sanctions against Israel appeared as a tacit approval of its extreme measures against the population of the West Bank, which it had occupied and tried to colonize in defiance of United Nations resolutions. Early missions by the victor of the Gulf War against Iraq, General Colin Powell, did not procure an indefinite Israeli withdrawal or earn any Arab support, but his persistent diplomacy did succeed in the passing by the Security Council of a strong United Nations resolution, requiring the return to Iraq of weapons inspectors, charged with eliminating all military methods of terrorism by nuclear bomb or poison gas. Failure to comply would ensure another American assault.

In a way, the global war against terror could provoke other unsolved conflicts in its name. There can be no end to nuclear proliferation, for if your enemy has the bomb, you must try to acquire it yourself. As the nuclear deterrents of Israel could obliterate Baghdad, not to mention Cairo or Damascus, Saddam Hussein would always have a good Islamic reason to manufacture missiles with warheads, let alone Egypt or Syria. The American–

Russian deal to cut their nuclear capacity by two-thirds would never deter dozens of other states from developing launch pads against their foes.

This menace was already the most dangerous in the world in Kashmir. There the confusion between freedom fighters and terrorists continued to threaten several more Hiroshimas to come. By backing Islamic militants in cross-border raids across the ceasefire line, successive Pakistani governments stirred the cauldron after three previous border wars. General Musharraf's wise support of the American campaign in Afghanistan backfired in the intolerable assault of Muslim terrorists in 2002 on the Indian Parliament where a dozen died. Under pressure from fundamentalist groups and his own army, Musharraf failed to crack down on the infiltrators, who killed another thirty-three people at an Indian army base.

So the ancient religious war between Hindu and Muslim, never resolved after the Moghul massacre at Delhi and the bloodiness of Partition when the British left, still promised a nuclear solution, particularly from out-gunned Pakistan. With hardline religious politicians backing another confrontation, there was little room for manoeuvre. The Americans had to send in their experienced Secretary of Defense Donald Rumsfeld to try to knock warheads together. Yet national pride and faith could at the best reach a truce, hardly an abiding peace.

The problem of the global war declared by America was that it lacked a strategy. While all generals were always accused of fighting the last war during the next one, the efforts of President Bush to put together a Homeland Security system by cobbling together many intelligence agencies was as doomed as his international coalition against terror. As with the anarchists of the nineteenth century, there was no protection against their bombs detonating in any urban centre. The problem was that a Victorian bomb might only kill dozens while a nuclear 'dirty bomb' could now kill hundreds of thousands of people and contaminate a city.

The means of terror had multiplied. Modern communications

had also made it easier for terrorists to signal to each other and move quickly about the world under false identities. American intelligence believed that al-Qaeda had the support of some 7,000,000 radical Muslims in many countries with more than 100,000 martyrs prepared to die for the cause, and at least 1,000 planted in sleeper cells in the United States and Europe. As with the anarchist threat, the price of security was increasing surveillance.

A military and legal adviser to four American Presidents, Philip Bobbitt, gave a bleak forecast of the future of terror in *The Shield of Achilles*, who was brought down at Troy by his vulnerable heel. Bobbitt foresaw a New York rendered into ruins as ancient Rome, with scavengers living among the rubble after the attacks of the barbarians and the plague. He found that history was saturated 'with the suffering imposed by people who have no limits at all to what they're willing to impose because their goal was limitless.' The present problem was that the multiple enemy was hard to target, as had been the Assassins and the anarchists. 'When you don't know who your adversary is, deterrence is of very little use.'

The anarchists were destroyed by a totalitarian Marxist doctrine as the Mafia in Sicily were castrated by the Fascists. Just so Arabic fundamentalism can only be destroyed by Western materialism. The good may remain rigidly in religious creeds. The goods shall only go to those who earn them. At the end of the day, most people would rather live well than believe what they are taught. The running of most Muslim states by corrupt regimes, which create an abyss between the elite and the poor and also preach a holy war to bury their misdeeds, can be overcome by the fair distribution of wealth, encouraged by the overmighty Western powers. The capitalist version of the solution of inequality, proven in Europe and the United States by the market economy, is the only answer to religious fundamentalism, once wiser governments adopt these policies in the Near East.

Where can one take refuge except in poetry? As Rilke wrote about the First World War in the opening of his *Duino Elegies*:

> For Beauty's nothing
> but beginning of Terror we're still just able to bear.
> and why we adore it so is because it serenely
> disdains to destroy us. Every angel is terrible.

I do not wish to intrude into this small text any more than the supreme Thucydides did briefly into his *Peloponnesian War*. But I did write a poem on the completion of this book of millennial nightmares, which seems to express more concisely what I have been trying to say:

> Terror is a fall from grace.
> Terror wears a human face.
> I am sick. There's no solace
>   For the likes of me.
>
> Terror hovers in the air.
> Terror is the blood of fear.
> I am scared and I am here.
>   Save the likes of me.
>
> Terror's murder on the cheap.
> Terror's bodies in a heap.
> I'm too near and in too deep.
>   SOS for me.
>
> Terror as a new-born child
> Puts red hands towards the wild.
> Wonder at that cruelty
>   Killing all and me.
>
> Stalin, Hitler and Pol Pot,
> Terror's uncles, may they rot.
> They lived on, when we did not.
>   Why such infamy?

Pentagon and Towers fall.
Terror strikes at us withal.
Each is each, and yet global
        Horror reaches me.

Auschwitz ended poetry.
Yet words we need, and so we try
To describe atrocity,
        Or we live and die.

Without a record, for you see,
If terror's anonymity
Hides the millions where they lie –
        Who are you? Who am I?

The only thing is to be.
Terror's in the mortuary.
Our family lives. And fears pass
        As the blades of grass.

Notes

Acknowledgements

The author and publishers would like to thank all those who have given permission to reproduce the illustrations and quotations in this book, which are acknowledged in the following Section Notes. Every effort has been made to trace copyright holders.

1. Ancient Terrors

On the history of Greece, nobody has yet written better than J. B. Bury, whose work was first published in 1900 in London. Niccolò dei Machiavelli remains in *The Prince* the supreme philosopher of the tactics of terror of Renaissance Italy. My *Jerusalem: The Endless Crusade* (London, 1996) describes the destruction there. Excellent on early religious conflicts is Karen Armstrong, *Holy War: The Crusades and their Impact on Today's World* (rev. ed., New York, 1991), also *A History of God* (London, 1993). The *Confessions* of St Augustine remain seminal.

2. The Texts of Holy Terror

These texts are derived from the Torah, the Bible, of which I use the King James Version, and the Qur'ān. For the crusades and the Grail romances, reference may be made to my *The Discovery of the Grail* (London, 1998). For a succinct description, *The Arabs in History* (London, 1950) by Bernard Lewis is most judicious.

3. The Horror of the Crusades

All enquiries into the crusaders still begin and end with Sir Stephen Runciman's *A History of the Crusades* (3 vols, Cambridge, 1951–4). Generally useful on the subject are Zoé Oldenbourg, *The Crusades* (London, 1966); Richard Barber, *The Knight and Chivalry* (London, 1970); and Amin Maalouf, *The Crusades Through Arab Eyes* (London, 1984). On the Cathars, Zoé Oldenburg remains the authority in her *Massacre at Montségur: A History of the Albigensian Crusade* (New York, 1961).

4. The Old Man of the Mountains

An examination with endnotes of the relations between the Knights Templars and the Assassins has already been made in my *The Sword and the Grail* (London, 1993).

5. The Anabaptists and Millennial Terror

Definitive on the Anabaptists is Norman Cohn, *The Pursuit of the Millennium* (London, 1957). After that, the best account is in George H. Williams, *The Radical Reformation* (London, 1962). There are also excellent sections on the Anabaptists as well as the Black Death in Otto Friedrich, *The End of the World: A History* (New York, 1986).

6. Sacred Terror and the French Religious Wars

Other than contemporary chronicles, the leading modern source is Mark P. Holt, *The French Wars of Religion, 1562–1629* (Cambridge, 1995).

7. Beast and Pest: The Origins of Bioterror

The Italian historian of the siege of Kaffa was Gabriel de Mussis. The specialist on the spread of diseases is R. S. Bray, *Armies of Pestilence* (Lutterworth Press, 1996). Also important are Howard W. Haggard, *Devils, Drugs, and Doctors* (London, 1929); H. Zinnser, *Rats, Lice and*

History (London, 1935); and Jared Diamond, *Guns, Germs and Steel* (London, 1997). Invaluable is Johannes Nohl, *The Black Death: A Chronicle of the Plague* (London, 1926). For the Spaniards in the Americas, essential reading is Bernal Diaz del Castillo, *The Discovery and Conquest of Mexico* (New York, 1956); Miguel Leon-Portilla, *The Broken Spears* (Boston, 1962); and William H. Prescott, *History of the Conquest of Mexico and History of the Conquest of Peru* (1 vol. ed., New York, 1957). For the introduction of epidemics to North America, see the important *Plagues and Peoples* (New York, 1976) by William H. McNeill, also David Horowitz, *The First Frontier* (New York, 1978).

8. The Outlaw and the Guerrilla

The authoritative works on these subjects are by Eric J. Hobsbawm in his *Primitive Rebels* (London, 1959) and *Bandits* (London, 1969). Also useful are Maurice Keen, *The Outlaws of Medieval Legend* (London, 1961) and Christopher Hibbert, *Highwaymen* (London, 1967). For the Scottish risings, see Bruce Lenman, *The Jacobite Risings in Britain, 1689–1746* (London, 1980). For Irish conspiracies, essential are the essays in *Secret Societies in Ireland*, ed. T. Desmond Williams (Dublin, 1973). For the influence of the Masonic Lodges in the American Revolution, see my *The Secret Scroll* (London, 2000).

9. The Illuminati and the French Revolution

The most accessible source is Nesta H. Webster, *Secret Societies and Subversive Movements* (London, 1924). Also significant is comte Le Couteulx de Canteleu, *Les Sectes et Sociétés Secrètes* (Paris, 1863).

10. The Terror

Of the multitude of works on the Terror, recommended are Donald Greer, *The Incidence of the Terror during the French Revolution* (Cambridge, Mass., 1935); George Rudé, *The French Revolution* (London, 1988); J. M. Roberts, *The French Revolution* (Oxford, 1978);

Richard Cobb, *Reactions to the French Revolution* (Oxford, 1972); *The French Revolution and the Creation of Modern Political Culture: 'The Terror'* (vol. 4, ed. K. M. Baker, Oxford, 1994); T. B. Rose, *The Enragés: Socialists of the French Revolution* (Melbourne, 1965); and Alfred Cobban, *A History of Modern France* (vol. 2, London, 1961).

11. Nationalist Secret Societies

For an understanding of the apocalyptic streak in revolutionary movements, J. L. Talmon, *Political Messianism: The Romantic Phase* (New York, 1960) is essential reading. The nationalist secret societies are covered in detail in the essays to be found in *Secret Societies*, ed. Norman Mackenzie (London, 1967).

12. The Early Art and Literature of Terror

Important is *Representing the French Revolution: Literature, Historiography, and Art*, ed. J. A. W. Heffernan (University Press of New England, 1992). For further analyses of the psychology of fear in literature, see my *The Naked Savage* (London, 1991). Kurt W. Treplow, *Vlad III Dracula: The Life and Times of the Historical Dracula* (Oxford, 2000) is essential reading.

13. Black Terror

Useful on the African slave trade is James Pope-Hennessy, *Sins of the Fathers* (London, 1967). Also important are K. G. Davies, *The Royal African Company* (London, 1957) and all of Basil Davidson's works on early African society, especially *Black Mother: Africa: The Years of Trial* (London, 1961), in which the author draws important parallels between feudal Europe and the Africa of the slavers. On the economic side, Eric Williams' *Capitalism and Slavery* (new ed., London, 1964) is most important, as is the revisionist work by Eugene D. Genovese, *The Political Economy of Slavery: Studies in the Economy and Society of the Slave South* (London, 1966) and *Roll, Jordan, Roll: The World the Slaves Made* (New York, 1975). The controversial work on slavery by

Robert W. Fogel and Stanley L. Engerman, *Time on the Cross: The Economics of African Negro Slavery* (Boston, 1974), was revised in two volumes in 1990 to complement Fogel's *Without Consent or Contract: The Rise and Fall of American Slavery* (New York, 1989).

14. Terror and the Warrior

Gwyn Jones is excellent in *A History of the Vikings* (Oxford, 1968): he quotes *The Danish History* of Saxo Grammaticus. Useful is Richard Holmes, *Redcoat: The British Soldier in the Age of Horse and Musket* (London, 2001); also George F. Scheer and Hugh F. Rankin, *Rebels and Redcoats* (New York, 1957), and Lawrence James, *The Savage Wars: British Campaigns in Africa, 1870–1920* (London, 1985).

15. Thuggee

On this subject, the essential work remains W. H. Sleeman, *A Journey through the Kingdom of Oude in 1849–50*, ed. P. D. Reeves (Cambridge, 1971). Also useful is F. I. S. Tuher, *The Yellow Scarf: Life of Thuggee Sleeman* (London, 1961).

16. The Secret Societies of China

In *Secret Societies*, op. cit., Barbara E. Ward has an admirable article on Chinese secret societies. I am also indebted to the many works on China of Jonathan Spence, particularly his *To Change China: Western Advisers in China, 1620–1960* (New York, 1969).

17. The Anarchists

The best short study of this subject is *Zero: The Story of Terrorism* (London, 1951) by Robert Payne. For Bakhunin, I have particularly used Anthony Masters, *Bakhunin: The Father of Anarchism* (London, 1974) and *The Political Philosophy of Bakhunin*, ed. G. P. Maximoff (New York, 1953). On the situation in the Balkans, useful are Herbert Vivian, *Secret Societies: Old and New* (London, 1927) and M. Edith Durham, *The Sarajevo Crime* (London, 1923).

18. The Anarchy of the West

For the best description of the life of the Mountain Men, see Ray Allen Billington, *The Far Western Frontier, 1830–1860* (New York, 1956). Also excellent is Lewis O. Saum, *The Fur Trader and the Indian* (Seattle, 1965). Important on the significance of the gun in the American psyche is Michael A. Bellesiles, *Arming America: The Origins of a National Gun Culture* (New York, 2000).

19. The Ku Klux Klan

The definitive essay on the Ku Klux Klan is written by David Annan in *Secret Societies*, op. cit.

20. The Mafia

The classic work on the Mafia remains *The Honoured Society* (London, 1964) by Norman Lewis. The full background of the later Ku Klux Klan and the Mafia in the United States may be found in my *Prohibition: The Era of Excess* (New York, 1962).

21. The Irish Rebellion

Interesting on the subject are the observations of a member of the staff of the chief of police in Ireland, Captain H. B. C. Pollard, *The Secret Societies of Ireland: Their Rise and Progress* (London, 1922), also the essays in *Secret Societies*, op. cit. The contemporary Irish historian was Joseph Mitchel. Essential reading remains Cecil Woodham-Smith, *The Great Hunger: Ireland, 1845–9* (London, 1964).

22. State Terror and the Bolsheviks

For further reading, most important are Isaiah Berlin, *Karl Marx: His Life and Environment* (Oxford, 1939); Sidney Hook, *From Hegel to Marx* (London, 1936); and H. Marcuse, *Reason and Revolution: Hegel and the Rise of Social Theory* (London, 1941). Also valuable are Otto

Friedrich, *The End of the World*, op. cit., and Hélène Carrère d'Encausse, *Lenin* (New York, 2001).

23. The Revolt of Labour

Of contemporary British historians, Henry Cockburn, *Memorials of His Time* (Edinburgh, 1856) is significant, also *The Luddites*, ed. Lionel Munby (London, 1971). Relevant are Donald Richter, *Riotous Victorians* (Ohio University Press, 1981) and Warren Sylvester Smith, *The London Heretics, 1870–1914* (New York, 1968). Also important is Malcolm Thomis and Peter Holt, *Threats of Revolution in Britain, 1789–1848* (London, 1977). There is an excellent book by Donald L. McMurry, *Coxey's Army* (University of Washington, 1968). The trilogy of John Dos Passos, *USA*, was published in a complete edition by the Modern Library in 1939 in New York.

24. The Psychology of World War

Two seminal books have informed me throughout of the thinking of the First World War. Robert Wohl, *The Generation of 1914* (Cambridge, Mass., 1980) is masterly in its insights and quotations. Paul Fussell, *The Great War and Modern Memory* (Oxford, 1975) set a new standard in historical recording, which recently led to the interesting work by Joanna Bourke, *An Intimate History of Killing* (London, 1999). Essential reading on the postwar period remains Robert Graves and Alan Hodge, *The Long Week-end: A Social History of Great Britain, 1918–1939* (London, 1940). I am dependent upon the excellent Everyman translation of Henri Barbusse, *Under Fire* (London, 1926). The other war classic, *All Quiet on the Western Front*, by Erich Maria Remarque, was first published in 1929 worldwide. Also essential are Denis Mack Smith, *Mussolini* (London, 1981), and Robert Payne, *Zero*, op. cit., while James A. Aho, *This Thing of Darkness: A Sociology of the Enemy* (Seattle, Washington, 1994) is interesting. Tristan Tzara made his statement in the *Manifeste du Mouvement Dada*, while Naphta's words come from Thomas Mann's *The Magic Mountain*, V, 'Of the City of God and Deliverance from Evil'.

25. The Road to Barcelona

Again, I am deeply indebted to Robert Wohl, *The Generation of 1914*,
op. cit., who quotes from Vicens Vives, *Approaches to the History of
Spain*. The quotations are from Robert Graves and Alan Hodge, *The
Long Week-end*, op. cit. George Orwell's *Homage to Catalonia* was
first published in 1938 in London. The most accessible book on *The
Spanish Civil War* remains the work of that title by Hugh Thomas,
published in 1961 in London. For research on nuclear fission in the
1930s, see my *The Red and the Blue* (London, 1986). C. P. Snow's
comments in the scientific magazine *Discovery* of 1939 may be found
in his 'The Moral Un-Neutrality of Science' of 1960, printed in *Public
Affairs* (London, 1971).

26. The Failed American Revolution

R. and H. Lynd, *Middletown in Transition* (New York, 1937) was the
successor to their pathbreaking *Middletown* (New York, 1929); they
examined the town of Muncie, Indiana. Richard Neustadt, *Presidential
Power*, was published in 1963 in Boston. The quotations are from F.
Dunne, *Dissertations by Mr Dooley* (New York, 1906) and the super-
lative Wilbur J. Cash, *The Mind of the South* (New York, 1941). There
is a good analysis of the private armies of America in J. Shalloo, *Private
Police* (Ph.D., Univ. of Philadelphia, 1933) and of the Ford Service
Department's connection with criminal racketeers in L. Morris, *Not So
Long Ago* (New York, 1949) and K. Sward, *The Legend of Henry Ford*
(New York, 1948). See also E. Lavine, *Gimme* (New York, 1931) and
L. Velie, *Labor, U.S.A.* (New York, 1959). 'Bread Line' was published
in January 1932, in the *Atlantic Monthly*.

27. The Shame of Japan

R. J. Rummel, *Death by Government*, was published in 1995 in New
Brunswick, NJ. See also Arnold C. Brackman, *The Other Nuremberg:
The Untold Story of the Tokyo War Crimes Tribunals* (New York,
1987). Most percipient is the article 'Occidentalism' by Ian Buruma and

Avishai Margalit in the *New York Review of Books*, December 2001, as is D. C. Holtorn, *Modern Japan and Shinto Nationalism* (Chicago, 1943). The witness, Dr Nagatomi Hakudo, is quoted in the matchless book by Iris Chang, *The Rape of Nanking* (New York, 1997); her account of this atrocity is the most appalling in the history of modern terror.

28. Fear, Strange Mercy and Annihilation

This section generally derives from my *War Like a Wasp: The Lost Decade of the Forties* (London, 1989). Edward Higham, *William Medium*, was published in 1947 in London, while David Gascoyne's *Paris Journal 1937–1939* was also published in London in 1978. Liam O'Flaherty's views of air domination came from *Shame the Devil* (London, 1934). 'Losses' derived from Randall Jarrell, *Selected Poems* (London, 1956). The quotation from Elias Canetti was from *The Human Province* (London, 1985). 'S.S. City of Benares' was published in *Poems of G. S. Fraser* (Leicester, 1981), while Denis Saunders's 'Almendro' was part of an anthology, *Return to Oasis* (London, 1980). Hamish Henderson, 'Elegies for the Dead in Cyrenaica' is reprinted with the author's permission. Francis Bacon spoke to me about *Painting, 1946*. William Golding wrote in the *Guardian*, 20 November 1975.

29. The Final Solution

The quotations from Goering and Goebbels come from the majestic work by Michael Burleigh, *The Third Reich* (London, 2000), which breaks new ground in explaining why ordinary German people carried out Hitler's programmes of annihilation. I am also indebted to Robert Payne's analysis of Hitler's thinking in *Zero*, op. cit.: he quotes Richard Wagner. The quotation from David Rousset is from his *L'Univers Concentrationnaire* (Paris, 1946). Hannah Arendt's opinions on the banality of evil, *The Origins of Totalitarianism* (London, 1951), remain challenging. Also important are Alan Bullock, *Hitler: A Study in Tyranny* (London, 1961); Karl Bracher, *The German Dictatorship*

(London, 1970); Joachim Fest, *Hitler* (London, 1974); and Ian Kershaw, *Hitler, 1937–1945: Nemesis* (London, 2000).

30. African Secret Societies

For the Afrikaner Broederbond and the Mau Mau, see *Secret Societies*, op. cit. Albert Camus, *The Plague*, was first published in 1947 in Paris. Most useful for an understanding of the Islamic influence on the Algerian revolution is John L. Esposito, *The Islamic Threat: Myth or Reality?* (Oxford, 1999).

31. The Gulag Lies

George Orwell published *Animal Farm* in 1946 in London and *Nineteen Eighty-Four* in 1949 in London. *The Gulag Archipelago* by Aleksandr Solzhenitsyn was published in 1986 in New York. The estimate of 66,000,000 dead came from the work of the émigré Professor of Statistics, Kurganov. There is an incisive book on Smyrna 1922: *The Destruction of a City* by Majorie Housepian (London, 1972). The American correspondent was George Horton, who wrote *The Blight of Asia* (New York, 1926).

32. The Forced Refugees

The quotation on premeditated genocide is taken from Helen Fein, *Accounting for Genocide* (New York, 1979). On the first deportation to Syria, the quotation is in the brilliant article by Richard G. Hovannisian, 'The Armenian Question, 1878–1923' in *A Crime of Silence: The Armenian Genocide* (London, 1985). Lord Curzon spoke at a War Cabinet meeting on 25 June 1918, quoted in the excellent book by Manough J. Somakian, *Empires in Conflict: Armenia and the Great Powers, 1895–1920* (London, 1995). Lord Mountbatten's Viceroy's Personal Report is dated 17 April 1947. Sardar Patel and General Rees are quoted by H. V. Hodson in his excellent work, *The Great Divide: Britain–India–Pakistan* (rev. ed., Oxford, 1985).

33. The Problem of Palestine

For more information, see my *Jerusalem: The Endless Crusade* (London, 1996). The most informative account of this period is by Dov Joseph, who served as the military governor of Jerusalem for the new state of Israel and wrote of his experiences in *The Faithful City: The Siege of Jerusalem, 1948* (London, 1962). I have quoted from his own text and used his quotations from Sir Alan Cunningham to Ben-Gurion. Emmanuel Litvinoff, *Road to Jerusalem: Zionism's Imprint on History* (London, 1965) is admirably impartial on the issue, and he quotes David Ben-Gurion's evidence to the United Nations Special Committee. Most relevant is Yigal Lossin, *Pillar of Fire: The Rebirth of Israel – A Visual History* (Jerusalem, 1983). Ronald Storrs is quoted in *The High Walls of Jerusalem* by Ronald Sanders, published in 1983 in New York. Jabotinsky's views appear in Karen Armstrong's *Holy War: The Crusades and their Impact on Today's World* (rev. ed., New York, 1991). The former British commander of the Arab Legion put the Jordanian point of view on Israel and its history in John Bagot Glubb, *Peace in the Holy Land* (London, 1971). Folke Bernadotte's *To Jerusalem* was published in 1951 in London.

34. The Killing Fields of Asia

The quotations from Mao Zedong are drawn from the analytic *For Mao: Essays in Historical Materialism*, ed. Philip Corrigan and Harvie Ramsey (London, 1979). The quotation of Mao's poem comes from the excellent book by Stanley Karnow, *Mao and China: From Revolution to Revolution* (New York, 1973). On the atrocities in Vietnam, Joanna Bourke, *An Intimate History of Killing* (London, 2000), is compelling reading. William Calley, *Body Count*, was published in 1971 in London. Generally excellent is Jonathan Spence, *The Gate of Heavenly Peace: The Chinese and their Revolution, 1895–1980* (London, 1982).

35. Guevara: Swimming in a Dry Sea

For further reading on Che Guevara, essential are J. L. Anderson, *Che Guevara: A Revolutionary Life* (London, 1997), and Jorge G. Castañeda, *Compañero: The Life and Death of Che Guevara* (London, 1997). See also my *Guevara* (rev. ed., Sutton Books, 2000). Most important are Guevara's own works: *Episodes of the Cuban Revolutionary War* (New York, 1996), and *Guerrilla Warfare* (London, 1968). The most exact and illuminating book on modern terrorism across the globe is by Walter Laquer, *The New Terrorism: Fanaticism and the Arms of Mass Destruction* (London, 1999).

36. The Broadcast Horror

On bioterror, I am dependent on the brilliant work of Edmund Russell, *War and Nature: Fighting Humans and Insects with Chemicals from World War I to Silent Spring* (Cambridge, 2001). He particularly emphasizes the scale of the use of bioterror which is now possible. Cornelius Ryan wrote in *Collier's* magazine on 27 November 1953. Bertrand Russell wrote in the *Nation* on 6 July 1963; President Nixon spoke on 25 November 1969. An important book, *The New Fascists*, was written by Paul Wilkinson and published in a revised edition in 1983 in London. My observation on assassination comes from my memoir of the 1960s, *In Love and Anger* (London, 1994).

37. The Unused Deterrence

The quotations from the Cabinet minute and Sir Henry Tizard and Sir William Penney come from my *The Red and the Blue: Cambridge, Treason and Intelligence* (Boston, 1986). The admirable *Nuclear Warriors: Soldiers, Combat and Glasnost* by Richard Holmes was published in 1991 in London: he quotes Richard S. Macnamara. Again Walter Laquer is my guide in his superb *The New Terrorism*, op. cit. John Deutch warned in 1996 of an 'electronic Pearl Harbor'.

38. Ethnic Terror

Anthony Mockler wrote a knowledgeable book on *Mercenaries*, published in 1970 in London. William Shawcross also wrote an incisive book on ethnic terror, *Deliver Us From Evil: Warlords & Peacekeepers in a World of Endless Conflict* (London, 2000). He quotes Sergio Viera de Mello on the Hutu refugee camps in Zaire, and Henry Kissinger on the virtue of intervention.

39. Return to Holy War

As well as texts already cited, I am deeply indebted to the most significant book by Mark Juergensmeyer, *Terror in the Mind of God: The Global Rise of Religious Violence* (rev. ed., Berkeley, 2000). Also most important are Bruce Hoffman, *Inside Terrorism* (New York, 1998); *Origins of Terrorism: Psychologies, Ideologies, Theologies, States of Mind*, ed. Walter Reich (New York, 1990); Paul Wilkinson, *Political Terrorism* (London, 1974); and *Terrorism in Context*, ed. Martha Crenshaw (Philadelphia, 1995). David Chidester, *Salvation and Suicide* (Indianapolis, 1980), interprets Jim Jones and the Jonestown People's Temple, while Dick J. Reavis, *The Ashes of Waco: An Investigation* (New York, 1995), reports on that tragedy.

Important material can be found in Chaim Herzog, *The Arab–Israeli War: War and Peace in the Middle East* (rev. ed., New York, 1984), and in Sydney D. Bailey, *Four Arab–Israeli Wars and the Peace Process* (London, 1990). Robin Wright in *Sacred Rage: The Crusade of Modern Islam* (London, 1986) is good on the Israeli invasion of Lebanon and its consequences. I am indebted to the seminal work of Samuel P. Huntington, *The Clash of Civilisations and the Remaking of World Order* (New York, 1997).

40. The Revenge of Islam

Other than the texts already mentioned, particularly significant is John K. Cooley, *Unholy Wars: Afghanistan, America and International Terrorism* (rev. ed., London, 2000). *Newsweek* reported Saddam Hussein's remarks on his withdrawal from Kuwait in 1992, also those of Richard Cheney and Yitzhak Rabin. The Kuwaiti roving ambassador spoke on the BBC on 25 February 1991, as did the citizens of Baghdad. Karen Armstrong quoted the prayer of Kibbutz Dati in her *Holy War*, op. cit. Osama bin Laden spoke to Hamid Mir, as reported in the *Sunday Times*, 11 November 2001. M. J. Gohari, *The Taliban: Ascent to Power* (Oxford, 2000) published the full text of the fatwa of Osama bin Laden.

41. Countdown to Kabul

The religious judge was Sayed Abdur Rahman and was quoted in *The Taliban: Ascent to Power*, op. cit., which describes its Wahhabi origins. I am also indebted to important articles by Ian Buruma and Avishai Margalit, 'Occidentalism', the *New York Review of Books*, 17 January 2002, and Fareed Zakaria, 'The Roots of Rage: Islam & The West', *Newsweek*, 15 October 2001.

42. The Future of Terror

Bernard Lewis wrote his quoted article, 'Muslims, Christians and Jews: The Dream of Co-existence' in the *New York Review of Books*, 26 March 1992. He has also written many admirable works on Islamic civilization, summed up in his *The Middle East* (London, 1995). Also important and quoted are Avishai Margalit and Moshe Halbertal, *Idolatry* (Cambridge, Mass., 1994) and Kanan Mikiya, *Cruelty and Silence: War, Tyranny, Uprising and the Arab World* (New York, 1993). Mirko Mirković quoted Stefan Zweig in his speech to the 34th International Writers' Meeting in Bled in May 2001.

Envoi

The speech of George W. Bush at West Point was reported in the *New York Times*, 3 June 2002. See Samantha Power, *A Problem from Hell: America and the Age of Genocide* (New York, 2002). See also her article, 'Genocide and America', in the *New York Review of Books*, 14

March 2002. Philip Bobbitt, *The Shield of Achilles* (London, 2002) was also quoted in the London *Times*, 24 June 2002. The *Duino Elegies* of Rainer Maria Rilke were translated by J. B. Leishman and Stephen Spender and published in 1939 in New York.

Index

labour revolts (*cont.*)
Lafayette, Marie-Joseph-Paul-Yves-Roch-Gilbert du Motier, marquis de 65, 71, 73, 84, 110
Lamartine 86, 87, 88
Lampião, Captain (Virgulino Ferreira da Silva) 360
Lancelot 17–18
Land League 178
Languedoc 23–4, 24, 25, 36, 44
Latin America 299–300
Lawrence, St 17
Lazar, Prince 324
League of the Elect 39
League of the Just 85
League of Outlaws 85
Ledru-Rollin, Alexandre-Auguste 87, 89
Lenin, V. I. 135, 186, 187, 189–90, 190, 191–3, 361
Lesbos 4
Leviticus 47
Lewis, Bernard, 'The Dream of Co-existence' 355
Lewis, John L. 224, 225
Liao dynasty 126
Liberia 321, 322
Libya 334
Life and Death of Jack Straw (Peele) 57
Lin Piao 285
Lin Tung-chi 125
Lincoln, Abraham 139, 145
Lindberg kidnap case (1932) 156
literature, of terror 93–9
Little Big Horn, Battle of the 54
Liu Pei 126
Lloyd George, David 184
Lockerbie 327
Lodhi, Makeen 121
London, Jack 129
Long, Huey 222, 228
Louis XIII, King 46
Louis-Philippe, King 84, 86
Luciano, Charles 'Lucky' 168, 170, 172, 174
Luddites 194
Lumumba, Patrice 294, 317
Luther, Martin 38, 39, 40
Luxor: murder of tourists (1997) 341–2

McAdoo, William Gibbs 154
MacArthur, General Douglas 196, 234, 239
MacDonald, Ramsay 210
McGuiness, Martin 350

Machiavelli, Niccolò dei 4, 42, 43, 46, 74, 208
Mackenzie, William Lyon 139
McKinley, William 134
Macmillan, Harold 313
Macnamara, Robert S. 315
McVeigh, Timothy 306, 329
Mafia 30, 56, 124, 129, 158–74, 367
    American
        and big business 169–70, 173
        and Capone 165–7
        establishment of 162
        killing of elder generation 168
        and money laundering 173–4
        and organized crime 163
    centralization of 172
    and clannishness 165
    differences between Sicilian and American 163–4, 168
    new era of cooperation among gangsters 165, 167
    origins and roots of 158
    Sicilian
        Allied invasion of Sicily (1943) 170
        blood feuds 161
        attempted eradication of 172–3
        and family 158–9
        initiation ceremony 161
        Mori's campaign against 168–9
        and Salvatore Giuliano 171–2
        organization 160–1
        transformation from outlaw bands to rulers 159–60
Magus, Simon 12
Mahabharata 200, 204
Maistre, Joseph de 75
Malan, Dr Daniel 252–3
Mameluks 33
Mandela, Nelson 255
Manhattan Project 312
Mann, Thomas, *The Magic Mountain* 211
Manz, Felix 38
Mao Zedong 239, 283–7, 288, 299
Marat, Jean-Paul 73, 76, 78, 92
Marat, Assassinated (David) 91–2
Marie-Antoinette 76
Marinetti, Filippo 207
Marx, Karl 71, 79, 85, 87, 130, 131, 132, 186, 194, 210
Masonic Lodges 63, 64–5, 81: *see also* Freemasons
Masoud, Ahmad Shah 347–8

OTHER BOOKS

AVAILABLE FROM PAN MACMILLAN

RICHARD ENGLISH ARMED STRUGGLE	1 4050 0108 9	£20.00
CHRISTOPHER HOPE BROTHERS UNDER THE SKIN	1 4050 0555 6	£17.99
JOHN SIMPSON STRANGE PLACES, QUESTIONABLE PEOPLE	0 330 35566 X	£7.99
JOHN SERGEANT GIVE ME TEN SECONDS	0 330 48490 7	£7.99

All Pan Macmillan titles can be ordered from our website,
www.panmacmillan.com, or from your local bookshop
and are also available by post from:

Bookpost, PO Box 29, Douglas, Isle of Man IM99 1BQ
Credit cards accepted. For details:
Telephone: 01624 677237
Fax: 01624 670923
E-mail: bookshop@enterprise.net
www.bookpost.co.uk

Free postage and packing in the United Kingdom

Prices shown above were correct at the time of going to press.
Pan Macmillan reserve the right to show new retail prices on covers
which may differ from those previously advertised in the text
or elsewhere.